The Power Chess Program
Book 2

Nigel Davies

B.T. Batsford Ltd, *London*

First published in 1999
© Nigel Davies 1999

ISBN 0 7134 8420 9

British Library Cataloguing-in-Publication Data.
A catalogue record for this book is
available from the British Library.

Printed in Great Britain by
Creative Print and Design (Wales), Ebbw Vale
for the publishers
B.T. Batsford Ltd
9 Blenheim Court
Brewery Road
London N7 9NT
A member of the Chrysalis Group plc

A BATSFORD CHESS BOOK

Contents

Symbols

+	check
#	mate
x	captures
!!	a brilliant move
!	a good move
!?	an interesting move
?!	a dubious move
?	a bad move
??	a blunder
1-0	White wins
0-1	Black wins
½-½	draw
Ct	Candidates tournament
Cm	Candidates match
Ch	Championship
WCh	World championship
Cht	Team championship
tt	Team tournament
Ol	Olympiad
Izt	Interzonal tournament
Zt	Zonal tournament
corr	Correspondence game
m	Match

Introduction

Welcome to year two of the *Power Chess Program* which can be studied either together with or independently from Book 1.

What is it that makes a strong chess player? Is it a knowledge of opening theory (as many people seem to believe) or perhaps being able to calculate more moves ahead than the opponent? A quick eye perhaps, fierce will to win or just patience?

Through my work as a chess trainer I have come across all sorts of theories as to what it is that makes someone good at chess, not all of them very sound. As a result it is quite difficult for an amateur player with a limited amount of time to know exactly how to improve.

With these thoughts in mind I set about developing a training program which would target the two main areas in which stronger players distinguish themselves. The first is their ability to see ahead clearly and deeply and be able to make disciplined calculations. The second is in recognising a large number of strategic patterns and being able to apply this to similar positions with good judgement and creativity.

The *Power Chess Program* is a two year course in which month by month I present different strategic themes and issues and then back this up with thematic test positions to get the reader actively involved. It is only through this active involvement that the strategic ideas really hit home, simply reading about them is not enough!

I have arranged the chapters in terms of 'weeks' and 'months' with the aim of encouraging a regular weekly study session of about 3-5 hours. For each week's lesson you should firstly read through the notes and then set about the test positions.

These positions are divided into two types. The 'key move' positions (KM13/1: to KM24/4) are fairly lightweight and you might allow yourself around 10 minutes each to find the next move. The analysis positions (A13/1: to A24/4) are much more difficult and I suggest you spend around 30 minutes on these. I recommend that you do not take more than the allotted time so as to avoid frustration and encourage quick, disciplined decisions. I also suggest that you try not to move the pieces as this will help develop visualisation skills.

You should also note that these positions are not necessarily tactical forced wins. Sometimes it is a good positional move that is required, sometimes you may be called on to find the best chance in a losing position. This conforms much more to the reality of chess than the standard two-movers we see all the time in newspapers. These lack any kind of challenge because you know there is something there!

I will not try to kid you that this course is an easy option and that merely opening this book will improve your chess. Several of my students have fallen by the wayside after a few months.

What I can say is that everyone who has persevered and worked systematically through it has experienced an upswing in their results, sometimes a quite dramatic improvement.

The *Power Chess Program* can also be studied in conjuntion with a personal tuition package. For more details you can contact me at my web site (www.checkerwise.co.uk).

It remains for me to wish you well with the Power-Chess Program and leave you with the words of John F. Kennedy:

"There are costs and risks to a program of action, but they are far less than the long-range risks and costs of comfortable inaction."

GM Nigel Davies,
Manchester, June 1999.

1 The Art of Attack

In Book 1, month one, we looked at various aspects of king safety and attack. This month we will look in more detail at the art of attack using the games of some of its greatest exponents.

In week one we will see the attack on the king in the most basic form in which the hapless monarch is being pursued by a number of the opponent's pieces. In week two we will see examples of direct attacks upon a king's fortress, in week three we see how a preliminary softening up process can be effective.

Last but not least I will give a rather more philosophical view of the attack by comparing chess strategy with the views on warfare expounded by the Chinese general Sun Tzu in his book *The Art of War*.

The greatest genius of the attack was, in my opinion, Alexander Alekhine who amazed his contemporaries with his ability to generate attacking positions. He seemed to have a unique ability to bring about attacking positions against the strongest of opposition and from all kinds of positions. For this reason I have featured Alekhine's games this month more than those of any other player.

Month 13/Week 1:
The King Hunt

There is nothing more dramatic or easily comprehensible in chess than the sight of a king running across the board whilst trying to evade blows by the opposing pieces. This is romantic chess in its purest form though in today's scientific era it is rather more difficult to bring about such scenarios than it was in the past.

The reason is that players are much more careful about the safety of their king and would prefer to make almost any concession rather than suffer the indignity of having their king hunted down. All the same this does sometimes happen ...

The first game this week sees attack and defence in balance with White having enough for a draw by perpetual check but not more than this. In the second game there is the rather more common scenario of the hunted king getting cut down in the cross-fire.

O'Kelly - Penrose
Varna Olympiad 1962

1 e4 c5 2 ♘f3 ♘c6 3 d4 cxd4 4 ♘xd4 e6 5 ♘c3 ♕c7 6 ♗e2 a6 7

0-0 ♘f6 8 ♗e3 ♗b4 9 ♘xc6 bxc6
10 ♗d3 d5 11 exd5 cxd5 12 ♗d4
♗e7 13 ♖e1 0-0

With White's pieces pointing
menacingly towards the kingside
this could be described as 'brave'.

**14 ♕f3 ♗b7 15 ♖e3 ♖fe8 16
♖ae1 ♖ad8 17 ♕h3 ♘e4!**

If 17 ... g6 there is 18 ♖f3 ♘e4 19
♕xh7+ ♔xh7 20 ♖h3+ ♔g8 21
♖h8#.

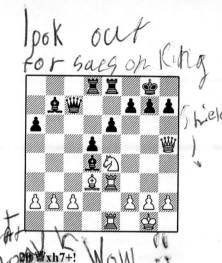

18 ♕h5!

There are several tempting possibilities, none of which brings home
the bacon. 18 ♗xg7 fails after 18 ...
♔xg7 19 ♖g3+ ♔h8 20 ♕h6 ♖g8,
18 ♘xe4 allows 18 ... dxe4 19
♗xe4 ♗xe4 20 ♖xe4 ♕xc2 and 18
f3 is met by 18 ... f5! 19 fxe4 dxe4.

18 ... ♗f6!

The only defence. The plausible
18 ... g6 loses to 19 ♕xh7+ ♔xh7
20 ♖h3+ ♔g8 21 ♖h8# and 18 ... f5
is met by 19 ♖h3 h6 20 ♗xg7 ♘g5
21 ♕g6.

19 ♘xe4

Both sides are finding their best
moves. After 19 ♖xe4 Black can defend himself with 19 ... dxe4 20
♗xf6 gxf6 21 ♗xe4 f5.

19 ... ♗xd4

20 ♕xh7+!

Not only spectacular but at this
stage rather necessary. 20 ♘g5 allows Black to take the initiative with
20 ... h6 21 ♖h3 ♕f4 etc.

This sacrifice is reminiscent of a
famous game between Edward
Lasker and Sir George Thomas
played in London in 1910 which
went 1 d4 f5 2 ♘c3 ♘f6 3 ♘f3 e6 4
♗g5 ♗e7 5 ♗xf6 ♗xf6 6 e4 fxe4 7
♘xe4 b6 8 ♗d3 ♗b7 9 ♘e5 00 10
♕h5 ♕e7 11 ♕xh7+! ♔xh7 12
♘xf6+ ♔h6 13 ♘eg4+ ♔g5 14 h4+
♔f4 15 g3+ ♔f3 16 ♗e2+ ♔g2 17
♖h2+ ♔g1 18 ♔d2# In the present
case it only leads to a draw.

20 ... ♔xh7!

Black has to sail into the eye of
the storm. 20 ... ♔f8 21 ♘g3 ♗xe3
22 ♖xe3 ♔e7 23 ♕xg7 gives White
a ferocious attack.

**21 ♘f6+ ♔h6 22 ♖h3+ ♔g5 23
♘h7+ ♔g4**

And not 23 ... ♔f4? because of 24
♖h4#.

24 ♗e2+ ♔f4 25 ♗d3

White must repeat moves as 25
♖h4+? is met by 25 ... ♔e5 and 25
♗h5? by 25 ... ♗xf2+ 26 ♔xf2
♕xc2+ 27 ♔g1 ♕xh7!.

25 ... ♔g4 26 ♗e2+ ♔f4 27 ♗d3

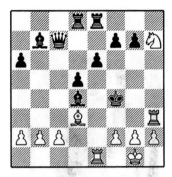

27 ... ♚g4

Black has little choice but to repeat moves, 27 ... ♗xf2+ 28 ♔xf2 ♕c5+ 29 ♔f1 ♕e7 30 ♖f3+ ♔g4 gives White the chance to search for a win. White too has to accede to the draw as 28 ♔f1 is met by 28 ... ♗xf2! 29 ♔xf2 ♕f4+.

½:½

Evans - Berger
Amsterdam Izt 1964

1 e4 c6 2 d4 d5 3 ♘c3 dxe4 4 ♘xe4 ♗f5 5 ♘g3 ♗g6 6 ♘f3 ♘d7 7 h4 h6 8 h5 ♗h7 9 ♗d3 ♗xd3 10 ♕xd3 ♕c7 11 ♗d2 ♘gf6 12 0-0-0 e6 13 ♔b1 c5 14 c4 cxd4?!

This proves to be very dangerous for Black with his king still hanging around in the middle of the board. It would be wiser to castle queenside at this point.

15 ♘xd4 a6

This allows White a winning sacrificial breakthrough but the position is already very difficult for Black. He had originally intended 15 ... ♘e5 but then White can play 16 ♕e2 ♘xc4 17 ♘xe6! ♘xd2+ 18 ♖xd2 fxe6 19 ♕xe6+ ♕e7 (Or 19 ... ♗e7 20 ♘f5 ♔f8 21 ♖c1+-) 20 ♕c4

with a winning attack. The best try was 15 ... 0-0-0! but then White has a very dangerous attack after 16 ♘b5 ♕b8 17 ♘e4. If Black continues with 17 ... ♘xe4 18 ♕xe4 a6 there follows 19 ♗f4 e5 20 ♖xd7 ♖xd7 21 ♗xe5 ♕a8 22 ♘c7 ♖xc7 23 ♕f5+ ♔b8 (Or 23 ... ♖d7 24 ♖d1+-) 24 ♕xf7 or if 18 ... ♘f6 there is 19 ♕e3 a6 20 ♘a7+ ♔c7 21 ♗a5+ b6 22 ♖xd8+-.

16 ♘xe6!

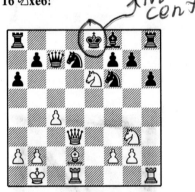

♪in center

16 ... fxe6 17 ♕g6+ ♔d8 18 ♖he1 ♔c8

White's attack keeps coming in all lines. If 18 ... e5 there is 19 ♗c3 ♔c8 20 f4! and 18 ... ♕xc4 is met by 19 ♗c3.

19 ♖xe6 b6 20 ♕f5!

Quiet but deadly. The threat is 21 ♗f4.

20 ... ♔b7 21 ♗f4 ♕c5

Black no longer has any prospect of defence. After 21 ... ♕c8 there is 22 ♘e4 ♗a7 (Or 22 ... ♘xe4 23 ♕xe4+ ♔a7 24 ♖c6! etc) 23 ♘xf6 ♘xf6 24 ♖xf6 gxf6 25 ♖d7+.

22 ♖xf6 1:0

Upon 22 ... ♘xf6 there follows 23 ♖d7+ ♔c6 24 ♖c7#.

KM13/1: 1) White to play

KM13/1: 2) White to play

KM13/1: 3) Black to play

KM13/1: 4) Black to play

A13/1: a) White to play.

A13/1: b) Black to play.

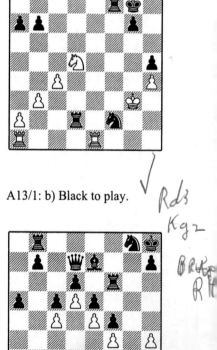

Month 13/Week 2:
Direct Assaults

With the great rise in the standard of technique, players of all standards are only too aware of the danger of an exposed king. Accordingly they will attempt to construct some sort of fortress and then bolster it at the slightest sign of trouble.

It is relatively rare for a direct attack to succeed when the defender concentrates all his efforts on beating back the attack. Successful direct attacks may come about in situations in which the players castle on opposite wings and are engaged in violent mutual attacks. Or they might occur when one side has a considerable lead in mobility or development, as for example in the following encounter.

Alekhine - Eliskases
Podebrady 1936

1 e4

Alekhine was equally adept at playing both 1 e4 and 1 d4. Nowadays most players are able to adopt a wide range of openings, in Alekhine's time it was more usual to specialize.

1 ... e5 2 ♘f3 ♘c6 3 ♗b5 a6 4 ♗a4 ♘f6 5 0-0 ♗e7 6 ♖e1 b5 7 ♗b3 d6 8 c3 ♘a5 9 ♗c2 c5 10 d3

The most usual move is 10 d4 but the modest text also has its points. Perhaps Alekhine, with a subtle insight into his opponent's psychology, knew that Eliskases would react in the way that he does.

10 ... ♘c6 11 ♘bd2 0-0 12 ♘f1 ♖e8 13 ♘e3 d5?

This 'liberating' move gives White's pieces more scope than those of his opponent. The patient 13 ... ♗f8 was in order.

14 exd5 ♘xd5 15 ♘xd5 ♕xd5 16 d4!

The refutation of Black's impatient thirteenth move. The position is opened up before Black has completed his development and while his pieces, especially the knight on c6, are on vulnerable squares.

16 ... exd4 17 ♗e4 ♕d7

Black's knight on c6 is giving him major problems. After 17 ... ♕d6? there is 18 ♗f4.

18 cxd4 ♗f6

After 18 ... ♗b7 White would create a powerfully supported passed pawn with 19 d5 ♘d8 20 ♘e5 ♕d6 21 ♗f4. But now lightning strikes from another direction.

19 ♗g5!

A very unpleasant move for Black to meet as it threatens to remove a key defender whilst further advancing White's development.

After 19 ... ♗xd4 there is 20 ♗f5! ♖xe1+ 21 ♕xe1 ♕d6 22 ♕e8+ ♕f8 23 ♗xh7+ winning the queen while 19 ... ♗xg5 20 ♘xg5 g6 21 dxc5 leads to a hopeless endgame for Black. So the following exchange sacrifice is forced.

19 ... ♖xe4 20 ♖xe4 ♗xd4 21 ♘xd4 ♘xd4 22 ♕h5! ♗b7 23 ♖h4

23 ... ♕f5
23 ... h6? loses immediately to 24 ♗xh6 ♘f5 25 ♗xg7 ♔xg7 26 ♕g5+ etc.

24 ♗e3! ♖d8?
Losing on the spot but by now the position is hopeless. After 24 ... ♕xh5 25 ♖xh5 ♘c2 26 ♖d1 ♘xe3 27 fxe3 c4 28 ♖c5 the endgame is quite hopeless for Black.

25 ♖xd4 1:0

In the following game we see Bobby Fischer on the attack against the Soviet Champion of the time, Leonid Stein. Stein made the mistake of pursuing his queenside counter-play rather than falling back into defence.

Fischer - Stein
Sousse Interzonal 1967

1 e4 e5 2 ♘f3 ♘c6 3 ♗b5 a6 4 ♗a4 ♘f6 5 0-0 ♗e7 6 ♖e1 b5 7 ♗b3 d6 8 c3 0-0 9 h3 ♗b7 10 d4 ♘a5 11 ♗c2 ♘c4 12 b3 ♘b6 13 ♘bd2 ♘bd7 14 b4 exd4 15 cxd4 a5 16 bxa5 c5 17 e5

White's attack starts to take shape, the first step being to drive Black's knight from f6

17 ... dxe5 18 dxe5 ♘d5 19 ♘e4 ♘b4!

Fischer gave 19 ... ♖xa5 20 ♘eg5! h6 21 ♕d3 g6 22 ♘e6! as an example of the danger Black faces in this position. Stein's move drives White's bishop to b1 which helps to keep his queen's rook out of play.

20 ♗b1 ♖xa5 21 ♕e2 ♘b6?
Black should safeguard his king with 21 ... ♖e8 followed by ... ♘f8.

22 ♘fg5

22 ... ♗xe4
After 22 ... h6 there is 23 ♘h7 ♖e8 24 ♘hf6+! ♗xf6 25 ♘xf6+ ♕xf6 26 exf6 winning the exchange and 22 ... g6 23 e6 f5 24 ♘f7 24 ♘f7 followed by 25 ♗b2 gives White a crushing attack.

23 ♕xe4 g6 24 ♕h4 h5 25 ♕g3 ♘c4 26 ♘f3

The Art of Attack 13

According to Fischer himself it was more precise to play 26 e6 f5 and only then drop the knight back to f3. The point is that this would side-step the tougher defence that Black should have adopted on his 28th move.

Keres gave 26 ♘xf7 ♖xf7 27 ♗xg6 but 27 ... ♖g7 is not very clear.

26 ... ♔g7

Keres recommended 26 ... ♘d3 27 ♗xd3 ♕xd3 but after Fischer's 28 ♗g5! White comes in on the dark squares.

27 ♕f4 ♖h8 28 e6! f5

According to Fischer Black should have tried 28 ... ♗f6! after which 29 exf6 ♗xa1 30 f8=♕+ ♕xf8 31 ♕c7+ ♔g8 32 ♗xg6 ♘d5 33 ♕b7 ♘f6 34 ♗f4 ♖h7! 35 ♗xh7+ ♘xh7 36 ♕d5+ ♕f7 37 ♕xf7+ ♔xf7 38 ♖xa1 leads to a position in which Black could still put up tough resistance. Now White uncorks a cracking move.

29 ♗xf5!

29 ... ♕f8

The bishop is immune as after 29 ... gxf5 there follows 30 ♕g3+ ♔h7

(Or 30 ... ♔f8 31 ♕g6 ♕e8 32 ♗h6+-) 31 ♘g5+! ♗xg5 32 ♗xg5 ♕d3 33 ♕c7+ ♔g6 34 ♕f7+! ♔xg5 35 ♕g7+ ♔f4 36 ♖ad1+-.

30 ♗e4?

White should have clinched matters with 30 ♘h4! ♗xh4 31 ♕xh4 ♕xf5 32 ♕e7+ ♔g8 33 ♕d8+ ♔g7 34 ♕c7+ ♔g8 35 e7.

30 ... ♕xf4 31 ♗xf4 ♖e8?

Missing his chance, 31 ... ♖xa2 was much better. Now White wins material.

32 ♖ad1 ♖a6 33 ♖d7 ♖xe6 34 ♘g5 ♖f6

If 34 ... ♖a6 there is 35 ♗b1 ♔f6 36 ♘e4+ ♔f7 37 ♘xc5.

35 ♗f3 ♖xf4 36 ♘e6+ ♔f6 37 ♘xf4 ♘e5 38 ♖b7 ♗d6 39 ♔f1

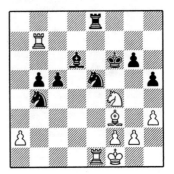

39 ... ♘c2

39 ... ♘xf3 is met by 40 ♖xe8 ♘d2+ 41 ♔e2 ♗xf4 42 ♖f8+ ♔g5 43 ♖xf4 ♔xf4 44 ♔xd2 etc.

40 ♖e4 ♘d4 41 ♖b6 ♖d8 42 ♘d5+ ♔f5 43 ♘e3+ ♔e6 44 ♗e2 ♔d7 45 ♗xb5+ ♘xb5 46 ♖xb5 ♔c6 47 a4 ♗c7 48 ♔e2 g5 49 g3 ♖a8 50 ♖b2 ♖f8 51 f4 gf 52 gf ♘f7 53 ♖e6+ ♘d6 54 f5 ♖a8 55 ♖d2 ♖xa4 56 f6 1:0

KM13/2: 1) Black to play

KM13/2: 2) White to play

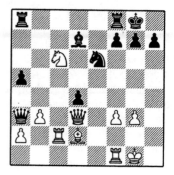

KM13/2: 3) White to play

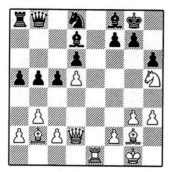

KM13/2: 4) White to play

A13/2: a) White to play

A13/2: b) White to play

Month 13/Week 3:
The Softening Up Process

It is rather difficult to win games with a direct assault due to the fact that the opponent will normally do his very best to bring over reserves for defence. Usually it is necessary to set about weakening the pawn structure around the opposing king and exchange off the key defensive pieces.

This area of attacking play tends to require a higher level of skill than that of a simple breakthrough. The pieces must often be arranged so that they exploit the emerging weaknesses in the opponent's structure.

Keres - Unzicker
Match, Hamburg 1956

1 e4 e5 2 ♘f3 ♘c6 3 ♗b5 ♘f6 4 0-0 ♘xe4 5 d4 ♗e7 6 ♕e2 ♘d6 7 ♗xc6 bxc6 8 dxe5 ♘b7 9 ♘c3 0-0 10 ♘d4 ♗c5 11 ♖d1 ♗xd4 12 ♖xd4 d5 13 exd6 cxd6 14 b4!

An excellent move which fixes Black's pawn weaknesses, may eventually threaten b4-b5 and keeps Black's knight out of play.

14 ... ♖e8 15 ♗e3 ♗e6 16 ♕f3

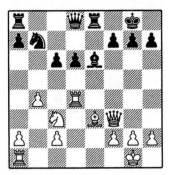

16 ... ♕d7?

A poor move which moves the queen away from the defence of the kingside dark squares. Keres recommended 16 ... d5! after which White should keep a small advantage with 17 ♗f4! rather than play 17 b5 c5! 18 ♖dd1 d4 19 ♕xb7 ♕a5 when Black wins back the piece with good chances of equality.

17 ♘e4 ♗f5?

A further mistake after which Black's position becomes desperate. He should play 17 ... ♗d5 after which 18 ♘f6+? gxf6 19 ♖g4+ ♔f8 leaves White with no good follow-up. The best would be to play 18 c4 ♗xe4 19 ♖xe4, retaining an edge due to the poor position of Black's knight on b7, though Black could still obtain some counter-play with 19 ... a5.

18 ♘g3!

A very strong pawn sacrifice after which another Black piece is decoyed from the defence of the kingside. After 18 ... ♗g6 White can play the powerful 19 h4!, so he is obliged to capture the pawn on c2.

18 ... ♗xc2 19 ♖c1 ♗a4 20 ♘h5

20 ♘f5 was even stronger because it would prevent Black's next move.

20 ... f5! 21 ⬜f4 ⬜e7

After 21 ... ⬜f8 there follows 22 d4! ⬜f7 23 ♗xg7! with a fork on f6 should Black take the bishop. So he has to let the pawn on f5 go.

22 ⬜xf5 ⬜f7

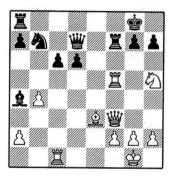

23 ♘xg7!

A very unpleasant surprise for Black. After 23 ... ♔xg7 White wins with either 24 ♗h6+ or 24 ♕g4+ and the attempt to bring reinforcements over with 23 ... ⬜af8 is answered by 24 ♘e6! ⬜xf5 (If 24 ... ♕xe6 there is 25 ♕g4+ ♕g6 26 ⬜g5+- or if 25 ... ♔h8 then 26 ♗d4+ ⬜f6 27 ⬜xf6 ♕xg4 28 ⬜xf8#) 25 ♕g4+ ♔h8 26 ♘xf8 etc. Accordingly Black has very little choice.

23 ... ⬜xg7 24 ♗h6 ♕e7

After 24 ... ⬜f7 there is 25 ⬜g5+ ♔h8 26 ♕c3+- and 24 ... ⬜e8 25 h4 is decisive due to the threat of 26 ♗xg7 and 27 ⬜g5.

25 ♗xg7 ♕xg7

25 ... ♔xg7 doesn't help either after 26 ♕c3+ ♔g8 27 ⬜f3 threatening 28 ⬜g3+ and 28 ⬜e1.

26 h4 h6

There was no longer a good defence to 27 ⬜g5. 26 ... ⬜f8 is answered by either 27 ⬜e1 or 27 ⬜xf8+

♕xf8 28 ♕g4+ ♔h8 29 ♕d4+ ♔g8 (29 ... ♕g7 30 ♕xa7) 30 ⬜c3.

27 ⬜c4 1:0

An impressive game by Keres in the way that he built up an attack with minimal means. In the next game we see something even more remarkable with Alekhine conjuring up a devastating attack from what seems like thin air:

Alekhine - Sterk
Budapest 1921

1 d4 d5 2 ♘f3 ♘f6 3 c4 e6 4 ♘c3 ♘bd7 5 e3 ♗d6 6 ♘b5

Not one of Alekhine's happier ideas. Although it can claim to be original, it just loses time.

6 ... ♗e7 7 ♕c2 c6 8 ♘c3 0-0 9 ♗d3 dxc4 10 ♗xc4 c5! 11 dxc5

White's opening has not been a success and he can only claim to have a rather sterile equality. After 11 0-0 ♘b6 12 ♗d3 cxd4 13 exd4 ♗d7 White would have inadequate compensation for his isolated d-pawn.

11 ... ♗xc5 12 0-0 b6

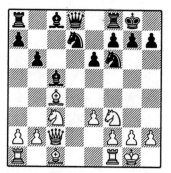

13 e4!?

Typical of Alekhine in that he tries to create complex problems despite his unsuccessful opening. 13 b3 was the safe move.

13 ... ♗b7 14 ♗g5

After 14 e5? there follows 14 ... ♘g4! 15 ♘g5 g6 16 ♘xe6 ♕h4 17 h3 ♕g3 followed by mate.

14 ... ♕c8! 15 ♕e2 ♗b4! 16 ♗d3

16 e5 is still poor because of 16 ... ♘g4 and 16 ♖ac1 would be met by 16 ... ♗xc3 17 ♗d3! ♘c5! 18 ♖xc3 ♗xe4! 19 ♗xf6 ♗xd3 with a clear advantage for Black. Watch how Alekhine now creates problems from a position which seems to offer him nothing.

16 ... ♗xc3 17 ♖fc1!

The saving resource, the point of which is that after 17 ... ♘c5 18 ♖xc3 ♗xe4 19 ♗xf6 ♗xd3 White can play 20 ♕e3! (the point of 17 ♖fc1 rather than 17 ♖ac1) 20 ... gxf6 21 b4 ♗g6 22 bxc5 bxc5 23 ♖xc5 After Black's queen moves there is 24 h4 with attacking chances for the pawn.

17 ... ♘xe4?

After this Black gets into difficulties due to the exposed position of his knight on c5.

18 ♗xe4 ♗xe4 19 ♕xe4 ♘c5 20 ♕e2! ♗a5 21 ♖ab1 ♕a6 22 ♖c4 ♘a4

An ingenious attempt to save the game, 23 b4?! would be met by 23 ... ♘c3. But Alekhine has prepared a devastating blow on the other side of the board.

23 ♗f6! ← Look for shots toward king

An unexpected and quite beautiful idea which commences a mating attack. The immediate threat is 24 ♖g4! ♕xe2 25 ♖xg7+ followed by mate next move.

23 ... ♖fc8! 24 ♕e5

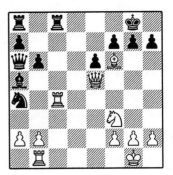

24 ... ♖c5

There is no longer any defence for Black. After 24 ... ♕xc4 there is 25 ♕g5 ♔f8 26 ♕xg7+ ♔e8 27 ♕g8+ ♔d7 28 ♘e5+ ♔c7 29 ♕xf7+-, 24 ... ♖xc4 is answered by 25 ♕g5 ♖g4 26 ♕xg4 g6 27 ♕xa4+- and 24 ... gxf6 25 ♖g4+ leads to mate in two.

25 ♕g3! g6 26 ♖xa4 ♕d3 27 ♖f1 ♖ac8 28 ♖d4 ♕f5 29 ♕f4 ♕c2 30 ♕h6 1:0

KM13/3: 1) White to play

KM13/3: 2) White to play

KM13/3: 3) Black to play

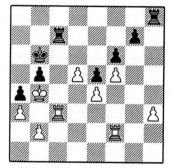

A13/3: 4) White to play

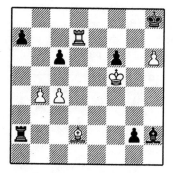

A13/3: a) White to play

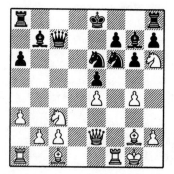

A13/3: b) White to play

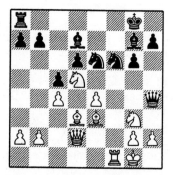

Month 13/Week 4:
The Tao Of Attack

"When you are concentrated into one while the opponent is divided into ten, you are attacking at a concentration of ten to one, so you outnumber the opponent. If you can strike few with many, you will thus minimise the number of those with whom you do battle.

"Your battleground is not to be known, for when it cannot be known, the enemy makes many guard outposts, and since multiple outposts are established, you only have to do battle with small squads. So when the front is prepared, the rear is lacking and when the rear is prepared the front is lacking. Preparedness on the left means lack on the right, preparedness on the right means lack on the left. Preparedness everywhere means lack everywhere." (Sun Tzu in *The Art Of War*)

Sun Tzu's book on military strategy, *The Art of War*, contains many useful insights for chess players. The passage above describes the concept of attacking the opponent where he is at his weakest.

Translating this into chess terms one of the most effective weapons of attack is to decoy defenders away from their king. The normal method of doing this is to set up pressure on one part of the board before suddenly switching the direction of the attack when the opponent's pieces are tied down.

This is one of the most advanced strategies of attack which very few players have mastered. The greatest exponent of this art was Alekhine who would crown masterly positional play on one side of the board with a sudden switch to the other flank.

Alekhine - Asztalos
Kecskemet 1927

1 ♘f3 d5 2 c4 e6 3 d4 ♘f6 4 ♗g5 h6 5 ♗xf6 ♕xf6 6 ♘c3 c6

These days this line is known as the 'Moscow Variation' and gives Black a solid position with a pair of bishops but a certain lack of mobility. It is fascinating to watch how Alekhine keeps Black's position under control whilst gradually preparing an attack.

7 ♕b3 ♘d7 8 e4 dxe4 9 ♘xe4 ♕f4 10 ♗d3 ♗e7 11 0-0 0-0 12 ♖fe1 ♖d8 13 ♖ad1 ♕c7 14 ♘g3 ♘f8 15 ♕c3!

The idea behind this is to play ♘h5 followed by d4-d5 Black parries this threat but only at the cost of queenside weaknesses.

15 ... a5 16 a3 a4 17 ♘e5 ♕a5 18 ♕c1 ♗d7 19 c5!

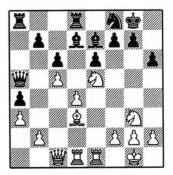

Intending to plant a knight on b6 which virtually forces Black's reply. But new problems now arise due to the weakness of the c6 pawn.

19 ... b5 20 ♗e4 ♕c7 21 ♕c3 ♗e8 22 ♘e2!

Beginning a new and deadly plan. The idea of bringing this knight to b4 forces Black to exchange off one of the pieces attacking c6 (the knight on e5) with ... ♘f8-d7. But this knight is needed to defend the kingside.

22 ... ♖a6 23 ♘c1 ♘d7 24 ♘xd7 ♖xd7 25 ♘d3 ♖d8 26 ♘e5 ♗f8 27 h4! ♖aa8 28 ♗b1 h5 29 ♕f3 g6 30 g4!

Finally Alekhine commences his attack, but just at the moment when Black is too passively placed to offer any real defence.

30 ... hxg4 31 ♕xg4 ♗g7 32 ♗a2! b4

If 32 ... ♕e7? there is an immediate win with 33 ♘xg6 fxg6 34 ♖xe6 etc.

33 ♗c4! bxa3 34 bxa3 ♕a5 35 ♕e4 ♕c7 36 ♕f4 ♖ab8 37 h5 gxh5 38 ♔h1 ♖b7 39 ♖g1 ♕e7 40 ♖xg7+! ♔xg7 41 ♖g1+ ♔h7 42 ♘xf7! 1:0

After 42 ... ♕xf7 there is 43 ♗d3+ ♕g6 44 ♗xg6+ ♗xg6 45 ♖xg6 ♔xg6 46 ♕e4+ ♔g7 47 ♕e5+! which would soon pick up one of Black's rooks.

Rather than having to actively decoy the opposing forces, similar effects can be obtained by simply having superior mobility. In his writings Sun Tzu expounded the benefits of superior mobility at some length:

"Appear where they cannot go, head for where they least expect you. To travel hundreds of miles without fatigue, go over land where there are no people. To unfailingly take what you attack, attack where there is no defence."

In the next game Alekhine takes on one of the great masters of defence, the Hungarian Grandmaster Geza Maroczy and launches a devastating attack simply because Maroczy' pieces lack enough mobility to counteract Alekhine's sudden kingside assault.

Alekhine - Maroczy
Bled 1931

1 d4 d5 2 ♘f3 ♘f6 3 c4 e6 4 ♗g5 ♘bd7 5 e3 h6 6 ♗h4 ♗e7 7 ♘c3 0-0 8 ♖c1 c6 9 ♗d3 a6 10 0-0 dxc4 11 ♗xc4

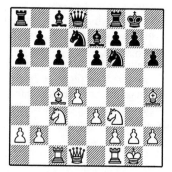

11 ... c5?!

Black should try to get his queen-side developed with 11 ... b5!? 12 ♗d3 c5 or 12 ... ♗b7 Alekhine's next move exploits this omission of 11 ... b5 and makes it difficult for Black to develop.

12 a4! ♕a5 13 ♕e2 cxd4! 14 exd4 ♘b6 15 ♗d3! ♗d7 16 ♘e5 ♖fd8 17 f4

With Black's pieces rather passively deployed on the queenside, White plays very sharply for an attack on the opposing king. Alekhine pointed out that White could also try 17 ♕f3!? in this position.

17 ... ♗e8 18 ♘g4 ♖xd4 19 ♗xf6 ♗xf6 20 ♘xf6+ gxf6 21 ♘e4

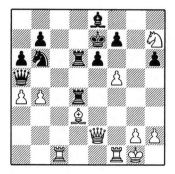

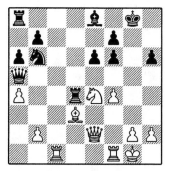

21 ... ♖ad8?

Black should have held onto the f-pawn with 21 ... f5!? 22 ♘f6+ ♔f8 though after 23 b3! White nevertheless has very dangerous attacking chances. Now his king gets driven into the middle of the board.

22 ♘xf6+ ♔f8 23 ♘h7+! ♔e7

Maroczy may have missed Alekhine's last move which has the point that 23 ... ♔g8? is answered by 24 ♕g4+ ♔h8 25 ♕h4 ♖xd3 26 ♕xh6 etc.

24 f5! ♖8d6 25 b4!

Typical Alekhine, the attack is crowned with a blow on another part of the board. The point of this move is that White's queen will penetrate the opposing position via e5 in the game or h5 after 25 ... ♖xb4. Alekhine gave the line 25 ... ♖xb4 26 ♕h5! e5! 27 f6+ ♔d8 28 ♕xh6 ♖xd3 29 ♕f8 ♖d7 30 ♖c5 ♕xa4 31 ♖xe5+-

25 ... ♕xb4 26 ♕e5! ♘d7 27 ♕h8! ♖xd3

If 27 ... ♕b6 there is 28 a5!+- or if 27 ... ♕a5 then 28 ♖c8+-.

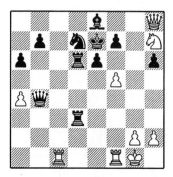

28 f6+! 1:0

Black is mated after either 28 ... ♘xf6 29 ♕xf6+ ♔d7 30 ♘f8# or 28 ... ♔d8 29 ♕xe8+! ♔xe8 30 ♖c8#.

KM13/4: 1) White to play

KM13/4: 2) White to play

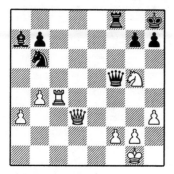

KM13/4: 3) Black to play

KM13/4: 4) White to play

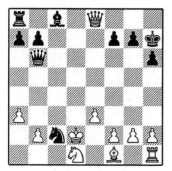

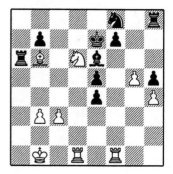

A13/4: a) Black to play

A13/4: b) White to play

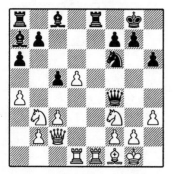

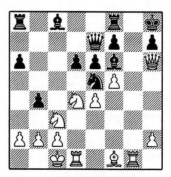

2 The Initiative

The initiative in chess roughly equates to possession of the ball in soccer. The player who holds the initiative is able to make threats and force his opponent onto the defensive. This may prove to be a temporary effect which dissipates after a few accurate defensive moves or it may be the prelude to a genuine attack. To use a hackneyed old proverb, it all depends on the position.

In week one of this month's material we will look at positions in which one of the players takes the initiative with decisive effect. In week two we will look the concept of gambit play in which possession of the initiative is paid for with material.

In week three we will see a fierce struggle for the initiative in which both sides eschew defence in favour of pursuing their own threats. Week four features the generation of another type of initiative which is more a case of supercharging the potential of your pieces rather than achieving any kind of direct attack.

Month 14/Week 1:
Taking The Initiative

The Israeli Grandmaster Valery Beim once described our colleague, Leonid Gofstein, as an 'initiative player' and he felt that it was important to deprive Gofstein of the initiative even if it meant taking certain positional risks: "When he gets even the smallest initiative he starts to feel himself very good."

There are a number of players like this who simply love to force the pace and the names of attacking players such as Tal, Alekhine, Kasparov come to mind as well as those of lesser lights such as Gofstein, Kupreichik and Denker.

The greatest of them all was, in my opinion, Alexander Alekhine. His games involve a restless striving for the initiative with either colour and to this end he was prepared to take great risks.

Here are two masterpieces in which Alekhine took the initiative in the early middle-game and never let it go.

Alekhine - Euwe
Amsterdam WCh 1935

1 d4 d5 2 c4 c6 3 ♘f3 ♘f6 4 ♘c3 dxc4 5 a4 ♗f5 6 ♘e5 ♘bd7 7 ♘xc4 ♕c7 8 g3 e5 9 dxe5 ♘xe5 10 ♗f4 ♘fd7 11 ♗g2 ♗e6 12 ♘xe5 ♘xe5 13 0-0 ♗e7

In view of what happens it looks sensible to firmly defend the knight on e5 with 13 ... f6.

14 ♕c2 ♖d8 15 ♖fd1 0-0 16 ♘b5 ♖xd1+ 17 ♖xd1 ♕a5 18 ♘d4 ♗c8

The position seems quiet enough but now Alekhine takes the

initiative and keeps it. His next move sets about undermining Black's important pawn on c6 whilst gaining time on the queen.

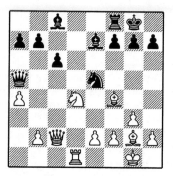

19 b4! ♕c7

After 19 ... ♗xb4? White wins with 20 ♘b3 ♕c7 21 ♕e4 ♗c3 (21 ... ♗d6 22 ♕d4) 22 ♖c1 ♗b2 23 ♖c2 f5 24 ♕b4. So Black is forced to retreat.

20 b5 c5 21 ♘f5 f6?

It is quite understandable that Black wants to defend his knight on e5 securely but now White's advantage assumes decisive proportions. 21 ... ♗f6 was relatively best though still unpleasant after 22 ♘d6 ♖d8 23 ♘c4.

22 ♘e3 ♗e6 23 ♗d5! ♗xd5 24 ♖xd5 ♕a5

After 24 ... ♖d8 there is 25 ♗xe5 fxe5 26 ♕f5+-.

25 ♘f5 ♕e1+ 26 ♔g2 ♗d8 27 ♗xe5 fxe5 28 ♖d7 ♗f6 29 ♘h6+! ♔h8 30 ♕xc5 1:0

If 30 ... ♖e8 there is 31 ♕d5 gxh6 32 ♕f7 ♗e7 33 ♖xe7 etc.

Aaron Nimzowitsch wrote a lot about restricting his opponent's possibilities and the concept of zugzwang. It must have been embarrassing for him to find his own

weapons used against him as they were in the following encounter.

Alekhine - Nimzowitsch
San Remo 1930

1 e4 e6 2 d4 d5 3 ♘c3 ♗b4 4 e5 c5 5 ♗d2 ♘e7 6 ♘b5 ♗xd2+ 7 ♕xd2 0-0 8 c3 b6?!

Rather than his somewhat passive move Black should probably prefer 8 ... ♘f5. Now White takes a lot of space without having to worry about being counter-punched.

9 f4 ♗a6 10 ♘f3 ♕d7 11 a4 ♘bc6 12 b4! cxb4 13 cxb4 ♗b7 14 ♘d6 f5?

Nimzowitsch might have felt that a blocked position would not suit the ferocious Alekhine but now White takes the initiative. He should have stopped the advance of White's a-pawn with 14 ... a5!? after which Alekhine wrote that he would have preferred 15 ♗b5 axb5 16 0-0 to 15 b5 ♘b4.

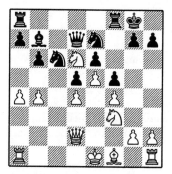

15 a5! ♘c8

And not 15 ... bxa5? because of 16 b5! when Black's pieces would find themselves in an even more parlous state. Black hurries to exchange off White's monstrous knight on d6 but finds himself under tremendous pressure on the c-file.

16 ♘xb7 ♕xb7 17 a6

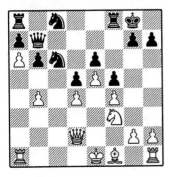

17 ... ♕f7

If 17 ... ♕e7 there is 18 ♗b5! ♘xb4? 19 ♖b1, trapping the knight. In the game continuation Black is unable to defend both the c6 and c7 squares in the long run.

18 ♗b5 ♘8e7 19 0-0 h6 20 ♖fc1 ♖fc8 21 ♖c2 ♕e8

If Black tried to exchange rooks on the c-file with 21 ... ♘d8 there would follow 22 ♖ac1 ♖xc2 23 ♖xc2 ♖c8 24 ♖xc8 ♘xc8 25 ♕c3 followed by ♕c7.

22 ♖ac1

White could have trebled major pieces on the c-file more effectively by starting this process with 22 ♖a3. In any case Black cannot defend against this plan in the long run.

22 ... ♖ab8 23 ♕e3 ♖c7 24 ♖c3! ♕d7

With the desperate idea of making room for the king on d8 so that it can protect the rook on c7. Unfortunately for Black even this cannot save him.

25 ♖1c2 ♔f8 26 ♕c1 ♖bc8

Has Black managed to defend himself? White's next move provides the answer.

27 ♗a4!

The threat of 28 b5 forces Black to give up a pawn in order to gain time to defend the rook on c7. But then he finds himself in zugzwang!

27 ... b5 28 ♗xb5 ♔e8 29 ♗a4 ♔d8 30 h4! h5 31 ♔h2 g6 32 g3 1:0

Black can play a couple of irrelevant moves but will then be forced to play ... ♕e8. After that b4-b5 will win a piece because the rook on c7 is unguarded.

KM14/1: 1) White to play

KM14/1: 2) Black to play

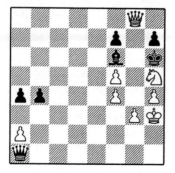

KM14/1: 3) Black to play

KM14/1: 4) Black to play

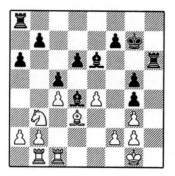

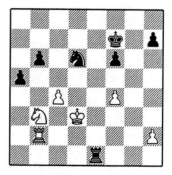

A14/1: a) White to play

A14/1: b) White to play

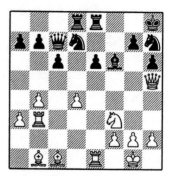

Month 14/Week 2:
Gambit Play

It is of course unlikely that anyone will give you the initiative on a plate and usually you have to fight for it. There is also the option of paying for the initiative by sacrificing some material though in this case you need to judge that your compensation will be adequate.

Sacrificing material for the initiative in the opening is called a gambit, the best-known examples of gambit being the King's, Queen's or Evans Gambits. It is also worth noting that there are often gambit opportunities in many other openings which have no official name but offer the means of taking the initiative. Such lines are stock-in-trade for many masters of the attack.

As I noted in the previous section Alexander Alekhine eagerly sought the initiative with either colour and to this end would occasionally try out daring gambit lines. In the following game he plays a gambit of dubious merit but the suprise effect turns out to be devastating.

Pirc - Alekhine
Bled 1931

1 d4 d5 2 c4 e6 3 ♘c3 c5 4 cxd5 cxd4!?

The Schara-Hennig Gambit which aims at fast development. The following queen manoevre leads to the same position as 5 ♕xd4 ♘c6 6 ♕d1 exd5 7 ♕xd5 ♗d7.

5 ♕a4+ ♗d7 6 ♕xd4 exd5 7 ♕xd5 ♘c6 8 ♗g5

The accepted means of meeting this line is with 8 ♘f3 ♘f6 9 ♕d1 ♗c5 10 e3 ♕e7 11 ♗e2 0-0-0 12

0-0 g5 13 b4!?, returning the pawn in order to open lines against Black's king. Yet some players are still quite happy to play Black.

8 ... ♘f6 9 ♕d2 h6 10 ♗xf6 ♕xf6 11 e3 0-0-0 12 0-0-0?

White's king is very insecurely placed on the queenside and Black quickly develops a decisive initiative. White should try Kotov's recommendation of 12 ♘d5! ♕g6 13 ♘e2 intending ♘e2-f4, and ♕c3.

12 ... ♗g4 13 ♘d5

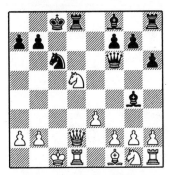

13 ... ♖xd5! 14 ♕xd5 ♗a3!

The brilliant point of Alekhine's exchange sacrifice which piles up the pressure. Recovering the exchange with 14 ... ♗xd1 15 ♕xd1 would be far less effective after 15 ... ♕xf2 16 ♕g4+ f5 17 ♕e2.

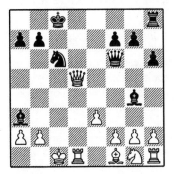

15 ♕b3!

The best try. After 15 bxa3 Black wins with 15 ... ♕c3+ 16 ♔b1 ♖d8-+ and 15 ♖d2 is met by 15 ... ♗xb2+ 16 ♖xb2 ♕c3+ 17 ♔b1 ♕e1+ 18 ♔c2 ♖d8-+.

15 ... ♗xd1 16 ♕xa3 ♕xf2 17 ♕d3

17 ... ♗g4!
And not the immediate 17 ... ♖d8? because of 18 ♘h3 ♕f6 19 ♕c3.

18 ♘f3 ♗xf3
Once again timing is everything. After 18 ... ♖d8?! White has 19 ♕e2.

19 ♕f5+ ♔b8 20 ♕xf3 ♕e1+ 21 ♔c2
Or if 21 ♕d1 there follows 21 ... ♕xe3+ 22 ♕d2 ♕e6 23 ♕f4+-+.

21 ... ♖c8 22 ♕g3+ ♘e5+ 23 ♔b3 ♕d1+ 24 ♔a3 ♖c5 0:1

Amongst the series of Soviet World Champions who followed Alekhine none of them were to incorporate traditional gambits in their opening repertoires, not even the brilliant Mikhail Tal. It was only Bobby Fischer who followed Alekhine's example by reviving the Evans and Bishops Gambits and more recently Kasparov has shown an appreciation of the benefits of such openings. He recently brought back the Evans Gambit to the surprise of some of his world class opponents:

**Kasparov - Anand
Riga 1995**

1 e4 e5 2 ♘f3 ♘c6 3 ♗c4 ♗c5 4 b4!
This move distinguishes the Evans which for years has been the Cinderella of chess openings. White takes the initiative on move four at the cost of a pawn.

4 ... ♗xb4 5 c3 ♗e7 6 d4 ♘a5

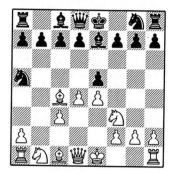

7 ♗e2!
In conjunction with his next move this constituted a new idea at the time of the game.

In an earlier quickplay game against Nigel Short, Kasparov tried 7 ♘xe5 though this probably doesn't trouble Black too much after 7 ... .♘xc4 8 ♘xc4 d5 9 exd5 ♕xd5 10 ♘e3 ♕d8. It is difficult to believe that 7 ♗xf7+ ♔xf7 8 ♘xe5+ ♔f8 will give White enough for his piece.

After 7 ♗e2 Black's safest option may well be the solid 7 ... d6 after which 8 ♕a4+ c6 9 dxe5 dxe5 10 ♘xe5 ♘f6 11 0-0 leaves Black with a choice between 11 ... ♕c7 and 11 ... b5!?.

7 ... exd4? 8 ♕xd4! ♘f6 9 e5 ♘c6

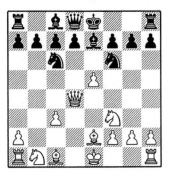

10 ♕h4!

Another improvement on theory from Kasparov's arsenal of ideas, this time improving on a game Melts-Gajewski, USSR 1981 in which 10 ♕f4 ♘h5 11 ♕a4 g6 was played.

10 ... ♘d5 11 ♕g3! g6 12 0-0 ♘b6 13 c4

In addition to this move White might try an immediate 13 ♗h6!?, preventing Black from castling kingside. If Black then challenges the e5 pawn with 13 ... d6 then 14 ♗b5 will make it difficult for Black's king to find shelter.

13 ... d6 14 ♖d1 ♘d7

Another possibility is 14 ... ♗d7 when once again White can prevent Black from castling kingside with 15 ♗h6!?. White could now try 15 ♗f4 with the idea of meeting 15 ... 0-0 with 16 exd6 ♗f6 17 ♗g5! but Black can play the irritating 15 ... dxe5 16 ♘xe5 ♗h4! when 17 ♕e3 can be met by 17 ... ♘cxe5 18 ♗xe5 0-0.

15 ♗h6!? ♘cxe5 16 ♘xe5 ♘xe5 17 ♘c3 f6 18 c5!

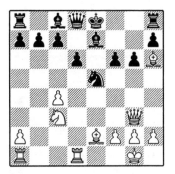

Kasparov continues to pursue his initiative with great energy and in his notes did not comment on Black's next move. Yet according to GM Ian Rogers Black can play 18 ... ♗d7 and emerge unscathed. If this is true it might be worth considering different methods of playing the attack, Kasparov mentioned 17 c5!? without further comment.

18 ... ♘f7(?) 19 cxd6 cxd6 20 ♕e3 ♘xh6 21 ♕xh6 ♗f8 22 ♕e3+ ♔f7 23 ♘d5

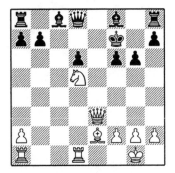

23 ... ♗e6?!

The last chance to stay alive was with 23 ... ♗d7 but then Kasparov gives both 24 ♗c4+ ♔g7 25 ♖d4 and 24 ♖ac1 ♗c6 25 ♗c4+ as being clearly better for White.

24 ♘f4 ♕e7 25 ♖e1 1:0

After 25 ... ♗h6 there is 26 ♗c4+ or 25 ... d5 then 26 ♗f3+-.

KM14/2: 1) White to play

KM14/2: 2) Black to play

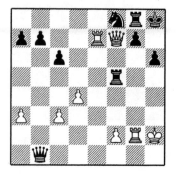

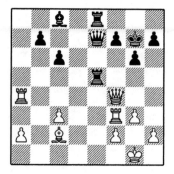

KM14/2: 3) Black to play

KM14/2: 4) White to play

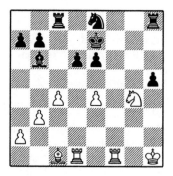

A14/2: a) Black to play

A14/2: b) White to play

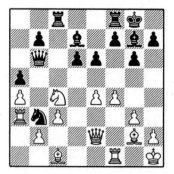

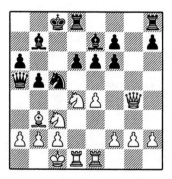

Month 14/Week 3:
Diamond Cut Diamond

So far we have looked at examples in which the initiative is the exclusive property of only one of the players whether or not he has to offer material for it. Yet such cases are not really the norm in the modern game, todays players tend to dislike purely defensive roles and will try to counterattack.

In order to obtain a position with counterplay your choice of opening can be quite important. Modern Grandmasters rarely choose the most orthodox forms of the Queen's Gambit Declined not because of any intrinsic defect with this defence but rather because Black is striving only to equalize. More aggressive lines such as the King's Indian, Nimzo-Indian and Gruenfeld are far more frequently played.

The most challenging opening of all may well be the Sicilian Defence which accounts for its massive popularity. The following two games show why.

The first features one of the great pioneers of the Sicilian, Mark Taimanov, use it with success in a critical Soviet Championship game. The second is the game in which Garry Kasparov won the World title from Karpov and persuaded him to switch to the move 1 d4.

Lutikov - Taimanov
USSR Championship,
Moscow 1969

1 e4 c5 2 ♘f3 ♘c6 3 d4 cxd4 4 ♘xd4 e6 5 ♘c3 ♕c7 6 ♗e3 a6 7 ♗d3 b5 8 ♘xc6 ♕xc6 9 ♗d4 ♗b7

10 ♕e2 ♘e7 11 f4 b4 12 ♘b1 ♘g6 13 ♕f2 ♗d6!

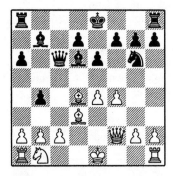

Immediately giving White problems with his f4 pawn—after 14 e5 there follows 14 ... ♗e7 15 0-0 ♘h4 with tremendous pressure on the long diagonal whilst 14 ♗xg7 is met by 14 ... ♘xf4 15 ♗xh8 ♘xd3+ 16 cxd3 ♕c1+ 17 ♔e2 ♕xh1.

14 ♗e3 0-0 15 ♘d2 ♖ac8 16 h4!?
The struggle for the initiative is in full swing, White playing for the attack in spite of the strong pressure on his game.

16 ... ♕c7! 17 e5 ♗c5 18 h5 ♗xe3 19 ♕xe3 ♘e7 20 ♘c4
20 ♘e4 ♘f5 21 ♕f2 d6 22 exd6 ♘xd6 23 ♘xd6 ♕xd6 24 0-0-0 ♕c5 would leave Black with an excellent game. White has no attack and his position has been seriously weakened.

20 ... ♘f5 21 ♕d2
After 21 ♗xf5 Black could choose between the solid 21 ... ♕xc4 22 ♗d3 ♕d5 and the more adventurous 21 ... exf5!? 22 ♘d6 ♕xc2 23 ♘xc8 ♖xc8.

21 ... ♗d5 22 ♘e3 ♘xe3 23 ♕xe3 ♕c5 24 ♕g3
After 24 ♕xc5 ♖xc5 the endgame would favour Black. Rather than

surrender the initiative in such a way, Lutikov plays for the attack.

24 ... h6 25 ♖h4!? ♕g1+?

Throughout his career Taimanov was prone to impetuous decisions and here he gives a thoughtless check. 25 ... ♔h8 26 ♖g4 ♖g8 was stronger when White's is unable to strengthen his attack.

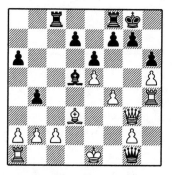

26 ♔d2?!

After 26 ♔e2 Black would have to play 26 ... ♖xc2+ 27 ♗xc2 ♗c4+ 28 ♔d2 (28 ♔f3? ♕xa1 29 ♖g4 ♕f1+ 30 ♔e3 ♕e2+ 31 ♔d4 ♕xc2-+) 28 ... ♕d4+ 29 ♔c1 ♕g1+ with a draw by perpetual check and not 26 ... ♕d4? 27 f5 ♕xb2 28 f6 ♖xc2+ 29 ♗xc2 ♕xc2+ 30 ♔f1.

26 ... ♕d4

Retracing his steps. White's attack breaks through after either 26 ... ♕xg2+? 27.♕xg2 ♗xg2 28.♖g1 ♗d5 29 ♖hg4 or 26 ... ♕xa1? 27.♖g4 whereas now Black can meet 27 ♖g4? with 27 ... ♗e4 28 ♖xg7+ ♔h8.

27 f5!

Lutikov continues to play with gusto and the game now approaches its climax. With his queen attacked and 28 f6 threatened, Black has only one saving clause.

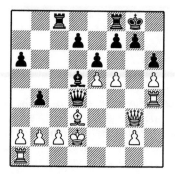

27 ... ♖xc2+!! 28 ♔xc2 b3+ 29 ♔d1

After 29 axb3 ♗xb3+ Lutikov probably assumed that 30 ♔xb3 was forced whereupon Black's attack continues with 30 ... ♖b8+. What he must have missed was that 30 ♔d2 ♕xb2+ 31 ♔e3 was possible when the outcome still isn't clear. After 29 ♔d1 White's pieces lack coordination.

29 ... ♕g1+ 30 ♕e1 ♕xg2!

White's pieces are so poorly placed that Black can afford the luxury of quiet play with one rook less.

31 ♕f1 ♗f3+ 32 ♔e1 ♕xb2! 33 ♖b1 ♕xe5+ 34 ♔f2 bxa2 35 ♖e1 ♕f6 36 ♔g3 ♗g2!

A study-like idea. If 37 ♕xg2 there follows 37 ... a1=♕ or if 37 ♔xg2 then 37 ... ♕xh4.

37 ♕g1 exf5 38 ♕d4 ♕g5+ 39 ♔h2 ♗e4 40 ♖hxe4 fxe4 41 ♕xe4 ♕xh5+ 0:1

**Karpov - Kasparov
Moscow WCh 1985**

1 e4 c5 2 ♘f3 d6 3 d4 cxd4 4 ♘xd4 ♘f6 5 ♘c3 a6 6 ♗e2 e6 7 0-0 ♗e7 8 f4 0-0 9 ♔h1 ♕c7 10 a4 ♘c6 11 ♗e3 ♖e8

This is all rather well-known theory which featured in the later match between Anand and Kasparov.

12 ♗f3 ♖b8 13 ♕d2 ♗d7 14 ♘b3 b6 15 g4

The battle-lines are now clearly drawn, White is aiming for a kingside attack and first wants to drive Black's knight from f6, Black meanwhile must regroup his pieces in preparation for queenside or central counter-play. This is the kind of position in which you *must* play actively.

15 ... ♗c8 16 g5 ♘d7 17 ♕f2 ♗f8 18 ♗g2 ♗b7 19 ♖ad1 g6 20 ♗c1 ♖bc8

Kasparov later recommended the immediate 20 ... ♘c5! as being more precise.

21 ♖d3 ♘b4 22 ♖h3 ♗g7

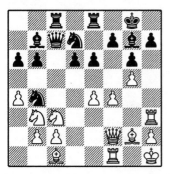

A critical position which was subjected to serious analytical scrutiny after the match. Without going into too much detail it emerged that 23 f5 would subject Black to serious pressure, Kasparov's intention of 23 ... exf5 24 exf5 ♘e5 being strongly met by 26 ♖f4! ♗xg2+ 27 ♔xg2 ♕c6+ 28 ♔g1 gxf5 29 ♘d4 ♕c5 30 ♗e3 rather than the precipitous 26 ♕xh7+ ♔f8 27 ♘d2 ♗xg2+ 28 ♔xg2 ♕c6+ 29 ♘f3 gxf5 30 ♕xf5 ♘d5 31 ♔g1 ♘xc3 32 bxc3 ♕c5+

33 ♖f2 ♖c7 when Black has counterplay. Yet in his notes to the game Karpov held that his move is also good.

23 ♗e3 ♖e7! 24 ♔g1 ♖ce8 25 ♖d1 f5 26 gxf6 ♘xf6 27 ♖g3

According to Karpov White should play 27 ♗xb6 ♕b8 28 a5! ♖f7 29 ♕d2 ♘h5 30 ♘e2 followed by 31 c3 with a very unpleasant position for Black.

27 ... ♖f7 28 ♗xb6 ♕b8 29 ♗e3 ♘h5 30 ♖g4 ♘f6 31 ♖h4

And here 31 ♖g3 ♘h5 would lead to a draw by repetition. However Karpov rejected this because he had to win.

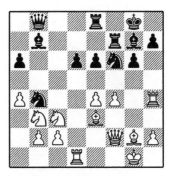

31 ... g5! 32 fxg5 ♘g4!

After 32 ... ♘xe4 White can sacrifice his queen with 33 ♕xf7+ ♔xf7 34 ♘xe4 and obtain a dangerous attack.

33 ♕d2 ♘xe3 34 ♕xe3 ♘xc2 35 ♕b6 ♗a8 36 ♖xd6?

36 ♕xb8 ♖xb8 37 ♗h3! (Agzamov) was still quite playable for White but Karpov burns his bridges in a final attempt to win.

36 ... ♖b7 37 ♕xa6 ♖xb3 38 ♖xe6 ♖xb2 39 ♕c4 ♘h8 40 e5 ♕a7+ 41 ♔h1 ♗xg2+ 42 ♔xg2 ♘d4+ 0:1

KM14/3: 1) White to play

KM14/3: 2) Black to play

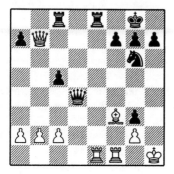

KM14/3: 3) White to play

KM14/3: 4) Black to play

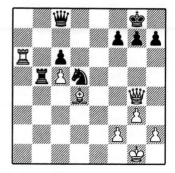

KM14/3: a) White to play

A14/3: b) Black to play

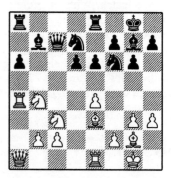

Month 14/Week 4:
Charging the Currents

In this last section I will attempt to deal with a rather less tangible form of the initiative in which a player 'charges the currents' of a position rather than sets up direct threats. When the sacrifice of material is involved this is especially difficult to judge and very few players have really mastered this most difficult aspect of the game.

I think that the greatest exponent of this art was Leonid Stein who would frequently give up light material such as pawns or rook for bishop without any clearly visible return. Yet after a few moves it would become apparent that an initiative was starting to develop and ultimately this would be transformed into an attack.

Korchnoi - Stein
USSR Ch, Tallinn 1965

1 d4 ♘f6 2 c4 g6 3 ♘c3 ♗g7 4 e4 d6 5 f3 0-0 6 ♗e3 e5 7 d5 ♘h5 8 ♕d2 f5 9 0-0-0 ♘d7 10 ♗d3

10 ... fxe4!?

Had it not been made by a great master such as Stein, this move would be condemned as a mistake because it gives White the e4 square as a base of operations. Yet Stein sees it as the start of a process of undermining White's pawn structure.

11 ♘xe4 ♘f4 12 ♗c2 ♘f6

In a later game against Hort, Stein varied at this point with 12 ... ♘b6 13 b3 a5 14 g3 ♘h5 15 g4 ♘f4 16 ♘e2 a4 17 ♘2c3 ♗d7 18 ♔b2 and should now have played 18 ... ♕b8! rather than 18 ... ♘c8. This would lend weight to the idea that his play in the present game was not entirely reliable.

13 ♘c3

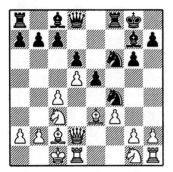

13 ... b5!?

A brilliantly imaginative pawn sacrifice for which there seems to be very little return. A more normal way to prepare ... b7-b5 would be with 13 ... a6.

14 ♘xb5

After 14 cxb5 Black would gain a strong initiative with 14 ... a6, but it is difficult to see much compensation for Black after 14 g3 ♘4h5 15 ♘xb5 ♗a6 16 ♘e2.

14 ... ♗a6 15 ♘a3

Apparently quite solid but this is not an attractive square for the

knight. At this point 15 g3 is a move
too late, Black can play 15 ...
♘4xd5 because the knight on b5 is
hanging.
   **15 ... ♖b8 16 g3 ♘4h5 17 b3
♗b7!**
Clearly announcing his intention
to undermine the d5 pawn with 18
... c6!. By now it is becoming clear
that Black has compensation for his
pawn but this has been a distinctly
gradual process.
   18 ♘b1 c6!

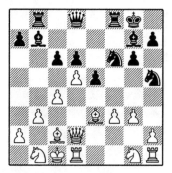

19 dxc6 ♗xc6 20 ♕xd6
White goes a second pawn up but
there are serious weaknesses around
his king. Black also has pressure on
both of the long diagonals.
   **20 ... ♕e8 21 ♖e1 ♖f7 22 ♗d2
♗f8 23 ♕d3**
Snatching another pawn would be
too much, 23 ♕xe5 ♖e7 24 ♕c3
♖xe1+ 25 ♗xe1 ♗b4 26 ♕xb4
♖xb4 27 ♗xb4 ♘g4 28 fxg4 ♗xh1
29 gxh5 ♕e3+ picks up the knight
on g1 as well.
   23 ... e4 24 ♕c3
Stubbornly refusing to give back
any booty. 24 fxe4 ♘g4 25 ♘f3
♘f2 26 ♕e2 ♘xh1 27 ♖xh1 was
White's best practical chance.
   24 ... ♗g7! 25 ♘h3

25 **♕a5 ♖e7!** would quietly
increase the pressure.

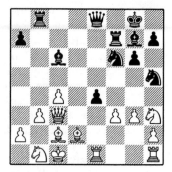

25 ... ♘g4! 26 fxg4
White finally admits that he must
return some material and gives up
his queen in order to try and stem
the tide of Black's attack. After 26
♕a5 there would follow 26 ... ♖xf3
27 ♘g5 (Or 27 ♕xa7 e3 28 ♗c3
♖f7) 27 ... ♖f5 28 ♕xa7 ♖xg5 29
♗xg5 ♕e5 30 ♗d2 ♕b2+ 31 ♔d1
♖a8 32 ♕b6 ♖xa2 etc.
   **26 ... ♗xc3 27 ♘xc3 ♘f6 28 g5
♘d7 29 ♘xe4 ♕f8 30 ♗c3 ♖f3 31
♗b2 ♖e8 32 ♔b1**
If 32 ♘f6+ there is 32 ... ♘xf6 33
gxf6 ♖xf6 34 ♗xf6 ♗xh1 etc.
   **32 ... ♗xe4 33 ♗xe4 ♖xe4 34
♖xe4 ♖f1+ 35 ♖e1 ♕f5+ 36 ♔a1
♖xh1 37 ♖xh1 ♕xh3 38 ♗d4 ♕g2
39 ♖g1 ♕d2 40 ♗xa7 ♘e5 41 ♗c5
♘d3 42 ♗a3 ♘b4 43 ♗xb4 ♕d4+
44 ♔b1 ♕xg1+ 0:1**

I found this and other Stein games
truly inspiring, there was something
in this form of sacrifice that went
beyond the conventional idea of
compensation. In my own games I
have tried to emulate such play, as
for example in the following
encounter.

Davies - Manor
Israeli League 1995

**1 ♘f3 ♘f6 2 g3 b5 3 ♗g2 ♗b7 4
0-0 e6 5 d3 d5 6 ♘bd2 ♘bd7?!**
After White plays e2-e4-e5
Black's other knight will need this
square. Black probably thought that
my next move would lose a pawn.
7 e4! c5
It turns out that 7 ... dxe4 8 dxe4
♘xe4 9 ♘g5 ♕xg5 10 ♘xe4 ♕d8
11 ♘f6+ gxf6 12 ♗xb7 ♖b8 13
♗c6 ♗d6 14 ♗e3 recovers the
pawn at the very least.
8 ♖e1 dxe4
Rather than have his king's knight
shut out of play after 8 ... ♗e7 9 e5
♘g4 10 h3 ♘h6 11 g4 Black tries to
lend the position some original
touches. But the text has the drawback that after White plays e4-e5 his
knight will be able to use the excellent e4 square.
**9 dxe4 c4 10 e5 ♘d5 11 a4 a6 12
♘e4 ♘c5**

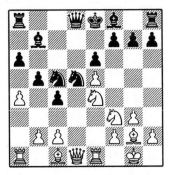

13 ♘fg5! h6
After 13 ... ♗e7 there is 14 ♘xc5
♗xc5 15 ♘e4 ♗e7 16 ♕g4 when
Black cannot castle because of 17
♗h6. After 13 ... ♘xa4 I intended
14 ♕h5! g6 (Or 14 ... ♕d7 15 ♘xh7
0-0-0 16 ♘xf8) 15 ♕f3 ♕d7 16
♘f6+ ♘xf6 17 ♕xb7! (17 ♕xf6

♖g8 18 ♗xb7 ♕xb7 19 ♘xe6 ♗e7
20 ♘g7+ ♔f8 21 ♘e6+=) 17 ...
♕xb7 18 ♗xb7 ♖a7 19 ♗xa6 ♖xa6
20 exf6 with a clear advantage in
the endgame.
**14 ♘xc5 ♗xc5 15 ♘e4 ♗e7 16
♕g4 ♔f8 17 axb5 axb5 18 ♗d2 g6
19 ♘d6!**
Another pawn sacrifice which this
time Black accepts rather than try to
live with the knight on d6.
**19 ... ♖xa1 20 ♖xa1 ♗xd6 21
exd6 ♕xd6 22 ♕d4! e5 23 ♗b4!!**

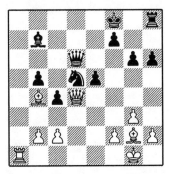

Certainly one of the nastiest
moves I have played, with the queen
already hanging White puts a bishop
en prise as well! Taking the queen is
bad for Black because of (23 ...
exd4) 24 ♗xd6+ ♔e8 (Or 24 ...
♔g7 25 ♗e5+ f6 26 ♖a7 fxe5 27
♖xb7+-) 25 ♖a7 ♔d7 26 ♗e5 ♖e8
27 ♖xb7+- so he goes for the bishop
instead.
23 ... ♕xb4 24 ♕xe5 ♔g8
Or 24 ... f6 25 ♕b8+-.
25 ♖a7!
The point of White's combination. After 25 ... ♗c6 there follows
26 ♗xd5 ♗xd5 27 ♕xd5 ♕e1+ (Or
27 ... ♕f8 28 ♕xb5 etc) 28 ♔g2
♕e6 29 ♕xe6 fxe6 30 ♔f3+-.
**25 ... ♘e3 26 ♕xe3 ♗xg2 27
♔xg2 ♕d6 28 ♕e8+ ♕f8 29 ♕xb5
c3 30 bxc3 h5 31 h4 ♔g7 32 ♕e5+
♔h7 33 ♕f6 1:0**

KM14/4: 1) White to play

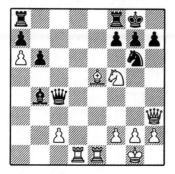

KM14/4: 2) White to play

KM14/4: 3) White to play

KM14/4: 4) White to play

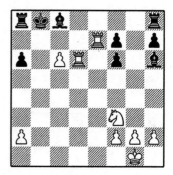

A14/4: a) White to play

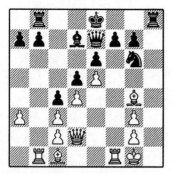

A14/4: b) Black to play

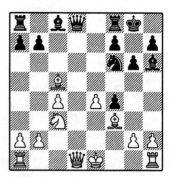

3 The Art of Defence

Good defensive play requires all round chess ability, from calculating ability to positional judgement, imagination and a cool nerve. Whilst chess literature has lavished attention on the art of attack, relatively little has been written about defence. Yet good defensive play has been one of the outstanding hallmarks of every World Champion since Steinitz.

This month we will look at various aspects of defence. In week one we will examine the simple method of exchanging off pieces whilst in week two we will see how it is possible to neutralise threats before they arise with the art of prophylaxis. In week three we shall look at the concept of blockade of which Tigran Petrosian was the greatest master. Week four is devoted to what may be the most effective defensive strategy of all, taking the initiative away from the opponent with a timely counterattack.

Month 15/Week 1: Arms Reduction

One of the most simple and effective methods of defence is simply reduce the number of arms. I do not advocate indiscriminate exchanges in which pieces are exchanged just for the sake of it and in fact this can lead to disaster. But to exchange off the most dangerous opposing pieces for those which are relatively poorly placed can lead to a general improvement in your position and neutralise any danger.

Such a strategy is commonly used when one player gives up a pawn for piece activity. If his active pieces can be exchanged off he will be left with little or nothing for the pawn as, for example, in the following encounter:

Boleslavsky - Kotov
Zurich Ct 1953

1 d4 d5 2 c4 dxc4 3 ♘f3 ♘f6 4 e3 e6 5 ♗xc4 c5 6 0-0 a6 7 ♕e2 cxd4 8 exd4 ♗e7 9 ♘c3 b5 10 ♗b3 ♗b7 11 ♗g5 0-0 13 ♖ad1

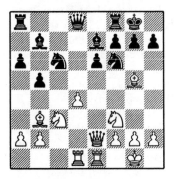

13 ... ♘a5
Bronstein commented in his notes that everyone thought that this was a mistake as it allows White a breakthrough in the centre. Yet perhaps

Kotov saw that 13 ... ♘b4 is answered strongly by 14 d5! ♘bxd5? 15 ♘xd5 ♗xd5 16 ♗xd5 ♘xd5 17 ♗xe7 ♕xe7 18 ♖xd5 whilst after the text move he could give up a pawn and obtain compensation.

14 d5! ♘xb3 15 dxe6 ♕b6 16 axb3 fxe6 17 ♘d4! ♗d6 18 ♕xe6+ ♔h8 19 ♘f3 ♖ad8

It looks as if Black has excellent compensation for the lost pawn in the form of open lines, a menacing bishop pair and weakened White queenside pawns. But Boleslavsky neutralises the danger by initiating a series of exchanges.

20 ♗f4! ♗xf3 21 ♖xd6 ♖xd6 22 ♕xd6 ♕xd6 23 ♗xd6 ♖e8 24 ♖xe8+ ♘xe8 25 ♗e5!

An excellent move which pins Black's knight to the back rank. Without this possibility the opposite coloured bishops would give Black excellent drawing chances.

25 ... ♗c6 26 b4! h5 27 f3 ♔h7 28 ♘e2 g5 29 ♔f2 h4 30 g3 hxg3+ 31 hxg3 ♔g6 32 g4! ♗b7

Or if 32 ... ♘f6 there is 33 ♗xf6 ♔xf6 34 ♔e3 ♔e5 35 ♘c3+-.

33 ♔e3 ♗c6 34 ♘c3 ♗b7 35 ♘e4 ♗d5 36 ♘c5 ♔f7 37 ♘xa6 ♔e6 38 ♗c3 ♗a8 39 ♘c5+ ♔f7 40

♘e4 ♔g6 41 ♗e5 ♗d5 42 ♘d2 ♔f7 1:0

In a way this was a rather straightforward example, the next one is far more complex. After getting a poor position from the opening we see Bent Larsen fight for his life against Boris Spassky, who at the time of the game was the reigning World Champion. On move 13 we see a brilliant offer of an exchange sacrifice which forces the exchange of queens. And then Larsen fights for the full point in a complex endgame.

Spassky - Larsen
USSR-Rest of the World,
Belgrade 1970

1 d4 ♘f6 2 c4 e6 3 ♘f3 b6 4 ♘c3 ♗b7 5 ♗g5 ♗e7 6 e3 0-0 7 ♗d3 c5 8 0-0 ♘c6 9 d5 ♘b4 10 d6 ♗xd6

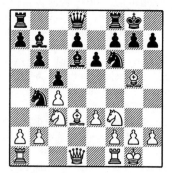

11 ♗xh7+

This appears to lead to a very attractive position for White but 11 ♗xf6 gxf6 (11 ... ♕xf6?? 12 ♗e4+-) 12 ♗xh7+ ♔xh7 13 ♕xd6 was probably even stronger. Spassky might have overlooked Black's 13th move.

11 ... ♔xh7 12 ♕xd6 ♗xf3 13 gxf3 ♘e8!

A brilliant defensive idea which aims to exchange Black's public enemy number one, the queen on d6. In playing this way Black offers an exchange sacrifice which Spassky quite rightly declines.

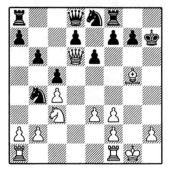

14 ♕e7!
Spassky rightly makes a bee-line for Black's d-pawn rather than going for bigger fish. After 14 ♗xd8?! ♘xd6 15 ♗e7 ♘xc4 16 ♗xf8 ♖xf8 Black has excellent compensation whilst 14 ♕xf8 is met by 14 ... ♕xg5+ 15 ♔h1 ♕f5 after which rejecting a draw by repitition with 16 ♖g1 looks too risky because of 16 ... ♕xf3+ 17 ♖g2 ♘d3.
14 ... ♕xe7 15 ♗xe7 ♖g8 16 ♖fd1 ♘c6 17 ♖xd7 ♘e5 18 ♖b7 ♘xc4 19 ♘e4 ♘a5 20 ♖d7 ♘c6 21 f4 ♖c8 22 ♖c1 a5 23 a3

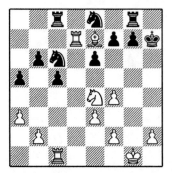

23 ... ♔g6?!

A very risky move which aims to activate Black's king with the board still full of pieces. In doing so he turned down the safe 23 ... ♘xe7 24 ♖xe7 ♖c7 which would probably lead to a draw.

Larsen is renowned for his fighting qualities and given the choice between a safe line and taking a risk to try and win he would generally take the risk. On this occasion it pays off but it could so easily have backfired.
24 ♔g2 ♖h8 25 ♔f3
In his notes to the game Spassky felt he could have put Black in serious trouble with 25 ♖g1 ♘xe7 26 ♔f3+ ♔h6 27 ♖xe7 ♖c7 28 ♖xc7 ♘xc7 29 ♘d6 ♖f8 30 ♘c4 ♖b8 31 ♖d1 which ties up Black's pieces whilst preparing to infiltrate.
25 ... ♖xh2 26 ♘g5 e5! 27 ♖g1 exf4 28 ♗d6! ♘xd6 29 ♖xd6+ f6 30 ♘e6+ ♔f5 31 ♘xf4 ♘e5+ 32 ♔e2 ♖e8 33 ♖xb6
And here White could have played 33 ♘e6! ♘c4 34 ♘xg7+ ♔e5 35 ♘xe8.
33 ... ♘c4 34 ♖b3 g5 35 ♘d5 ♖e5 36 ♖d1 g4 37 ♔f1??
A time-trouble blunder, giving away a rook. Larsen's brinkmanship triumphs.

37 ... ♖h1+ 38 ♔e2 ♖xd1 0:1

KM15/1: 1) Black to play

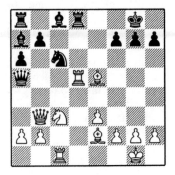

KM15/1: 2) White to play

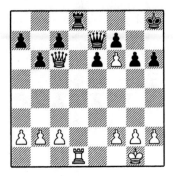

KM15/1: 3) White to play

KM15/1: 4) White to play

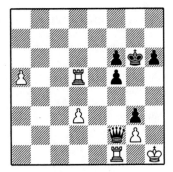

A15/1: a) Black to play

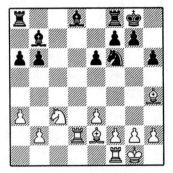

A15/1: b) Black to play

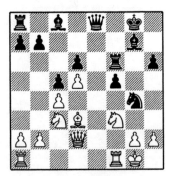

Month 15/Week 2:
Prophylaxis

In his brilliant writings on chess, Aaron Nimzowitsch introduced some rather mystical concepts such as *overprotection* and prophylaxis. In this section we shall look at *prophylaxis*, the art of inhibiting the opponent's active possibilities before they really arise. In a sense this is a kind of chessboard vaccination rather than attempting a cure once the disease has already developed.

To some extent it is rather difficult to put such ideas into words. Instead let me show you one of the most famous of all prophylactic moves after which I really started to understand this concept.

The player who played it was Anatoly Karpov, whose flair for snuffing out danger is legendary. It is taken from the 1974 Candidates final which, because Fischer did not defend his title, effectively proved to be a World Championship match.

Karpov - Korchnoi
Moscow Cm 1974

1 e4 c5 2 ♘f3 d6 3 d4 cxd4 4 ♘xd4 ♘f6 5 ♘c3 g6

This choice of opening was dictated by Korchnoi's wish to test Karpov out in sharp and murky positions.

6 ♗e3 ♗g7 7 f3 ♘c6 8 ♕d2 0-0 9 ♗c4 ♗d7 10 h4 ♖c8 11 ♗b3 ♘e5 12 0-0-0 ♘c4 13 ♗xc4 ♖xc4 14 h5 ♘xh5 15 g4 ♘f6

A well known Dragon position in which it was felt that the game would be won by whoever got their attack in first. Prior to this game White had tried various attacking moves such as 16 e5 or 16 ♗h6 though this latter move can be met by 16 ... ♗xh6 17 ♕xh6 ♖xc3. In fact the c3 square is the focal point of Black's pressure on the h8-a1 diagonal, which goes a long way towards explaining White's next move.

16 ♘de2!

Very untypical of the Dragon in that White usually goes hell for leather at Black's king. But the point is that it reinforces the c3 square and goes a long way towards neutralising Black's attack.

16 ... ♕a5

A natural enough move but later on it was discovered that Black should also take prophylactic measures of his own with 16 ... ♖e8, preventing the exchange of his crucial dark-squared bishop with 17 ♗h6.

17 ♗h6 ♗xh6 18 ♕xh6 ♖fc8 19 ♖d3! ♖4c5 20 g5 ♖xg5

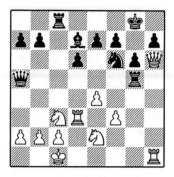

21 ♖d5! ♖xd5 22 ♘xd5 ♖e8

Neither 22 ... ♕d8 23 ♘ef4 ♕f8 24 ♘xf6+ exf6 25 ♕xh7# nor 22 ... ♘h5 23 ♘xe7+ ♔h8 24 ♘xc8 helps Black very much.

23 ♘ef4 ♗c6

23 ... ♗e6 is met by 24 ♘xe6 fxe6 25 ♘xf6+ exf6 26 ♕xh7+ ♔f8 27 ♕xb7+-.

24 e5!

The *coup de grâce*. 24 ... dxe5 is met by 25 ♘xf6+ exf6 26 ♘h5 gxh5 27 ♖g1+ followed by mate.

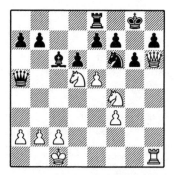

24 ... ♗xd5 25 exf6 exf6 26 ♕xh7+ ♔f8 27 ♕h8+ 1:0

Games such as this, and Nimzo-witsch's books, have made quite a big impression on my own style of play. In my 'mature' years I have become very conscious of trying to gauge my opponent's intentions in order to meet them half way. This kind of thinking is rather typical of my favourite *Modern Defence* in which Black tends to adapt his strategy to White's chosen set-up.

**Baker - Davies
Crewe 1996**

1 e4 g6 2 d4 ♗g7 3 ♘c3 d6 4 f4 e6!?

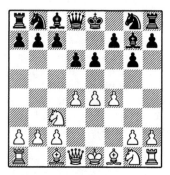

Already a prophylactic idea against the possibility of White playing f4-f5. The way I see it is that if I prevent White from moving his f-pawn forward his bishop on c1 will never be able to exchange itself for my bishop on g7. And in that case my king position should keep a vital defender.

5 ♘f3 ♘e7 6 ♗e2 ♘d7 7 0-0 b6 8 ♕e1?!

The start of a somewhat primitive plan to mate Black on the kingside. I answer this charge on the flank by hitting back in the centre.

8 ... ♗b7 9 ♔h1 0-0 10 ♕h4?!

White himself should adopt pro-phylactic measures and try to prevent the coming ... c7-c5 lever with 10 ♗e3 and 11 ♖d1.

10 ... c5 11 ♗e3 ♘f6!

An unpleasant move for White to meet after which 12 e5 is answered by 12 ... ♘f5 and 12 ♗d3 by 12 ... c4!. Rather than go for a passive and miserable defence White gamely sacrifices two pawns for piece activity. But it can never really be enough.

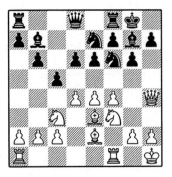

12 ♖ad1 ♗xe4! 13 ♘xe4 ♘xe4 14 f5 gxf5!
Assuring central control by capturing *towards* the centre. In this particular position this is more important than the integrity of the kingside pawn shield.
15 dxc5 bxc5 16 ♘g5 ♘xg5 17 ♗xg5 f6 18 ♗e3 ♖c8!

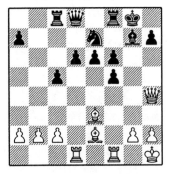

A very important prophylactic move which effectively neutralises White's play. Not only does it defend against the threat of 19 ♗xc5 but it prepares to eject a White bishop from d3 with the push ... c5-c4.
19 ♖f3 ♘g6 20 ♕h5 ♖f7! 21 ♖h3 ♗f8 22 ♖g1 c4 23 g4 f4 24 ♗d4 e5 25 ♗c3 ♕e8!
Another key prophylactic move after which Black's defences are very solid and his central pawn mass can start to move forwards. 25 ... d5 would be premature and could have been met by 26 g5 f5 27 ♗xe5!! ♘xe5 28 g6 ♖g7 29 ♕xh7+!! etc.

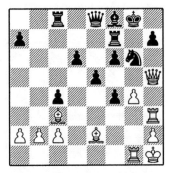

26 g5 f5 27 ♗f3 ♕e6
Once again Black carefully secures his defences. He should not play 27 ... e4 because of 28 ♕xg6+.
28 ♖e1 ♖d7
The last prophylactic move which finally puts an end to any mating combinations based on ♕xg6. The rest is fairly simple.
29 ♔g1 d5 30 ♔h1 e4 31 ♗g2 ♕f7 32 ♗f6 f3 33 ♗xf3 exf3 34 ♕xf3 d4 35 ♕xf5 ♕d5+ 36 ♕xd5+ ♖xd5 37 ♖d1 ♗g7 38 ♖f3 ♗xf6 39 gxf6 ♔f7 40 b3 cxb3 41 cxb3 ♖c6 42 ♖h3 h5 43 ♖hd3 ♖cd6 0:1

KM15/2: 1) Black to play

KM15/2: 2) White to play

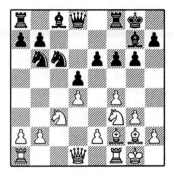

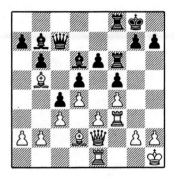

KM15/2: 3)White to play

KM15/2: 4) Black to play

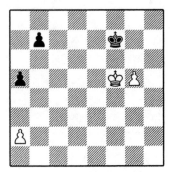

A15/2: a) White to play

A15/2: b) White to play

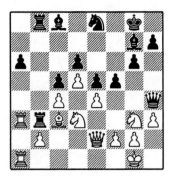

Month 15/Week 3:
Blockade

One of Nimzowitsch's most famous phrases was: "First restrain, next blockade and lastly destroy." Whilst this was coined primarily with regard to enemy pawn weaknesses the same process can apply in part to the art of defence. Prophylaxis might be seen as restraining the opponent's aggressive intentions and this can develop into a blockade, the construction of a truly impregnable position into which there are no inroads. A counterattack may or may not be the next development.

Nigel Short put this process quite picturesquely in his book *New Ideas In The French Defence*: "More cautious players like myself prefer to nullify our opponent's play and then blow their heads off." But the greatest master of this art was undoubtably Tigran Petrosian who sometimes seemed to understand Nimzowitsch's ideas better than Nimzowitsch himself.

Petrosian had a rare gift for constructing quite impenetrable positions and he would often find a delicate positional sacrifice of a pawn or the exchange in order to do exactly that. Witness for example this game against Polugayevsky in which he sacrifices the exchange to construct an impenetrable line of defence on the dark squares.

Polugaevsky - Petrosian
Moscow 1983

1 ♘f3 g6 2 d4 ♗g7 3 c4 d6 4 ♘c3 e5 5 e4 ♘c6 6 dxe5 ♘xe5 7 ♘d4 a6!?

The start of an interesting plan by Petrosian which he was later to criticise in his notes to the game.
8 ♗e2 c5
The consistent follow-up to Black's last move though it does leave the d-pawn backward. Black is playing for an outpost on d4.
9 ♘c2 ♗e6

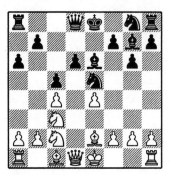

10 ♘d5?
After this Black gets time to implement his plan. White should have taken this opportunity to play the dynamic 10 f4 after which 10 ... ♘xc4 11 f5 gxf5 12 exf5 ♗xf5 13 0-0 (and not 13 ♗xc4? ♕h4+) would give White a winning attack according to Petrosian. Black would in fact be forced to retreat with 10 ... ♘c6 after which 11 ♗e3 would leave him unable to occupy the d4 square.
10 ... ♗xd5 11 exd5
Whichever pawn White recaptures with he plugs the hole on d5. 11 cxd5 ♘e7 is also far from clear.
11 ... ♘e7! 12 0-0 0-0 13 ♖b1 ♘f5 14 b4?
14 b3 would have been better as now Black acquires an outpost on c5. Polugaevsky no doubt felt he should punish Black for his provocative opening play.

14 ... cxb4 15 ♖xb4 ♕c7

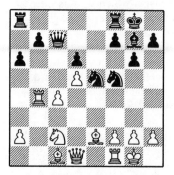

16 ♗b2 ♖fe8 17 ♘d4?!

Continuing to play ambitiously but probably already missing Petrosian's 19th move. White should play simply 17 g3.

17 ... ♘xd4 18 ♗xd4 ♘d7 19 ♗e3

After 19 ♗xg7 ♔xg7 Black would simply stand better because of his dark-square outposts. It now seems that White is well placed with two bishops and pressure on the b-file. But with the sacrifice of the exchange Black sets up a complete blockade of the position.

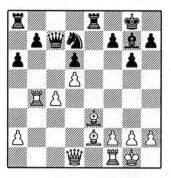

19 ... ♖xe3! 20 fxe3 ♘c5 21 ♕c2 ♖e8 22 ♖f3?!

22 ♖bb1 is the best, in order to centralise the rook with ♖be1.

22 ... ♗h6 23 ♕c3?!

Preparing the fatal blunder. 23 ♖b1 is correct.

23 ... ♕e7

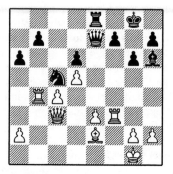

24 ♖b6??

Here it is, the losing move. Polugayevsky was hoping for 24 ... ♗xe3+ 25 ♖xe3 ♕xe3+ 26 ♕xe3 ♖xe3 27 ♗f3 when White lifts the blockade of d5.

24 ... ♘a4 0:1

Here's another example of this kind of exchange sacrifice which also shows what happens when an irresistible force meets an immovable object. The master of attack, Mikhail Tal, meets one of the greatest masters of defence.

Tal - Petrosian
USSR Ch, Riga 1958

1 e4 e5 2 ♘f3 ♘c6 3 ♗b5 a6 4 ♗a4 ♘f6 5 0-0 ♗e7 6 ♖e1 b5 7 ♗b3 0-0 8 c3 d6 9 h3 ♘a5 10 ♗c2 c5 11 d4 ♕c7 12 ♘bd2 ♗d7 13 ♘f1 ♘c4 14 ♘e3 ♘xe3 15 ♗xe3 ♗e6 16 ♘d2 ♖fe8 17 f4 ♖ad8 18 fxe5 dxe5 19 d5 ♗d7 20 c4 ♖b8 21 a4 b4 22 a5 ♖f8 23 ♗a4 ♗xa4 24 ♖xa4 ♖bd8 25 ♕f3 ♖d6 26 ♘b3 ♘d7 27 ♖aa1 ♖g6 28 ♖f1 ♗d6 29 h4 ♕d8 30 h5 ♖f6 31 ♕g4

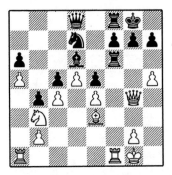

After conducting the early part of the game in excellent fashion White has a rather obvious positional advantage due to his passed d-pawn, greater control of space, better bishop and the weakness on c5. In addition to this White is preparing an attack on the opposing king and threatens 32 ♗g5 ♖xf1+ 33 ♖xf1 ♕c7 (33 ... f6 34 ♕e6+) 34 ♗h6 winning the exchange. Things look bleak for Petrosian but he has conceived a brilliant blockading idea.

31 ... ♖f4! 32 ♗xf4

It looks natural enough to take the rook but perhaps White should have played 32 ♖xf4! exf4 33 ♗xf4 after which his dark-square bishop can challenge for control of the e5 square. Both 33 ... ♘e5 34 ♕g3 ♘xc4 35 e5 and 33 ... ♕f6 34 ♗xd6 ♕xd6 35 ♖f1 look better for White.

32 ... exf4 33 ♘d2 ♘e5

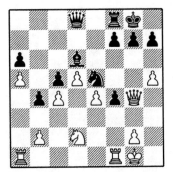

This knight is really superbly placed and holds Black's entire position together. Over the next few moves Tal's play betrays signs of growing frustration that he is unable to penetrate Black's position despite his material advantage.

34 ♕xf4 ♘xc4 35 e5 ♘xe5 36 ♘e4 h6 37 ♖ae1?

He should settle for 37 ♘xd6 ♕xd6 38 ♖fe1 f6 39 ♖ad1.

37 ... ♗b8 38 ♖d1 c4 39 d6 ♘d3 40 ♕g4 ♗a7+ 41 ♔h1 f5 42 ♘f6+ ♔h8 43 ♕xc4 ♘xb2 44 ♕xa6 ♘xd1 45 ♕xa7 ♕xd6 46 ♕d7 ♕xf6 47 ♕xd1 ♖b8

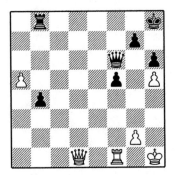

The tables have been turned and now Black has a material advantage. White managed to hang on for a draw—but only just.

48 ♖f3 ♖a8 49 ♕e1 ♖xa5 50 ♕xb4 ♖e5 51 ♕f4 ♔h7 52 ♔h2 ♖d5 53 ♖f1 ♕g5 54 ♕f3 ♖e5 55 ♔g1 ♖c5 56 ♕f2 ♖e5 57 ♕f3 ♖a5 58 ♔h2 ♔h8 59.♔g1 ♖a2 60 ♕d5 ♖c2 61 ♕a8+ ♔h7 62 ♕f3 ♖c1 63 ♖xc1 ♕xc1+ 64 ♔h2 ♕c7+ 65 ♔h3 ♕e5 66 g4 fxg4+ 67 ♔xg4 ♕g5+ 68 ♔h3 ♕f6 69 ♕e4+ ♔g8 70 ♕e8+ ♕f8 71 ♕xf8+ ♔xf8 72 ♔g4 ♔f7 73 ♔f5 ½-½

KM15/3 1) Black to play

KM15/3: 2) White to play

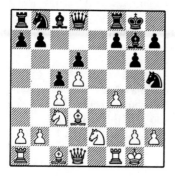

KM15/3: 3) Black to play

KM15/3: 4) White to play

A15/ 3: a) Black to play

A15/3: b) Black to play

Month 15/Week 4:
Counterattack

The well-worn cliché states that attack is the best form of defence and this holds just as true in chess as in many other spheres. The rather obvious reason for this is that if someone is busy fending off the opponent's threats he will not have the time to develop threats of his own and his forces will be obliged to take up a defensive rather than offensive posture.

In the field of defence and counterattack I have found the writings of Emanuel Lasker a constant source of inspiration and especially his brilliant and underrated book, Lasker's *Manual of Chess*. It was through Lasker that I understood that the idea of making the least possible concession whilst employing every other piece in counterattack: *the principle of economy*.

Very often I see defenders adopt a completely passive posture in the face of rather empty threats after which the attacker gets the leeway to reinforce his attack. The *principle of economy* indicates that the defender should gauge exactly how dangerous the threats are and defend only against those and nothing more. This demands a cool nerve and accurate calculating ability, both of which Lasker had in great abundance.

Winawer - Lasker
Nuremberg 1896

1 e4 e5 2 ᘯf3 ᘯc6 3 ♗b5 ᘯf6 4 0-0 ᘯxe4 5 d4 ♗e7 6 ♕e2 ᘯd6 7 ♗xc6 bxc6 8 dxe5 ᘯb7 9 ᘯd4 0-0 10 ᘯc3 ♗c5 11 ᘯf5?!

It would have been better to play 11 ♖d1. Lasker meets this attacking fling with great poise.

11 ... d5! 12 ♕g4 ♗xf5 13 ♕xf5 ♖e8 14 ♗f4 ♗d4!

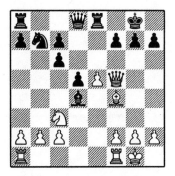

The first in a series of powerful and instructive moves which see Lasker defend his kingside with the minimum number of pieces whilst setting out to inflict permanent damage on White's position and ultimately force him back into defence.

15 ♖fe1 ᘯc5 16 ♖ad1 ♗xc3! 17 bxc3 ♕c8! 18 ♕h5 ♕a6! 19 ♖e3 ♕xa2

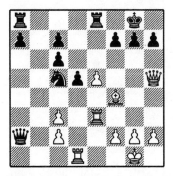

A key move in Black's plan of counterattack. The point is not so much that it wins a pawn but that it creates a passed a-pawn. As it strolls down the board this pawn will distract White's forces from the attack.

20 ♖c1 ♕c4 21 ♖f3 ♘e6 22 ♗d2
♖e7 23 ♖h3 ♕e4 24 f3
24 f4 was a better try.
24 ... ♕g6 25 ♕h4 ♖d7 26 f4
♕e4!

27 g4
Winawer goes for an all-out attack but in doing so weakens his position. According to Tarrasch White should have tried 27 ♖d3 followed by ♖e1, but this would ease the pressure on Black's kingside.
27 ... ♘f8! 28 ♕f2 a5 29 ♖e3 ♕c4 30 f5 a4 31 ♖f1 a3 32 ♖ee1

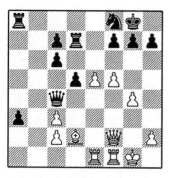

Retreating another piece from its aggressive posture in order to stop the a-pawn. Lasker's counter-attack is clearly bearing fruit and the rest of the game is little more than a mopping up operation.

32 ... a2 33 h3 c5 34 ♔h2 d4 35 ♕f3 c6! 36 e6 fxe6 37 fxe6 ♘xe6 38 ♕xc6 ♖da7 39 ♖a1 ♖f8 40 ♖fe1 ♘d8 41 ♕b6 ♖af7 42 ♗g5 ♖f2+ 43 ♔g3 ♕xc3+ 0:1

The following game takes the idea of counterattack one step further, deep into the realm of psychology. In his brilliant book entitled *Dynamic Chess Strategy* Suba recommended two secret weapons to the defender:
"When the opponent has a strong attack on the king, his blood pressure is getting higher and you can 'blackmail' him with 'lost endings'. This can cause him to deviate from the right path—it is unlikely that he will abandon the idea of mate so easily.
"The second one is complementary to the first. When your opponent has a strategic advantage and virtually controls the board, or when he attacks something that he cannot defend by reasonable means, then the 'threat' or 'blackmail' with non-existant attacks on the king may induce a mistake. As you can see, in both cases a static principle is opposed by a dynamic one, and reciprocally the psychological factor speculated upon is 'inertia', the difficulty in switching from one to the other."
In the following game we see Suba putting his ideas into practice when he found himself in a poor position against Jan Timman. When Timman obtained a positional advantage he was clearly reluctant to get drawn into the complications which Suba offered and in his need for security made the fatal mistakes.

Suba - Timman
Las Palmas 1982

1 c4 e5 2 g3 ♘f6 3 ♗g2 d5 4
cxd5 ♘xd5 5 ♘c3 ♘b6 6 ♘f3 ♘c6
7 d3 ♗e7 8 0-0 0-0 9 a3 a5 10 ♗e3
♖e8 11 ♖c1 ♗g4 12 ♘e4?!
A poor move by Suba which
lands him in difficulties. Black's
reply is very strong.
12 ... ♘d4! 13 ♗xd4 exd4 14
♖e1?!
White should try to simplify the
position with 14 ♘c5 ♗c8 15 ♘a4
but Suba, playing White, did not
want to admit that he was already
worse.
14 ... a4! 15 ♕c2 c6 16 ♘c5 ♗c8
17 ♕d2 ♗f6 18 ♖c2 g6 19 h4!?

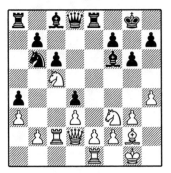

A very instructive moment from a
psychological point of view. Black
has control over the position and no
doubt wanted to maintain this control and play a quiet and secure
positional game. Suba on the other
hand goes out of his way to create
as much of a mess as possible.
19 ... h6 20 ♖b1 ♗g7 21 b3!
Suba made the wry comment that
this move was heavily criticised in

the press because it weakens the
queenside and added: "I apologize
to commentators for my attempt to
breathe instead of waiting for a slow
but sure death."
21 ... ♕e7! 22 ♘h2!
Preventing Black's knight from
going to c3 via d5. So Timman
takes an alternative route.
22 ... axb3 23 ♖xb3 ♘a4 24
♘xa4 ♖xa4 25 ♕c1 ♗e6?
A blunder borne out of the difficulties that White is creating for his
opponent. Black should play either
25 ... ♖a7 or 25 ... ♗f8.

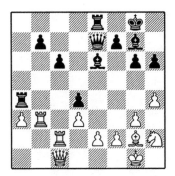

26 ♖xb7! ♕xb7 27 ♗xc6 ♕a7 28
♗xe8 ♖xa3 29 ♘f1?!
29 ♕f4 was better.
29 ... ♖a1 30 ♕f4 ♕a5?
The last mistake. 30 ... ♕a8! 31
♗c6 ♕c8 32 g4 ♗b3 33 ♖c5 ♗f8
34 ♗d5 ♗xc5 35 ♕xf7+ ♔h8 36
♕f6+ forces White to force a draw.
31 ♗xf7+! ♗xf7 32 ♖c8+ ♗f8 33
♕d6 ♕a3 34 ♖xf8+ ♔g7 35 ♕xa3
♖xa3 36 ♖d8 ♖a2 37 ♖xd4 ♖xe2
38 ♘e3 ♗e6 39 ♖e4 ♖e1+ 40 ♘f1
♖xe4 41 dxe4 ♔f6 42 f4 g5 43
hxg6+ hxg6 44 ♔f2 1:0

KM15/4: 1) Black to play

KM15/4: 3) White to play

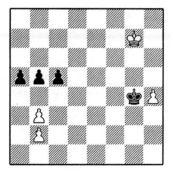

KM15/4: 3) Black to play

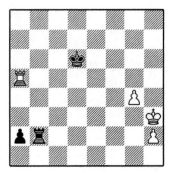

KM15/4: 4) Black to play

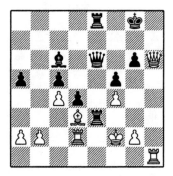

A15/4: a) Black to play

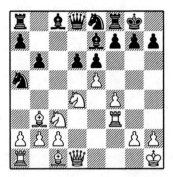

A15/4: b) Black to play

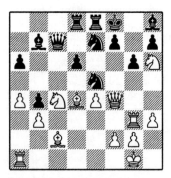

4 Winning 'Won' Positions

How many times do we hear that someone was 'winning' but then finally drew or lost? People tell me about 'won positions' all the time but my normal reaction is to ask what the final result was and then brutally point out that this is really all that counts.

I have noticed even at grandmaster level that there is in fact a very high percentage of 'won' positions that are not converted into actual wins. In my own practice I have noticed that I often do much better in tournaments when I get poor positions out of the opening.

This is probably due largely to the fact that my opponents become less vigilant whilst I on the other hand become fully concentrated in my efforts to stave off defeat. As the Swedish GM Lars Karlsson likes to say: "It's easier to fight for your life than it is to kill someone".

To win 'won positions' requires a cool head, not to overreach in the attempt to force resignation whilst being decisive enough to know when to pounce. In week one of this month's material we will see examples of the ball being placed quite firmly in the net whilst in week two we will look at the art of proceeding securely, the main aim being to deprive the opponent of counterplay.

In weeks three and four we will look at the defence of very difficult and even lost positions. Week three is devoted to the so-called 'swindle' whilst in week four we see how one can create the most difficulties for the opponent and maximise his chances of slipping up.

Month 16/Week 1:
Deadly Finishing

From a psychological point of view the player with the 'won game' finds himself under all kinds of pressures including the thought that the point should be in the bag if only he doesn't 'mess it up'. This can lead to a desire to be careful which can manifest itself in excessive caution. Opportunites to decide the game are missed and before you know where you are there is no win at all.

The greatest masters know when to pounce and finish their games with precision and energy when this is the kind of play the position requires. Amongst the World Champions I would single out Alexander Alekhine and Bobby Fischer as being outstanding exponents of the crisp finish.

In the following two games we see Alekhine in action.

Alekhine - Marshall
Baden-Baden 1925

1 d4 ♘f6 2 c4 d5 3 cxd5 ♘xd5 4 e4 ♘f6 5 ♗d3 e5 6 dxe5 ♘g4 7 ♘f3

And not 7 f4? because of 7 ... ♗c5 8 ♘h3 ♕h4+.

7 ... ♘c6 8 ♗g5!

Alekhine rejected 8 ♗f4?! because of 8 ... ♘b4 9 ♗b5+ ♗d7 10 ♗xd7+ ♕xd7 11 ♕xd7+ ♔xd7 with a better for Black.

8 ... ♗e7 9 ♗xe7 ♕xe7 10 ♘c3 ♘cxe5 11 ♘xe5 ♕xe5?!

According to Alekhine Black should have played 11 ... ♘xe5 though even then White would maintain slightly the better game with 12 ♗e2 0-0 13 f4 ♘g4 (Or 13 ... ♖d8 14 ♘d5) 14 ♗xg4 ♕h4+ 15 g3 ♕xg4 16 ♕xg4 ♗xg4 17 ♔f2 ♖ad8 18 h3.

12 h3 ♘f6 13 ♕d2! ♗d7 14 ♕e3!

A quiet but very strong move by Alekhine which prepares to advance the f-pawn.

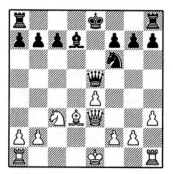

14 ... ♗c6?

Black should have played 14 ... ♕a5! in order to defend his a7 pawn and prepare queenside castling. The kingside proves to be uninhabitable after Alekhine advances his e- and f-pawns.

15 0-0-0 0-0 16 f4 ♕e6

White wins a pawn after 16 ... ♕a5 17 e5 ♘d5 18 ♘xd5 ♗xd5 19 ♗xh7+ ♔xh7 20 ♕d3+ followed by ♕xd5.

17 e5 ♖fe8 18 ♖he1 ♖ad8

After 18 ... ♘d7?! White continues with 19 g4.

19 f5 ♕e7 20 ♕g5 ♘d5 21 f6 ♕f8

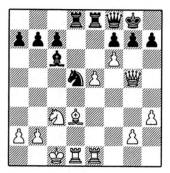

22 ♗c4!

The first in a series of hammer-blows which decide the game within the space of a few moves. Having obtained such a strong position many players would be tempted to want to keep what they have gained. But Alekhine pursues his attack with unrelenting precision.

22 ... ♘xc3 23 ♖xd8 ♖xd8 24 fxg7!

A much more convincing line than 24 e6 ♖d5!.

24 ... ♘xa2+

If 24 ... ♕e8 there follows 25 ♗xf7+ ♔xf7 26 ♖f1+ ♔e6 27 ♖f6+ ♔d5 28 ♖f8+-.

25 ♔b1!

And not 24 ♗xa2 ♕c5+.

25 ... ♕e8 26 e6!

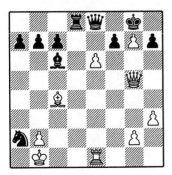

26 ... ♗e4+ 27 ♔a1

Another precise move. 27 ♖xe4 ♖d1+ 28 ♔c2 ♕a4+ 29 b3 ♘b4+ 30 ♔xd1+- also wins but the text is more convincing.

27 ... f5

27 ... fxe6 is also quite lost for Black after 28 ♗xe6+ ♕xe6 29 ♕xd8+ ♔xg7 30 ♕d4+-.

28 e7+ ♖d5 29 ♕f6 ♕f7 30 e8=♕+ 1:0

Alekhine - Opocensky
Paris 1925

1 d4 d5 2 c4 c6 3 ♘c3 ♘f6 4 e3 ♗f5 5 cxd5 ♘xd5

After 5 ... cxd5 there is 6 ♕b3 with the better game for White.

6 ♗c4 e6 7 ♘ge2 ♘d7 8 e4 ♘xc3 9 ♘xc3 ♗g6 10 0-0 ♕h4 11 d5! exd5 12 g3 ♕f6 13 exd5

13 ... ♗c5?

Black's first and probably decisive mistake. According to Alekhine he had to play 13 ... ♘e5 14 ♗e2! ♗c5 and should White renew the threat of f2-f4 with 15 ♔g2 he should try 15 ... h5!. White would then be almost forced to play 16 h4 followed by 17 ♗g5 when the position is quite dynamic and there is everything still to play for.

14 ♖e1+ ♔f8 15 ♗f4 ♘b6 16 ♗b3 h5 17 h4

White is playing to prevent Black from coordinating his rooks.

17 ... ♔g8 18 dxc6 bxc6 19 ♖c1 ♗d4 20 ♘e4 ♗xe4 21 ♖xe4 c5

After 21 ... ♗xb2? White wins with 22 ♖c5 ♘d5 23 ♗xd5 cxd5 24 ♖xd5+-.

22 ♕e2 g6 23 ♗g5 ♕d6 24 ♕f3 ♕f8

25 ♖xd4!

Once again finishing matters in the most convincing fashion. White eliminates Black's most important defender after which his game falls apart.

25 ... cxd4 26 ♖c6! ♔h7

After 26 ... ♔g7 Alekhine intended 27 ♖xg6+ ♔xg6 (Or 27 ... fxg6 28 ♕b7+-) 28 ♕f6+ ♔h7 29 ♗xf7 ♖g8 30 ♕f5+ ♔h8 31 ♗f6+-.

27 ♗xf7 ♖c8 28 ♖xg6 1:0

KM16/1: 1) White to play

KM16/1: 2) White to play

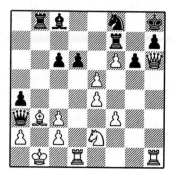

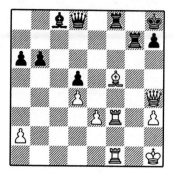

KM16/1: 3) White to play

KM16/1: 4) White to play

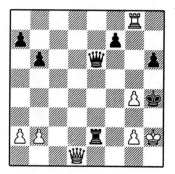

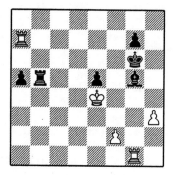

A16/1: a) White to play.

A16/1: b) White to play (Black has moved his king)

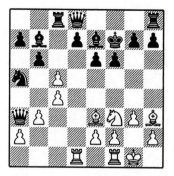

**Month 16/Week 2:
Ironclad Technique**

The British Grandmaster Jon Speelman has a number of favourite expressions, one of which is 'trying too hard to win'. This is one he uses when one side has a big advantage and then overreaches in his efforts to put the ball in the net.

In the last section we saw Alekhine dispose of his opponents in short order, but it isn't always advisable to try and win in such quick and dramatic style. Sometimes what is called for is the gradual improvement of your position whilst suppressing the opponent's counterplay.

The greatest master of this art is undoubtably Anatoly Karpov who often seems to win his games with the most minute advantages and without allowing his opponents the slightest counterchance. The suppression of his opponent's counterplay is a characteristic feature of Karpov's play. He will often carry a slight advantage into the endgame in which the absence of queens makes matters much simpler.

In the following game he disposes of Kasparov in the most convincing style.

**Karpov - Kasparov
London WCh 1986**

1 d4 ♘f6 2 c4 g6 3 ♘c3 d5 4 ♗f4 ♗g7 5 e3 c5 6 dxc5 ♕a5 7 ♖c1 ♘e4 8 cxd5 ♘xc3 9 ♕d2 ♕xa2 10 bxc3

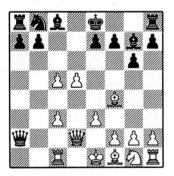

10 ... ♕xd2+!?
The main line is 10 ... ♕a5. The text was rather new at the time of the game and has been far less well explored.

11 ♔xd2 ♘d7 12 ♗b5 0-0 13 ♗xd7 ♗xd7 14 e4 f5 15 e5 e6
The real novelty, evidently prepared by Kasparov for this game. Black allows White a supported passed pawn on d6 but hopes to get counterplay with his bishop pair.

15 ... ♖ac8 had been tried previously but then 16 c4 ♖xc5 17 ♗e3 ♖a5 18 f4 e6 19 d6 leaves Black with the problem of how to find counterplay.

16 c4 ♖fc8 17 c6! bxc6 18 d6 c5?
Black had to play 18 ... g5 but then 19 ♗xg5 ♗xe5 20 c5 ♖cb8 21 ♘f3 ♗b2 22 ♖c2 seems to leave Black without much play.

19 h4! h6 20 ♘h3!!
A beautiful move which ruins Black's plans. Kasparov and his seconds had apparently prepared the whole line up to this point but now they only looked at 20 ♘f3. Over the board Karpov finds a much stronger idea which prepares to close the a8-h1 diagonal with a timely f2-f3 and manoeuvre the knight from h3 to f2 and d3.

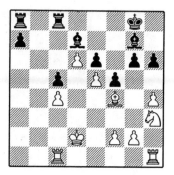

20 ... a5 21 f3 a4 22 Ihe1!

Another deeply instructive move by Karpov, protecting the e-pawn prepares ♘h3-f3. The immediate 22 ♘f2 would have been met by 22 ... g5.

22 ... a3 23 ♘f2 a2 24 ♘d3 Ia3 25 Ia1!

Another fine move. 25 ♗e3 Ixd3+ 26 ♔xd3 ♗xe5 allows Black's king's bishop to breathe again.

25 ... g5

25 ... Ib8 was a suggestion of Ricardo Calvo who gave the line 26 Iec1 g5 27 hxg5 hxg5 28 ♗xg5 Ibb3 29 ♘xc5 Ib2+ 30 ♔e1 ♗xe5 31 ♘xd7 ♗xd6 with complications. Probably this is all unnecessary as 26 ♔e2! Ibb3 27 ♘xc5 looks good.

26 hxg5 hxg5 27 ♗xg5 ♔f7?

27 ... Ib8 28 ♔e2 Ibb3 29 ♘xc5 Ib2+ 30 ♔f1 is an easy enough win for White.

28 ♗f4 Ib8 29 Iec1 ♗c6 30 Ic3 Ia5 31 Ic2 Iba8 32 ♘c1 1:0

The next game also features victory by suppression but this time an altogether different type of player is the one doing the suppressing. Leonid Stein was noted for his restless and dynamic style, he also understood very well that at times you

need to inhibit your opponent's counterplay.

Stein - Bilek
Moscow 1967

1 e4 c5 2 ♘f3 g6 3 d4 ♗g7 4 d5 d6 5 ♘c3 ♘f6 6 ♗e2 0-0 7 0-0 ♗g4 8 ♘d2 ♗xe2 9 ♕xe2 ♘bd7

Black's failure to get anything like adequate play in this game makes it necessary to look for improvements early on. 9 ... Ie8 is more interesting so that after 10 ... e6 11 dxe6 Black would be able to put his knight on c6.

10 ♘c4 ♘b6 11 ♘e3!

Avoiding the exchange of knights and preparing an advance of his a-pawn.

11 ... Ie8 12 a4 e6 13 dxe6

And not 13 a5? ♘bxd5 14 exd5 exd5 which wins back the knight with interest.

13 ... Ixe6 14 a5 ♘bd7 15 f3 Ib8 16 Id1

An instructive position. White has obtained control of the d5 square and this alone will cause Black grave difficulties. If White prevents Black from **16 ... ♘e5 17 ♘c4 ♘xc4 18 ♕xc4 ♘d7 19 ♘d5 ♘e5 20 ♕a4 g5?**

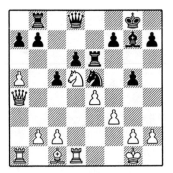

A horrible move by Bilek which makes his position even worse. No doubt he was worried about his one well-placed piece, the knight on e5, being driven away with f3-f4. But the hole on f5 is far too great a price to pay.

21 ♖a3 ♘c6 22 ♘e3 ♗d4

Black must eliminate the knight even at the cost of this vital bishop.

23 ♔h1 ♗xe3 24 ♗xe3 ♕f6 25 ♖d5 h6 26 ♖b3

Threatening 27 a6, which could presently have been answered by 26 ... ♕xb2.

26 ... a6 27 h3 ♘e5

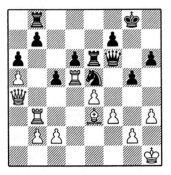

28 ♕a1!

A powerful regrouping. The queen is en route for the d1 square from where it will intensify the pressure on d6.

28 ... ♕g6

28 ... ♘xf3 fails to 29 ♖f5!.

29 ♕d1 ♘c4 30 ♗d2 b5 31 axb6 ♖xb6 32 ♖xb6 ♘xb6 33 ♖d3 f5

By undermining the e4 pawn Black hopes to regain control of d5. But the further weakening of his king position proves to be intolerable.

34 ♖b3 ♘d7 35 ♖b7 ♖e7 36 exf5 ♕xf5 37 ♗c3 d5 38 b4 d4 39 bxc5

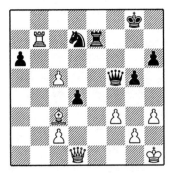

The game now reaches its final stage. Black has repaired the strategic weakness of his d-pawn but ultimately loses due to the weakness of his king and the superiority of bishop over knight in such a wide-open position.

39 ... ♕d5

Or 39 ... dxc3 40 c6.

40 ♖c7 ♕e5 41 ♖c8+ ♔f7 42 ♕xd4 ♕xd4 43 ♗xd4 ♘f8 44 c6 ♘e6 45 ♗b6 ♖e8 46 ♗d8!

The killer. After 46 ... ♖xd8 47 ♖xd8 ♘xd8 48 c7 and 46 ... ♘xd8 47 c7 both result in the pawn promoting.

46 ... a5 47 ♖b8 a4 1:0

KM16/2: 1) White to play

KM16/2: 2) Black to play

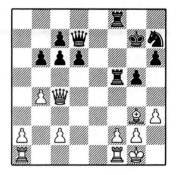

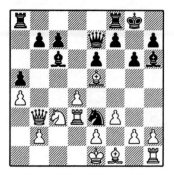

KM16/2: 3) White to play

KM16/2:4) Black to play

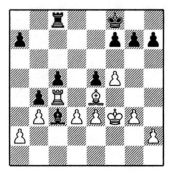

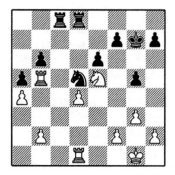

A16/2: a) White to play

A16/2: b) White to play

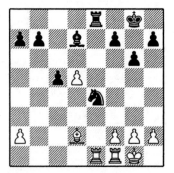

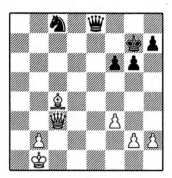

Month 16/Week 3:
The 'Swindle'

'Swindling' is generally regarded as a disreputable way to win your games. I could not disagree more and in fact rather dislike the term.

The fact is that if your opponent loses his way in a winning position then it is entirely his fault and probably a reflection of his overall playing strength. So don't apologise to your opponents if you outplay them from a lost position.

There are no moral laws to say that it is right and proper that 'winning' positions should be won.

Emanuel Lasker was one of the greatest 'swindlers' in the history of the game. He believed that a position could never be so bad as not to hold out the prospect of defence and he saved many positions in which others would have resigned.

Lasker - Nimzowitsch
St. Petersburg 1914

1 e4 c6 2 d4 d5 3 ♘c3 dxe4 4 ♘xe4 ♘f6 5 ♘xf6+ gxf6 6 ♗e2 ♗f5 7 ♗f3 ♕a5+ 8 c3 h5 9 ♗xh5 ♘d7 10 ♗g4 ♗xg4 11 ♕xg4 0-0-0 12 ♘e2 e6 13 ♗f4 ♕b5 14 0-0-0 ♘b6 15 ♘g3?

15 b3 would have left White with a safe but difficult game according to Lasker. Now Black regains his pawn with interest.

15 ... ♕d5 16 ♔b1 ♕xg2 17 ♖dg1 ♕xf2

Emerging a pawn up. In theory Black should no doubt be able to win this position in the end, in practice it turns out to be a very difficult matter.

I find it deeply instructive the way Lasker ultimately manages to 'swindle' his opponent. He doesn't gamble everything on one desperate charge but sets himself the task of preventing his opponent from winning.

18 ♘e4 ♕h4 19 ♕f3 ♘c4 20 ♔a1 f5 21 ♘g5 ♗d6 22 ♗c1 ♖d7 23 ♖g2 ♗c7 24 ♖hg1 ♘d6 25 ♕e2 ♘e4 26 ♘f3 ♕h3

26 ... ♕h5 may well have been better but this isn't such an important point for the illustration of the theme. What matters is how Lasker sets about putting up resistance.

27 a3!?

Most players would probably have tried to free themselves with 27 ♘g5 but after 27 ... ♘xg5 28 ♗xg5 f4! 29 ♕e4 (29 ♖f2 ♖g8!) 29 ... f3 30 ♖f2 ♖g8 31 ♕xf3 ♕xf3 32 ♖xf3 ♗xh2 Black retains his advantage in a considerably simpler position.

Lasker decides instead to await events because he saw that Black must regroup his pieces in order to achieve anything. And during this regrouping procedure he hopes to get an opportunity to create counter-play ...

27 ... a6 28 ♗e3 ♖hd8 29 ♔a2 ♖h8 30 ♔a1 ♖hd8 31 ♔a2

31 ♘g5 ♕h4! prevents White's bishop from taking up residence on f6 which would in fact happen after 31 ... ♘xg5 32 ♗xg5.

31 ... ♖e8 32 ♖g8 ♖xg8 33 ♖xg8+ ♖d8 34 ♖g7 ♖d7 35 ♖g8+ ♖d8 36 ♖g7 ♖f8 37 c4 ♘f6?

Nimzowitsch starts to lose his nerve and allows Lasker the chance he has been waiting for. 37 ... ♕h8! 38 ♕g2 (Or 38 ♖g2) 38 ... ♘f6 would have been good for Black and would probably win in the long run.

38 ♗g5! ♘h5?

Black takes fright at the thought of 38 ... ♘e4 39 ♗e7 but then 39 ... ♖e8 40 ♖xf7 ♕g4! threatening 41 ... ♕g8 would have been very unpleasant for White. Clearly Black had missed the following stunning blow:

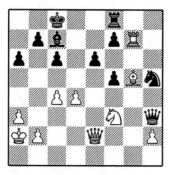

39 ♖xf7! ♖xf7 40 ♕xe6+ ♖d7

Nimzowitsch might have been close to panic but then seen that he can draw. If 40 ... ♔b8 there follows 41 ♕e8+! (and not 41 ♕xf7 ♕xf3) 41 ... ♔a7 (41 ... ♗d8 42 ♗xd8) 42 ♕xf7 etc.

41 ♘e5 ♗xe5 42 ♕e8+ ½-½

42 ... ♔c7 43 ♕xe5+ leaves Black unable to escape perpetual check.

Frank Marshall was another arch-swindler, if not quite in Lasker's overall class. In the following game we clearly see frustration creep into White's play as an excellent position starts to evaporate. And in his efforts to pursue an illusory advantage he weakens his position ... .

Vidmar - Marshall
New York 1927

1 d4 ♘f6 2 ♘f3 e6 3 c4 ♗b4+ 4 ♗d2 ♗xd2+ 5 ♘bxd2 d5 6 e3 0-0 7 ♕c2 ♘bd7 8 ♗d3 h6?!

A dubious-looking move with a dubious-looking follow-up. The sound course was to play 8 ... c6 followed by 9 ... ♕e7

9 0-0 c5!? 10 cxd5 ♘xd5 11 dxc5 ♘b4 12 ♗h7+ ♔h8 13 ♕c4 ♘a6 14 ♗c2 ♘dxc5 15 b4 ♘d7 16 ♖fd1 ♘b6 17 ♕b3 ♕d5 18 ♕b2 ♗d7 19 ♘e4 ♕b5 20 a3 ♗c6

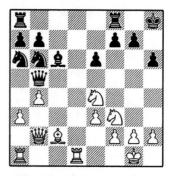

21 ♘d4?

It turns out that this loses most of White's advantage. As Alekhine pointed out in the tournament book White could increase the pressure with either 21 ♗d3 or 21 ♘e5.

21 ... ♕e5 22 f4?

Mistakes rarely come alone and this move seriously weakens

White's position. He should have played 22 ♕b1 when White still has the better game.

22 ... ♕c7 23 ♘xc6 bxc6 24 ♗d3 ♘b8 25 ♖ac1 ♘d5

Beginning the counterplay against White's weakened centre.

26 ♕f2 a5! 27 b5 ♕b6!

The threat against the b5 and e3 pawns forces White's reply and leads to a significant improvement in Black's position.

28 bxc6 ♘xc6 29 ♘c5 ♖ad8 30 g4?

White is finding it difficult to believe that his advantage has disappeared and tries to launch an unjustified attack. In reality this just weakens his position.

30 ... ♘de7 31 h4? ♖d5!

Marshall strikes back, threatening the knight on c5. White's reply is more or less forced and would have been good for him had Black been forced to retreat.

32 e4

32 ... ♖d4!

This must have come as a shock to White. The point is that 33 ♘d7 ♕d8 34 ♘xf8 ♖xd3 35 ♖xd3 ♕xd3

(35 ... ♕xd3 36 f5 exf5 37 exf5 ♔g8 38 f6 gxf6) traps White's errant knight.

33 f5 exf5 34 gxf5 ♘e5! 35 ♗e2

35 ♕xd4?? ♘f3+ would lose the queen.

35 ... ♖xd1+ 36 ♖xd1 ♖d8 37 ♖xd8+ ♕xd8 38 f6 ♘7c6 39 fxg7+ ♔xg7 40 ♔g2

40 ♘d3 ♘xd3 41 ♕g3+ ♔h7 42 ♗xd3 ♕d4+ 43 ♔f1 ♘e5 is also very unpleasant.

40 ... ♘g6 41 ♔h3

Or 41 h5 ♕g5+ 42 ♔f1 ♘f4.

41 ... ♕d6!

Threatening to win a piece with 42 ... ♘f4+. White's position continues to get worse.

42 ♔g2 ♘d4 43 ♘b7

43 ♘d3 ♘xe2 44 ♕xe2 ♕xd3! wins a piece.

43 ... ♕e5 44 ♔f1 ♘f4 45 ♕g3+ ♔h7 46 ♗d3 ♘de6! 47 ♗a6 ♕a1+ 48 ♕e1 ♕b2!

Commencing the final attack.

49 ♕e3 ♕g2+ 50 ♔e1 ♕c2 51 ♕f3 ♘g2+ 52 ♔f1 ♘ef4! 53 ♔g1 ♘xh4 54 ♕f1 ♕xe4 55 ♘c5 ♕e3+ 56 ♔h1 ♕xc5 57 ♗d3+ f5! 0:1

KM16/3: 1) Black to play

KM16/3: 2) White to play

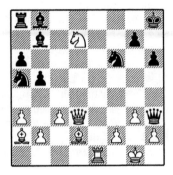

KM16/3: 3) White to play

KM16/3: 4) White to play

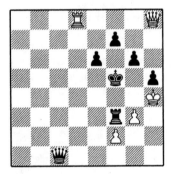

A16/3: a) Black to play

A16/3: b) Black to play

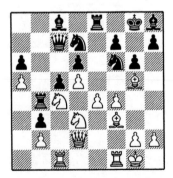

Month 16/Week 4:
Never Say Die!

It started to become clear from the examples given last week that the best way to pull off a 'swindle' is not just to try an isolated trick. The right thing to do is to make it as difficult as possible for your opponent to win the position, to put as many obstacles in his path as possible.

One of the most inspiring books I have read is *The Art of the Middle Game* by Paul Keres and Alexander Kotov. Keres wrote a superb chapter entitled 'How to Defend Difficult Positions'. The advice contained within this chapter has undoubtably helped me save many lost positions:

"When the player with the upper hand is continually confronted by new problems, when, at every moment, one renders the win as difficult as possible, then it is likely that his powers will eventually weaken and he may make some mistake."

In the following game Keres practiced what he preached:

Bronstein - Keres
Amsterdam Ct 1956

1 e4 e5 2 ♘f3 ♘c6 3 ♗b5 a6 4 ♗a4 ♘f6 5 0-0 ♗e7 6 ♖e1 b5 7 ♗b3 d6 8 c3 0-0 9 h3 ♘a5 10 ♗c2 c5 11 d4 ♕c7 12 ♘bd2 cxd4 13 cxd4 ♘c6 14 ♘b3 ♗b7 15 ♗g5 h6 16 ♗h4 ♘h5 17 d5 ♘d8 18 ♗xe7 ♕xe7 19 ♘fd4!

Black's opening has hardly been a success and White's pressure mounts move by move.

19 ... ♘f4 20 ♘f5 ♕f6 21 ♖e3 ♔h7 22 a4 bxa4 23 ♖xa4 ♗c8 24 ♖b4 ♘b7 25 ♖c3 g6 26 ♘e3 a5 27 ♖b6 ♕d8 28 ♘c4 ♖a7 29 ♘c1 ♕g5 30 ♖g3 ♕e7 31 ♘e2 ♘xe2+ 32 ♕xe2 ♖d8 33 ♖a3 ♗d7 34 ♕e3 ♖c8 35 ♗d3 ♗e8!

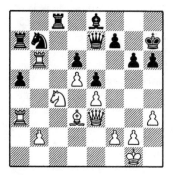

36 b4!

Keres tried to lure White into taking the d-pawn but after 36 ♘xd6 ♘xd6 37 ♖xd6 ♕xd6 38 ♕xa7 ♕b4 he would get good counterplay (39 ♕xa5 can be met by 39 ... ♖c1+ 40 ♔h2 ♕xb2 41 ♖a2 ♕b3).

36 ... a4 37 ♔h2 ♖aa8 38 ♗e2 ♖c7 39 b5! ♕d8 40 ♖a2 ♔g7 41 ♖c6!

Bronstein's sealed move which was undoubtably the best. Black can hardly accept the exchange sacrifice as 41 ... ♗xc6 42 dxc6 ♘c5 43 ♘xe5 is hopeless. So Keres tries to distract White with the lure of the a4 pawn.

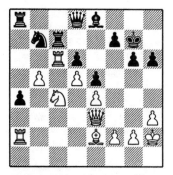

41 ... ♖b8 42 ♖d2!

An excellent move which simply maintains the advantages of White's position. Rushing in with 42 ♖xa4 ♗xc6 43 dxc6 would allow Black to gain a tempo with 43 ... ♘c5 and bring the knight to e6 and d4.

42 ... h5 43 ♖d1

The most effective way to win would have been with, say, 43 ♕c3! after which White is threatening things like 44 ♘xe5, 44 ♘xd6 and even 44 f4. But Bronstein was getting into time-trouble and doubtless wanted to keep it simple.

43 ... ♔g8 44 ♔g1 ♔h7 45 ♕a3 ♕e7

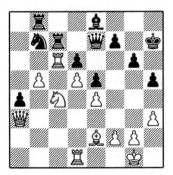

46 ♕xa4?

A serious mistake which gives Black his chance. Bronstein had used more valuable time to discover that the line 46 ♘xd6 ♗xc6 47 dxc6 ♘xd6 48 ♕xd6 (Or 48 ♖xd6 ♖d8 49 ♖d3 ♕xa3 50 ♖xa3 ♖d4) 48 ... ♕xd6 49 ♖xd6 a3 50 ♖d2 (50 ♗c4 a2 51 ♖d1 ♖xc6!) 50 ... ♖a7 is far from clear. But 46 ♕c3! would have been strong.

46 ... ♘c5 47 ♕c2

47 ♕a5 was a better chance when Black should first go 47 ... ♖a7! rather than the immediate 47 ...

♗xc6 as after 48 dc the move 48 ... ♘xe4 can be met by 49 ♗f3!.

47 ... ♗xc6! 48 dxc6 ♖xb5!

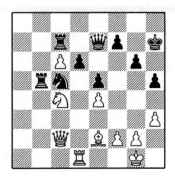

49 ♘xd6

Bronstein is unable to adjust in time to the change of fortunes and continues to play for a win. 49 ♘e3! ♖b8 50 ♘d5 ♕d8 51 ♘xc7 ♕xc7 would have given White an equal game. Probably he thought that Black has to play 49 ... ♖a5 50 ♕c3 ♖xc6 51 ♕xa5 ♖xd6 with what is probably a drawn endgame

49 ... ♖b6! 50 ♗b5?

The losing move. 50 ♕xc5 ♖cxc6 51 ♕xb6 ♖xb6 52 ♘c8 ♕c5 53 ♘xb6 ♕xb6 would still have held the game with careful play.

50 ... ♘e6 51 ♗a4

On 51 ♕c4 there is 51 ... ♘d4 52 ♕d5 ♘xb5 53 ♘xb5 ♖cxc6 etc.

51 ... ♘d4 52 ♕c5 ♖bxc6! 53 ♗xc6 ♖xc6 0:1

White lost on time but his position is already hopeless.

In the last example this month we see Bobby Fischer perform a miraculous escape against a Swiss amateur. The message is that strong players make their own luck.

**Walther - Fischer
Zurich 1959**

1 e4 c5 2 ♘f3 d6 3 d4 cd 4 ♘xd4 ♘f6 5 ♘c3 a6 6 ♗g5 e6 7 f4 ♗e7 8 ♕f3 ♘bd7 9 0-0-0 ♕c7 10 ♗d3 b5 11 ♗xf6 ♘xf6 12 ♖he1 ♗b7

Fischer pointed out that he should have played 12 ... b4! followed by ... ♗b7 and maybe ... d5. This opportunity repeats itself on the next move because White omits the mandatory 13 a3.

13 ♔b1 ♖c8?

Giving up the possibility of castling queenside. 13 ... b4! was still the right move.

14 g4 ♘d7 15 g5 ♘b6?

The very last chance to play ... b5-b4.

16 f5! e5

16 ... b4? 17 fxe6 is hopeless and 16 ... ♗xg5? is met by 17 ♗xb5+! ♔e7 18 fxe6 fxe6 19 ♘xe6! etc.

17 f6! gxf6

17 ... exd4 18 ♘d5 ♗xd5 19 exd5 is absolutely deadly.

18 gxf6 ♗f8 19 ♘d5 ♘xd5 20 exd5 ♔d8 21 ♘c6+! ♗xc6 22 dxc6 ♕xc6 23 ♗e4 ♕b6

Fischer is quite lost here but he hangs on by the skin of his teeth.

24 ♕h5 ♔c7 25 ♗f5! ♖d8 26 ♕xf7+ ♔b8 27 ♕e6 ♕c7 28 ♖e3! ♗h6 29 ♖c3 ♕b7 30 f7 ♗g7 31 ♖cd3 ♗f8 32 ♕xe5! dxe5 33 ♖xd8+ ♔a7 34 ♖1d7 h5 35 ♖xb7+ ♔xb7 36 c3 ♔c7 37 ♖a8

After 37 ♖e8!, either here or on the next move, Fischer would have resigned. Now the win is more difficult.

37 ... ♔d6 38 ♖xa6+ ♔e7 39 ♖e6+

A simpler way would have been 39 ♖a7+ ♔f6 40 ♗d3.

39 ... ♔xf7 40 ♖xe5 b4 41 cxb4 ♗xb4 42 h3 ♔f6 43 ♖b5 ♗d6 44 ♗e4 ♖e8 45 ♖f5+ ♔g7 46 ♗f3 ♖e1+ 47 ♔c2 ♖f1 48 ♖d5

Black was threatening to repeat the position with 48 ... ♖f2+ 49 ♔b1 (49 ♔b3? ♗g6!) 49 ... ♖f1+ etc.

48 ... ♖f2+ 49 ♖d2

49 ♔b1 ♗a3 50 bxa3 ♖xf3 51 ♖xh5 ♖xa3 is also lost.

49 ... ♖xd2+ 50 ♔xd2 h4 51 ♔d3 ♔f6 52 ♔c4 ♔e7 53 ♔b5 ♔d7

54 a4?

White misses his last chance. The Swiss endgame composer Fontana pointed out that 54 b4! ♔c7 55 ♔a5! ♔b8 56 b5 ♗a3 57 b6 ♔c8 58 ♔a6 ♔b8 59 ♗g2! puts Black in zugzwang (59 ... ♔c8 60 ♔a7 ♗c5 61 a4).

54 ... ♔c7 55 b4 ♔b8 56 a5 ♔a7 57 ♔c4 ♗g3 58 ♔b3 ♗e1 59 ♔a4 ♗d2 60 ♗h5 ♗e1 61 b5 ♗f2 62 ♗e2 ♗e3 63 ♔b3 ♗d2 64 b6+ ♔b7 65 ♔a4 ♔c6 66 ♗b5+ ♔c5 67 ♗e8 ♗e1 ½-½

White's pawns are unable to advance any further. 68 b7 is met by 68 ... ♗g3 69 a6 ♔b6.

KM16/4: 1) White to play

KM16/4: 2) White to play

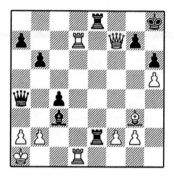

KM16/4: 3) Black to play

KM16/4: 4) White to play

A16/4: a) Black to play

A16/4: b) Black to play

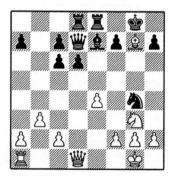

5 Endgame Themes

Many people believe that because the opening comes first it is more important to study this phase of a game before anything else. After all, if you can't get good positions to start with then what's the use of knowing how to convert a slight advantage in the endgame?

I see this question rather differently. In the opening we start out with the most complex position and through exchanges gradually derive simpler ones. If one is unable to understand fully how a few pieces cooperate together then how can we appreciate positions with a full orchestra of pieces? It is no accident that many of the greatest masters, notably Karpov and Capablanca, have recommended studying the endgame before other aspects of chess.

The process of studying the endgame can have a profound influence on one's whole game by developing a general understanding of chess and enabling players to think in a more logical and methodical manner. A player who is confident in his ability to win in the endgame can play both opening and middlegame in a more restrained manner. Being unafraid to enter an endgame can mean that straining to play for mate will be a thing of the past.

In week one of this month I will touch upon the art of knowing which piece to exchange while week two is concerned with stretching the defence by attacking several weaknesses. In week three we will look at the art of reducing the opponent's active possibilities rather than immediately pursuing one's own active plans. Week four is devoted to the kind of systematic thinking that works particularly well in endgames and can benefit one's game as a whole.

Month 17/Week 1:
The Art of Exchanging

Knowing which pieces to exchange and which to leave on the board is one of the thorniest issues on the chessboard and of particular importance in the endgame where it can even be decisive. There are certain configurations of pieces which have drawish tendencies, others will simply suit the pawn structure better.

Generally speaking the best way to exploit a material advantage is through simplification but thoughtless exchanges can lead to a draw. rook or opposite coloured bishop endgames will have drawish tendencies whilst the simplest endgames are those with pawns.

In the following game we see the former World Champion Mikhail Botvinnik make a brilliant decision to exchange the rooks seeing that the resulting pawn endgame is a win.

Taimanov - Botvinnik
Moscow 1967

1 d4 d5 2 c4 c6 3 ♘f3 ♘f6 4 ♘bd2 g6 5 e3 ♗g7 6 ♗e2 0-0 7 0-0 b6 8 b4 ♗b7 9 ♗b2 ♘e4 10 ♘xe4 dxe4 11 ♘d2 f5 12 c5 ♘d7 13 ♕b3+ ♔h8 14 d5 cxd5 15 ♗xg7+ ♔xg7 16 ♗b5 bxc5 17 bxc5 ♖c8 18 ♕c3+ ♖f6 19 ♘b3 ♔g8 20 ♖ac1 a6 21 ♗xd7 ♕xd7 22 ♖fd1 ♗c6 23 ♘a5 f4 24 exf4 ♖xf4 25 ♘xc6 ♖xc6 26 ♕e5 ♖f5 27 ♕xe4 dxe4 28 ♖xd7 ♖fxc5 29 ♖e1 ♖c1 30 ♔f1 ♔f7 31 ♖d4?

According to Botvinnik White should have played 31 ♖xc1 ♖xc1+ 32 ♔e2 ♖c2+ 33 ♔e3 ♖xa2 34 ♖d4! with a likely draw. Now he drifts into trouble.

31 ... ♖xe1+ 32 ♔xe1 ♖c2 33 ♖a4?

At this point 33 ♖xe4 ♖xa2 34 g4! followed by ♔f1-g2 was the best chance.

33 ... e3! 34 fxe3 ♖xg2 35 h4 h5 36 ♔f1 ♖g4!!

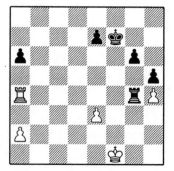

A brilliantly worked out move by Botvinnik which shows great confidence in his calculations. Pawn endgames can be the simplest to win but this one requires great subtlety and finesse.

37 ♖xg4 hxg4 38 ♔g2 g5! 39 h5

Black is also winning after 39 ♔g3 ♔g6 40 ♔xg4 gxh4 41 ♔xh4 ♔f5 42 ♔g3 ♔e4 43 ♔f2 a5 44 ♔e2 a4 45 a3 e6! 46 ♔d2 ♔f3 47 ♔d3 e5-+.

39 ... ♔g7 40 ♔g3 ♔h7!

And not 40 ... ♔h6 41 ♔xg4 a5 42 e4 when it is White who wins.

41 ♔xg4 ♔h6 0:1

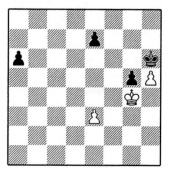

Taimanov sealed the move 42 e4 but he resigned when Botvinnik demonstrated a win with 42 ... a5 43 a4 e5 44 ♔f5 ♔xh5 45 ♔xe5 g4 46 ♔f4 ♔h4 47 e5 g3 48 e6 g2 49 e7 g1=♕ 50 e8=♕ ♕f2+ 51 ♔e5 ♕e1+ etc. Had White played 42 a4 then 42 ... a5 43 e4 e5 would lead to the same thing and not 42 ... e6? 43 a5 or 42 ... e5 43 a3.

In the next game we see Bobby Fischer demonstrate the art of exchanging in classic style. Fischer was simply outstanding when it came to fluently translating one type of advantage into another, even by the high standards of World Champions.

Fischer - Petrosian
Buenos Aires Cm 1971

1 e4 c5 2 ♘f3 e6 3 d4 cxd4 4
♘xd4 a6 5 ♗d3 ♘c6 6 ♘xc6 bxc6
7 0-0 d5 8 c4! ♘f6 9 cxd5 cxd5 10
exd5 exd5 11 ♘c3 ♗e7 12 ♕a4+!
♕d7 13 ♖e1!

Fischer heads for a clear endgame
edge rather than taking a hot rook
with 13 ♗b5 axb5 14 ♕xa8 0-0.

13 ... ♕xa4 14 ♘xa4 ♗e6 15
♗e3 0-0

16 ♗c5!

The exchange of Black's good
bishop is rather a standard proceed-
ure and White thereby gains control
of an outpost on c5 Black should
probably have answered this with
16 ... ♗xc5 17 ♘xc5 ♖fb8!, trying
for counter-play on the b-file.

16 ... ♖fe8 17 ♗xe7 ♖xe7 18 b4!
♔f8 19 ♘c5 ♗c8 20 f3 ♖ea7

20 ... ♖xe1+ 21 ♖xe1 ♘d7 looks
better but would nevertheless leave
Black facing White's queenside
pawn majority and the weakness of
his a-pawn and the d4 square.

21 ♖e5 ♗d7

Clearly intending 22 ... ♗b5 and
should White prevent this with 22
a4 the b4 pawn would be a target.
Fischer's reply is just brilliant.

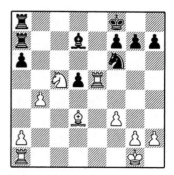

22 ♘xd7+!

Exchanging off Black's bad
bishop like this looks like a begin-
ner's move. In fact it allows White
to further penetrate his opponent's
defences.

22 ... ♖xd7 23 ♖c1

Threatening 24 ♖c6.

**23 ... ♖d6 24 ♖c7 ♘d7 25 ♖e2 g6
26 ♔f2 h5 27 f4**

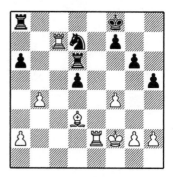

27 ... h4?

Petrosian's resistance starts to
crumble. 27 ... ♘b6 28 ♖ee7 ♖f6
was more tenacious.

**28 ♔f3 f5 29 ♔e3 d4+ 30 ♔d2
♘b6 31 ♖ee7 ♘d5 32 ♖f7+ ♔e8 33
♖b7 ♘xb4 34 ♗c4 1:0**

There is nothing Black can do
about the threat of 35 ♖h7 ♖f6 36
♖h8+ ♖f8 37 ♗f7+.

KM17/1: 1) White to play

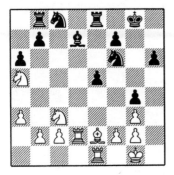

KM17/1: 2) White to play

KM17/1: 3) Black to play

KM17/1: 4) White to play

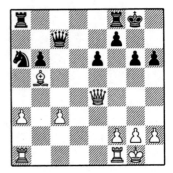

A17/1: a) White to play

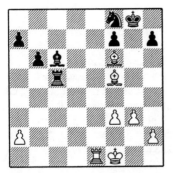

A17/1: b) White to play

Month 17/Week 2:
On The Rack

It is usually not enough to attack a single weakness. Your opponent defends it and then what do you do?

One answer to this problem is to create a second weakness in another part of the board. The superior mobility of the attacking side will enable him to switch from one weakness to the other faster than the defender can respond.

In the following two games Alekhine puts his opponents on the rack as his uses this strategy of creating a second target:

Alekhine - Euwe
London 1922

1 d4 ♘f6 2 ♘f3 g6 3 ♗f4 ♗g7 4 ♘bd2 c5 5 e3 d6 6 c3 ♘c6 7 h3 0-0 8 ♗c4! ♖e8 9 0-0 e5 10 dxe5 ♘xe5 11 ♗xe5! dxe5 12 ♘g5! ♗e6

An unfortunate necessity as after 12 ... ♖f8 13 ♘de4 Black is in terrible trouble whether he chooses 13 ... ♕xd1 14 ♖fxd1 ♘xe4 15 ♘xe4 b6 16 ♘d6, 13 ... ♕e7 14 ♘d6! or 13 ... ♘xe4? 14 ♗xf7+!.

13 ♗xe6 fxe6 14 ♘de4 ♘xe4 15 ♕xd8 ♖exd8 16 ♘xe4

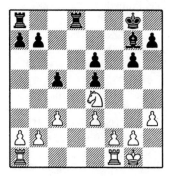

White has obtained a clear advantage out of the opening. His knight is a tower of strength compared with Black's bad bishop on g7 and Black has weak doubled e-pawns. Yet how is White to convert these advantages into a full point?

16 ... b6 17 ♖fd1 ♔f8 18 ♔f1! ♔e7 19 c4! h6 20 ♔e2 ♖xd1 21 ♖xd1

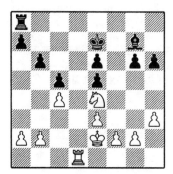

21 ... ♖b8

By avoiding the exchange of rooks Black makes things much more difficult. Alekhine noted that after 21 ... ♖d8? 22 ♖xd8 ♔xd8 White plays 23 h4! intending to fix Black's kingside with g2-g4-g5. He can then play b2-b3 followed by ♔d3, ♘c3, ♔e4; ♘d3 and finally advance with f2-f4!. If Black takes this pawn White recaptures with the knight and wins the pawn on g6. If Black doesn't capture he loses the e5 pawn.

22 ♖d3 ♗h8 23 a4!

White sets about creating a weakness on the queenside. Black cannot play 23 ... a5 since 24 ♖b3 would win his b-pawn. So he has to allow the opening of the a-file which White then occupies with his rook.

23 ... ♖c8 24 ♖b3 ♔d7 25 a5!
♔c6 26 axb6 axb6 27 ♖a3 ♗g7 28
♖a7! ♖c7

Black now sees nothing better
than exchange the rooks but now
White has a quicker way to win.

29 ♖a8! ♖e7 30 ♖c8+ ♔d7 31
♖g8 ♔c6 32 h4!

White can systematically
strengthen his position because
Black has no counterplay what-
soever. The idea now is to seal in
Black's bishop with g2-g4-g5

32 ... ♔c7 33 g4 ♔c6 34 ♔d3
♖d7+ 35 ♔c3 ♖f7 36 b3 ♔c7 37
♔d3 ♖d7+ 38 ♔e2 ♖f7 39 ♘c3!

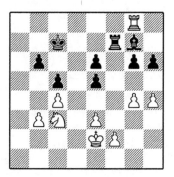

The beginning of the final stage.
White intends to post this knight on
b5, an even stronger square than e4.
This latter outpost will be occupied
by his king.

39 ... ♖e7 40 g5 hxg5 41 hxg5
♔c6 42 ♔d3

White could also win by bringing
his knight to h4 via e4, d2 and f3.
But he prefers to stick to the original
plan.

42 ... ♖d7+ 43 ♔e4 ♖c7 44 ♘b5
♖e7 45 f3 ♔d7

The only move for after 45 ...
♔b7 there is 46 ♘d6+ followed by
47 ♘e8 winning the bishop.

46 ♖b8 ♔c6 47 ♖c8+ ♔d7

If 47 ... ♖f7 there is 48 ♖c8+ or if
47 ... ♔b7 White wins with 48
♘d6+ ♔a7 49 ♖g8.

48 ♖c7+ ♔d8 49 ♖c6! ♖b7 50
♖xe6 1:0

In the next game Alekhine gives
another masterful demonstration of
this type of plan, this time setting
about opening a second front on the
kingside (32 g4!) to exploit his extra
pawn.

Alekhine - Vidmar
Hastings 1936-7

1 d4 d5 2 c4 e6 3 ♘c3 ♘f6 4
♗g5 ♘bd7 5 e3 ♗e7 6 ♘f3 0-0 7
♖c1 c6 8 ♕c2 a6 9 cxd5 ♘xd5 10
♗xe7 ♕xe7 11 ♗c4 ♘xc3 12 ♕xc3
c5 13 dxc5 ♕xc5?

Black should play 13 ... ♘xc5
after which 14 ♗e2 ♘e4 15 ♕d4
♘f6 16 0-0 leaves White with only
a slight pull. An interesting alternative would be 14 ♗d5!?.

14 ♗b3! b6

After 14 ... ♕xc3 15 ♖xc3 a
White rook would cause Black serious problems by landing on c7. But
now White pursues attacks his opponent's queen until he gaims a material advantage.

15 ♕d2 ♕h5 16 ♗d1!

The immediate 16 ♖xc8? would
have been bad because of 16 ...
♖axc8 17 ♕xd7 ♖fd8-+ but now it
is a threat. Black's reply is forced.

16 ... ♘c5 17 b4! ♘e4 18 ♕d4
♗b7 19 0-0

Vidmar is trying to lure his opponent into departing from the logical
path with 19 ♕xb6?! ♗d5 20 a3
♕g6 (21 0-0 ♘d2!). But Alekhine
refuses to be tempted.

19 ... b5 20 ♘e5 ♕h6 21 ♘c6
♗xc6 22 ♖xc6 ♘f6 23 ♗f3

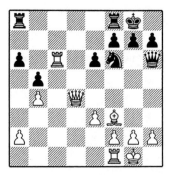

Reaching the kind of position that Alekhine had in mind when he first played 16 ♗d1. The bishop is very effective on this diagonal and Black's queen cannot help come to the aid of his queenside.

23 ... ♖ad8 24 ♖d6 ♖xd6 25 ♕xd6 ♕h4 26 a3 ♕c4 27 ♕xa6 ♘d5 28 a4! ♘c7

Alekhine pointed out that 28 ... ♕xb4 loses to 29 ♗xd5 exd5 30 ♕xb5.

29 ♕c6 ♕xc6 30 ♗xc6 bxa4 31 ♖a1 ♖b8 32 ♖xa4 ♔f8 33 g4!

The start of the winning plan. White's b-pawn on its own can be blockaded so White sets about creating another weakness. He will achieve this objective with a gradual advance of his kingside pawns.

33 ... ♔e7 34 b5! e5 35 f4! f6

It would have been better to exchange on f4 but then White would gain the d4 square for his rook.

36 fxe5 fxe5 37 ♖a2 ♖b6 38 ♖b2 h6 39 ♔f2 ♔e6 40 ♔f3 ♘d5

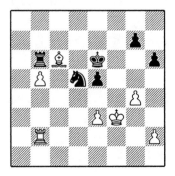

41 h4!

Naturally White avoids a rook endgame which would increase Black's drawing prospects. He chooses instead to consistently carry out his plan.

41 ... ♘e7 42 ♗e4 ♘d5 43 ♖b3 ♔d6 44 g5! hxg5 45 hxg5 ♔e6 46 ♗d3 ♔d6 47 ♖a3 ♘c7 48 ♖a7 ♖b8 49 ♔e4

The threat of 50 ♔f5 forces another weakness after which White begins the invasion.

49 ... g6 50 ♖a3! ♖b6 51 ♗c4 ♖b8 52 ♖d3+ ♔c5 53 ♖d7!

Finally White's rook invades the opposing camp. Black is in no position to defend the new weaknesses.

53 ... ♘e8 54 ♗f7 ♘d6+ 55 ♔xe5 ♖b6 56 e4 ♘xb5 57 ♖d5+! ♔b4 58 ♖d8 ♘a7 59 ♖d6 ♘c6+ 60 ♔d5 ♘e7+ 61 ♔e6 ♘c6 62 ♔f6 ♔c5 63 ♖d5+ ♔b4 64 e5 ♔c4 65 ♖d1+ ♔c5 66 ♖c1+ ♔d4 67 e6 ♔e3 68 ♗xg6 ♘d4 69 ♗f7 ♘e2 70 ♖e1 ♔f2 71 ♖xe2+ 1:0

KM17/2: 1) Black to play

KM17/2: 2) White to play

KM17/2: 3) White to play

KM17/2: 4) Black to play

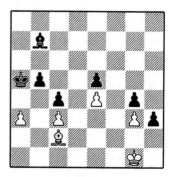

A17/2 a) Black to play

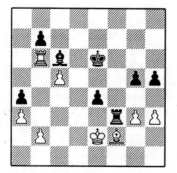

A17/2: b) Black to play

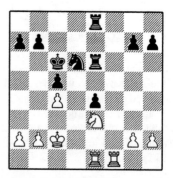

Month 17/Week 3:
Python Technique

Last month we looked at the idea of restricting the opponent's counterplay in order to win won positions. This month we will take this idea one step further and look at the art of gradually running the opponent out of decent moves, perhaps even going as far as to put him in *zugzwang*. This strategy of strangulation is far from being negative, sometimes it can represent the only logical way to play a position and prove far more effective than a quick attack. If your opponent has no active moves it can have quite a depressing effect .

Here are two examples on this theme, the first being a classic example of the minority attack in which Kotov gives Black a weak c-pawn and then tightens his grip on the other side of the board.

Kotov - Pachman
Venice 1950

1 d4 e6 2 c4 ♘f6 3 ♘c3 d5 4 ♗g5 ♗e7 5 e3 0-0 6 ♘f3 ♘bd7 7 ♖c1 a6 8 cxd5 exd5 9 ♗d3 ♖e8 10 0-0 c6 11 ♕c2 ♘f8 12 a3 g6 13 b4 ♘e6 14 ♗xf6 ♗xf6 15 a4 ♘g7 16 b5 axb5 17 axb5 ♗f5 18 ♗xf5 ♘xf5 19 bxc6 bxc6 20 ♘a4

A rather typical minority attack type position in which White has saddled Black with a weak c-pawn. The next part of the game shows White gradually trying to infiltrate the opposing camp.

20 ... ♖c8 21 ♕c5 ♘d6 22 ♘d2 ♖e7 23 ♖b1 ♖b7 24 ♖xb7 ♘xb7 25 ♕a7 ♘d6 26 ♕a6 ♕c7 27 ♖c1 ♗d8 28 ♘c5 ♕a5 29 ♕d3 ♕b5 30

g3 ♗b6 31 ♖b1 ♕xd3 32 ♘xd3 ♗a5 33 ♘b3 ♗d8 34 ♘bc5 ♗e7 35 ♘d7 ♖c7 36 ♘b8 ♘c4 37 ♖a1 ♖c8 38 ♘d7 ♖c7 39 ♖a8+ ♔g7 40 ♘7e5 ♘xe5 41 ♘xe5 ♗d6 42 ♘d3 ♔f6?

A serious mistake which allows White to fix a second weakness. Had Black seen what was coming he would have played 42 ... h5.

43 g4!

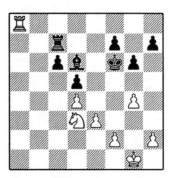

A very instructive move, reminiscent of Alekhine's 32 g4 in the previous section. White takes space on the kingside and sets about fixing a second weakness.

43 ... ♔e6

White would meet 43 ... ♔g5 with 44 h3 h5 45 f4+ ♔h4 46 ♔g2.

44 ♔g2 ♖b7 45 ♖e8+ ♖e7 46 ♖h8 f6 47 h4 ♖b7 48 ♔f3 ♖f7 49 ♖e8+ ♖e7 50 ♖d8! ♖a7 51 ♘c5+ ♔e7 52 ♖c8!

After the immediate 52 ♖h8 Black would escape with 52 ... ♗xc5 53 dxc5 ♖a5 54 ♖xh7+ ♔f8. The point is that defending c6 with 52 ... ♖c7 would be met with 53 ♖h8 so Black decides to go active in any case.

52 ... ♗xc5 53 dxc5 ♔d7 54 ♖h8 ♔e6

If 54 ... ♖a5 there follows 55 ♖xh7+ ♔e6 56 ♖g7.

55 ♖d8 ♔e7?!

According to Speelman 55 ... ♖c7 was a better defence.

56 ♖d6 ♖a6 57 g5!

Clearing the way for his king to enter the opposing camp.

57 ... fxg5 58 hxg5 ♔f7 59 ♔g3

And not 59 ♔f4 ♖a4+ 60 ♔e5?? ♖e4#.

59 ... ♔e7 60 f3 ♖a3 61 ♔f4 ♖a4+ 62 ♔e5 ♖a3 63 ♖xc6 ♖xe3+ 64 ♔xd5 ♖d3+

After 64 ... ♖xf3 White wins with 65 ♖c7+ ♔e8 66 ♖xh7.

65 ♔e4 ♖c3 66 f4 ♖c1 67 ♖c7+

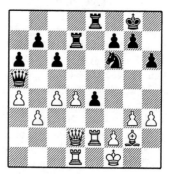

67 ... ♔d8?

The last mistake. Speelman pointed out that Black can still draw with 67 ... ♔e6 68 ♖xh7 ♖c4+ 69 ♔f3 ♖xc5 70 ♖g7 ♖c6! 71 ♖xg6+ (71 ♔g4 ♔d5 72 ♖f7 ♖e6 73 ♖f6 ♔d6 fails to make progress) 71 ... ♔f5 72 ♖xc6 stalemate!

68 ♖xh7 ♖xc5 69 ♖f7 1:0

The next example is a typical Karpov performance—he gradually increases the pressure until his opponent cracks. The exchange of minor pieces on move 57 is particularly interesting. Rook endgames are traditionally thought of as having drawish tendencies but Karpov sees that it the way to penetrate his opponent's defences.

Karpov - Hort
Tilburg 1979

1 e4 c6 2 ♘c3 d5 3 ♘f3 dxe4 4 ♘xe4 ♘f6 5 ♘xf6+ exf6 6 ♗e2 ♗d6 7 0-0 0-0 8 d4 ♖e8 9 ♖e1 ♗f5 10 ♗e3 ♘d7 11 h3 ♗e4 12 ♘d2 f5 13 ♘xe4 fxe4 14 c4 ♕c7 15 ♗f1 ♗h2+ 16 ♔h1 ♗f4 17 ♕d2 ♗xe3 18 ♕xe3

This position looks fairly innocent but White has more space and a bishop against knight. Slowly but surely Karpov sets about increasing these advantages.

18 ... ♘f6 19 ♖ad1 ♖ad8 20 ♖d2 h6 21 g3 ♕a5 22 b3 ♖d7 23 ♗g2 ♖ed8 24 ♖ed1 ♕g5 25 ♔g1 a6 26 ♖e2 ♔f8

With a bishop against a knight the exchange of queens favours White as queens work together well with knights. In this positon White would get added support for his d-pawn after 26 ... ♕xe3 27 fxe3.

27 ♕c3 ♕f5 28 a4 ♔g8 29 ♕e3 ♖e8 30 ♔f1 ♕a5 31 ♕d2

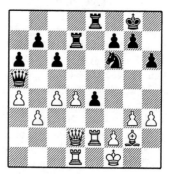

31 ... ♕xd2?!

Black should still decline the exchange of queens (with 31 ... ♕f5 for example) despite the fact that he no longer gives White and extra center pawn by doing so. Now

White is able to advance his king-side pawns and improve the position of his king.

32 Xexd2 e3 33 Xe2 exf2 34 Xxe8+ ♘xe8 35 ♔xf2 a5 36 ♔e3 ♔f8 37 Xb1 ♔e7 38 g4 ♔d8 39 b4

White has set gaining space on both sides of the board. His last move marks Black's b-pawn out as a weakness.

39 ... Xe7+ 40 ♔d3 axb4 41 Xxb4 ♔c7 42 Xb1 ♘f6 43 a5

Continuing the work started with 39 b4 by fixing Black's b-pawn to the b7 square.

43 ... ♘d7 44 Xa1 ♘b8 45 h4 ♘a6 46 Xb1 ♘b8 47 ♗f3 ♘d7 48 Xa1 Xe8 49 Xf1 Xe7 50 ♗g2 ♘b8 51 Xf4 ♘d7 52 Xf1 ♘b8 53 ♗e4 ♘a6 54 Xb1 ♘b8 55 ♗f5 ♘d7 56 Xa1 g6?

The decisive mistake? Black should have avoided this weakening move and kept the minor pieces on the board with 56 ... ♘b8. Karpov's reply must have come as a great surprise.

57 ♗xd7! Xxd7 58 Xf1 ♔b8 59 Xf6 ♔a7 60 h5

This is the real point of White's exchange on move 57. His rook on f6 is powerfully placed to attack Black's kingside.

60 ... ♔a6?!

Black should play 60 ... gxh5 61 gxh5 ♔a6 with chances to save the game. He might have missed White's reply.

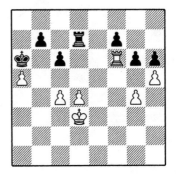

61 g5!

Deadly. Whether Black captures the g- or h-pawn White obtains a powerful passed pawn which ties Black's rook down to a hopelessly passive position.

61 ... hxg5 62 h6 ♔xa5 63 h7 Xd8 64 Xxf7 b5 65 cxb5 ♔xb5

After 65 ... cxb5 White wins with 66 ♔e4+-.

66 Xb7+! ♔a6 67 Xg7 Xh8 68 ♔e4 ♔b5 69 ♔f3 ♔c4 70 Xd7 ♔d3 71 ♔g4 Xxh7 72 Xxh7 ♔xd4 73 Xd7+ 1:0

KM17/3: 1) White to play

KM17/3: 2) White to play

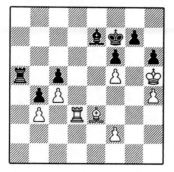

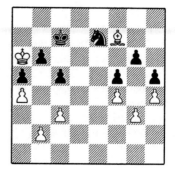

KM17/3: 3) White to play

KM17/3: 4) Black to play

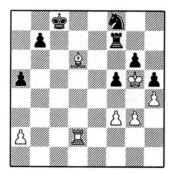

A17/3: a) Black to play

A17/3: b) White to play

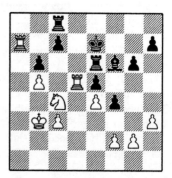

Month 17/Week 4:
Steadily Forward

Calculation is an inefficient means of thinking about chess and computers are much better at it than we are. What human players do have is an intuitive feel for where their pieces are best placed.

Smyslov has sometimes been called 'The Hand' because his finely developed intuition would enable him to play good moves almost without thinking at all. Other players with this kind of highly developed feel for chess include Karpov and the legendary Capablanca.

In his excellent book *Think Like a Grandmaster* Kotov recalls the following story:

"Once in a lobby of the Hall of Columns of the Trade Union Centre in Moscow a group of masters were analysing an ending. They could not find the right way to go about things and there was a lot of arguing about it. Suddenly Capablanca came into the room. He was always fond of walking about when it was his opponent's turn to move. Learning the reason for the dispute the Cuban bent down to look at the position, said, 'Si, si,' and suddenly redistributed the pieces all over the board to show what the correct formation was for the side that was trying to win. I haven't exaggerated. Don José literally pushed the pieces round the board without making moves. He just put them in fresh positions where he thought they were needed.

"Suddenly everything became clear. The correct scheme of things had been set up and now the win was easy. We were delighted by
Capablanca's mastery, and soon had further proof of the need to think schematically about the ending."

Kotov then went on to give a position from one of Capablanca's games in this tournament:

Capablanca - Ragozin
Moscow 1936

1 d4 ♘f6 2 c4 e6 3 ♘c3 ♗b4 4 ♕b3 ♘c6 5 e3 d5 6 ♘f3 0-0 7 a3 dxc4 8 ♗xc4 ♗d6 9 ♗b5 e5 10 ♗xc6 exd4 11 ♘xd4 bxc6 12 ♘xc6 ♕d7 13 ♘d4 ♕g4 14 0-0 ♗a6 15 h3 ♕h4 16 ♘f3 ♕h5 17 ♖e1 ♖ab8 18 ♕a4 ♗b7 19 e4 h6 20 ♗e3 ♖fe8 21 ♗d4! ♘h7 22 ♗xa7 ♖a8 23 ♕b5 ♕xb5 24 ♘xb5 ♖xe4 25 ♖xe4 ♗xe4 26 ♘d2 ♗d3 27 ♘xd6 ♖xa7 28 ♘6e4 ♘f8 29 ♘c5 ♗f5 30 ♘f3 ♘e6 31 ♖c1 ♔f8 32 ♘xe6+ ♗xe6

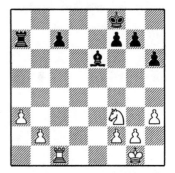

After facing an interesting pawn sacrifice in the opening Capablanca has emerged a pawn up in the endgame. Yet how exactly should he go about winning?

For Capablanca it would be rather easy to see a good configuration for the White pieces by putting his knight on d4, rook on c3 and then king up and set about improving the position still further.

33 ♘d4 ♖b7 34 b4 ♗d7 35 f4 ♔e7 36 ♔f2 ♖a7 37 ♖c3 ♔d6 38 ♖d3 ♔e7 39 ♔e3 ♖a4 40 ♖c3

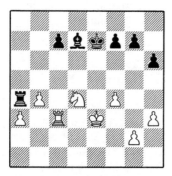

Stage one is complete and White has to decide how to advance his passed a-pawn still further. For this he needs his knight on c3 and sets about bringing it there.

40 ... ♔d6 41 ♖d3 ♔e7 42 ♖c3 ♔d6 43 ♘e2 g6 44 ♖d3+ ♔e6 45 ♔d4 ♖a6 46 ♖e3+ ♔d6 47 ♘c3

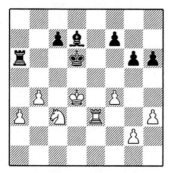

Mission accomplished. The a-pawn is immune because of (47 ... ♖xa3) 48 ♘e4+ and Black is actually unable to bring his king to a better square. This allows White the time to bring his king across to support his a-pawn which ensures its further advance.

47 ... f5 48 b5 ♖a8 49 ♔c4 ♗e6+ 50 ♔b4 c5+ 51 bxc5 ♗g8 52 ♘b5+ ♔xc6 53 ♖d3 g5 54 ♖d6+ ♔b7 55 fxg5 hxg5 56 ♖g6 ♖f8 57 ♖xg5 f4 58 ♘d4 ♖c8 59 ♖g7+ ♔b6 60 ♖g6+ ♔b7 61 ♘b5 ♖f8 62 ♘d6+ ♔b8 63 h4 1:0

Throughout his career Capablanca used his brilliant understanding of where his pieces belonged to guide him. Whilst in his match against Alekhine this was not enough he was considered unbeatable for many years and his pieces always seemed to be in harmony. It was almost impossible to lay a glove on him and in his whole career he lost just a handful of games.

Here is another example of Capablanca's schematic thinking.

Janowsky - Capablanca
New York 1916

1 d4 ♘f6 2 ♘f3 d5 3 c4 c6 4 ♘c3 ♗f5 5 ♕b3 ♕b6 6 ♕xb6 axb6 7 cxd5 ♘xd5 8 ♘xd5 cxd5 9 e3 ♘c6 10 ♗d2

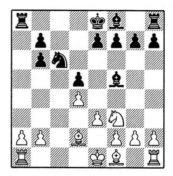

10 ... ♗d7!
Beautifully thought out. Capablanca sees that his plan is to transfer his knight to c4 and he needs to play ... b6-b5 in order to

support it on this outpost. Accordingly he assigns his bishop to prepare the advance of the b-pawn and moves it from what seems like the more active square.

Had Janowsky understood what Black wanted he would have answered this with 11 ♗b5.

11 ♗e2 e6 12 0-0 ♗d6 13 ♖fc1 ♔e7 14 ♗c3 ♖hc8 15 a3?

Now it will be difficult for White ever to play b2-b3.

15 ... ♘a5 16 ♘d2 f5!

First of all Capablanca stops any counterplay based on e3-e4.

17 g3 b5 18 f3 ♘c4

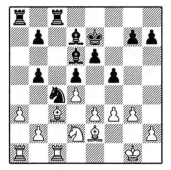

"Black's first plan is completed. White now will have to take the knight, and Black's only weakness, the doubled b-pawn, will become a source of great strength at c4. Now for two or three moves Black will devote his time to improving the general strategic position of his pieces before evolving a new plan, this time a plan of attack against White's position."—Capablanca.

19 ♗xc4 bxc4 20 e4 ♔f7 21 e5?

Probably the losing move. Without the danger of any White

counterplay Black has a free hand to build an attack. White had to play 21 exd5 exd5 22 f4 intending ♘f3-e5.

21 ... ♗e7 22 f4 b5 23 ♔f2 ♖a4 24 ♔e3 ♖ca8 25 ♖ab1 h6!

Now Capablanca aims to open a second front on the kingside. The defender is unable to deal with threats on both sides of the board due to his lack of manoeuvrability.

26 ♘f3 g5 27 ♘e1 ♖g8 28 ♔f3 gxf4 29 gxf4 ♖aa8 30 ♘g2 ♖g4 31 ♖g1 ♖ag8 32 ♗e1

White wants to defend his kingside by bringing his bishop to f2 and playing ♘g2-e3. But the loss of coordination between his rooks allows Black to pounce.

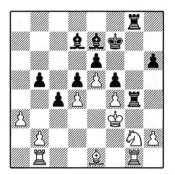

32 ... b4 33 axb4

33 ♗xb4 ♗xb4 34 axb4 h5 leaves White helpless against the advance of the h-pawn.

33 ... ♗a4 34 ♖a1 ♗c2 35 ♗g3 ♗e4+ 36 ♔f2 h5 37 ♖a7 ♗xg2 38 ♖xg2 h4 39 ♗xh4 ♖xg2+ 40 ♔f3 ♖xh2 41 ♗xe7 ♖h3+ 42 ♔f2 ♖b3 43 ♗g5+ ♔g6 44 ♖e7 ♖xb2+ 45 ♔f3 ♖a8 46 ♖xe6+ ♔h7 0:1

KM17/4: 1) White to play

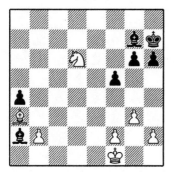

KM17/4: 2) White to play

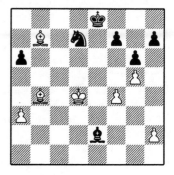

KM17/4: 3) Black to play

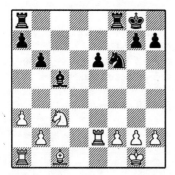

KM17/4: 4) White to play

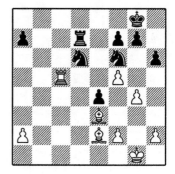

A17/4: a) White to play

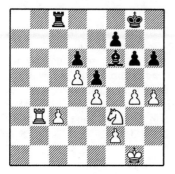

A17/4: b) White to play

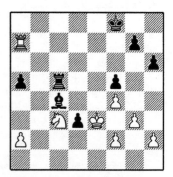

6 Endgame Battles

This month we will continue looking at endgames and in particular some which can arise from major opening systems.

In such sharp openings as the Sicilian Dragon and King's Indian Defence one would imagine that the endgame would be very far away. But in fact these lines can lead to typical endgame scenarios which we shall examine in weeks one and two. In week three we will look at one of the most common types of position is that in which both sides exchange their d and c-pawns. Finally in week four we will round off the treatment of endgames with two highly instructive games in which Karpov wins drawn positions.

Month 18/Week 1:
Dragon Endgames

The Sicilian Dragon is renowned as one of the sharpest of openings yet it typically leads to endgames with an unusual material balance. Such scenarios often come about when White sacrifices a pawn in an attempt to accelerate his attack (h4-h5) and then Black defuses it by giving up material of his own.

Most typical of all is the sacrifice of the exchange on c3 by Black which we shall see in the first game between Boris Spassky and Leonid Stein. In the second we see even more violent play which leads to an endgame in which Black has four pawns for a rook!

Spassky - Stein
USSR 1967

1 e4 c5 2 ♘f3 d6 3 d4 cxd4 4 ♘xd4 ♘f6 5 ♘c3 g6 6 ♗e3 ♗g7 7 f3 ♘c6 8 ♕d2 0-0 9 ♗c4 ♕a5 10 0-0-0 ♗d7 11 h4 ♖fc8 12 ♗b3 ♘e5 13 h5 ♘xh5 14 ♔b1 ♖xc3!

This exchange sacrifice is one of Black's main resources in the Dragon.

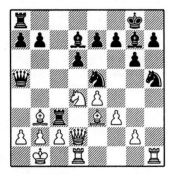

15 ♕xc3

Keeping queens on the board with 15 bxc3 can lead to a draw after 15 ... ♖c8 16 ♗h6 ♘c4 17 ♗xc4 ♖xc4 18 ♗xg7 ♔xg7 19 g4 ♘f6 20 e5 dxe5 21 ♘b3 ♕xc3 22 ♕h6+ ♔g8 23 ♖xd7 ♕xc2+ 24 ♔a1 ♕c3+ etc as in Klovan-Zaitsev, Jurmala 1969 If White plays 22 ♕xc3 instead with the idea of winning material after 22

... ♖xc3 23 g5, Black can obtain an overwhelming mass of passed pawns with 23 ... ♗c6 24 gxf6+ exf6 25 ♘d2 ♖xf3! 26 ♘xf3 ♗xf3.

15 ... ♕xc3 16 bxc3 ♖c8

An important type of position which deserves close examination. Black has a pawn for the exchange and has created serious weaknesses in White's pawn structure. The main problem with this structural damage from White's perspective is that he is unable to organise any effective pawn levers and penetrate Black's defences with his rooks. As we saw in month two, rooks really need to break into the enemy ranks in order to show their full strength.

17 ♔b2

After 17 ♗g5 Black can take the initiative with 17 ... ♗f6! 18 ♗xf6 ♘xf6 19 ♔b2 b5. In a game Scholl-Tatai, Beverwijk 1967 Black gradually assumed the initiative after 17 ♘e2 a5 18 a3 a4 19 ♗a2 ♗b5 20 ♖he1 ♘c4 21 ♗xc4 ♗xc4 22 ♗d4 ♘f6 23 ♘c1 e5 24 ♗e3 d5 25 ♗g5 dxe4 26 fxe4 ♗e6 27 ♔b2 ♘d7 28 ♗e3 ♖c4 29 ♗f2 f5.

17 ... a5 18 a3 ♘f6 19 ♗f4 ♘e8 20 ♗g5 a4 21 ♗a2 ♘c6! 22 ♖d2 22 ♘xc6 ♖xc6 23 ♗xe7 ♖xc3 24 ♔b1 ♖xa3 favours Black.

22 ... ♘f6 23 ♘xc6 ♗xc6 24 ♖d4

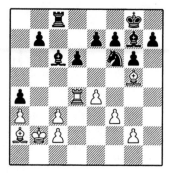

24 ... h5!

Another instructive move which safeguards the h-pawn so as to bring his king to the centre. Coming down the h-file is one of White's only hopes if he wants to activate his rooks.

25 ♔c1 ♔f8 26 ♔d2 ♖a8 27 ♖b4 ♖a5 28 ♗e3 e6!

Another instructive move, making room for Black's king on e7. Spassky keeps playing for a few more moves but there is hardly any prospect of breaking down Black's defence.

29 c4 ♘d7 30 c3 ♗f6 31 ♗b1 ♗g5 32 ♗c2 ♗xe3+ 33 ♔xe3 ♔e7 34 ♔f2 ♘c5 35 ♖bb1 ♘d7 36 ♖b4 ♘c5 37 ♖bb1 ♘d7 ½-½

Westerinen- Ernst
Gausdal 1991

1 e4 c5 2 ♘f3 d6 3 d4 cxd4 4 ♘xd4 ♘f6 5 ♘c3 g6 6 ♗e3 ♗g7 7 f3 0-0 8 ♕d2 ♘c6 9 ♗c4 ♗d7 10 0-0-0 ♖c8 11 ♗b3 ♘e5 12 h4 ♘c4 13 ♗xc4 ♖xc4 14 h5 ♘xh5 15 g4 ♘f6 16 ♘b3

This quiet move has been quite popular in this position. Black's best reply may well be 16 ... ♕c7 as the text commits him to an extraordinary line of play.

16 ... Ēe8 17 e5 ♘xg4!

Forced! 17 ... dxe5 18 g5 leaves the bishop on d7 hanging.

18 fxg4 ♗xg4 19 Ēdg1 ♗xe5

Once again this is the only way to play it. 19 ... h5 is bad because of 20 e6! ♗xe6 21 ♗d4 ♗g4 22 Ēxg4! hxg4 23 ♗xg7 ♔xg7 24 ♕h6+ with a strong attack and 19 ... dxe5 fails against 20 ♕xd8 Ēxd8 21 ♘d2.

20 ♗d4

Trying to remove the Dragon bishop in order to leave Black's kingside weak. Black's reply is remarkable.

20 ... Ēxd4! 21 ♘xd4 h5 22 ♘d5 e6 23 ♘e3 ♕b6 24 c3 ♗xd4 25 ♕xd4 ♕xd4 26 cxd4 f5

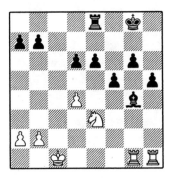

Do Black's connected passed pawns give him adequate compensation for the rook? It would be a brave man indeed to stick his neck out on that one, perhaps in some future game White will demonstrate a way to activate his rooks and halt the advance of Black's pawns. One thing that does seem fairly clear is that Black's position is easier to play in practice.

27 ♔d2

White might have eliminated the bishop with 27 ♘xg4 though Black retains his dangerous pawn mass.

27 ... ♔g7 28 Ēc1 ♗f3 29 Ēh3 ♗c6 30 ♘c4 ♔f6 31 ♘a5 ♗g2 32 Ēh2 ♗d5 33 Ēc7 Ēe7 34 Ēxe7 ♔xe7

Now only the bishop remains to support the Black pawns. Actually it does an excellent job from its outpost on d5 which makes me wonder if it shouldn't have been eliminated earlier on.

35 ♔d3 b5 36 ♘b3 ♔f6 37 ♘c1 f4 38 ♔d2 ♔f5 39 ♘d3 ♔g4 40 Ēe2 g5 41 ♘b4 ♔f3 42 ♘xd5 exd5 43 ♔e1 h4 44 Ēf2+ ♔g3 45 ♔f1 h3 46 ♔g1 g4 47 Ēc2 ♔h4 48 Ēc7 g3 49 Ēxa7 ♔g4 50 Ēg7+ ♔f3 51 a3

The only way to create a passed pawn. 51 b3 is met by 51 ... b4.

51 ... ♔e2 52 Ēe7+ ♔d3

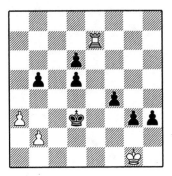

53 Ēf7?

Falling at the last hurdle, White could have held the game by cold-bloodedly creating a passed pawn with 53 b3!. After 53 ... f3 54 a4 bxa4 55 bxa4 h2+ 56 ♔h1 f2 57 Ēf7 ♔e2 58 Ēe7+ ♔d2 59 Ēf7 we would see a draw by repetition.

53 ... ♔e3 54 Ēe7+ ♔xd4 55 Ēf7 ♔e3 56 Ēe7+ ♔f3 57 Ēe6 h2+ 58 ♔h1 ♔f2 0:1

KM18/1: 1) White to play.

KM18/2: 2) Black to play

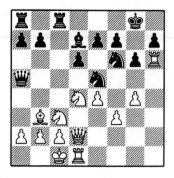

KM18/2: 3) White to play

KM18/2: 4) White to play

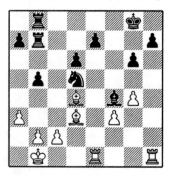

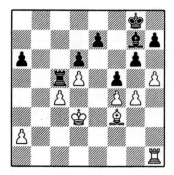

A18/1: a) White to play

A18/1: b) White to play

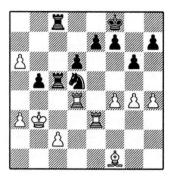

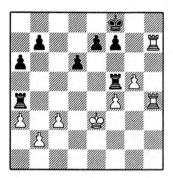

Month 18/Week 2:
King's Indian Exchange

One of the best ways for Black to play for a win after 1 d4 is with the dynamic and complex King's Indian Defence. It is no accident that this opening has appealed to such fighting players as Bobby Fischer and Garry Kasparov.

Some White players are loathe to get embroiled in the kind of complex battle which the King's Indian usually leads to and instead have sought out simpler ways to play against it. One of these is to exchange pawns on e5 and then swap the queens as well. They hope for a slight initiative based on a lead in development and that Black's bishop on g7 will prove ineffective. But the downside is that by playing c2-c4 and d2-d4 White weakens his d4 square.

In the following games we see Kasparov and then Fischer exploit this weakness, with a little help from their opponents of course!

Danailov - Kasparov
Dortmund 1980

1 c4 g6 2 ♘f3 ♗g7 3 ♘c3 d6 4 d4 ♘f6 5 e4 0-0 6 ♗e2 e5 7 dxe5 dxe5 8 ♕xd8 ♖xd8 9 ♗g5 ♘bd7!?

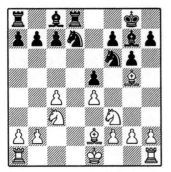

In my own King's Indian days I liked this move as well, inspired to some extent by the present game. Black develops another piece and the knight often heads for d4 via c5 and e6

10 ♘d5
A dubious reply after which Black is very comfortably placed. White should play 10 0-0-0 after which 10 ... ♖f8! 11 ♘d5 c6 12 ♘e7+ ♔h8 13 ♗e3 ♖e8 14 ♘xc8 ♖axc8 15 c5 ♗f8 16 b4 b6 was about equal in Cvetkovic-Kuzmin, Linz 1990.

10 ... c6 11 ♘e7+ ♔f8 12 ♘xc8 ♖dxc8
Black already stands very well as he can set about controlling the d4 square.

13 0-0-0?!
After Black's reply White is forced to capture on f6 which gives Black a clear edge. 13 ♘d2 ♘c5 14 f3 ♘e6 15 ♗e3 was relatively best.

13 ... ♘c5 14 ♗xf6 ♗xf6 15 ♗d3 a5 16 ♖he1 ♖e8! 17 ♗f1 ♗d8!
The point of putting the rook on e8—the bishop is being re-routed to a better diagonal.

18 g3 a4 19 ♔c2 ♗a5 20 ♖e3 ♖ad8 21 ♖xd8 ♖xd8 22 ♗h3 f6

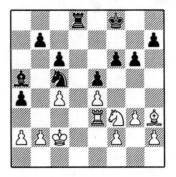

A very unpleasant move to meet, Black quietly protects his e-pawn and asks White what he intends to do. White's problems stem from being unable to bring his rook round to challenge for control of the d-file.

23 ♖e2 ♔e7 24 ♗g2 ♘d3 25 a3 ♘c5 26 h4 h5 27 ♖e3 g5!

Decisively increasing the pressure by setting about displacing White's knight from f3.

28 hxg5 fxg5 29 ♖e2 ♘b3 30 ♔b1 ♔f6 0:1

White has no move. 31 ♔c2 is met by 31 ... g4, 31 ♗h1 by 31 ... ♖d1+ and 31 ♔a2 by 31 ... ♖d1.

Larsen - Fischer
Monte Carlo 1967

1 d4 ♘f6 2 c4 g6 3 ♘c3 ♗g7 4 e4 d6 5 ♗e2 0-0 6 ♘f3 e5 7 0-0 ♘c6 8 ♗e3 ♖e8 9 dxe5

The exchange on e5 is the only serious try. After 9 d5 ♘d4 10 ♘xd4 exd4 11 ♗xd4 ♘xe4 Black recovers the pawn with a comfortable position.

9 ... dxe5 10 ♕xd8 ♘xd8 11 ♘b5 ♘e6 12 ♘g5 ♖e7 13 ♖fd1

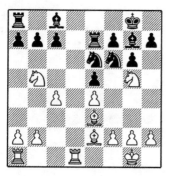

13 ... b6!

At the time of the game this was a novelty. After 13 ... c6 Larsen intended the brave 14 ♘xa7 ♗d7 15

♘xe6 ♗xe6 16 f3, though this is far from clear after 16 ... ♖d7 intending ... ♖d4!. The state of White's knight on a7 would give Black definite compensation for his pawn.

14 c5!?

Typical enterprise from Larsen, 14 ♘xe6 followed by 15 f3 would be drawish. Black's reply is forced as 14 ... bxc5 is virtually losing after 15 ♘xe6 ♗xe6 16 ♗xc5 ♖d7 17 f3.

14 ... ♘xc5 15 ♖d8+ ♗f8

15 ... ♘e8? is bad because of 16 ♗xc5 bxc5 17 ♘xc7 ♖xc7 18 ♖xe8+ ♗f8 19 ♘xh7+- and after 15 ... ♖e8 White would play 16 ♖xe8+ ♘xe8 17 ♗xc5 bxc5 18 ♗c4.

16 ♘xa7 ♖xa7 17 ♖xc8 ♔g7

Black would do better to play 17 ... h6! after which 18 ♘f3 ♔g7 19 ♗xc5 bxc5 20 ♗d3 is equal.

18 f3 ♘e8

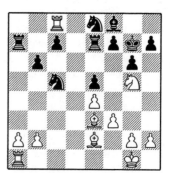

19 a3?

Over the next few moves White gradually goes astray due to his reluctance to part with his bishop pair. 19 ♗xc5 bxc5 20 ♖b8 would give White chances because of his a-pawn though the opposite coloured bishops would make this very difficult to advance.

19 ... ♘d6 20 ♖d8

20 **Rb8 Nd7** 21 **Rd8 Nb7** 22 **Rc8 Nd6** would draw by repetition, Larsen typically wants to win.

20 ... h6 21 Nh3 Ne6 22 Rb8 Re8 23 Rxe8 Nxe8 24 Bb5

White should bring his knight into play with 24 Nf2.

24 ... Nd6 25 Bf1 Nb7! 26 Nf2 Bc5! 27 Bxc5 Nbxc5 28 Rd1 h5!

Keeping White's knight out of the g4 square. 28 ... Nd4 is met by 29 Ng4 f6 30 f4.

29 Rd5

29 Nd3 Nxd3 30 Bxd3 Nd4 31 Kf2 would probably still hold the endgame despite Black's powerful knight.

29 ... Kf6 30 h4 Ke7! 31 Bc4

And not 31 Rxe5? c6.

31 ... c6 32 Rd2 Nd4!

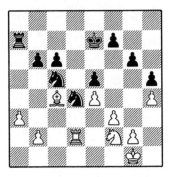

Mission accomplished. Black is clearly better now and White makes matters worse by failing to bite the bullet.

33 Kf1 f5! 34 b4

34 Nd3 was a better chance to hang on.

34 ... b5! 35 Bg8

Both 35 bxc5 bxc5 and 35 Bxb5 Ncb3 would lose for White.

35 ... fxe4! 36 fxe4 Nd7 37 Rd3 Ra6! 38 Rc3 c5! 39 g4?

39 bxc5 b4 40 Rc1! was better. Now Black's c-pawn will decide matters.

39 ... c4 40 gxh5 gxh5 41 Bd5 Nf6 42 Rg3 Nxd5 43 exd5 Rf6 44 Kg2 Nf5 45 Rh3 Rg6+ 46 Kf3 Nd4+ 47 Ke3

After 47 Ke4 there is 47 ... Kd6 48 Rh2 Rg3.

47 ... Rg2 48 Rh1 Kd6 49 Ne4+ Kxd5 50 Nc3+ Ke6

Threatening 51 ... Rc2 and, after the knight moves, 51 ... Re2 is mate.

51 Rc1 Rh2 52 a4 Rh3+ 53 Kf2 Nb3 54 Kg2 Nxc1 55 Kxh3 bxa4 56 Nxa4 Ne2 57 b5 c3 58 b6 c2 59 Nc5+ Kd5 60 Nb3

60 Nd3 is met by 60 ... Nf4+ 61 Nxf4+ exf4 62 b7 c1=Q 63 b8=Q Qh1# and 60 b7 by 60 ... c1=Q 61 b8=Q Qh1#.

60 ... Kc6 61 Kg2 Kxb6 0:1

KM18/2: 1) Black to play

KM18/2: 2) Black to play

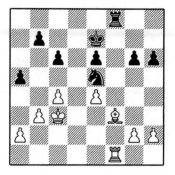

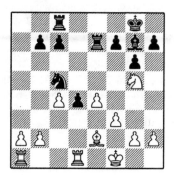

KM18/2: 3) Black to play

KM18/2: 4) Black to play

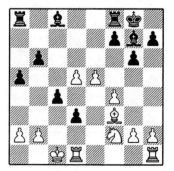

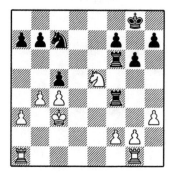

A18/2: a) Black to play

A18/2: b) White to play

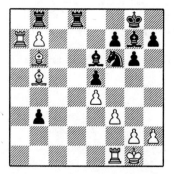

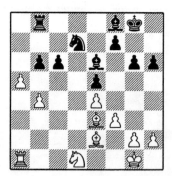

Month 18/Week 3:
Open d-and c-files

Positions in which both sides have had the d- and c-pawns exchanged are very common indeed and often involve the exchange of queens as well. In many cases these positions will assume a drawish character because the exchange of rooks will also often follow. But should one side have a lead in development he might penetrate the opponent's defences with a rook and develop a serious initiative.

In the following two games this is precisely what happens.

Botvinnik - Balashov
Hastings 1966-7

1 c4 ♘f6 2 ♘c3 e6 3 d4 ♗b4 4 e3 0-0 5 ♗d3 d5 6 a3 dxc4 7 ♗xc4 ♗d6

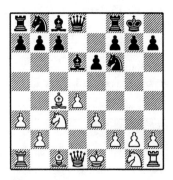

8 f4

An attempt to exploit the relative inexperience of his young opponent as Botvinnik admitted himself in his notes. In fact it turns out to be a psychological error as Balashov reacts very well. White should play 8 ♘f3.

8 ... c5! 9 dxc5 ♗xc5 10 b4

Again very ambitious but rather weakening. 10 ♘f3 was better.

10 ... ♗b6 11 ♕xd8 ♖xd8 12 ♘f3 ♗d7!

Threatening to exploit the loose position of White's pieces with 13 ... ♖c8. Over the next few moves White has to be very careful.

13 ♗d2 ♖c8

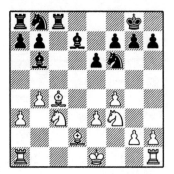

14 ♘e5

The only move, 14 ♗d3 loses a pawn after 14 ... ♗xe3 Black's best move is now 14 ... ♗e8! after which White could only keep the balance with 15 ♔e2 ♘c6 16 ♘xc6 ♗xc6 17 ♖hg1 ♗xg2 18 ♗xe6. The following simplification eases White's defence.

14 ... ♘g4 15 ♘xg4 ♖xc4 16 ♘e5 ♖c7 17 ♘xd7 ♘xd7 18 ♔e2 ♘f6 19 ♖ac1 ♖d8 20 ♖hd1 ♖cd7 21 ♗e1 ♘d5?!

This loses time after which the active position of White's king finally starts to become significant. Black should play something like 21 ... ♔f8 with a likely draw in prospect and not 21 ... ♘g4 22 ♖xd7 ♖xd7 23 ♘a4! etc.

22 ♘xd5 ♖xd5 23 ♖xd5 ♖xd5

23 ... exd5 is better but Black didn't want an isolated pawn.

24 a4 f6?

This puts Black in serious trouble as White's rook now penetrates his ranks He should play 24 ... ♖d7 25 a5 ♗c7 with a defensible position.

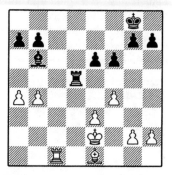

25 a5 ♗d8 26 ♖c8 ♔f7

26 ... a6 is met by 27 b5! axb5 28 a6 bxa6 29 ♗a5 etc.

27 e4 ♖d7 28 b5 ♗e7 29 ♗d2 ♗d6 30 ♖a8 b6

Now Black gets a weak a-pawn which with bishops on the board is hopeless for him. He should play 30 ... ♗c5 31 ♗e3 ♗xe3 32 ♔xe3 b6 33 axb6 axb6 34 ♖b8 would offer better practical chances than the game.

31 a6 ♗c5 32 ♗c3 ♔e7 33 h3 ♔d6 34 ♖c8 ♖c7?

A time-trouble error which shortens Black's resistance.

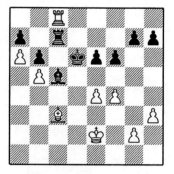

35 e5+ ♔d7 36 ♖g8 f5 37 ♖xg7+ ♔d8 38 ♖g8+ ♔d7 39 ♖h8 ♗e7 40 ♗d4 ♖c2+ 41 ♔d3 ♖a2 42 ♖a8 1:0

In the second game we see another World Champion in action, Anatoly Karpov. But on this occasion we see the rare sight of him being on the receiving end of a masterly technical performance:

Ribli - Karpov
Amsterdam 1980

1 d4 ♘f6 2 c4 e6 3 g3 d5 4 ♗g2 ♗e7 5 ♘f3 0-0 6 0-0 dxc4 7 ♕c2 a6 8 ♕xc4 b5 9 ♕c2 ♗b7 10 ♗f4 ♘d5 11 ♘c3 ♘xf4 12 gxf4 ♘d7 13 ♖fd1 ♕c8 14 ♘e4!

A significant improvement by Ribli which gives White an edge. 14 ... ♗xe4 15 ♕xe4 c5? 16 ♘g5! wins the exchange and 15 ... ♘f6 16 ♕c6 leaves Black facing c-file pressure.

14 ... c5 15 dxc5 ♘xc5 16 ♘xc5 ♕xc5

16 ... ♗xc5 17 ♖ac1 ♗e7 18 ♘e5! also leaves Black facing serious difficulties.

17 ♕xc5 ♗xc5 18 ♖ac1 ♖fc8 19 ♘e5!

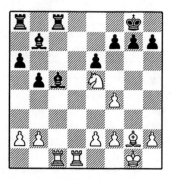

19 ... ♗xg2 20 ♔xg2 f6

In the later game Gavrikov-Azmaiparashvili, USSR 1981, Black attempted to strengthen Karpov's play with 20 ... ♖c7 White nevertheless maintained an edge with 21 e3 ♖ac8 22 ♖d7 a5 23 b3 f6 24 ♖xc7 ♖xc7 25 ♘f3 ♔f7 26 ♘d4 b4 27 ♘b5 ♖c6 28 ♔f3.

21 ♘f3 ♗f8

21 ... ♔f7 22 ♖d7+ ♗e7 23 ♖cc7 is unpleasant.

22 e3 g6

22 ... ♔f7 23 ♖d7+ ♔e8 24 ♖cc7 is once again better for White.

23 b3

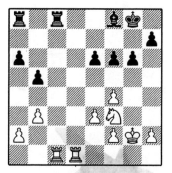

23 ... ♗b4

After 23 ... ♗a3 White plays 24 ♖xc8+ ♖xc8 25 ♖d7 ♖c2 26 ♘d4 and now 26 ... ♖xa2 is met by 27 ♘xe6 and 26 ... ♖d2 by 27 ♖b7! rather than 27 ♖d8+?! ♔f7 28 ♘xe6 ♖xa2!.

24 h3

24 ♖xc8+ ♖xc8 25 ♖d7 is no longer good as after 25 ... ♖c2 26 ♘d4 ♖xa2 27 ♘xe6 ♗e1 Black counterattacks f2 and 28 ♖g7+ ♔h8 29 ♖f7 can be met by 29 ... h5.

**24 ... ♔f8 25 ♘d4 ♔f7 26 a4!
bxa4 27 bxa4 ♗c5**

If 27 ... a5 there is 28 ♘b5 ♖xc1 (28 ... ♔e7 29 ♘c7 ♖ab8 30 ♖c6+-) 29 ♖xc1 ♖e8 30 ♔f3 with advantage.

28 ♖c4! ♗a3

28 ... ♗xd4 29 ♖cxd4 ♖e8 30 ♖b4 is also very unpleasant for Black.

29 ♖xc8 ♖xc8 30 ♖b1 ♖c4

30 ... ♖c7 31 ♖b8 still sees White's rook come in.

31 ♖b7+ ♗e7 32 ♖a7 e5

32 ... ♖xa4?? 33 ♘c6 wins a piece.

33 fxe5 fxe5 34 ♘f3 ♖xa4 35 ♘xe5+ ♔f6 36 ♘c6 ♗c5 37 ♖xh7 ♖a2 38 ♔f3 a5 39 h4 a4 40 ♔e4!

Unexpectedly conjuring up mating threats.

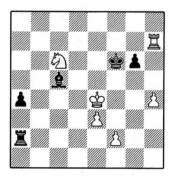

40 ... ♗f8

40 ... ♖xf2 41 ♘d8+- threatens mate with 42 ♖f7.

41 ♖a7 ♗d6 42 f4 ♖h2 43 ♖a6 ♔f7 44 ♘e5+ ♗xe5 45 ♔xe5 ♔g7 46 ♖a7+ ♔h6 47 ♖xa4 ♖xh4 48 ♔f6 ♖h5 49 e4 ♖h4 50 e5 ♖h5 51 e6 ♖f5+ 52 ♔e7 ♔g7 53 ♔d6 ♖f8 54 ♖a7+ ♔f6 55 ♖d7 1:0

KM18/3: 1) White to play

KM18/3: 2) White to play

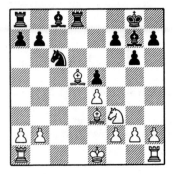

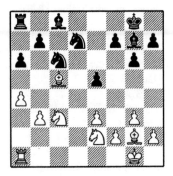

KM18/3: 3) White to play

KM18/3: 4) White to play

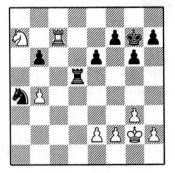

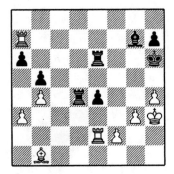

A18/3: a) White to play

A18/3: b) White to play

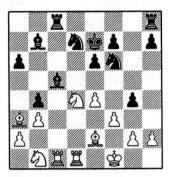

Month 18/Week 4:
Winning 'Drawn' Games

This will be the final week devoted to endgames, I hope that the last couple of months have shown how difficult and interesting they can be. The greatest masters treat this phase of the game with the greatest care and attention and can often eek out wins from what seems like unpromising material.

In the following games we see Karpov win two 'totally drawn' positions with logical and well directed play whilst his opponents seemed to be somewhat at a loss as to how to proceed. There is nothing magical about what he did in these games, it was simply a question of patience, determination and excellent technique:

Estevez - Karpov
Leningrad Izt 1973

1 d4 ♘f6 2 c4 e6 3 ♘f3 d5 4 ♘c3 ♗e7 5 ♗g5 0-0 6 e3 h6 7 ♗h4 b6 8 ♗e2 ♗b7 9 ♗xf6 ♗xf6 10 cxd5 exd5 11 b4 c6 12 0-0 a5 13 a3 ♕d6 14 ♕b3 axb4 15 axb4 ♘d7 16 ♖fd1 ♖xa1 17 ♖xa1 ♗e7

Putting pressure on the b-pawn like this is a risky attempt to create some problems as it allows White to activate his pieces. 17 ... ♖a8 18 ♖xa8+ ♗xa8 19 ♕a4 ♗b7 20 ♕a7 ♕b8 would be rather drawish.

18 ♖a7 ♖b8 19 ♘a2 ♗c8 20 ♕c2 ♗f6 21 ♘c1 ♘f8 22 ♘d3 ♗f5 23 ♕a4 ♘d7 24 ♖a8 ♖xa8 25 ♕xa8+ ♔h7 26 ♕a6 g6 27 ♕b7 ♔g7 28 h3 h5 29 ♕a7 ♗d8 30 ♕b7 ♕c7 31 ♕a8 ♗e7 32 ♘de5 ♗xb4 33 ♕xc6?!

Assuming perhaps that a draw would be automatic after the queens come off; in fact it helps Black relieve his position and the two bishops come more into their own. 33 ♘xc6 was better when I prefer White.

33 ... ♕xc6 34 ♘xc6 ♗d6

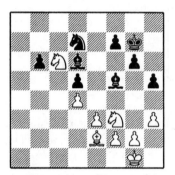

The game has been simplified to what looks like a fairly even endgame. White has the more harmonious pawn structure but Black's b-pawn is passed. Black has the two bishops though these are not especially effective given the closed nature of the position.

35 ♗b5?

The bishop proves to be a poor blockader of Black's b-pawn. White should play 35 ♘a7! followed by ♘b5 when the knight would be doing an excellent job.

35 ... ♘f6 36 ♘d2?!

White is drifting. He should play 36 ♘ce5.

36 ... ♘e8!

Setting about removing the b-pawn's blockader in preparation for its advance.

37 f3 ♘c7 38 ♗e2 ♗c2 39 ♔f2 ♗a4 40 ♘e5 b5 41 ♘d3?

White's sealed move and another inaccuracy. He should play 41 g4!

and after 41 ... h4 advance his king-side pawn majority with 42 f4. Alexander Kotov suggested another good plan, the blockade of Black's b-pawn at b3 with 41 ♘c6 followed by 42 ♘a5.

41 ... h4!

Fixing g2 as a weakness.

42 ♘b2?

Continuing to drift. Once again White can try to blockade the b-pawn with 42 ♘c1. The other plan is a counterattack with 42 e4.

42 ... ♗b4! 43 ♘b1 ♗b3 44 ♗d3 ♗c4 45 e4?!

White finally understands that a plan is required but this rather be-lated activity backfires. He should sit tight with 45 ♔e2 or 45 f4.

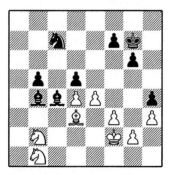

45 ... g5!

Further restraining White's king-side. With his next move White leaves himself with an isolated d-pawn and opens the position for Black's bishops a little more.

46 exd5 ♗xd5 47 ♘d1 ♗c6!

With the structure having changed Karpov sets about making a new plan. Over the next few moves he arranges his pieces so that they put pressure on White's isolated d-pawn whilst preparing the advance of the b-pawn.

48 ♘bc3 ♗d7 49 ♘e4 ♗e7 50 ♘c5?

White cracks under the pressure—this leads to the loss of a pawn. He had to centralise the king with 50 ♔e3.

50 ... ♗xc5! 51 dxc5 ♘e6 52 ♘c3 b4 53 ♘e4 b3 54 ♘d2 ♘xc5 55 ♗b1 ♔f6! 56 ♔e3 0:1

After playing 56 ♔e3 White's flag fell before he could press his clock. Black could win either with 56 ... ♗f5! or aim to mop up White's kingside pawns with 56 ... ♗c6 57 ♔d4 ♘e6+ 58 ♔c3 ♘f4.

Ljubojevic - Karpov
Milan 1975

1 e4 e5 2 ♘f3 ♘c6 3 ♗b5 a6 4 ♗a4 ♘f6 5 0-0 ♗e7 6 d4 exd4 7 e5 ♘e4 8 ♘xd4 0-0 9 ♘f5 d5 10 exd6 ♗xf5 11 dxe7 ♘xe7 12 ♗b3 ♕xd1 13 ♖xd1 ♖ad8 14 ♖e1

It seems quite surprising that a draw wasn't agreed at this point, presumably neither player offered one, could it have been out of pride? The position is really quite equal and should not be lost by a strong grandmaster.

14 ... ♘c5 15 ♘c3 ♖d7 16 ♗e3 ♘xb3 17 cxb3 ♖fd8 18 ♖ad1 f6 19 ♖xd7 ♖xd7 20 ♖d1 ♖xd1+ 21 ♘xd1 ♘d5

All of a sudden it isn't equal any more. The text threatens to win a pawn with 22 ... ♗b1 23 a3 ♗c2 and if White prevents this with 23 ♘c3 Black can play 23 ... ♘xe3. Ljubojevic makes the right decision in giving up a pawn to reach an endgame with opposite colour bishops.

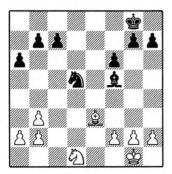

22 ♗d2 ♗b1 23 a3 ♗c2 24 ♘e3 ♘xe3 25 ♗xe3 ♗xb3 26 f3 ♔f7 27 ♗f4 c6 28 ♗d6

This still doesn't lose but White is getting careless. He should probably centralise his king with 28 ♔f2.

28 ... ♔e6 29 ♗f8 g6 30 ♔f2 a5 31 ♔e3?!

Again slightly careless as this gives Black the opportunity to put his pawns on dark squares. He should play 31 ♗c5 and 32 ♗b6.

31 ... b6 32 h4 c5! 33 g4?

This does little but weaken the kingside making it easier for Black to penetrate on this flank with his king. White should bring his bishop back into play with 33 ♗h6 followed by 34 ♗f4.

33 ... ♗d1

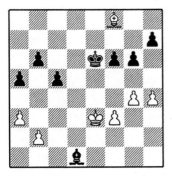

34 ♔e4?

Once again a careless move by White and this time the decisive mistake. White should play either 34 ♗h6 or exchange one of the kingside pawns with 34 h5.

34 ... a4! 35 h5 gxh5 36 gxh5 f5+ 37 ♔e3 ♔d5 38 h6 ♔c4 39 f4 ♔b3

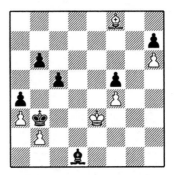

40 ♗g7?!

The best practical chance was 40 ♔d2 after which 40 ... ♔xb2 41 ♔xd1 ♔xa3 42 ♔c2 ♔b4 43 ♔b2 holds on. Black needs to find 41 ... c4! 42 ♗e7 b5 43 ♗f8 c3 44 ♗g7 b4! 45 axb4 a3 46 ♔e2 ♔c2-+.

40 ... ♔c2! 41 ♗e5 ♗h5 42 ♗f6 ♗f7 43 ♗e5 ♗b3 44 ♗g7 b5 45 ♗f8

Or 45 ♗c3 b4 46 axb4 cxb4 47 ♗xb4 ♔xb2 followed by pushing the a-pawn.

45 ... c4 46 ♗g7 b4! 47 ♔d4

47 axb4 c3 48 bxc3 ♗c4 49 b5 ♗xb5 would again cost White his bishop.

47 ... c3! 48 bxc3 bxa3 49 c4 a2 50 ♔c5 ♔b1 51 ♔b4 a1=♕ 52 ♗xa1 ♔xa1 53 c5 ♔b2 54 c6 a3 55 c7 ♗e6 56 ♔c5 a2 57 ♔d6 ♗c8 0:1

KM18/4: 1) White to play

KM18/4: 2) White to play

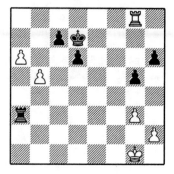

KM18/4: 3) White to play

KM18/4: 4) Black to play

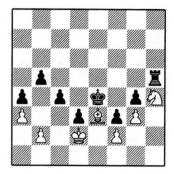

A18/4: a) Black to play

A18/4: b) Black to play

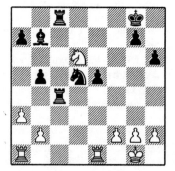

7 Masters of Attack

One of the best ways to improve your chess is to study the games of a single great player whose style of play most closely resembles your own. In so doing you will get many insights into how to deal with various practical and theoretical problems.

The way that people think about chess is extremely varied, in fact everyone has their own way of trying to find their next move. It can also be very difficult to define someone's style of play as many great players are equally adept at all sorts of positions.

In spite of this I have identified what I consider to be the four main categories of player, masters of attack, strategists, technicians and tacticians. I will look at each of these categories in turn, examining the styles of outstanding Grandmasters from each of them.

My 'Masters Of Attack' are Rudolf Spielmann, Leonid Stein, Mikhail Tal and Garry Kasparov. This particular choice is designed to illustrate the different ways in which players who like to attack set about building their game. In Spielmann we have an old-fashioned gambiteer whose methods were, to put it mildly, direct. Stein infused positions with tension, Tal would fluently pursue the initiative whilst Kasparov backs up his great natural talent with deep preparation and research.

Month 19/Week 1:
Rudolf Spielmann—Gambiteer

Rudolf Spielmann (1883-1942) was the last gambiteer to be successful at the highest levels of competitive chess. The construction of Spielmann's games was old-fashioned even by 1920s standards, his style being more reminiscent of the gambiteers of the romantic 19th century.

Spielmann's results were highly erratic due partly to his style of play but mainly to his extremely sensitive temperament. He could easily become depressed by a defeat and sink to the bottom of a tournament for good. But he could equally produce the most stunningly brilliant games:

Spielmann - Tarrasch
Karlsbad 1923

1 e4 e5 2 f4

Typical of Spielmann's style. Tarrasch declines the gambit in an attempt, no doubt, to curb his adversary's aggressive intentions.

2 ... ♗c5 3 ♘f3 d6 4 c3 ♗g4

Opening theory doesn't have a very high opinion of this move, preferring 4 ... ♘f6 instead.

5 fxe5 dxe5 6 ₩a4+ ♗d7 7 ₩c2
♘c6 8 b4 ♗d6 9 ♗c4 ♘f6 10 d3
♘e7 11 0-0 ♘g6 12 ♗e3 b5 13
♗b3 a5 14 a3 axb4 15 cxb4 0-0

After 15 ... ♗xb4? White plays 16
♘g5 0-0 17 ♘xf7 ♖xf7 18 ♗xf7+
♔xf7 19 ₩b3+ ♗e6 20 ₩xb4, winning back the piece with interest.

16 ♘c3 c6 17 h3 ₩e7 18 ♘e2
♗b8 19 ♔h2 ♗a7 20 ♗g5 h6 21
♗xf6 ₩xf6 22 ♘fd4 ₩d6 23 ♘f5
♗xf5 24 ♖xf5 ♘f4 25 ♖f1 g6?

Allowing White the chance of
some remarkable pyrotechnics.
Black should play 25 ... ♘e6, clos-
ing the a2-g8 diagonal.

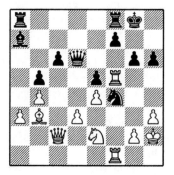

26 ♖1xf4! exf4 27 e5! ₩e7 28
♖f6! ♔g7

After 28 ... ₩xe5 there follows 29
♖xg6+ ♔h7 30 d4!, forcing Black
to give up his queen with 30 ...
₩xe2. But Black could defend more
tenaciously with 28 ... ♔h8.

29 d4 ♗xd4 30 ♗xf7! ♗xe5

Or 30 ... ♖xf7 31 ₩xg6+ ♔f8
32 ♘xd4 ♖xf6 33 exf6 ₩f7
34 ₩xh6+ ♔e8 35 ₩xf4+-.

31 ₩xg6+ 1:0

Later in his career Spielmann
made a conscious effort to play in a
more mature and restrained style. In

this respect the following game can
be seen as an abysmal failure:

Spielmann - S.Rubinstein
Vienna 1933

1 d4 ♘f6 2 c4 e6 3 ♘c3 d5 4 ♘f3
♗e7 5 ♗g5 0-0 6 e3 b6 7 ♗d3 ♗b7
8 ♗xf6 ♗xf6 9 cxd5 exd5

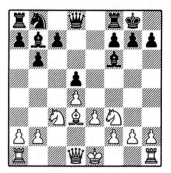

10 h4!?

The gambiteer in Spielmann
shows himself with this undisguised
threat to sacrifice the bishop on h7.
Should Black play 10 ... h6 White
would continue with 11 g4 in order
to prise open lines with g4-g5. After
10 ... g6 he would continue with 11
h5 ♖e8 12 hxg6 hxg6 13 ₩c2 ♘d7
14 ♗xg6! fxg6 15 ₩xg6+ ♗g7 (or
15 ... ♔f8 16 ♘g5 ♗xg5 17
♖h7!+-) 16 ♘g5 ₩f6 17 ♖h8+
♔xh8 18 ₩h7#.

Black would have been well advised to respond with the calm 10 ...
♖e8 but instead he launches a
counterattack in the centre:

10 ... c5 11 ♗xh7+!? ♔xh7 12
♘g5+ ♔h6 13 ₩d3

13 ₩c2! would have been better
in order to side-step the possibility
of 17 ... ♗a6. Of course it was very
difficult to foresee this improvement

and Black missed it when it was right under his nose.

13 ... g6 14 h5!

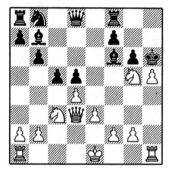

11 ... ♗xg5

Black has little choice but to accept the sacrifice as 14 ... ♔g7 15 hxg6 ♖h8 16 ♘xf7 ♖xh1+ 17 ♔d2 ♖xa1 18 ♘xd8 ♗xd8 19 ♕f5 ♗f6 20 ♕h5 is hopeless. Yet Black could have tried 14 ... ♔xg5 after which neither 15 f4+ ♔h6 16 hxg6+ ♔g7 17 ♖h7+ ♔g8 18 0-0-0 ♗g7 nor 15 ... ♔g4!? 16 ♘d1 ♗h4+ 17 ♘f2+ ♗xf2+ 18 ♔xf2 cxd4 19 g3 dxe3+ are at all clear.

15 hxg5+ ♔g7 16 ♖h7+ ♔f6 17 0-0-0!

The best chance. Attempting to recover one of the pieces with 17 f4 would be met by 17 ... ♗h4+ 18 ♖xh4 ♖h8, taking over the h-file. Had White played 13 ♕c2 he would have been able to meet this line with 19 ♕f2! and maintained a strong attack.

17 ... c4?

After this White's attack becomes irresistible. Black could have played 17 ... ♗a6! 18 ♕c2 ♘c6 19 dxc5

♘b4 with excellent counterplay—another reason why 13 ♕c2 was better.

18 ♕e2 ♔e7 19 f4 ♗f6 20 e4!

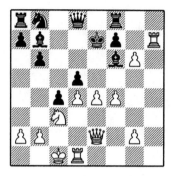

The decisive breakthrough. Black's king is now hopelessly exposed.

20 ... dxe4

Or 20 ... ♔e8 21 e5 ♗e7 22 gxf7+ ♔d7 23 g4 with a massive attack.

21 ♘xe4 ♔d7 22 d5 ♘a6 23 g7! ♖g8

Or if 23 ... ♖e8 there is 24 g8=♕ ♖xg8 25 ♖xf7+ ♗e7 26 d6+-

24 ♖h6! ♗xg7 25 ♖d6+ ♔c7 26 ♕xc4+!

An important check which decides the game by breaking the coordination of Black's rooks. 26 ... ♘c5 is met by 27 ♖xd8 ♖axd8 (or 27 ... ♔xd8 28 ♘d6+-) 28 b4+- so there is little choice.

26 ... ♔b8 27 ♖xd8+ ♖xd8 28 ♔b1 ♘c7 29 d6 ♘e6 30 f5 ♗xe4+ 31 ♕xe4 ♘c5 32 ♕c6 ♖c8 33 ♕d5 ♖d8 34 ♕xf7 ♖d7 35 ♕g8+ ♔b7 36 ♕d5+ ♔b8 37 ♕c6 a5 38 ♕xb6+ ♘b7 39 ♕c6 ♖d8 40 ♕c7+ 1:0

KM19/1: 1) White to play

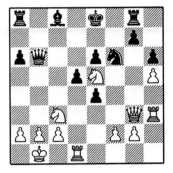

KM19/1: 2) White to play

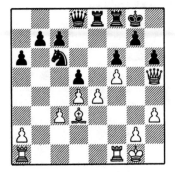

KM19/1: 3) White to play

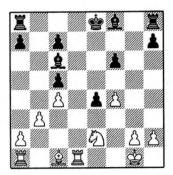

KM19/1: 4) White to play

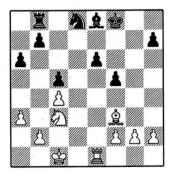

A19/1: a) White to play

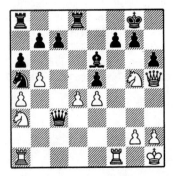

A19/1: b) White to play

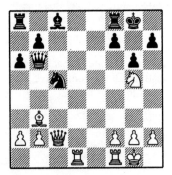

Month 19/Week 2:
Leonid Stein—Dynamic Currents

Leonid Stein (1934-73) is one of my own favourite players. One of the leading Soviet Grandmasters of the 1960s he came into prominence relatively late in life and then died tragically young.

Stein's style of play was very dynamic and aggressive yet unlike Spielmann and Tal, he did not so much try to attack right out of the opening as infuse the position with tension. So in the early part of the game he might avoid the sharpest lines and instead steer the game towards tense and complicated positions which would suddenly ignite in the middle-game. It was there that his tremendous combinative gift would show itself to advantage:

Stein - Evans
Amsterdam Izt 1964

1 e4 e5 2 ♘f3 ♘c6 3 ♗b5 a6 4 ♗a4 ♘f6 5 0-0 ♗e7 6 ♖e1 b5 7 ♗b3 d6 8 c3 0-0 9 h3 ♘b8 10 d3

A fairly restrained move (10 d4 is more usual) which in many ways is rather typical of Stein. He usually preferred to switch the main emphasis of the struggle to the middle-game rather than indulge in theoretical discussions.

10 ... c5 11 ♘bd2 ♕c7 12 ♗c2 ♘c6 13 ♘f1 d5

A forthright but committal continuation. 13 ... ♖e8 or 13 ... ♗b7 would have been more solid.

14 ♘e3 dxe4

More or less forced after which the d5 square is a serious weakness. After 14 ... d4 there is 15 ♘d5! and 14 ... ♖d8 can be met by 15 exd5

♘xd5 16 ♘xd5 ♖xd5 17 d4 threatening 18 ♗e4.

15 dxe4 ♖d8 16 ♕e2 g6

Defending against the threats of both 17 ♘f5 and 17 ♘d5 ♘xd5 18 exd5 ♖xd5 19 ♕e4. But nevertheless Black has serious latent weaknesses which Stein proceeds to exploit.

17 a4 ♖b8 18 axb5 axb5 19 ♘g5 h6 20 ♘d5!

Just as Black might have hoped he was consolidating the position it explodes in his face. From here on Stein just never lets up landing one blow after another on Black's shaky defence.

20 ... ♘xd5 21 exd5

21 ... hxg5

There is little choice. If 21 ... ♖xd5 White has 22 ♕f3+- and 21 ...

&xg5 22 &xg5 hxg5 23 dxc6 ♕xc6
24 ♕xe5 &b7 25 ♕xg5 (25 ... ♖d2
26 &e4) wins a pawn without any
apparent compensation.

**22 dxc6 ♕xc6 23 ♕xe5 &b7 24
♕g3 ♕f6**

Necessary in order to defend the
g-pawn but now comes the point of
20 ♘d5 which Stein must have seen
in advance.

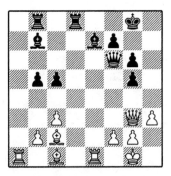

**25 ♖xe7! ♕xe7 26 &xg5 f6 27
&f4**

The second point. White is hitting
both the g6 pawn and the rook on
b8.

**27 ... ♖a8 28 ♖xa8 &xa8 29
&xg6 ♕g7 30 &e3 c4**

After 30 ... ♖c8 there is 31 &h6
♕xh6 32 &f5+, winning back the
exchange. Now comes the final
point of White's attacking plan.

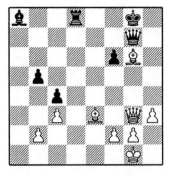

31 &f7+! ♔xf7

Everything fits in perfectly.

31 ... ♔f8 can be met by 32 &c5+
and 31 ... ♔h8 by 32 ♕h4+ ♕h7 33
♕xf6+ etc.

**32 ♕c7+ ♔g6 33 ♕xd8 &c6 34
&d4 ♕f7 35 ♕d6 1:0**

The following game is in some
respects rather similar but this time
Stein is playing Black. Once again
he conjures up a devastating attack,
this time using his beloved King's
Indian Defence.

Eliskases - Stein
Mar del Plata 1966

**1 d4 ♘f6 2 c4 g6 3 ♘c3 &g7 4
e4 d6 5 f3 0-0 6 &e3 b6**

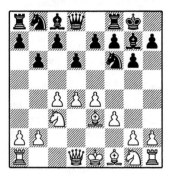

The double fianchetto line was
popular at the time but has since
been abandoned by most King's Indian players. This game was played
in the days when it was assumed
that Black had to prepare ... c7-c5
with something but in current practice it has been discovered that 6 ...
c5 can be played immediately. After
7 dxc5 dxc5 8 ♕xd8 ♖xd8 9 &xc5
♘c6 Black gets a prolonged initiative for the pawn.

7 ♖c1

A rather old-fashioned looking reply which would be more appropriate in a Queen's Gambit Declined than the dynamic King's Indian. He should probably play 7 ♗d3.

7 ... c5 8 ♘ge2

And not 8 ♗d3? ♘g4 9 fxg4 cxd4 which recovers the pawn with a tremendous position.

8 ... ♘c6 9 g3?

Another pedestrian developing move which shows a lack of appreciation of the danger White faces. He should probably have played 9 d5.

9 ... e5! 10 dxe5 ♘xe5 11 ♘g1?

A horribly retrograde move after which White's position goes rapidly downhill. 11 ♘f4 was more natural though Eliskases might have been concerned about 11 ... g5 12 ♘fd5 g4.

11 ... ♖e8 12 ♗e2 a6 13 ♕d2 ♗e6 14 b3 ♘c6 15 ♗d1

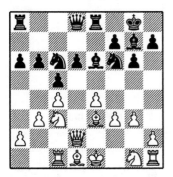

15 ... ♘d4!

A blow reminiscent of Stein's 20 ♘d5 in the previous game. Over the next few moves he doesn't count the cost in either pieces or pawns but plays single-mindedly to smash open the positon with White's king in the centre. The theme is very old

but, in the context of the King's Indian, thoroughly modern.

16 ♗xd4 cxd4 17 ♘ce2

For the time being the pawn is immune as 17 ♕xd4 loses to 17 ... ♘xe4 18 ♕xe4 ♗f5 etc. With his next move Stein offers it once again and this time it has to be taken.

17 ... d3! 18 ♕xd3

If 18 ♘f4 there is 18 ... d5, smashing open the centre.

18 ... b5 19 ♘f4

After 19 cxb5 axb5 Black's queen's rook would enter the fray. But White would have been better advised to play 19 ♘d4.

19 ... ♗f5 20 ♕f1

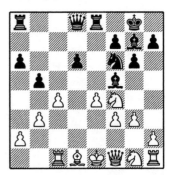

20 ... ♗xe4!

The culmination of Black's play over the last few moves as the last ramparts of the defense are swept away. 21 fxe4 ♘xe4 is horrific for White since in addition to the various discovered checks Black threatens 22 ... ♕a5+.

21 ♘ge2 ♗b7 22 ♘d5

White is staggering on in a hopeless position and by now he had time-trouble to add to his woes. The rest is a massacre:

22 ... ♗xd5 23 cxd5 ♘xd5 24 b4 ♘xb4 25 ♗b3 ♘d3+ 26 ♔d2 ♘xc1 27 ♘xc1 ♖c8 28 ♕d3 ♕f6 0:1

KM19/2: 1) Black to play

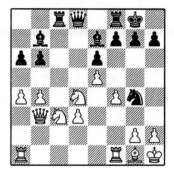

KM19/2: 2) White to play

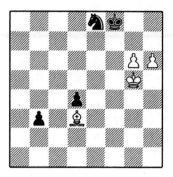

KM19/2: 3) Black to play

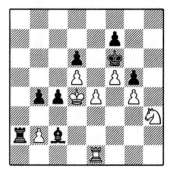

KM19/2: 4) Black to play

A19/2: a) White to play

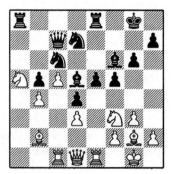

A19/2: b) Black to play

Month 19/Week 3:
Mikhail Tal—The Initiative

Mikhail Tal (1936-92) is thought by many to have been the greatest genius the game has ever produced. He climbed to the chess summit in record time to become World Champion at the age of 24 but then failed to live up to his early promise due to persistent problems with his health.

Tal's sight of the board and speed of calculation was just phenomenal and this, combined with a natural instinct for the initiative and attack, made him, at his best, virtually unstoppable. Nobody could live with him in wild positions.

Tal - Geller
USSR Ch, Riga 1958

1 e4 e5 2 ♘f3 ♘c6 3 ♗b5 a6 4 ♗a4 ♘f6 5 0-0 ♗e7 6 ♖e1 b5 7 ♗b3 0-0 8 c3 d6 9 h3 ♘a5 10 ♗c2 c5 11 d4 ♗b7 12 b4 cxb4 13 cxb4 ♘c4 14 ♘bd2 d5 15 exd5 exd4

15 ... ♘xd5 16 ♘xc4 bxc4 17 ♘xe5 ♘xb4 18 ♘xc4 ♘xc2 19 ♕xc2 ♖c8 20 ♕d3 leaves Black with inadequate compensation for the pawn.

16 ♘xc4 bxc4 17 ♕xd4

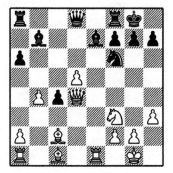

17 ... ♗xb4

After 17 ... ♘xd5 White has 18 ♕e4 g6 19 ♗h6 ♖e8 20 ♗a4 ♘c3 21 ♕xb7 ♘xa4 22 ♕c6! and after 17 ... ♗xd5 18 ♘e5 gives him good attacking chances. Geller's choice is the most reasonable and gives White the problem of how to defend both the rook on e1 and the pawn on d5. Tal's solution is inspired, sacrificing the exchange for lasting pressure.

18 ♖b1! ♗xe1

It's an offer Black can't refuse as 18 ... ♘xd5 is met by 19 ♗xh7+ ♔xh7 20 ♘g5+ ♔g8 21 ♕h4 ♘f6 22 ♖xb4+-.

19 ♖xb7 ♖e8

Black might have been well advised to play 19 ... ♕xd5!? 20 ♕xd5 ♘xd5 21 ♘xe1 ♖ab8 22 ♖xb8 ♖xb8 with a drawish endgame. Geller's move may be objectively correct but it is surely an unwise choice against Tal.

20 d6 ♕c8

Geller is playing well and probably expected 21 ♖c7 ♕e6 22 ♗g5 ♘d5 23 ♖c5 ♘c3 with good counterplay. Tal answers by throwing gasoline onto the fire.

21 ♗g5!?

A truly amazing move, giving up a whole rook to keep the initiative. Black in turn finds the best reply.

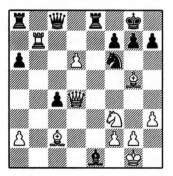

21 ... ♖e2!

After 21 ... ♕xb7 Tal intended 22 ♗xf6 gxf6 23 ♕h4 ♗xf2+ 24 ♔xf2 ♕b6+ 25 ♘d4 ♕xd6 26 ♕xh7+ ♔f8 27 ♕h6+-.

22 ♖c7 ♕e6 23 ♘xe1 ♖xe1+ 24 ♔h2 ♖d8! 25 ♗xf6 gxf6??

After a magnificently conducted defence, Geller finally slips up. He should have played 25 ... ♕xf6 after which 26 ♕xf6 gxf6 27 d7 ♔g7 (and not 27 ... ♔f8? 28 ♗xh7 ♖e2 29 ♔g3 ♖xa2 30 ♗f5) 28 ♗f5 ♖e5 29 ♖c8 ♖xf5 30 ♖xd8 ♖d5 would probably be drawn according to Tal.

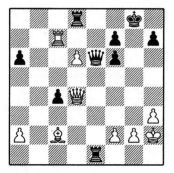

26 ♖e7 ♕xd6+

Geller had missed that 26 ... ♕xe7 is answered by 27 ♕g4+. Now he is simply left a piece down.

27 ♕xd6 ♖xd6 28 ♖xe1 ♖d2 29 ♖c1 ♖xf2 30 ♗e4 ♖xa2 31 ♖xc4 a5 32 ♖c8+ ♔g7 33 ♖c7 1:0

Tal's win over Botvinnik in their match in 1960 was a tremendous clash of styles and personalities, the serious, scientific Botvinnik against the devil-may-care Tal. Many leading Grandmasters were hoping that the defects in Tal's 'tricky' style would finally be exposed but the public were overjoyed when he emerged the winner.

The following game was the first in which Tal unleashed one of his famous speculative sacrifices. Would the mighty Botvinnik succeed in the defence where so many of his colleagues had failed?

Botvinnik - Tal
Moscow WCh 1960

1 c4 ♘f6 2 ♘f3 g6 3 g3 ♗g7 4 ♗g2 0-0 5 d4 d6 6 ♘c3 ♘bd7 7 0-0 e5 8 e4 c6 9 h3 ♕b6 10 d5 cxd5 11 cxd5 ♘c5 12 ♘e1 ♗d7 13 ♘d3 ♘xd3 14 ♕xd3 ♖fc8 15 ♖b1 ♘h5 16 ♗e3 ♕b4 17 ♕e2 ♖c4!? 18 ♖fc1 ♖ac8 19 ♔h2 f5 20 exf5 ♗xf5 21 ♖a1

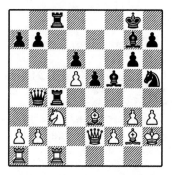

The position looks slightly better for White, he has more space, there is a hole on e4 and Black's piece activity looks like a temporary phenomenon. Rather than surrender the initiative Tal finds an extraordinary idea:

21 ... ♘f4!?

Giving up a piece in order to activate his king's bishop and weaken White's kingside.

22 gxf4 exf4 23 ♗d2?

23 a3! ♕b3 24 ♗xa7! was better after which Black should play 24 ... ♗e5! (and not 24 ... b6? 25.♕d1!+-)

25 ♗f3 b6 26 ♕d1 ♕xb2 27 ♖a2 ♖xc3 28 ♖xb2 ♖xc1 29 ♕e2 (and not 29 ♕d2? ♗e4!) 29 ... ♖8c3 with compensation for the queen.

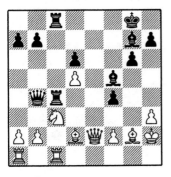

23 ... ♕xb2?

Black in turns slips up. He should have played first 23 ... ♗e5! after which 24 f3 ♕xb2 25 ♘d1 ♕d4 (25 ... ♕xa1!? 26 ♖xa1 ♗xa1 is also worth considering) 26 ♖xc4 ♖xc4 27 ♖c1 ♖xc1 28 ♗xc1 ♕xd5 29 ♗f1 is approximately equal.

24 ♖ab1! f3!

The only move. 24 ... ♗xb1 is bad because of 25 ♖xb1 ♕c2 26 ♗e4 ♖xe4 27 ♕xe4 ♕xd2 28 ♕e6+-.

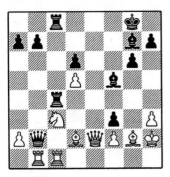

25 ♖xb2?

Botvinnik fails to meet the challenge. Salo Flohr pointed out that White could have obtained a clear advantage with 25 ♗xf3! ♗e5+ (or

25 ... ♗xb1 26 ♖xb1 ♕c2 27 ♗e4! ♖xe4 28 ♘xe4! ♕xb1 29 ♘xd6 ♖f8 30 ♕e6+ ♔h8 31 ♘f7+ ♖xf7 32 ♕xf7 ♕f5 33 ♕xf5 gxf5 34 ♔g3) 26 ♔g2 ♗xb1 27 ♖xb1 ♕c2 28 ♗e4! ♖xe4 29 ♘xe4 ♕xb1 30 ♘xd6!! ♗xd6 31 ♕e6+ ♔g7 32 ♕d7+! etc.

25 ... fxe2 26 ♖b3 ♖d4! 27 ♗e1

Or 27 ♗e3 ♖xc3 28 ♖bxc3 ♖d1 decides matters.

27 ... ♗e5+ 28 ♔g1

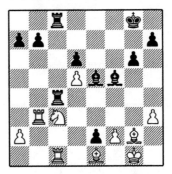

28 ... ♗f4

Black could have won much more quickly with 28 ... ♖xc3! after which 29 ♖bxc3 ♖d1 30 ♖c4 is met by 30 ... ♗f4! (31 ♖xf4 ♖xc1 32 f3 ♖xe1+ 33 ♔f2 ♖g1!-+). Tal may have missed this because the noise from the spectators forced the arbiters to move the game to a closed room.

29 ♘xe2 ♖xc1 30 ♘xd4 ♖xe1+ 31 ♗f1 ♗e4! 32 ♘e2 ♗e5 33 f4 ♗f6 34 ♖xb7 ♗xd5 35 ♖c7

Or 35 ♖xa7 ♖xe2 36 ♗xe2 ♗d4+ etc.

35 ... ♗xa2 36 ♖xa7 ♗c4 37 ♖a8+ ♔f7 38 ♖a7+ ♔e6 39 ♖a3 d5 40 ♔f2 ♗h4+ 41 ♔g2 ♔d6 42 ♘g3 ♗xg3 43 ♗xc4 dxc4 44 ♔xg3 ♔d5 45 ♖a7 c3 46 ♖c7 ♔d4 47 ♖d7+ 0:1

KM19/3: 1) White to play

KM19/3: 2) White to play

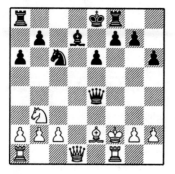

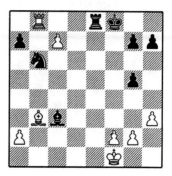

KM19/3: 3) White to play

KM19/3: 4) White to play

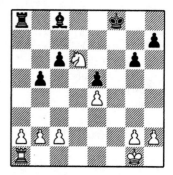

A19/3: a) Black to play

A19/3: b) White to play

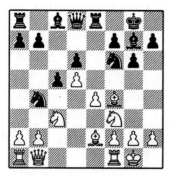

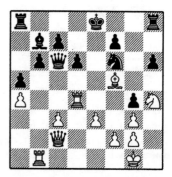

Month 19/Week 4:
Garry Kasparov—Heavy Duty
Preparation

The talent of Garry Kasparov (born in 1963) was spotted at a very early age after which he received the very best training the Soviet Union had to offer. The result was the development of arguably the strongest player in history.

Kasparov is the leading representative of the new generation of chess-player that has taken opening preparation to fantastic new levels of detail, aided not only by computer databases but a considerable amount of Grandmaster-power. Over the years he has assembled a team of seconds and opening analysts to develop the most thoroughly analysed opening arsenal and he wins many games with home analysis alone. This factor, the chess equivalent of a virtually unreturnable tennis serve, has given Kasparov a clear advantage in his games against his leading rivals.

In addition to the analytical excellence of his preparation, Kasparov is usually able to find the most unpleasant openings for his opponents to meet from a psychological perspective. In this he reminds us of his idol, Alexander Alekhine to whom he bears a great resemblance in his style of play.

Here is the 7th game of his 1993 World title match against Britain's Nigel Short in which he outplays his opponent from the opening and finishes matters with some brilliant attacking play.

Kasparov - Short
London WCh 1993

1 e4 e5 2 ♘f3 ♘c6 3 ♗b5 a6 4 ♗a4 ♘f6 5 0-0 ♗e7 6 ♖e1 b5 7 ♗b3 0-0

Threatening to play a Marshall Attack (with 8 c3 d5!) was certainly good psychology on Short's part so as to put Kasparov into the less comfortable role of defender. But Kasparov is having none of it and sidesteps Short's intention with the anti-Marshall line.

8 a4 ♗b7 9 d3 d6 10 ♘bd2 ♘d7 11 c3 ♘c5 12 axb5 axb5 13 ♖xa8 ♗xa8 14 ♗c2 ♗f6 15 b4 ♘e6 16 ♘f1! ♗b7

Black might have done better to play 16 ... d5!?.

17 ♘e3 g6 18 ♗b3 ♗g7 19 h4 ♗c8

It was also worth considering 19 ... h5 in order to prevent the further advance of White's h-pawn.

20 h5 ♔h8 21 ♘d5 g5?!

This turns out badly. Black should probably have tried 21 ... gxh5, precarious though this may be.

22 ♘e3 ♘f4 23 g3 ♘xh5 24 ♘f5 ♗xf5 25 exf5 ♕d7

26 ♗xg5! h6

Probably a mistake. After 26 ... ♕xf5 White wins with 27 ♗d5! but Black had two superior possibilities in 26 ... ♗f6 and 26 ... ♘f6. In either case the outcome would have been far from clear.

Kasparov claimed that his next move was also a mistake, suggesting instead that he should have played 27 ♔g2!? intending 28 ♖h1. His analysis continued: 27 ... ♕xf5 28 ♖h1 ♕g6 29 ♘xe5 dxe5 30 ♕xh5! ♕xh5 31 ♖xh5 ♔h7 32 ♗e3 when White has a clear advantage.

27 ♘h4 ♘f6 28 ♗xf6 ♗xf6 29 ♕h5 ♔h7 30 ♘g2

Once again Kasparov was critical of his own play and suggested 30 ♘f3 ♘e7 31 d4 exd4 32 cxd4 after which 32 ... ♘g8 is forced. After 30 ♘g2 the position is far from clear.

30 ... ♘e7 31 ♘e3 ♘g8 32 d4! exd4 33 cxd4 ♗xd4?

The losing move. Black has to play 33 ... ♗g5! after which both 34 ♘f1 and 34 f4 ♗f6 35 ♘g4 ♔g7 leave everything still to play for.

34 ♘g4

34 ... ♔g7

After 34 ... ♕d8 there follows 35 f6! ♗xf6 36 ♕f5+ ♔g7 37 ♗c2 ♖e8 38 ♖xe8 ♕xe8 39 ♕h7+ ♔f8

40 ♕xg8+! according to Averbakh. Also after the text White's attack comes crashing through.

35 ♘xh6! ♗f6

Or 35 ... ♘xh6 36 ♕g5+ ♔h7 37 f6 intending 38 ♗c2+.

36 ♗xf7! 1:0

Both 36 ... ♘xh6 37 ♕g6+ and 36 ... ♖xf7 37 ♕g6+ lead to mate.

The following game is a scary example of the depth of Kasparov's opening preparation. It looks to me as if White's entire concept of 16 ♖b4 and 17 ♖xb7 had been prepared beforehand and it left Black with a deeply unpleasant position. Perhaps Shirov could have defended better but he was clearly under terrible pressure after the initial surprise.

Kasparov - Shirov
Horgen 1994

1 e4 c5 2 ♘f3 e6 3 d4 cxd4 4 ♘xd4 ♘f6 5 ♘c3 ♘c6 6 ♘db5 d6 7 ♗f4 e5

Shirov, like Short, chooses a line in which Black tries to take the initiative early on, this time at the cost of certain structural weaknesses rather than a pawn. Kasparov's reaction is quite similar in that he chooses a line which limits Black's play rather than attempting to refute it from the outset.

As the game proceeds it turns out that Kasparov has prepared this line in great depth. His original rook manoeuvre on move 16 is followed by an astonishing exchange sacrifice.

8 ♗g5 a6 9 ♘a3 b5 10 ♘d5 ♗e7 11 ♗xf6 ♗xf6 12 c3 ♗b7 13 ♘c2 ♘b8 14 a4 bxa4 15 ♖xa4 ♘d7 16 ♖b4!

Kasparov finally unveils a novelty, deviating from the mundane 16 ♘ce3 0-0 17 ♖a3 ♗g5 18 ♘c4 ♗xd5 19 ♕xd5 ♗e7 as played in Tatai-Iruzubieta, Cannes 1992.

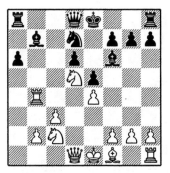

16 ... ♘c5

Had Black fully appreciated the strength of the following exchange sacrifice, he might have chosen 16 ... ♖b8!? instead.

17 ♖xb7! ♘xb7 18 b4

No dramatic follow up, just a simple pawn advance to control the c5 and a5 squares. Black's knight is now a truly miserable beast which can only reenter the game via d8.

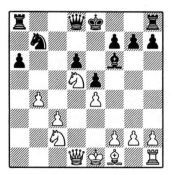

18 ... ♗g5 19 ♘a3 0-0 20 ♘c4 a5 21 ♗d3 axb4 22 cxb4 ♕b8 23 h4 ♗h6 24 ♘cb6 ♖a2 25 0-0 ♖d2 26 ♕f3 ♕a7 27 ♘d7

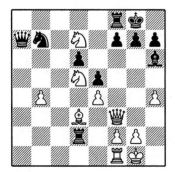

27 ... ♘d8?

One can understand Shirov's desire to improve the position of his knight on b7 but this is the decisive mistake. He should have tried to hang tough with 27 ... ♖a8! as the return of the exchange brings little in the way of relief.

28 ♘xf8 ♔xf8 29 b5 ♕a3 30 ♕f5 ♔e8 31 ♗c4 ♖c2 32 ♕xh7 ♖xc4 33 ♕g8+ ♔d7 34 ♘b6+ ♔e7 35 ♘xc4 ♕c5 36 ♖a1 ♕d4 37 ♖a3 ♗c1 38 ♘e3 1:0

KM19/4: 1) White to play

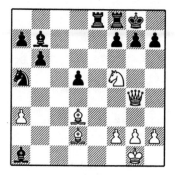

KM19/4: 2) White to play

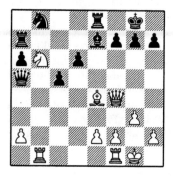

KM19/4: 3) White to play

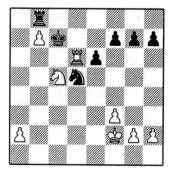

KM19/4: 4) White to play

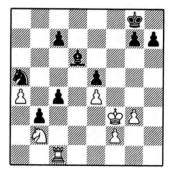

A19/4: a) White to play

A19/4: b) White to play

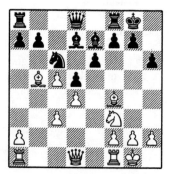

8 The Strategists

Strategically minded players aim to outplay their opponents using a superior understanding of positions. By knowing the kind of action a position requires they hope to be able to outmanoeuvre opponents who play in a less consistent way.

The four players under review this month were at times able to mystify their opponents with the depth of their positional insight.

Month 20/Week 1:
Wilhelm Steinitz
—Reason and Plans

Wilhelm Steinitz is regarded by many as being the father of modern positional chess. His insight into the nature of chess strategy was well ahead of his time and enabled him to triumph over players who were arguably more gifted in other respects.

Steinitz's teachings were studied by a number of younger masters of whom Siegbert Tarrasch tried to put them into a series of rather simplistic rules, a form which could be readily understood by the general public. Yet in my opinion this led to the real genius and meaning behind Steinitz's ideas being lost.

In his superb book, *Lasker's Manual of Chess*, Emanuel Lasker paid tribute to the man he succeeded as World Champion and came much closer to describing Steinitz's revolutionary way of thinking about chess. Lasker rightly claimed that Steinitz was the first player to understand that victory is not won by strength of will and genius alone but by making sound plans that conform to the requirements of the position. I can only add that in this way one's growth in chess mirrors reaching maturity in life, that someone grows up when the self-centred will of the child is finally tempered by reason, and objectivity.

In the following games Steinitz uses reason and good planning to triumph over two of the greatest masters of combination, Anderssen and Zukertort.

Anderssen - Steinitz,
London 1866

1 e4 e5 2 ♘f3 ♘c6 3 ♗b5 ♘f6 4 d3 d6 5 ♗xc6+?! bxc6 6 h3

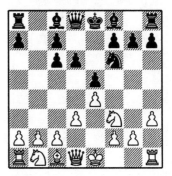

White's last two moves might be explained by the fact that Anderssen, like Chigorin, is reputed to have preferred knights to bishops. First of all he made an unprovoked exchange on c6 and then safeguarded his knight on f3 against 6 ... ♗g4.

There is no logical reason for this preference for the knight and I can only guess that it was the combinative properties of this piece that appealed to him.

6 ... g6

Already thinking in terms of a pawn advance on the kingside. In support of this plan Black's bishop will be well-placed on g7.

7 ♘c3 ♗g7 8 0-0 0-0 9 ♗g5 h6 10 ♗e3 c5

Preventing d3-d4 which would give open the centre and give White some chances.

11 ♖b1?!

Andersson wants to activate this rook with b2-b4 but this idea has no strategic basis. He should have continued trying to play for d3-d4 and to this end he should play 11 ♘c3-e2 followed by 12 c3.

11 ... ♘e8 12 b4 cxb4 13 ♖xb4 c5 14 ♖a4

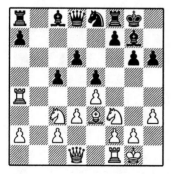

White continues 'attacking' by taking aim at Black's a-pawn. Unfortunately for Anderssen there is no justification for this and the rook is simply misplaced on this square. Meanwhile Steinitz continues his plan of a kingside pawn advance supported by his bishop pair.

14 ... ♗d7 15 ♖a3 f5 16 ♕b1 ♔h8 17 ♕b7 a5 18 ♖b1 a4

Safeguarding the queenside by quite economical means. With White's pieces offside Black's kingside attack is much more effective than it would otherwise have been.

19 ♕d5 ♕c8 20 ♖b6 ♖a7

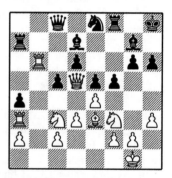

The rook prepares to swing over to the kingside to lend further force to Black's kingside pawn advance. This also has the incidental threat of 21 ... fxe4 22 dxe4 ♗xh3 etc.

21 ♔h2 f4 22 ♗d2 g5 23 ♕c4 ♕d8 24 ♖b1 ♘f6 25 ♔g1 ♘h7

Methodically protecting the g5 pawn in preparation for a further advance.

26 ♔f1 h5 27 ♘g1 g4 28 hxg4 hxg4 29 f3 ♕h4 30 ♘d1 ♘g5

Once again Black plays his pieces to squares where they support

Black's kingside breakthrough. Note the contrast between Steinitz's steady play and Anderssen's attempts to make superficial threats.

31 ♗e1 ♕h7 32 d4

Desperately trying to get the hapless rook on a3 into play, even at the cost of a-pawn. Steinitz declines these meagre gains and brings his plan to a successful conclusion.

32 ... gxf3 33 gxf3 ♘h3 34 ♗f2 ♘xg1 35 dxc5 ♕h3+ 36 ♔e1 ♘xf3+ 37 ♖xf3 ♕xf3 38 ♘c3 dxc5 39 ♗xc5 ♖c7 40 ♘d5 ♖xc5 41 ♕xc5 ♕xe4+ 42 ♔f2 ♖c8 43 ♘c7 ♕e3+ 0:1

In his matches against Johannes Zukertort, Steinitz faced one of the most gifted players of his day. Yet Zukertort lost heavily on both occasions because, like Anderssen, he lacked the positional understanding of Steinitz and his ability to create sound plans.

Zukertort - Steinitz
St Louis, WCh 1886

1 d4 d5 2 c4 e6 3 ♘c3 ♘f6 4 ♘f3 dxc4 5 e3 c5 6 ♗xc4 cxd4 7 exd4 ♗e7 8 0-0 0-0 9 ♕e2 ♘bd7 10 ♗b3 ♘b6 11 ♗f4 ♘bd5 12 ♗g3

As in the Anderssen game it is difficult to detect the thread which ties White's moves to the requirements of the position. It is as if he is playing his pieces to active squares in the hope that a combination will eventually present itself.

Steinitz meanwhile pursues a logical plan to put pressure on White's isolated d-pawn.

12 ... ♕a5 13 ♖ac1 ♗d7 14 ♘e5 ♖fd8 15 ♕f3 ♗e8 16 ♖fe1 ♖ac8 17 ♗h4 ♘xc3 18 bxc3 ♕c7 19 ♕d3

Even now Zukertort does not seem to have constructed any kind of plan. Lasker recommended 19 ♗g3 ♗d6 20 c4 at this point to gain space with the hanging pawns.

19 ... ♘d5 20 ♗xe7 ♕xe7 21 ♗xd5 ♖xd5 22 c4?!

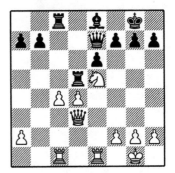

By now the advance of the hanging pawns lacks force due to the exchange of two sets of minor pieces. White no longer has the kind of attacking chances associated with this structure and should content himself with quietly trying to maintain his position.

22 ... ♖dd8 23 ♖e3? ♕d6 24 ♖d1 f6 25 ♖h3?! h6 26 ♘g4 ♕f4 27 ♘e3 ♗a4 28 ♖f3 ♕d6 29 ♖d2 ♗c6 30 ♖g3 f5 31 ♖g6

Over the last few moves Zukertort's rook has drifted ever further offside. He should retreat with 31 ♘d1.

31 ... ♗e4 32 ♕b3

Threatening 33 c5.

32 ... ♔h7 33 c5 ♖xc5 34 ♖xe6 ♖c1+ 35 ♘d1 ♕f4 36 ♕b2 ♖b1 37 ♕c3 ♖c8 38 ♖xe4 ♕xe4 0:1

KM20/1: 1) White to play

KM20/1: 2) Black to play

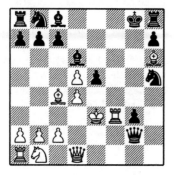

KM20/1: 3) Black to play

KM20/1: 4) White to play

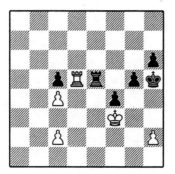

A20/1: a) White to play

A20/1: b) Black to play

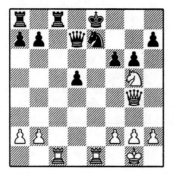

Month 20/Week 2:
Aaron Nimzowitsch
—Prophylaxis

The 1920s was a period in which established concepts in many different fields were challenged and re-evaluated. Chess was no exception and the so-called 'hypermodern' movement came to challenge the establishment.

The leading representatives of the hypermodern movement were Gyula Breyer, Richard Reti and Aaron Nimzowitsch. They preached ideas which were considered heresy by the likes of Dr. Tarrasch. Amongst their shocking views they held that the centre did not need to be occupied with pawns but could instead be controlled by pieces. In his original books on chess strategy, *My System* and *Chess Praxis*, Nimzowitsch also introduced words such as 'prophylaxis' into the chess vocabulary.

Many writers have implied that Nimzowitsch was an opponent of the classical view of strategy as laid down by Steinitz but I don't think this was really the case. I see them as being remarkably similar in spirit, both Steinitz and Nimzowitsch were tireless researchers into the nature of chess and were willing to stand alone against the rest of the world.

The following two games show Nimzowitsch's great originality and profound insight which was years ahead of its time. Even today Nimzowitsch is regarded as being required reading by the leading players.

Johner - Nimzowitsch
Dresden 1926

1 d4 ♘f6 2 c4 e6 3 ♘c3 ♗b4 4 e3 0-0 5 ♗d3 c5 6 ♘f3 ♘c6 7 0-0 ♗xc3 8 bxc3 d6

A plan of blockade which retains its popularity to this day. Yet the modern interpretation of this plan is to delay castling with 4 ... c5 5 ♗d3 ♘c6 6 ♘f3 ♗xc3+ which retains the option of castling queenside.

9 ♘d2 b6 10 ♘b3?!

An inaccuracy according to Nimzowitsch who suggested that White should play the immediate 10 f4 after which 10 ... e5 is met by 11 fxe5 dxe5 12 d5 with a balanced game.

10 ... e5 11 f4

11 d5 is strongly by met by 11 ... e4 12 ♗e2 ♘e5.

11 ... e4 12 ♗e2 ♕d7!!

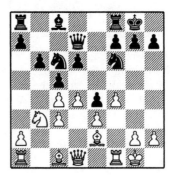

A really extraordinary looking move which must have been considered quite eccentric at the time. This is where we see real depth of understanding in that Nimzowitsch knew he must restrain White's kingside pawns from advancing with g2-g4. If he achieves this White will be left without a good plan.

13 h3?! ♘e7 14 ♕e1? h5!

Continuing his plan of restraint and if fact White is soon reduced to complete passivity. He should have tried 13 ♗d2 followed by 14 ♗e1 and 14 ♗d2 was also an improvement.

15 ♗d2 ♕f5! 16 ♔h2 ♕h7!

By now it's becoming clear that White will not be able to play g2-g4. With his next few moves Nimzowitsch saps the remaining energy from White's position by blockading his a-pawn and inducing d4-d5.

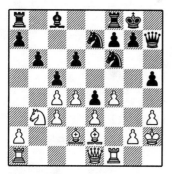

17 a4 ♘f5 18 g3 a5!

Preventing the exchange of White's weak a-pawn at the cost of a slight weakening of b6. White didn't play 18 a5 because of 18 ... ♘g4+ 19 hxg4 hxg4+ 20 ♔h1 g3 but 19 ♗xg4 hxg4 20 axb6 might have been a better chance than the game.

19 ♖g1 ♘h6 20 ♗f1 ♗d7 21 ♗c1 ♖ac8! 22 d5

After this White can do nothing but wait to see how Black will try to break through on the kingside.

22 ... ♔h8 23 ♘d2 ♖g8 24 ♗g2 g5 25 ♘f1 ♖g7 26 ♖a2 ♘f5 27 ♗h1 ♖cg8 28 ♕d1 gxf4

An important decision which had to be well judged. It opens the g-file for Black and the e-file for White.

29 exf4 ♗c8 30 ♕b3 ♗a6

31 ♖e2

White makes a bid for counterplay by attacking the e-pawn. After 31 ♗d2 Black could play an attractive combination with 31 ... ♖g6! 32 ♗e1 ♘g4+! 33 hxg4 hxg4+ 34 ♔g2 ♗xc4 35 ♕xc4 e3 with the decisive threat of 36 ... ♕h3+.

31 ... ♘h4 32 ♖e3

If White went for the e-pawn with 32 ♘d2 ♗c8 33 ♘xe4 he would fall victim to the beautiful 33 ... ♕f5 34 ♘f2 ♕xh3+! 35 ♘xh3 ♘g4#. If White varies with 33 ♕d1, Black has 33 ... ♗xh3! 34 ♔xh3 ♕f5+ etc.

32 ... ♗c8 33 ♕c2 ♗xh3! 34 ♗xe4

34 ♔xh3 ♕f2+ 35 ♔h2 ♘g4+ leads to mate.

34 ... ♗f5 35 ♗xf5 ♘xf5 36 ♖e2 h4 37 ♖gg2 hxg3+ 38 ♔g1 ♕h3 39 ♘e3 ♘h4 40 ♔f1 ♖e8! 0:1

Black threatens 41 ... ♘xg2 42 ♖xg2 ♕h1+ 43 ♔e2 ♕xg2+ and if White defends against this with 41 ♔e1 there is 41 ... ♘f3+ followed by 42 ... ♕h1+.

In the next game we see Nimzo-witsch play against one of the earliest examples of the Modern Benoni. Thrown onto his own re-sources Nimzowitsch shows a re-markable insight into the position.

Nimzowitsch - Marshall
New York 1927

1 c4 ♘f6 2 d4 e6 3 ♘f3 c5!?
In this tournament the ingenious Frank Marshall introduced this opening which later became known as the Modern Benoni. Black con-cedes some space in the centre in order to obtain a half-open e-file and a queenside pawn majority.
4 d5 d6 5 ♘c3 exd5 6 cxd5 g6

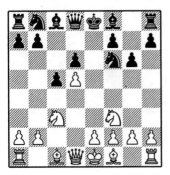

7 ♘d2!
Disregarding the rules about fast development, Nimzowitsch brings the knight to c4 where he feels it is best placed.
7 ... ♘bd7?! 8 ♘c4 ♘b6 9 e4 ♗g7?
Black should take this opportunity to rid himself of his badly placed knight on b6 with 9 ... ♘xc4 10

♗xc4 ♗g7. The modern preference is for 7 ... ♗g7.
10 ♘e3! 0-0 11 ♗d3 ♘h5
This quite reasonable move by Marshall came in for a lot of unfair criticism. The real mistake came later.
12 0-0 ♗e5 13 a4 ♘f4 14 a5 ♘d7 15.♘c4 ♘xd3 16 ♕xd3 f5?
A typical Marshall move which undermines White's centre and acti-vates Black's pieces. Unfortunately it proves too loosening.
17 exf5 ♖xf5 18 f4! ♗d4+ 19 ♗e3 ♗xc3 20 ♕xc3 ♘f6 21 ♕b3! ♖xd5?
This is refuted with an elegantly conducted attack and after 21 ... ♘xd5 White has 22 ♖ae1! when 22 ... ♗e6 is answered by 23 ♗xc5. The only chance was 21 ... ♘g4.

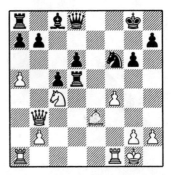

22 f5! gxf5
Or 22 ... ♗xf5 23 ♗g5 etc..
23 ♗g5 ♖d4
After 23 ... ♗e6 White plays 24 ♕xb7 ♖c8 25 ♖ae1! etc.
24 ♘b6+ c4 25 ♕c3 axb6 26 ♕xd4 ♔g7 27 ♖ae1! bxa5 28 ♖e8! ♕xe8 29 ♕xf6+ ♔g8 30 ♗h6 1:0

KM20/2: 1) White to play

KM20/2: 2) White to play

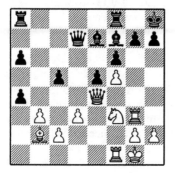

KM20/2: 3) Black to play

KM20/2: 4) Black to play

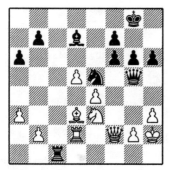

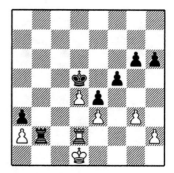

A20/2: a) White to play

A20/2: b) Black to play

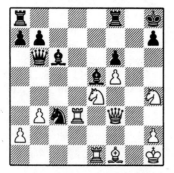

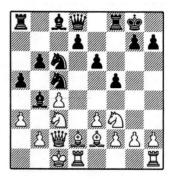

Month 20/Week 3:
Mikhail Botvinnik—The Scientist

When the Soviet Union emerged as the world's leading chess nation, its champion was Mikhail Botvinnik. Approaching chess from the point of view of a research scientist Botvinnik thoroughly analysed certain types of positions which were previously simply 'played'.

As a result of his research he developed a thorough mastery of every aspect of the game. Not only did he discover many new systems of development but worked them out thoroughly before the game even started. This new kind of preparation could at times leave even his most illustrious adversaries looking like amateurs.

In the following two games Botvinnik triumphs over two of the greatest players in history. In the first he beats the reigning World Champion, Alexander Alekhine.

Botvinnik - Alekhine
Amsterdam 1938

1 ♘f3 d5 2 d4 ♘f6 3 c4 e6 4 ♘c3 c5 5 cxd5 ♘xd5 6 e3 ♘c6 7 ♗c4 cxd4 8 exd4 ♗e7 9 0-0 0-0 10 ♖e1

10 ... b6?!

According to Botvinnik this was probably the decisive mistake, such is the strength of the pressure he now obtains. Black should first exchange knights on c3.

11 ♘xd5! exd5 12 ♗b5 ♗d7

12 ... ♘a5 might have been a better try though after 13 ♘e5. White retains a significant edge. The text leads to exchanges but White retains a clear advantage.

13 ♕a4 ♘b8

The only move as 13 ... ♖c8 is met by 14 ♗d2! threatening 15 ♖ac1.

14 ♗f4 ♗xb5 15 ♕xb5 a6 16 ♕a4 ♗d6 17 ♗xd6 ♕xd6 18 ♖ac1 ♖a7 19 ♕c2 ♖e7

White's last move ensures control of the c-file and leaves Black with the problem of what to play next. The text move leads to a bad endgame as would 19 ... f6 20 ♕f5 followed by 21 ♕e6+.

20 ♖xe7 ♕xe7 21 ♕c7 ♕xc7 22 ♖xc7

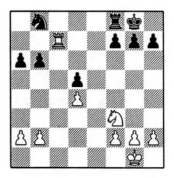

22 ... f6!

Alekhine is defending well, with the text move intending to drive White's rook from the 7th rank with 23 ... ♖f7. The answer to 23 ♖b7 would be 23 ... ♖c8.

23 ♔f1 ♖f7 24 ♖c8+ ♖f8 25 ♖c3!
Leaving Black with nothing to do but try to bring his king to the centre. In order to do this he has to make the following weakening advance of his kingside pawns.

25 ... g5 26 ♘e1 h5
26 ... h6 would be answered by 27 ♘c2 ♔f7 28 ♘e3 ♔e6 29 g4 followed by 30 ♘f5, but now Botvinnik finds a very unpleasant move.

27 h4! ♘d7
There was little else to be done as 27 ... gxh4 is answered by 28 ♘f3, recovering the pawn with advantage. After 27 ... ♔f7 Botvinnik intended 28 ♘f3 g4 29 ♘e1 ♔e6 30 ♘d3 ♔f5 31 g3 followed by 32 ♘f4.

28 ♖c7 ♖f7 29 ♘f3 g4 30 ♘e1 f5 31 ♘d3 f4
The only defence against 32 ♘f4. Botvinnik could now have won a pawn with 32 ♘b4 but he prefers to place Black in zugzwang.

32 f3 gxf3 33 gxf3 a5 34 a4 ♔f8 35 ♖c6 ♔e7 36 ♔f2 ♖f5 37 b3 ♔d8 38 ♔e2 ♘b8

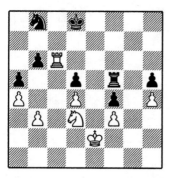

39 ♖g6!
Resisting the temptation to play 39 ♖xb6 which could be met by 39 ... ♔c7 followed by 40 ... ♘c6.

39 ... ♔c7 40 ♘e5 ♘a6 41 ♖g7+ ♔c8 42 ♘g6 ♖f6 43 ♘e7+ ♔b8 44 ♘xd5 ♖d6 45 ♖g5 ♘b4 46 ♘xb4 axb4 47 ♖xh5 ♖c6
White would answer 47 ... ♖xd4 with 48 ♖f5 ♔b7 49 ♖f6 ♔c7 50 h5 etc.

48 ♖b5 ♔c7 49 ♖xb4 ♖h6 50 ♖b5 ♖xh4 51 ♔d3 1:0

The following game was one of Botvinnik's most brilliant wins. To play it against the Cuban genius José Raúl Capablanca must have been especially satisfying.

Botvinnik - Capablanca
Amsterdam 1938

1 d4 ♘f6 2 c4 e6 3 ♘c3 ♗b4 4 e3 d5 5 a3
Botvinnik specialised in this line against the Nimzo-Indian, accepting a doubled pawn in return for the two bishops and central control. After Black's fourth move it is particularly effective because the doubled pawns will be dissolved. He should probably play 5 ... ♗e7.

5 ... ♗xc3+ 6 bxc3 c5 7 cxd5 exd5 8 ♗d3 0-0 9 ♘e2 b6 10 0-0 ♗a6
Certainly it is a good idea by Black to exchange off one of White's bishops but White nevertheless retains a potentially dangerous central pawn majority.

11 ♗xa6 ♘xa6 12 ♗b2 ♕d7 13 a4 ♖fe8?
Black has found himself in the kind of position which Botvinnik studied thoroughly at home and over the next few moves finds himself being thoroughly outplayed. The text move seems natural enough but it does little to challenge

White's long-term plan of advancing his central pawns. He should play 13 ... cxd4 14 cxd4 ♖fc8 with counterplay on the c-file.

14 ♕d3 c4?

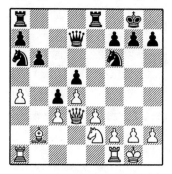

According to Botvinnik this is a really serious mistake. Capablanca had evidently assumed that White would be unable to advance his central pawns with e3-e4 whilst he could mobilise his queenside majority. Just how wrong he was will soon be revealed.

15 ♕c2 ♘b8 16 ♖ae1 ♘c6 17 ♘g3 ♘a5

White is systematically aiming for a central breakthrough with e3-e4 and there is little Black can do to prevent this. After 17 ... ♘e4 Botvinnik intended 18 ♘h1! ♘a5 19 f3 followed by returning his knight to g3 and playing e3-e4.

18 f3 ♘b3 19 e4 ♕xa4 20 e5 ♘d7 21 ♕f2 g6 22 f4 f5 23 exf6

White must keep the position open on the kingside.

23 ... ♘xf6 24 f5 ♖xe1 25 ♖xe1 ♖e8

This meets with a strong reply but even after 25 ... ♖f8 White would develop a menacing attack with 26 ♕f4!.

26 ♖e6!

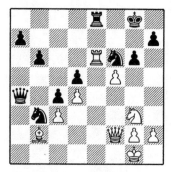

26 ... ♖xe6

The only move according to Botvinnik who gave the refutation of 26 ... ♔f7 as 27 ♖xf6+ ♔xf6 28 fxg6+ ♔xg6 (or 28 ... ♔e7 29 ♕f7+ ♔d8 30 g7+-) 29 ♕f5+ ♔g7 30 ♘h5+ ♔h6 31 h4 ♖g8 32 g4 ♕c6 33 ♗a3+-.

27 fxe6 ♔g7 28 ♕f4 ♕e8 29 ♕e5 ♕e7

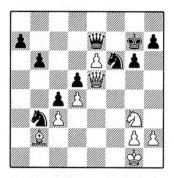

We have already met this position once in Book 1 of the Power-Chess program, month 5, week 1. For a detailed commentary on the following magnificent combination, please turn to these notes.

30 ♗a3!! ♕xa3 31 ♘h5+! gxh5 32 ♕g5+ ♔f8 33 ♕xf6+ ♔g8 34 e7! ♕c1+ 35 ♔f2 ♕c2+ 36 ♔g3 ♕d3+ 37 ♔h4 ♕e4+ 38 ♔xh5 ♕e2+ 39 ♔h4 ♕e4+ 40 g4 ♕e1+ 41 ♔h5 1:0

KM20/3: 1) Black to play

KM20/3: 2) White to play

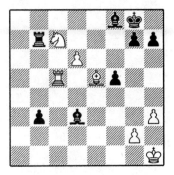

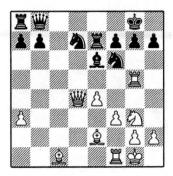

KM20/3: 3) White to play

KM20/3: 4) White to play

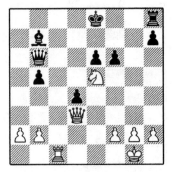

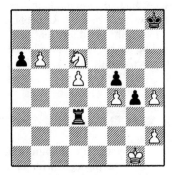

A20/3: a) Black to play

A20/3: b) Black to play

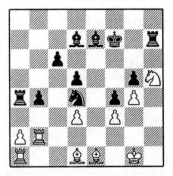

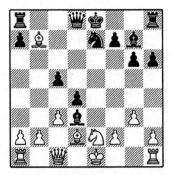

Month 20/Week 4:
Tigran Petrosian

In many ways Petrosian's style of play resembled that of Nimzowitsch. In the art of draining the energy from his opponent's position he was quite unparalleled and at his best he was regarded as being virtually unbeatable.

Petrosian became World Champion by edging out his rivals in the 1962 Curacao Candidates tournament and then defeating an ageing Botvinnik in 1963.

Despite the fact that everyone was familiar with Nimzowitsch's teachings Petrosian managed to baffle the strongest of opposition. In the following game he outplays former World Champion Machgielis Euwe.

Petrosian - Euwe
Zurich Ct 1953

1 ♘f3 ♘f6 2 g3 d5 3 ♗g2 ♗f5 4 d3 e6 5 ♘bd2 h6 6 0-0 ♗c5 7 ♕e1 0-0 8 e4 dxe4

The modern interpretation of this position would be to play 8 ... ♗h7 and then try to execute a queenside pawn advance. But here the bishop on c5 would be better placed on e7.

9 ♘xe4 ♘xe4 10 dxe4 ♗h7

11 b4!

Gaining time and space on the queenside. White has clearly gained the initiative from his seemingly quiet opening.

11 ... ♗e7 12 ♗b2 ♘a6 13 a3 c6 14 ♖d1 ♕c8 15 c4 ♘c7 16 ♕c3 ♗f6 17 ♘e5

The opening has resulted in a clearly favourable position for White, he has more space and a choice of plans whilst Black's position is cramped and passive. 17 e5?! would allow Black's bishop on h7 to breathe again.

17 ... ♖d8 18 ♗f3 ♘e8 19 ♖xd8 ♕xd8 20 ♖d1 ♕c7 21 c5

Increasing White's space advantage and taking control of the d6 square.

21 ..., a5 22 ♗g2 axb4 23 axb4 ♖d8 24 ♖xd8 ♕xd8 25 ♕c2 ♘c7 26 ♗f1 ♘b5 27 f4 ♔f8 28 ♔f2 ♗xe5?

Ridding himself of the annoying knight on e5 but the cure is worse than the disease. Black might have made more of a fight of it with 28 ... g5.

29 ♗xe5 f6 30 ♗b2 ♔e7 31 ♗c4 ♗g6 32 ♔e3 ♗f7 33 g4 ♕c7 34 e5!

After a lengthy period of preparation and manoeuvre, Petrosian finally begins a direct attack. Having had his position reduced to such a passive state Black is in little position to resist.

34 ... ♕d8 35 exf6+ gxf6 36 h4 ♘c7 37 ♕c3 ♘d5+ 38 ♗xd5 ♕xd5 39 ♕xf6+ ♔e8 40 ♕h8+ ♔d7 41 ♕g7

The game was adjourned at this point with Black in a virtually hopeless position. His only chance is that the exposed position of White's king may permit perpetual check should he be careless.

41 ... ♔e8

If 41 ... ♕b3+ there follows 42 ♗c3 ♔e8 43 h5!+-.

42 ♗f6 ♕b3+ 43 ♗c3 ♕d1 44 ♕h8+ ♔d7 45 ♕b8 ♕c1+

The checks also run out after 45 ... ♕g1+ 46 ♔d2 ♕f2+ 47 ♔d1 ♕f1+ 48 ♔c2 ♕e2+ 49 ♗d2.

46 ♗d2 ♕g1+ 47 ♔d3 ♕f1+ 48 ♔c2 ♕a6

Or if 48 ... ♕c4+ there follows 49 ♔b2 ♕d4+ 50 ♗c3 ♕f2+ 51 ♔a3.

49 h5! ♕a2+ 50 ♔d3 ♕b1+ 51 ♔e2 ♕e4+ 52 ♔f2 ♕d4+ 53 ♗e3 ♕xb4 54 ♕f8 ♕b2+ 55 ♔g3 ♕f6 56 ♕d6+ ♔c8 57 ♗d4 ♕d8 58 ♕xd8+ ♔xd8 59 ♗g7 ♔c7 60 ♗xh6 b6 61 cxb6+ ♔xb6 62 ♔h4 1:0

In the next game Petrosian manages to outwit the man who replaced him as World Champion three years later. Note the cunning delay of castling by Black.

Spassky - Petrosian
Moscow WCh 1966

1 d4 ♘f6 2 ♘f3 e6 3 ♗g5 d5 4 ♘bd2 ♗e7 5 e3 ♘bd7 6 ♗d3 c5 7 c3 b6 8 0-0 ♗b7 9 ♘e5 ♘xe5 10 dxe5 ♘d7 11 ♗f4

In view of the way things turn out it would have been better to exchange bishops and play f2-f4. On f4 the bishop provides a target for Black's coming kingside pawn storm.

11 ... ♕c7

The immediate 11 ... g5 12 ♗g3 h5 was even better, but Petrosian used to like to disguise his intentions.

12 ♘f3 h6 13 b4

White feels things are turning against him and tries to stir up trouble. After 13 ... cxb4 14 cxb4 ♗xb4 15 ♘d4 he would get good play for his pawn.

13 ... g5 14 ♗g3 h5 15 h4

15 h3 g4 16 hxg4 hxg4 would leave White unable to hold the pawn on e5.

15 ... gxh4!

15 ... g4 16 ♘g5 ♘xe5 17 ♗b5+ leads to wild position with Black's king in the centre. Petrosian prefers a line which minimises White's counterplay.

16 ♗f4 0-0-0 17 a4 c4!

Most players would reject this move because it gives White the d4 square but Petrosian has judged that it is more important to keep the queenside closed.

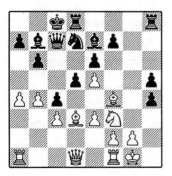

18 ♗e2?

The key moment. White should have played 18 ♗f5! sending the bishop en route for the h3 square from where it would defend the pawn on g2 The point is that after 18 ... exf5 19 e6 ♗d6 20 ♗xd6 ♕xd6 21 exd7+ ♖xd7 White can play 22 ♘d4! with superb play for his two pawn deficit.

Spassky rejected this move because he didn't want his bishop on h3. It was more important to defend the g2 pawn.

18 ... a6!

The logical follow up to the previous move. 19 a5 b5 seals things up completely and would leave Black free to attack White's king.

19 ♔h1 ♖dg8 20 ♖g1 ♖g4 21 ♕d2 ♖hg8 22 a5 b5 23 ♖ad1 ♗f8! 24 ♘h2

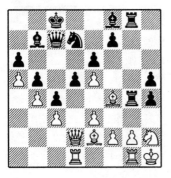

24 ... ♘xe5!

Giving up the exchange for massive compensation, Black has two pawns and his forces stand at the gates of the enemy palace.

25 ♘xg4 hxg4 26 e4

Attempting to get some counterplay before things get even worse.

26 ... ♗d6

And not 26 ... dxe4?? 27 ♗xe5 ♕xe5 28 ♕d8 mate.

27 ♕e3 ♘d7 28 ♗xd6 ♕xd6 29 ♖d4 e5 30 ♖d2

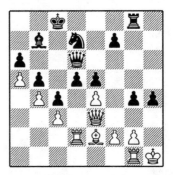

30 ... f5!

Mobilising Black's pawns with deadly effect. 31 exf6 ♘f6 32 ♕h6 ♕d8 intending ... ♖h8 would give Black an excellent attacking position.

31 exd5 f4 32 ♕e4 ♘f6 33 ♕f5+ ♔b8 34 f3

After 34 ♕e6 there is a nice variation in 34 ... ♕xe6 35 fxe6 ♘e4 when Black threatens a pretty mate with 36 ... ♘xf2+ and 37 ... g3#.

34 ... ♗c8 35 ♕b1 g3 36 ♖e1 h3 37 ♗f1 ♖h8 38 gxh3 ♗xh3 39 ♔g1 ♗xf1 40.♔xf1 e4 41 ♕d1 ♘g4! 42 fxg4 f3 43 ♖g2 fxg2+ 0:1

After 44 ♔xg2 there might follow 44 ... ♖h2+ 45 ♔g1 ♕h6.

KM20/4: 1) Black to play

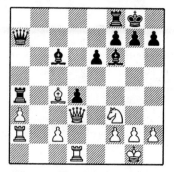

KM20/4: 2) White to play

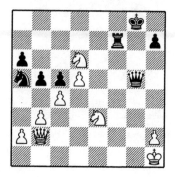

KM20/4: 3) White to play

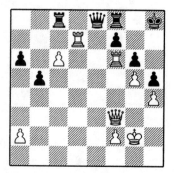

KM20/4: 4) White to play

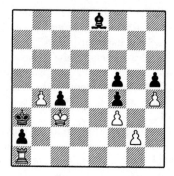

A20/4: a) Black to play

A20/4: b) Black to play

9 The Technicians

The term 'technician' may sound rather dull but it isn't meant to be. I am using it to describe players who, rather than straining to discover any great new ideas or launch ingenious attacks, set about making the most efficient use possible of the knowledge of their day.

I would actually include most modern professionals in the 'technician' category. Forty years ago there was still a pioneer spirit in chess in which new concepts were constantly being discovered. Nowadays it is not entirely true to say that there is nothing new to be found, but it is much harder to find original ideas which are actually playable.

Amongst club players there are very few who are technically orientated, most will tend to rely on sheer brain power to win their games, irrespective of technique. This makes the 'technicians' such particularly valuable models.

Month 21/Week 1:
José Raúl Capablanca

Much has been written about the ease and fluency with which Capablanca played chess and popularised the game with his personal charm. He rose to the summit in record time, beating Lasker in their match in 1921 and it came as a shock to the chess world when he lost his title just six years later. How could this have happened to the 'unbeatable' Cuban, the so-called Mozart of chess?

The fact is that although Capablanca had a truly brilliant chess talent he didn't work on his game. As a result his play became increasingly cautious as time went by; he tried to win by technique alone, avoiding sharp theory and complications alike.

The following game shows Capablanca at his lucid best. His pieces always seem to be on the right squares at the right time as he steadily moves forward:

Capablanca - Vidmar
New York 1927

1 e4 e5 2 ♘f3 ♘c6 3 ♗b5 a6 4 ♗a4 ♘f6 5 0-0 ♗e7 6 ♖e1 b5 7 ♗b3 d6 8 c3 ♘a5

Nowadays it is generally accepted that 8 ... 0-0 is a more flexible approach after which 9 d4 is answered by 9 ... ♗g4.

9 ♗c2 c5 10 d4 ♕c7 11 ♘bd2 0-0

Black might have taken this opportunity to play 11 ... ♗g4.

12 h3 ♘c6 13 d5 ♘d8 14 a4 b4?!

A serious positional mistake which concedes White a fine outpost for his knight on c4. Black should play 14 ... ♖b8.

15 ♘c4 a5?!

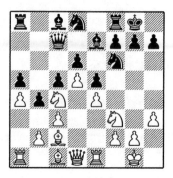

16 ♘fxe5!

A thematic tactical blow with which Capablanca forces a favourable endgame in which he has a strong bishop pair and weak pawns to attack. Vidmar should have played 15 ... ♘e8 which avoids this problem and starts the preparation for ... f7-f5.

16 ... ♗a6 17 ♗b3 dxe5 18 d6 ♗xd6 19 ♕xd6 ♕xd6 20 ♘xd6 ♘b7

Alternatively Black might have played 20 ... ♖b8 when White has a pleasant choice between 21 ♗c4 ♗xc4 22 ♘xc4 ♘c6 23 f3 and 21 ♘b5!? ♗xb5 22 axb5 ♖xb5 23 ♗c4. In either case White has a clear advantage.

21 ♘xb7 ♗xb7 22 cxb4 cxb4 23 f3 ♖fd8 24 ♗e3 h6 25 ♖ed1 ♗c6 26 ♖ac1 ♗e8 27 ♔f2 ♖xd1 28 ♖xd1 ♖c8 29 g4!

Staking out space on the kingside and threatening h2-h4 followed by g4-g5 and ♖d5. Black defends against this by bringing the bishop to e6 but this cure proves as deadly as the disease.

29 ... ♗d7 30 ♗b6 ♗e6

30 ... ♖a8 is met by 31 ♗c7 but now there follows a decisive simplification.

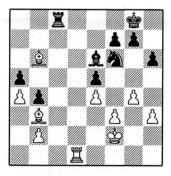

31 ♗xe6 fxe6 32 ♖d8+ ♖xd8 33 ♗xd8 ♘d7 34 ♗xa5 ♘c5 35 b3! ♘xb3 36 ♗xb4 ♘d4 37 a5 1:0

The tournament in New York was one of Capablanca's greatest triumphs. His greatest defeat came just a few months later when Alekhine beat him in a gruelling struggle.

Throughout this match Capablanca found himself at a considerable disadvantage in the opening where Alekhine was much better prepared. Only occasionally did the Cuban reach a favourable middlegame, as for example in game 3:

**Capablanca - Alekhine
Buenos Aires WCh 1927**

1 d4 ♘f6 2 ♘f3 b6 3 g3 ♗b7 4 ♗g2 c5 5 0-0 cxd4 6 ♘xd4 ♗xg2 7 ♔xg2 d5?

A mistake which allows White to open the game while he holds an advantage in development. 7 ... g6 was much safer.

8 c4! e6

After this Black finds himself in serious trouble. He should have taken the opportunity to exchange queens with 8 ... dxc4.

9 ♕a4+! ♕d7 10 ♘b5! ♘c6 11 cxd5 exd5

Black has little choice but to accept an isolated d-pawn as after 11 ... ♘xd5 there follows 12 e4! followed by 13 ♖d1.

12 ♗f4 ♖c8 13 ♖c1 ♗c5?

Understandably Black wants to develop his kingside but this loses two pieces for a rook. 13 ... ♘e4 was relatively best.

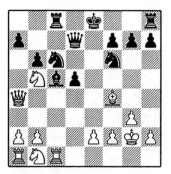

14 b4! ♗xb4

14 ... ♘xb4 loses the exchange after 15 ♘d6+ ♚d8 16 ♕xd7+ ♚xd7 17 ♘xc8.

15 ♖xc6! ♖xc6 16 ♕xb4 ♘e4 17 ♘d2 ♘xd2 18 ♕xd2

A classic example of Capablanca's tendency to avoid complications, even if they are favourable. It would have been even better to prevent Black from castling with 18 ♗xd2 as after 18 ... ♕e7 19 ♕b2 ♕e4+ 20 f3 ♕xe2+ 21 ♚g1 when there are too many threats.

18 ... 0-0 19 ♖d1 ♖c5 20 ♘d4 ♖e8 21 ♘b3 ♖cc8 22 e3 ♕a4

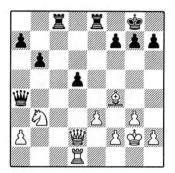

23 ♕xd5!

A finely judged decision. Capablanca is planning to win with a direct attack on Black's king and in exchange is prepared to give Black two united passed pawns on the queenside. The pawns in fact never really get going because of White's central control and active pieces.

23 ... ♖c2 24 ♖d2 ♖xa2 25 ♖xa2 ♕xa2 26 ♕c6! ♖f8 27 ♘d4 ♚h8 28 ♗e5!

The first threat appears, that of 29 ♗xg7+ ♚xg7 30 ♘f5+ followed by 31 ♕f6.

28 ... f6 29 ♘e6 ♖g8 30 ♗d4

Continuing the restraint of Black's queenside and simultaneously threatening 31 ♘xg7! ♖xg7 32 ♕xf6 ♕g8 33 h4! followed by 34 h5 and 35 h6.

30 ... h6 31 h4! ♕b1 32 ♘xg7!

A shattering blow. 32 ... ♖xg7 is answered by 33 ♕xf6 ♕h7 34 ♕f8+.

32 ... ♕g6 33 h5! ♕f7 34 ♘f5 ♚h7 35 ♕e4 ♖e8 36 ♕f4 ♕f8 37 ♘d6 ♖e7

Or 37 ... ♖d8 38 ♗xf6! ♖xd6 39 ♕f5+ ♚g8 40 ♕g6+.

38 ♗xf6 ♕a8+ 39 e4 ♖g7 40 ♗xg7 ♚xg7 41 ♘f5+ ♚f7 42 ♕c7+ 1:0

KM21/1: 1) White to play

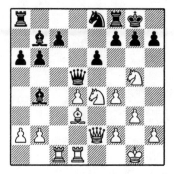

KM21/1: 2) White to play

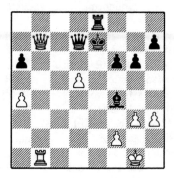

KM21/1: 3) White to play

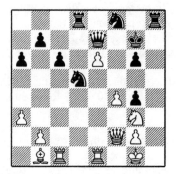

KM21/1: 4) White to play

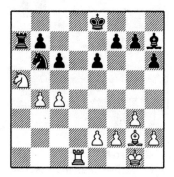

A21/1: a) White to play

A21/1: b) White to play

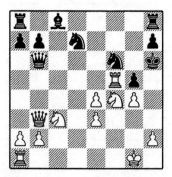

Month 21/Week 2:
Vassily Smyslov

Vassily Smyslov is one of the greatest post-war players and won a World Championship match against Botvinnik in 1957 only to lose the return in '58 Since then he has remained one of the world's leading players and at the time of writing is still an active competitor in tournaments.

Smyslov's style of play is one of great technical brilliance yet there were also other facets to his play. Unlike Capablanca he has invented new plans of development in the opening and there are, for example, several lines of the Gruenfeld Defence which bear his name. He was also noted for his combinative brilliance and would not be averse to a ferociously sharp struggle.

The following two games show Smyslov's superb endgame technique in action as he beats former World Champion Max Euwe and the future champion Mikhail Tal.

Smyslov - Euwe
Groningen 1946

1 e4 e5 2 ♘f3 ♘c6 3 ♗b5 a6 4 ♗a4 ♘f6 5 d3 d6 6 c3 g6 7 0-0 ♗g7 8 ♖e1 b5 9 ♗c2 0-0 10 ♗g5 h6 11 ♗h4 ♕e8

Black is aiming for play on the kingside. The Breyer manoeuvre of 11 ... ♘b8 and 12 ... ♘bd7 is an alternative.

12 ♘bd2 ♘h5 13 ♘f1 g5 14 ♗g3 ♘e7?!

In view of White's reply this looks like a mistake. Black had interesting alternatives in 14 ... ♘f4!? and 14 ... f5!?.

15 a4! ♘xg3

An unfortunate necessity as 15 ... ♗d7? is met by 16 ♘xe5, 15 ... ♗e6? by 16 ♘xg5 ♘xg3 17 ♘xe6 whilst 15 ... ♖b8 surrenders the a-file.

16 hxg3! ♗e6 17 d4 f6 18 ♗b3 ♗xb3 19 ♕xb3+ ♕f7 20 ♕xf7+ ♔xf7 21 ♘e3

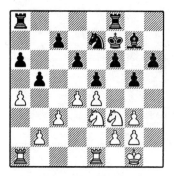

Over the last few moves White has made a lot of progress. The exchange of light-squared bishops in particular has weakened Black's light-squares and left him with a 'bad bishop' on g7.

Smyslov's willingness to go into an endgame is instructive; he felt that this was the best way to set about exploiting his advantage.

21 ... ♖fb8 22 axb5 axb5 23 d5 h5 24 ♔f1

An instructive move which brings the king nearer the centre. Such details are easily overlooked.

24 ... g4 25 ♘h4 ♗h6 26 ♘ef5 ♘g8 27 ♔e2 ♖a4 28 ♖xa4 bxa4 29 ♖b1 ♖b3

Attempting to force matters with 29 ... a3 would achieve nothing but a weakening of Black's a-pawn after 30 b4.

30 ♔d3 a3 31 ♔c2 ♖xb2+ 32 ♖xb2 axb2 33 ♔xb2

Euwe has been fighting hard to repair the earlier damage to his position and he probably felt he had good chances to draw this minor piece endgame.

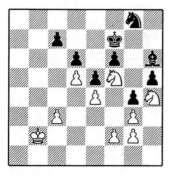

One of the critical lines occurs if Black exchanges off the remaining two minor pieces with 33 ... ♗g5 34 ♔b3 ♗xh4 35 gxh4 ♘e7 36 ♘xe7 ♔xe7. In fact White is winning this king and pawn endgame after 37 ♔c4 f5 (37 ... ♔d7 38 ♔b5) 38 f3! (38 exf5 ♔f6 39 ♔b5 ♔xf5 40 ♔c6 g3! 41 f3 e4! gives Black counterplay) 38 ... f4 39 ♔b5 ♔d7 40 c4 ♔d8 41 ♔c6 ♔c8 42 c5 dxc5 43 ♔xc5 ♔d7 44 ♔c4 ♔e7 45 ♔b4 ♔d6 46 ♔b5 g3 47 ♔b4! ♔e7 (or 47 ... c6 48 dxc6 ♔xc6 49 ♔c4 ♔d6 50 ♔b5) 48 ♔c4 ♔d6 49 ♔b5 ♔d7 50 ♔c5 ♔c8 51 d6 etc..

33 ... ♗d2 34 ♔c2 ♗e1 35 f3 ♘e7 36 ♘xe7 ♔xe7 37 fxg4 hxg4 38 ♘f5+ ♔f7 39 c4 ♔g6 40 ♔b3 ♔g5

Seeing that passive defence is hopeless Euwe decides to launch a counterattack. After 40 ... ♔f7 White would win with 41 ♔a4 ♔e8 42 ♔b5 ♔d7 43 ♘h6 ♗xg3 44 ♘xg4 ♗h4 45 ♘h6 ♗g5 46 ♘f5

♗c1 47 ♔a6 ♔c8 48 ♔a7 ♗g5 (or 48 ... ♗d2 49 ♔a8 ♗e1 50 g4 ♗f2 51 ♘e7+ ♔d7 52 ♘g8 ♗h4 53 ♔b8! ♗g5 54 ♔b7) 49 ♔a8 ♗c1 50 g4 ♗g5 51 ♘e7+ ♔d7 52 ♘c6 ♔c8 53 ♘a7+ ♔d7 54 ♔b7 etc.

41 ♔a4 ♗xg3 42 ♘xg3 ♔f4 43 ♘h5+ ♔xe4 44 ♘xf6+

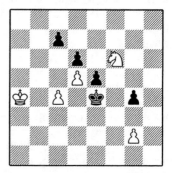

44 ... ♔f5

Or if 44 ... ♔f4 there follows 45 ♔b5 e4 (or 45 ... ♔f5 46 ♘h5 ♔g5 47 ♘g3 ♔f4 48 ♘f1 e4 49 ♔c6 e3 50 ♘xe3 etc.) 46 ♘xe4 ♔xe4 47 ♔c6 with White queening first.

45 ♘e8 e4 46 ♘xc7 e3 47 ♘b5! ♔f4

Or if 47 ... e2 there is 48 ♘d4+ ♔f4 49 ♘xe2+ etc.

48 ♘c3 ♔g3 49 c5 1:0

Smyslov - Tal
Bled Ct 1959

1 e4 c5 2 ♘f3

Smyslov was also a great connoisseur of the Closed Sicilian with 2 ♘c3 and 3 g3.

2 ... d6 3 d4 cxd4 4 ♘xd4 ♘f6 5 ♘c3 a6 6 ♗e2 e5 7 ♘b3 ♗e7 8 0-0 0-0 9 ♗e3 ♕c7 10 a4 ♗e6 11 a5 ♕c6 12 ♗f3 ♘bd7 13 ♘d5! ♗xd5 14 exd5 ♕b5 15 ♕d3!!

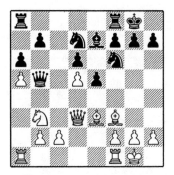

A brilliant decision. Smyslov has correctly forseen that the exchange of queens allows him to infiltrate Black's position on the c-file whilst the damage to his structure is just a temporary phenomenon.

15 ... ♖fc8 16 ♖fc1 ♛xd3

In view of the difficulties Black experiences in the endgame it might have been better to try 16 ... e4!?. After 17 ♗xe4 ♘xe4 18 ♛xe4 ♗f6 19 ♖ab1 ♖c4 20 ♘d4 ♗xd4 21 ♗xd4 ♖ac8 22 c3 ♘f6 Black has some counterplay for the pawn.

17 cxd3 g6

The attempt to block the c- file with 17 ... ♘c5?! is refuted by 18 ♘xc5 dxc5 19 d6 ♗xd6 20 ♗xb7.

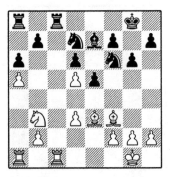

18 ♖c3! ♖xc3

Strategic capitulation, but then what else can Black do about the doubling of rooks on the c-file?

19 bxc3 ♖c8 20 c4 e4

Black couldn't allow White's pawn mass to remain intact but the position is still bad for him. He has some temporary piece activity but White's superior pawn structure and bishop pair must count in the end.

21 dxe4 ♖xc4 22 ♘d2 ♖c2 23 ♗d1 ♖c3 24 ♔f1 ♘c5 25 ♗d4 ♖d3 26 ♗xc5 dxc5

After 26 ... ♖xd2 27 ♗e3 ♖b2 28 ♖c1 Black's pawns start dropping.

27 ♔e2 ♖xd2+

The best practical chance. 27 ... ♖d4 28 f3 leaves Black facing threats such as 29 ♖b1 or 29 ♘c4.

28 ♔xd2 ♘xe4+ 29 ♔c2 ♘d6 30 ♗e2 ♗f6 31 ♖b1 ♔f8 32 ♔b3 ♔e7 33 ♗d3 ♔d7 34 f4 ♗d4 35 ♖f1 ♗e3 36 f5 ♗d2 37 fxg6 hxg6 38 ♖a1 ♔e7 39 ♖a2 ♗b4 40 h4 ♔f6 41 g4 ♗e1 42 h5 ♔g5 43 ♖a1 ♗d2 44 ♖h1 gxh5 45 gxh5 c4+ 46 ♗xc4 ♔h6 47 ♖f1!

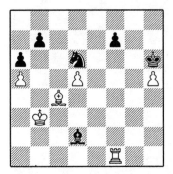

Giving up the h5 pawn to break through Black's defences.

47 ... ♔xh5 48 ♖f6 ♘e4 49 ♗e2+ ♔g5 50 ♖xf7 ♗e3 51 ♖e7 ♔f4 52 ♗d3 ♘d6 53 ♔b4 b6 54 axb6 ♗xb6 55 ♗xa6 ♗d4 56 ♖e6 ♗e5 57 ♔c5 ♘f7 58 ♗d3 ♗b2 59 ♗g6 ♘g5 60 ♖e8 ♗a3+ 61 ♔c6 ♘f3 62 ♖e4+ ♔g5 63 ♗h7 ♔h6 64 ♗f5 ♔g5 65 ♗g4 1:0

KM21/2: 1) White to play

KM21/2: 2) Black to play

KM21/2: 3) White to play

KM21/2: 4) White to play

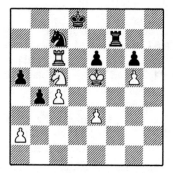
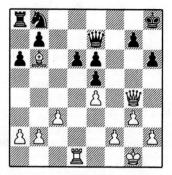

A21/2: a) White to play

A21/2: b) White to play

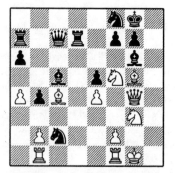
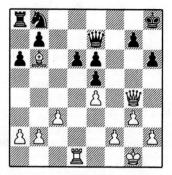

Month 21/Week 3:
Bobby Fischer

It was Bobby Fischer's sensational challenge for the World Championship that fanned the flames of my interest in chess. At the time of the 1972 Fischer-Spassky match in Reykjavik I was a boy of 12 who liked the game but whose interest might have faded after a year or two. The Reykjavik match changed everything.

From being an interesting pastime chess was turned into a symbol of something much greater, the ideological battle between East and West. In the mood of the time many young players developed a real passion for chess which accounted for the boom in its popularity.

Fischer's style is one of technical brilliance allied to fanatical determination. He didn't introduce anything very new but applied existing knowledge with tremendous energy and a hitherto unseen degree of perfection. Not even the might of the Soviet chess machine could stand against this one brilliant man.

The best game of the Reykjavik match was the tenth:

Fischer - Spassky
Reykjavik WCh 1972

1 e4 e5 2 ♘f3 ♘c6 3 ♗b5 a6 4 ♗a4 ♘f6 5 0-0 ♗e7 6 ♖e1 b5 7 ♗b3 d6 8 c3 0-0 9 h3 ♘b8

The Breyer Defence is Spassky's lifelong favourite. It was discovered by the Hungarian master Gyula Breyer who discovered that Black's queen's knight is much better placed on d7 than c6.

10 d4 ♘bd7 11 ♘bd2 ♗b7 12 ♗c2 ♖e8 13 b4 ♗f8 14 a4 ♘b6 15 a5 ♘bd7 16 ♗b2 ♕b8

Spassky is playing in very solid style, maintaining his centre like the best books tell us. Subsequent games however have tended to suggest that 16 ... ♖b8 is a better move.

17 ♖b1

With the positional threat of 18 c4, when Black's queen looks uncomfortable, staring down the b-file at a White rook. The immediate 17 c4 was also possible.

17 ... c5 18 bxc5 dxc5 19 dxe5 ♘xe5 20 ♘xe5 ♕xe5 21 c4 ♕f4 22 ♗xf6 ♕xf6

Fischer's great U.S. rival, Samuel Reshevsky, suggested the ugly 22 ... gxf6 to keep the queen on its strong position. Black would then threaten 23 ... ♖ad8 and ... ♗h6 is also in the offing.

23 cxb5 ♖ed8 24 ♕c1 ♕c3 25 ♘f3

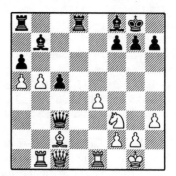

25 ... ♕xa5

A serious mistake which puts his queen offside. Either 25 ... axb4 or 25 ... c4 would have been better.

26 ♗b3! axb5 27 ♕f4 ♖d7

Already an 'only move'. After 27 ... c4 White has 28 ♗xc4 dxc4 29

🛳xb7 and if 29 ... f6 there is 30 e5! threatening 31 ♕xc4+, or 29 ... ♕h5 30 g4! ♕xh3 31 ♘g5.

28 ♘e5 ♕c7 29 🛳bd1 🛳e7

Black is already losing material but he hopes that his connected passed pawns on the queenside will give him chances in any endgame. 29 ... 🛳xd1 would lose immediately to 30 ♗xf7+ ♔h8 31 ♘g6+ hxg6 32 ♕h4#.

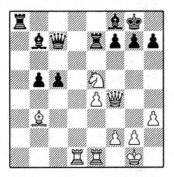

30 ♗xf7+ 🛳xf7 31 ♕xf7+ ♕xf7 32 ♘xf7 ♗xe4

Black would lose immediately after 32 ... ♔xf7 33 🛳d7+. In the following endgame Fischer manages to restrain Black's passed pawns whilst gradually mobilising his own kingside majority.

33 🛳xe4 ♔xf7 34 🛳d7+ ♔f6 35 🛳b7 🛳a1+ 36 ♔h2 ♗d6+ 37 g3 b4 38 ♔g2 h5 39 🛳b6 🛳d1 40 ♔f3 ♔f7

Hereabouts Black could have defended more accurately. At this point he should have tried the immediate 40 ... 🛳d5.

41 ♔e2 🛳d5 42 f4 g6 43 g4 hxg4 44 hxg4 g5 45 f5 ♗e5 46 🛳b5 ♔f6 47 🛳exb4 ♗d4 48 🛳b6+ ♔e5 49 ♔f3 🛳d8 50 🛳b8 🛳d7 51 🛳4b7 🛳d6 52 🛳b6 🛳d7 53 🛳g6 ♔d5 54 🛳xg5 ♗e5 55 f6 ♔d4 56 🛳b1 1:0

When the players sat down opposite each other again some twenty years later it was almost as if time had stood still. Another Ruy Lopez, another Breyer, another Fischer win and a remarkable achievement by Fischer after his long lay-off.

Fischer - Spassky
Sveti-Stefan m (Game 1) 1992

1 e4 e5 2 ♘f3 ♘c6 3 ♗b5 a6 4 ♗a4 ♘f6 5 0-0 ♗e7 6 🛳e1 b5 7 ♗b3 d6 8 c3 0-0 9 h3 ♘b8 10 d4 ♘bd7 11 ♘bd2 ♗b7 12 ♗c2 🛳e8 13 ♘f1

Fischer is the first to vary from the previous game.

13 ... ♗f8 14 ♘g3 g6 15 ♗g5

A somewhat unusual move from Fischer. The standard move is 15 a4.

15 ... h6 16 ♗d2 ♗g7 17 a4 c5 18 d5 c4

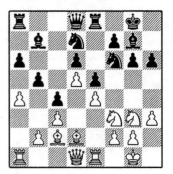

19 b4!

A strong move which fixes the b5 pawn and deprives Black's knight of the c5 square. If Black doesn't take en passant the position is simply better for White so 19 ... cxb3 20 ♗xb3 ♘c5 should be tried. In any case Black should be under pressure after Nigel Short's suggestion of 21 c4!.

19 ... ♘h7? 20 ♗e3 h5 21 ♕d2 ♖f8 22 ♖a3

Simplicity itself, White is planning to mass his major pieces on the a-file.

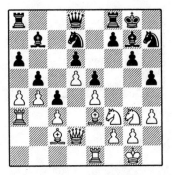

Should Black now force through ... f7-f5 with 22 ... h4 23 ♘f1 f5 there would follow 24 exf5 gxf5 25 ♘g5! ♘xg5 26 ♗xg5 ♗f6 27 ♗xf6 (or 27 ♗h6) followed by 28 ♖ea1 with play on both sides of the board. In playing for ... f7-f5 Spassky had misjudged the extent to which this would weaken his kingside.

22 ... ♘df6 23 ♖ea1 ♕d7 24 ♖1a2!

Preparing even to triple(!) major pieces on the a-file.

24 ... ♖fc8 25 ♕c1 ♗f8 26 ♕a1 ♕e8 27 ♘f1!

The start of a brilliant knight manoeuvre. Fischer's plan is to bring the knight to a3 via d2 and b1 when Black's b-pawn turns out to be virtually indefensible.

27 ... ♗e7 28 ♘1d2 ♔g7 29 ♘b1

Threatening 30 axb5 axb5 31 ♖xa8 ♖xa8 32 ♖xa8 ♕xa8 33 ♕xa8

♗xa8 34 ♘a3, simply winning Black's b5 pawn. With his next move Spassky tries to break out of the bind.

29 ... ♘xe4 30 ♗xe4 f5?!

With White's rooks ready to invade the 7th rank it would have been better to play 30 ... ♘f6. In any case there can't really be enough compensation.

31 ♗c2 ♗xd5 32 axb5 axb5 33 ♖a7 ♔f6 34 ♘bd2 ♖xa7 35 ♖xa7 ♖a8

36 g4!

Fischer is at his best when it comes to winning won games. Here he starts to demolish the flimsy defence of Black's king.

36 ... hxg4 37 hxg4 ♖xa7 38 ♕xa7 f4 39 ♗xf4!

Returning the piece to demolish Black's defensive ramparts.

39 ... exf4 40 ♘h4!

Even stronger than 40 ♕d4+.

40 ... ♗f7 41 ♕d4+ ♔e6 42 ♘f5 ♗f8 43 ♕xf4 ♔d7 44 ♘d4 ♕e1+ 45 ♔g2 ♗d5+ 46 ♗e4 ♗xe4+ 47 ♘xe4 ♗e7 48 ♘xb5 ♘f8 49 ♘bxd6 ♘e6 50 ♕e5 1:0

KM21/3: 1) White to play

KM21/3: 2) White to play

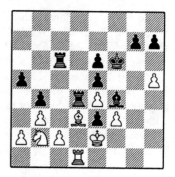

KM21/3: 3) White to play

KM21/3: 4) Black to play

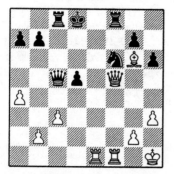

A21/3: a) White to play

A21/3: b) Black to play

Month 21/Week 4:
Anatoly Karpov

In many respects Anatoly Karpov's style of play might be seen as that of a modern Capablanca. He has the same easy and fluent style, his pieces always seem to be on the right squares and his endgame play is superb.

The main difference is that Karpov has enjoyed the full support of the Soviet chess machine with its teams of seconds and heavy emphasis on opening preparation. It made a formidable cocktail which has kept Karpov in the chess firmament for a quarter of a century.

The 14th game was one of the decisive encounters from Karpov's dramatic match with Korchnoi in Baguio City, 1978. Karpov's preparation gives him an edge which he turns into victory in superb style.

Karpov - Korchnoi
Baguio City WCh 1978

1 e4 e5 2 ♘f3 ♘c6 3 ♗b5 a6 4 ♗a4 ♘f6 5 0-0 ♘xe4 6 d4 b5 7 ♗b3 d5 8 dxe5 ♗e6 9 c3 ♗c5 10 ♘bd2 0-0 11 ♗c2 ♗f5 12 ♘b3 ♗g4 13 h3!

This straightforward move was actually new at the time. One of the points is that 13 ... ♗xf3 14 gxf3 ♕h4 is met by 15 ♘xc5 and 16 ♕xd5.

13 ... ♗h5 14 g4 ♗g6 15 ♗xe4 dxe4 16 ♘xc5 exf3 17 ♗f4 ♕xd1

With White having weakened his kingside I'm sure that Korchnoi would have liked to keep queens on the board. But 17 ... ♕e7 18 ♕d5 ♘a5 19 b4 leaves White controlling

a lot of space and the pawn on f3 cannot last for long.

18 ♖axd1 ♘d8 19 ♖d7 ♘e6 20 ♘xe6 fxe6 21 ♗e3 ♖ac8 22 ♖fd1 ♗e4 23 ♗c5 ♖fe8 24 ♖7d4 ♗d5 25 b3 a5 26 ♔h2 ♖a8 27 ♔g3 ♖a6?

A mistake by Korchnoi which overlooks the coming exchange sacrifice. He should have tried 27 ... ♗c6 followed by ... a4.

28 h4 ♖c6

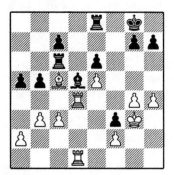

29 ♖xd5!

Simple and strong. White obtains a mass of advancing pawns for the exchange.

29 ... exd5 30 ♖xd5 ♖ce6 31 ♗d4 c6 32 ♖c5!

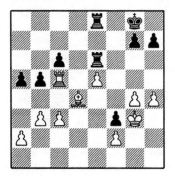

32 ... ♖f8?

After this further mistake there is little that Black can do to save the game. He had to try 32 ... ♖d8 33

♔xf3 ♖d5 after which 34 ♖xd5 cxd5 35 a3! g6 36 ♔g3 and 37 f4 gives White excellent winning chances. But it would still be a fight.

33 a4! bxa4 34 bxa4 g6 35 ♖xa5 ♖ee8 36 ♖a7 ♖f7

Or if 36 ... ♖a8 there is 37 ♖c7 ♖fc8 38 ♖xc8+ ♖xc8 39 ♗b6! ♔f7 40 ♔xf3 ♔e6 41 ♔e4 etc.

37 ♖a6 ♖c7 38 ♗c5 ♖cc8 39 ♗d6 ♖a8 40 ♖xc6 ♖xa4 41 ♔xf3 h5 42 gxh5 gxh5 43 c4 ♖a2 44 ♖b6 ♔f7 45 c5 ♖a4 46 c6! ♔e6

If Black snatches the h-pawn with 46 ... ♖xh4 there follows 47 c7 ♖c4 (or 47 ... ♖g4 48 ♖b8 ♖gg8 49 ♔e4 h4 50 f4 h3 51 f5) 48 ♖b8 h4 49 ♖xe8 ♔xe8 50 e6 h3 51 ♔g3 ♖c3+ 52 ♔h2.

47 c7 ♔d7 48 ♖b8 ♖c8 49 ♔e3 ♖xh4 50 e6+ 1:0

One of the things that has always amazed me about Karpov is his ability to win games with just a marginally better pawn structure. The following game from his match against Andrei Sokolov was one that I saw live and I have to say that I was deeply impressed. Without doing anything dramatic Karpov nursed a space advantage for most of the game. Suddenly, in an endgame with level material, Black's position turned out to be completely lost.

Karpov - Sokolov
Linares Cm 1987

1 d4 ♘f6 2 c4 e6 3 ♘f3 b6 4 g3 ♗a6 5 b3 ♗b4+ 6 ♗d2 ♗e7 7 ♘c3 0-0

Black might do better to consider the alternatives of 7 ... d5 immediately and 7 ... c6.

8 e4 d5 9 cxd5 ♗xf1 10 ♔xf1

The loss of castling rights is of minor importance as White's king can castle by hand. A more significant result of this last transaction is that White obtains a kingside pawn majority.

10 ... exd5 11 e5 ♘e4 12 ♕e2 ♘xc3 13 ♗xc3 ♕d7 14 ♔g2 ♘c6 15 ♖he1 ♘d8

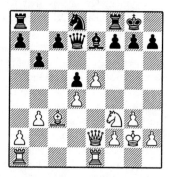

16 ♘g1!

I like this idea a lot. White's move may seem retrograde or passive but Karpov knows that his number one priority is to maintain his central pawn structure.

16 ... c5

Sokolov counterattacks in full recognition of the dangers posed by the pawn mass. The attempt to set up a blockade with 16 ... ♘e6 17 f4 f5? is met by 18 exf6 ♖xf6 19 f5!.

17 f4 cxd4 18 ♗xd4 ♕f5 19 ♖ad1 ♗b4 20 ♖f1 ♘e6 21 ♕d3!

An important moment. Recognising that his exposed king position is his main problem, Karpov is happy to exchange queens.

21 ... ♕xd3 22 ♖xd3 ♖ac8 23 ♘f3 ♖c2+ 24 ♖f2 ♖fc8 25 f5 ♘xd4 26 ♘xd4

Over the last few moves it has looked as if it is Black who has been making the running and Sokolov no doubt hoped he would have enough counterplay to draw. White's last move shows that he is still well on top as Black's rook can no longer maintain its strong position on c2.

26 ... Rxf2+ 27 Kxf2 Rc1 28 g4 Kf8 29 Kf3 Rf1+ 30 Kg3 Rc1 31 Kf4 h6

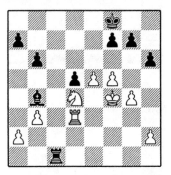

32 h4
Slowly but surely White advances his kingside pawn majority. As the pawns move forward Black's position becomes ever more cramped and there seems to be little he can do to achieve any kind of counterplay.

32 ... Ke8 33 Nf3 Rc2 34 a4 Rb2 35 Nd4 Be7 36 h5 a6

37 Kf3!
Preparing the transfer of his knight to f4 from where it bears down on d5 and attacks the e6 square.

37 ... Bc5 38 Ne2 d4 39 Nf4 Kd7 40 e6+ Ke8 41 Ke4 a5 42 Rf3! Rb1 43 Nd5! Rg1?

The losing move? Black had to try 43 ... Kf8! but then 44 e7+! Bxe7 45 Kxd4 Rg1 46 Kc4!! Rxg4+ 47 Kb5 would be good for White but not necessarily decisive.

44 Kd3! Rxg4 45 f6!

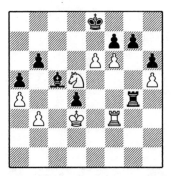

The decisive breakthrough. 45 ... fxe6 is answered by 46 f7+ Kf8 (or 46 ... Kd7 47 Nxb6+ Kc6 48 Nc4 etc) 47 Nc7 threatening 48 Ne6+.

45 ... Bd6 46 Nxb6! Rg5 47 fxg7 Rxg7 48 Nc4 Bb4 49 exf7+ Rxf7 50 Rxf7 Kxf7

So far Black has kept material parity but now his pawns start to fall.

51 Ne5+ Kf6 52 Nc6 Be1 53 Nxd4 Bb4 54 Nc6 Be1 55 Ke2 Bc3 56 Kd3 Be1 57 Kc4 Kg5 58 Nxa5! Bxa5 59 b4 Bd8 60 a5 Kxh5 61 Kb5 Bg5 62 a6 Be3 63 Kc6 1:0

KM21/4: 1) Black to play

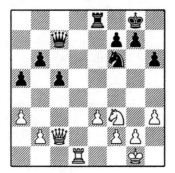

KM21/4: 2) White to play

KM21/4: 3) White to play

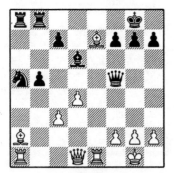

KM21/4: 4) Black to play

A21/4: a) White to play

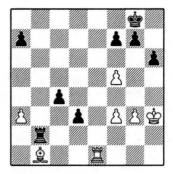

A21/4: b) White to play

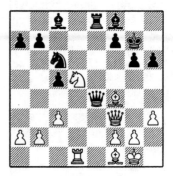

10 The Tacticians

Describing a player as a 'tactician' has often had a somewhat derogatory tone to it. In my view this is quite unjustified when you look at the evidence that strong tacticians have always been one of the dominant groups at the summit of world chess. One need only mention the names Emanuel Lasker and Viktor Korchnoi to understand that having a predominantly tactical style does not condemn someone to being a second rate player.

Tacticians tend to win most of their games by seeing things that their opponents miss. Even at the highest level there are many tactical oversights buried within the players' calculations. Superiority within this department is therefore the greatest weapon one can have and of far greater value than better strategic insight.

This month we will see tacticians from different generations, Lasker, Korchnoi, Alexei Shirov and finally the computer. Computers in particular are out-and-out tacticians, their play being guided by pure calculation and relatively primitive evaluation functions. In spite of this apparent handicap they are posing an ever greater threat to the all too fallible human brain.

Month 22/Week 1:
Emanuel Lasker

Emanuel Lasker was World Champion for no less than 27 years after he wrested the title from Wilhelm Steinitz in 1894. Despite this incredible record he has been quite underrated and in his day was accused of everything from luck to witchcraft to attempting to poison his opponents with cigar fumes. His critics claimed that he contributed nothing to the theory of the game and left no disciples but I detect a note of envy and even anti-Semitism in their words.

When I first became interested in chess Lasker was my idol. I admired the drama and courage contained within his outwardly unpretentious games. His writing too did not try to overwhelm the reader with over-elaborate theories and a mass of information but relied instead on common sense. By attempting to show that chess was subject to laws which were more universal in their nature, it seemed to me that he touched the soul of the game.

The following games show different aspects of Lasker's style. In the first we see him win a lost position against Pillsbury during the latter's greatest tournament triumph in Hastings 1895. In the second he overwhelms Bogoljubow with a display of superb technique.

Lasker - Pillsbury
Hastings 1895

1 e4 e5 2 ♘f3 ♘c6 3 ♗b5 g6 4 d4 exd4 5 ♘xd4
The modern preference is for 5 ♗g5 which certainly makes life more difficult for Black.
5 ... ♗g7 6 ♘xc6 bxc6 7 ♗c4 ♘e7 8 ♘c3 d6 9 0-0 ♗e6 10 ♗b3 0-0 11 ♗e3 c5 12 ♗xe6?!
This strengthens Black's centre. 12 ♕e2 was better.
12 ... fxe6 13 ♕d2 ♖b8 14 ♖ab1
And here 14 b3 was more economical.
14 ... ♘c6 15 b3 ♕h4 16 f3 ♘d4 17 ♘e2 ♗e5 18 f4?
Capping his previous poor play with the simple blunder of a pawn. 18 g3 had to be played.
18 ... ♘xe2+ 19 ♕xe2 ♗xf4 20 ♗xf4
In playing his 18th move Lasker might have thought that he could play 20 ♖xf4 ♖xf4 21 g3 at this point and only now saw 21 ... ♕g4.
20 ... ♖xf4 21 ♖xf4 ♕xf4 22 ♖f1 ♕e5

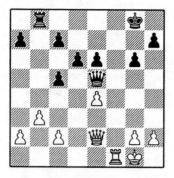

After 22 moves Black has achieved a winning position and after seeing his simple blunder of the pawn the reader might well wonder why I call Lasker one of the greatest tacticians in the history of the game. I started to understand Lasker when I realised that he was bored by plain sailing but stimulated by difficulties. Once faced with a challenge or a critical position he became utterly transformed.

White is a pawn down but he has some counterchances in the vulnerability of Black's king and the weakness of his a-pawn. Just watch how he uses these factors over the following moves:
23 ♕a6! ♕d4+ 24 ♔h1 ♕xe4 25 ♕xa7 ♕b7 26 ♕a4 c6 27 ♕e4 ♕d7 28 a4 e5 29 h3 ♖b4?
Apparently aggressive but in reality a poor position for the rook. Black should play 29 ... ♖e8, getting behind the passed e-pawn whilst maintaining watch over the a8 queening square.
30 ♕e1 e4 31 a5!

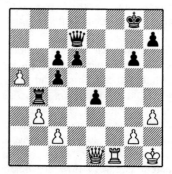

Suddenly White has genuine counterplay, his a-pawn is up and running. Black should still be better but his formerly simple task has been transformed into a very complex one.

31 ... d5 32 a6 ♕e7

Black should have brought his rook back with 32 ... ♖b8. His failure to admit this is his undoing.

33 ♕g3! e3

The vulnerablity of Black's king becomes apparent after 33 ... ♕a7 34 ♕d6 but he could do better with 33 ... ♖b6 (34 a7 ♕xa7 35 ♕d6 ♖b8).

34 ♖a1 ♕f6?

The decisive error. Black should play 34 ... ♕g7 to guard the a7 square.

35 ♖e1! d4 36 a7 ♕d8 37 ♖a1 ♕a8 38 ♕d6 ♖b7 39 ♕xc6 e2 40 ♕xb7 1:0

Lasker - Bogoljubow
Ostrava 1923

1 e4 e5 2 ♘f3 ♘c6 3 ♗b5 a6 4 ♗a4 ♘f6 5 0-0 ♗e7 6 ♖e1 b5 7 ♗b3 d6 8 c3 0-0 9 d4 exd4

The immediate 9 ... ♗g4 is better as now White gets use of the c3 square.

10 cxd4 ♗g4 11 ♘c3 ♘a5 12 ♗c2 c5 13 dxc5!

Spotting an opportunity to get a better endgame.

13 ... dxc5 14 e5! ♕xd1 15 ♖xd1 ♘d7 16 h3! ♗e6 17 ♘d5! ♗xd5 18 ♖xd5 ♘b6 19 ♖d1 ♖ad8 20 ♗g5! f6

Lasker is developing his initiative with the aid of concealed combinative ideas. 20 ... ♗xg5 21 ♘xg5 ♖xd1+ 22 ♖xd1 h6 fails because of 23 e6! hxg5 24 e7 ♖e8 25 ♖d8 or 23 ... fxe6 24 ♘h7+ ♔h8 25 ♘xe6 ♖f6 26 ♗e4!.

21 exf6 ♗xf6 22 ♗xf6 gxf6 23 ♖ac1 ♘bc4 24 b3 ♘d6 25 ♖d5!

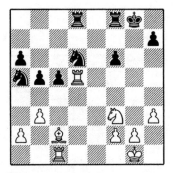

White's advantage is becoming decisive, this move attacks c5 and prepares to double rooks on the d-file.

25 ... ♘ab7 26 ♖cd1 b4

26 ... ♘f7 is answered by 27 ♖d7 ♘bd6 28 ♗xh7+! etc.

27 ♗d3 ♖a8 28 ♖e1 a5 29 ♖e7 ♖f7 30 ♖xf7 ♘xf7 31 ♖d7 ♘bd6 32 ♖c7 ♖d8! 33 ♗a6! ♖a8 34 ♗e2! ♖c8 35 ♖a7 ♘e5 36 ♘xe5! fxe5 37 ♗g4! ♖c6

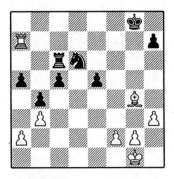

38 ♗d7!

Very accurate play. Lasker forces Black's rook to a worse square before cashing in.

38 ... ♖b6 39 ♖xa5 ♘e4 40 ♗f5 ♘c3 41 ♖xc5 ♖b5 42 ♖c8+ ♔g7 43 ♖c7+ ♔f6 44 ♗xh7 ♖d5 45 ♖c4 ♘xa2 46 f4 exf4 47 ♖xf4+ ♔g7 48 ♗c2 ♖d2 49 ♖f2 ♖d4 50 ♗f5 ♘c3 51 ♗e6 1:0

KM22/1: 1) White to play

KM22/1: 2) Black to play

KM22/1: 3) White to play

KM22/1: 4) White to play

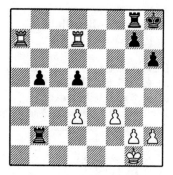

A22/1: a) White to play

A22/1: b) Black to play

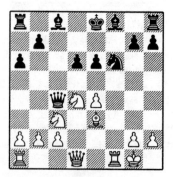

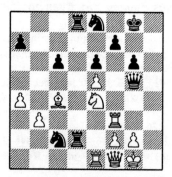

Month 22/Week 2:
Viktor Korchnoi

Viktor Korchnoi is one of the greatest post-war players, many would say the strongest player never to become World Champion. He played two World Championship matches against Anatoly Karpov and came desperately close to beating him in their Baguio City match in 1978.

A particularly impressive feature of Korchnoi's career is his amazing longevity. He maintained a position at the summit of World Chess for some 40 years and even now remains a force to be reckoned with. In this respect he showed a remarkable similarity to Lasker, his hero.

Although his style has developed and matured over the years into more of an all-court player, Korchnoi's most remarkable feature is the extent of his calculations. Every move is subject to deep calculation which few opponents could match. In addition to this Korchnoi is noted for an almost fanatical will to win which sometimes drives him to push too hard but has certainly brought a greater share of success than failure.

The following games are masterpieces of defence. In the first game Korchnoi turns the tables on his opponent with a brilliant counter-sacrifice, in the second the attacker is none other than Mikhail Tal.

Krogius - Korchnoi
USSR Ch, Riga 1958

1 e4 c5 2 ♘f3 e6 3 d4 cxd4 4 ♘xd4 a6 5 ♘c3 b5 6 ♗d3 ♕c7 7 0-0 ♗b7 8 ♕e2 ♘c6 9 ♘xc6 dxc6

10 a4 b4 11 ♘d1 c5 12 ♘e3 ♘e7 13 b3?!

13 ♘c4! was preferable. The text weakens the c3 and d4 squares and Korchnoi makes an immediate beeline for these weaknesses by bringing his dark-squared bishop to e5.

13 ... ♘c6 14 ♗b2 ♗d6 15 h3 ♗e5! 16 ♗xe5 ♘xe5 17 f4 ♘c6 18 e5 ♘d4 19 ♕h5 0-0-0 20 ♘c4?

Underestimating the following combination. White should continue developing with 20 ♖ad1.

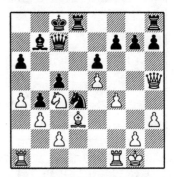

20 ... ♘xb3! 21 ♘d6+ ♖xd6! 22 exd6 ♕c6 23 d7+ ♔c7! 24 ♕e5+ ♔xd7 25 ♕xg7 ♘xa1

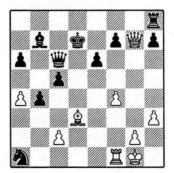

26 f5

Krogius certainly doesn't intend to give up without a fight. Another dangerous attacking try was 26 ♗b5!? axb5 27 ♖d1+ but this can be

defused with the spectacular 27 ...
♔c7 28 ♕e5+ ♔b6! 29 ♖d6 bxa4
30 ♖xc6+ ♗xc6 31 ♕xh8 ♘xc2 32
♕d8+ ♔b5 33 ♕d3+ c4 34 ♕xc2
a3, when the bishop and pawns
prove stronger than the queen. This
brilliant variation shows the depth
of Korchnoi's vision.

In the game continuation too
Korchnoi defuses the attack with a
spectacular counter-sacrifice.

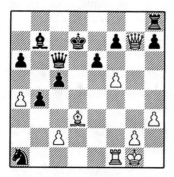

**26 ... ♕xg2+! 27 ♕xg2 ♗xg2 28
fxe6+ fxe6 29 ♔xg2 c4! 30 ♗e4**
Keeping the knight trapped but
Black's pawns are becoming more
dangerous. 30 ♗xc4 would be met
by 30 ... ♘xc2 31 ♖f7+ ♔d6 32
♗xa6 ♘d4 when Black's b-pawn is
the most dangerous on the board.

**30 ... ♘xc2 31 ♗xc2 b3 32 ♗e4
♔d6 33 ♖c1 ♔c5!**

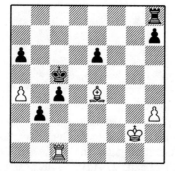

More neat play from Korchnoi. 34
♗d3 is answered by 34 ... ♔d4 35
♗xc4 ♖c8 36 ♖d1+ ♔xc4 37 ♖c1+
♔d3 38 ♖xc8 b2 when Black
achieves a winning pawn endgame.
Play might continue 39 ♖b8 ♔c2 40
♖c8+ ♔b3 41 ♖b8+ ♔a2 42 ♔f3
b1=♕ 43 ♖xb1 ♔xb1 44 ♔e4 ♔b2
45 ♔e5 ♔b3 46 ♔xe6 ♔xa4 47 ♔f7
♔b3 48 ♔g7 a5 49 ♔xh7 a4 50 h4
a3 51 h5 a2 52 h6 a1=♕ etc.

**34 ♔f3 ♔b4 35 ♔e3 c3 36 ♖b1
♔a3 37 ♖a1+ ♔b2 38 ♖b1+ ♔a2
39 ♖g1 c2 40 ♔d2 ♖d8+ 41 ♔c1
♖c8! 0:1**

During his glory years almost
everyone was afraid of Tal's daring
attacking play, all that is except
Korchnoi. Korchnoi was one of very
few players who keep up with Tal's
dazzling speed of calculation and
found the flaws that others missed.

**Tal - Korchnoi
USSR Ch, Riga 1958**

1 e4 e6 2 d4 d5 3 ♘c3 ♗b4 4 e5
c5 5 a3 ♗xc3+ 6 bxc3 ♘e7 7 ♕g4
♘f5 8 ♗d3 h5 9 ♕h3 cxd4 10 ♘f3
♕c7 11 ♖b1 dxc3 12 g4 ♘e7 13
gxh5 ♘bc6 14 ♗f4 ♘g6! 15 ♗g3!
♘gxe5

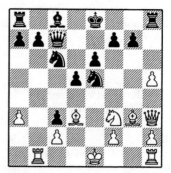

Black has played a very risky line. He had to take the e-pawn which would otherwise be a bone in his throat.

16 ♘xe5 ♘xe5 17 ♔f1

And not 17 ♔d1? because of 17 ... ♘xd3! 18 ♗xc7 ♘xf2+.

17 ... ♗d7

Black has no time for luxuries. Securing the knight on e5 with 17 ... f6 would be too dangerous after 18 ♖g1!.

18 ♕h4?

Giving Black the chance to wrest the initiative with 18 ... ♘f3! 19 ♕g4 ♘d2+ 20 ♔g2 e5 21 ♕xg7 0-0-0. A better line would have been 18 ♖e1 f6 19 ♗g6+.

18 ... f6? 19 ♗xe5! ♕xe5

19 ... fxe5 would have been good for White after 20 ♗g6+ ♔f8 21 ♕b4+ ♔g8 22 ♕xb7 etc.

20 ♖xb7 ♖b8 21 ♖xb8+ ♕xb8 22 ♕g4 ♔f8 23 ♖g1

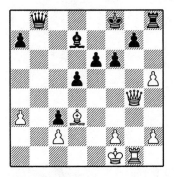

The position seems to be getting very scary for Black, not least because Mikhail Tal is the man sitting across the board. Korchnoi had seen all this in advance and found a creative way to blockade the kingside using White's own pawns!

23 ... g5! 24 hxg6

White could also consider 24 h4!? when Black replies with 24 ... ♕f4.

24 ... ♔g7 25 h4 a5!

Another deep move taking b4 from White's queen.

26 ♖g3 ♕b1+ 27 ♔g2

After 27 ♔e2 Black can reduce arms with 27 ... ♗b5.

27 ... ♕b7 28 h5 d4+ 29 ♗e4

After 29 f3 Black defends himself with 29 ... ♕d5 30 ♖h3 e5 31 ♗f5 ♗xf5 32 ♕xf5 d3! when Black's pawn on c3 suddenly plays a major part.

29 ... ♗c6?

Within sight of victory Korchnoi slips up. He should have played 29 ... ♕b5 with the idea that 30 ♖h3 is defused by 30 ... ♕g5.

30 ♗xc6 ♕xc6+ 31 ♔g1 ♕d5 32 ♕f4 ♕e5

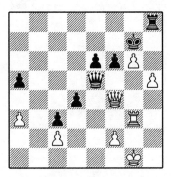

33 h6+??

With the game reaching boiling point Tal himself slips up. After 33 ♕f3 ♕d5 34 ♕f4 ♕e5 35 ♕f3 the game would end in a draw by repetition. The combination initiated by the text move has a huge hole.

33 ... ♖xh6 34 ♕xh6+ ♔xh6 35 g7 ♕xg3+! 0:1

The move Tal missed, taking out his passed pawn.

KM22/2: 1) White to play

KM22/2: 2) White to play

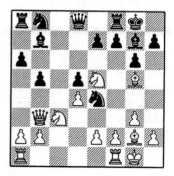

KM22/2: 3) White to play

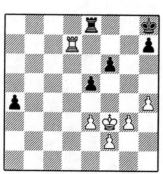

KM22/2: 4) Black to play

A22/2: a) White to play

A22/2: b) White to play

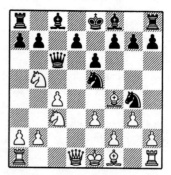

Month 22/Week 3:
Alexei Shirov

Shirov was born in Latvia in which Mikhail Tal was the national chess hero. This has resulted in a very different national playing style to that of many other former Soviet republics.

When I first saw some of Alexei Shirov's games they seemed to bear little relation to the kind of chess the rest of us are playing. One of the chess world's most exciting prospects, he seems to spread the pieces on the board like confetti and then brings off the most remarkable combinations.

For anyone who thinks that modern chess is dull, just take a look at the following two orgies of combination:

Shirov - Gelfand
Wijk aan Zee 1996

1 e4 c5 2 ♘f3 d6 3 d4 cxd4 4 ♘xd4 ♘f6 5 ♘c3 a6 6 ♗e3 e6 7 g4 e5 8 ♘f5 g6 9 g5 gxf5 10 exf5

This piece sacrifice is known to theory and stems from the artistic Hungarian player, Bela Perenyi, who died tragically young in a car crash.

10 ... d5 11 gxf6 d4 12 ♗c4! ♕xf6 13 ♘d5 ♕c6 14 ♗xd4 ♗b4+ 15 c3 ♕xc4 16 ♗e3!

Keeping all of his threats, 16 ♘f6+ would be premature because of 16 ... ♔e7 17 ♗xe5.

♖d8. This may all seem like quite extraordinary chess but in fact it is all theory. Gelfand's next move is new, 16 ... ♗e7 having been played in an earlier game.

16 ... ♗a5 17 ♘f6+ ♔e7 18 ♘d5+ ♔e8 19 ♘f6+ ♔e7 20 ♗g5

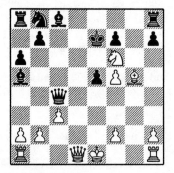

20 ... ♗c7
According to Shirov Black should have played 20 ... ♖d8 after which 21 ♘xh7+ f6! 22 ♗xf6+ ♔e8 23 ♕h5+ ♕f7 24 ♕xf7+ ♔xf7 25 ♗xd8 ♗xd8 produces a position which is difficult to assess. 20 ... h6? is bad because of 21 ♘e4+ hxg5 22 ♕d6+ followed by mate.

21 ♘e4+ ♔e8 22 ♕g4! b5 23 ♘f6+ ♔e7

It looks strange to walk into a potential discovered check but 23 ... ♔f8 is answered by 24 ♗h6+ ♔e7 25 ♕g5 with even more powerful threats in the offing. Now he hopes to exchange queens.

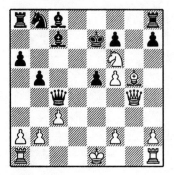

24 0-0-0!

Very cool play by White, amazingly his attack continues even after the exchange of queens. Note that White is still a piece down.

24 ... ♕xg4 25 ♘xg4+ ♔f8 26 ♗h6+ ♔e7 27 ♗g5+ ♔f8 28 ♗d8! ♗xf5

And not 28 ... ♖a7? because of 29 ♗xc7 ♖xc7 30 ♖d8+ ♔g7 31 f6+ etc.

29 ♗xc7 ♘c6

Black has no time to capture on g4 because of the threat of 30 ♖d8+ ♔g7 31 ♗xe5+ f6 32 ♗xf6+ etc. But Gelfand has conceived an amazing defensive idea.

30 ♘h6! ♗g6 31 ♖d6 ♘b4!!

No, this is not a misprint. Gelfand gives up his knight to create the possibility of a pin on the c-file.

32 cxb4 ♔g7

Black has finally found a safe haven for his king and he seems to be about to win his piece back as well. Should White get a pawn for it with 33 ♘xf7 and head for a draw? With his next move Shirov provides a negative answer, fanning the dying embers of his attack to create further difficulties for Black.

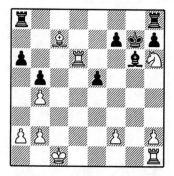

33 h4! ♖hc8 34 h5! ♖xc7+ 35 ♔d2 ♗e4 36 ♖g1+ ♔h8 37 ♔e3

Even White's king plays a part in the attack.

37 ... ♗b7 38 ♖gd1! ♖e8 39 ♘f5 ♗c8??

After conducting a long and difficult defence Gelfand finally cracks in time-trouble. He had to play 39 ... ♖c4 40 f3 ♖f4.

40 ♖d8! ♗xf5 41 ♖xe8+ ♔g7 42 ♖xe5 1:0

In keeping with the modern trend of extensive opening preparation, Shirov had clearly prepared the sacrifice he brings off in the next game. It proved to have devastating consequences for Black's treatment of this line of the Sicilian.

Shirov - Judit Polgar
Tilburg 1996

1 e4 c5 2 ♘f3 d6 3 d4 cxd4 4 ♘xd4 ♘f6 5 ♘c3 a6 6 ♗e2 e6 7 0-0 ♗e7 8 f4 0-0 9 ♗e3 ♕c7 10 g4 ♖e8 11 f5!? ♗f8 12 g5 ♘fd7

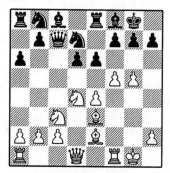

13 ♘xe6!!

Here it is, this totally unexpected sacrifice was a theoretical novelty at the time. An earlier game had seen the relatively harmless 13 fxe6.

13 ... fxe6 14 ♗h5 g6 15 fxg6 ♖e7

After 15 ... hxg6 16 ♗xg6 ♖e7 17 ♕h5 White's pieces charge into the attack. The text hopes to use White's own pawns as a defensive shield after 16 gxh7+ ♔h8 much as Korchnoi did against Tal. But Shirov finds new inroads into Black's camp by throwing gasoline onto the flames.

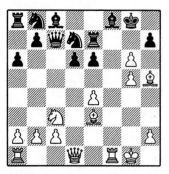

16 ♘d5!
Utterly brilliant! Before going any further with the demolition work on the kingside Shirov gives up a second piece to secure outposts for his forces in the centre.
16 ... exd5 17 ♕xd5+ ♔h8 18 gxh7
The point of White's 16th move is that he is now threatening 19 ♕g8#. This forces Black to take White's h7 pawn which is one of his own main defensive pieces.
18 ... ♖xh7 19 ♗g6 ♗g7
Black could also consider 19 ... ♖e7 20 ♖f3 ♘f6!? but then 21 ♗d4! ♖e5 22 ♖xf6! ♗g7 23 ♖f7 looks strong. In any case his king is coming under a withering attack.
20 ♗xh7 ♕d8
There is no time to recapture as 20 ... ♔xh7 is met by 21 g6+ ♔h8 22 ♕h5+ or 21 ... ♔xg6 22 ♕f5#. Black still has two pieces for a rook

but without any kingside pawn cover his king has little chance of survival in the long run.
21 ♗f5 ♘e5

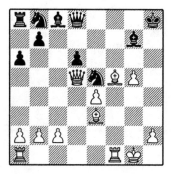

22 ♕d1!
The winning move. White's queen is on its way to h5 which induces a desperate reaction.
22 ... ♗xf5 23 exf5 ♕e8 24 g6 ♘g4
Hoping for 25 ♕xg4 ♕xe3+ but Shirov plays much better.
25 ♗d4! ♕e4 26 f6! ♘c6 27 fxg7+ ♔g8

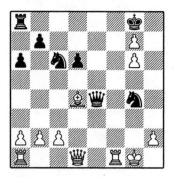

28 ♖f8+!
Finally crashing through in spite of all Black's efforts.
28 ... ♖xf8 29 gxf8=♕+ ♔xf8 30 ♕f1+ 1:0
Black is mated after 30 ... ♔e8 31 ♕f7+ ♔d8 32 ♗b6+ ♔c8 33 ♕c7#

KM22/3: 1) White to play

KM22/3: 2) White to play

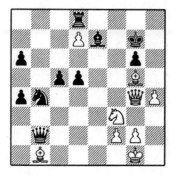

KM22/3: 3) White to play

KM22/3: 4) White to play

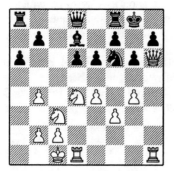

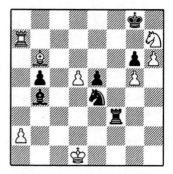

A22/3: a) Black to play

A22/3: b) Black to play

Month 22/Week 4:
The Machine

The arrival of the computer has created a revolution in the chess world. The fact that chess can be defined as a very complex mathematical problem has made it suitable for testing computer 'intelligence' against humans. The machine triumphed when Deeper Blue defeated Kasparov in a set six game match.

Computers 'play' a very different kind of chess to humans. They have poor evaluation functions (placing a heavy emphasis on material) but are supremely efficient calculators. The humans have been coming under growing pressure due to the supreme tactical ability of computers and incredible tenacity.

Here is the historic game that demonstrated the inferiority of organic players, at least in the eyes of the public. Personally speaking I would not have chosen Kasparov to represent the human race but he came, saw less and was conquered.

Deep Blue - Kasparov
New York m (Game 6) 1997

1 e4 c6

Kasparov decided that the Caro-Kann Defence was a more suitable weapon than his habitual Sicilian Defence. Many experts felt that it was a mistake on his part to play a defence with which he was less familiar but it is easy to be wise with the benefit of hindsight.

2 d4 d5 3 ♘c3 dxe4 4 ♘xe4 ♘d7

An interesting choice from Kasparov who had, prior to one of matches with Karpov, claimed that this line is 'unsound and would shortly be refuted'.

5 ♘g5 ♘gf6 6 ♗d3 e6 7 ♘1f3

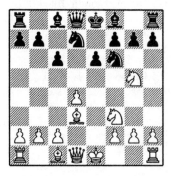

7 ... h6?!

This move is not considered to be the strongest by theory which recommends 7 ... ♗d6 instead. Given that Kasparov is the world's greatest expert on theory, this is a quite extraordinary decision.

8 ♘xe6!

This must have come as a shock to Kasparov who prefers to have the initiative himself rather than defend against a violent onslaught.

8 ... ♕e7?

8 ... fxe6 9 ♗g6+ ♚e7 10 0-0 ♕c7 11 ♖e1 ♚d8 is the only way for Black to play it. The text is a known mistake.

9 0-0 fxe6 10 ♗g6+ ♚d8 11 ♗f4

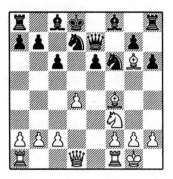

11 ... b5?!

In his notes to this game Seirawan was at pains to recommend 11 ... a5 at this point, though Black's position is unpalatable in any case. The text allows White get to Black's king by prising open the queenside.

12 a4! ♗b7 13 ♖e1 ♘d5 14 ♗g3 ♔c8 15 axb5 cxb5 16 ♕d3 ♗c6?

16 ... ♕b4 17 ♖xe6 ♗e7 was the last chance to make a fight of it.

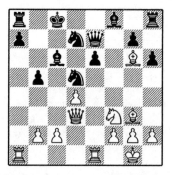

17 ♗f5! exf5 18 ♖xe7 ♗xe7 19 c4! 1:0

19 ... bxc4 20 ♕xc4 ♔b7 21 ♕a6 was mate but 19 ... ♘b4 20 ♕xf5 ♖f8 21 ♕e6 bxc4 22 ♘e5 would have been worth playing on a bit.

The next game features a commercially available program against a human club player with the human once again coming under heavy pressure. The machine proves to have an extensive 'book' repertoire and wins a pawn with the neat 27 ♘c7. Yet when positional intuition was required (31 c3) it had more difficulties and only won in the end because of tenacity and good clock handling.

HIARCS 5 - Quinn
Testing Match 1996

1 e4 c5 2 ♘f3 d6 3 d4 cxd4 4 ♘xd4 ♘f6 5 ♘c3 a6 6 ♗g5 e6 7 f4 ♗e7 8 ♕f3 ♕c7 9 0-0-0 ♘bd7 10 g4 b5 11 ♗xf5 ♘xf6 12 g5 ♘d7 13 f5 ♗xg5+

Taking the pawn is thought to be the best. The old line is 13 ... ♘c5 but then 14 f6 gxf6 15 gxf6 ♗f8 16 ♖g1! intending ♖g7 is very dangerous.

14 ♔b1 ♘e5 15 ♕h5 ♕e7 16 ♘xe6

Alternatively White can play either 16 ♖g1 or 16 fxe6.

16 ... ♗xe6 17 fxe6 g6 18 exf7+ ♔xf7 19 ♕e2 ♔g7 20 ♘d5 ♕d8 21 ♕f2 ♖f8 22 ♕d4

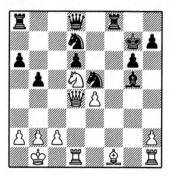

22 ... ♗f6

Hereabouts I don't like the way that Black played it. Perhaps 22 ... ♖c8 is better.

23 ♗e2 ♔g8 24 ♖df1 ♗g7 25 ♖xf8+ ♔xf8?!

25 ... ♕xf8 26 ♘c7 ♖c8 27 ♘xa6 ♘c4 28 ♕d5+ ♔h8 is a better try for Black.

26 ♖f1+ ♔g8 27 ♘c7!

Neatly winning a pawn. Presumably this took Black by surprise.

27 ... ♖c8 28 ♕d5+ ♔h8 29
♘xa6 ♘c4 30 ♗xc4 bxc4 31
♕b7?!

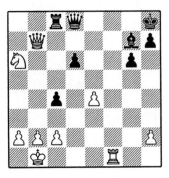

Having won material HIARCS
decentralises the queen and some
difficulties appear. I would prefer
31 c3, creating a solid support point
for the knight on b4.

31 ... ♕g8 32 h4 ♖f8 33 ♖xf8
♕xf8 34 a4 c3! 35 b4?!
Another dubious move. It is very
risky to allow the pawn on c3 to live
and what should have been a safe
technical win now becomes a life or
death struggle.

35 ... ♕f1+ 36 ♔a2 h5 37 ♕b8+
♔h7 38 ♕xd6 ♕c1
Suddenly threatening mate on b2
and when White runs with his king
the c2 pawn falls.

39 ♔b3 ♕b1+ 40 ♔c4 ♕xc2 41
♘c5 ♕a2+ 42 ♔b5 c2 43 ♘d3
♕b1 44 a5
White has to give up a piece as 44
♕c5 is met by 44 ... ♕d1 and if 45
♕c4 then 45 ... ♕xc3. This accident
is a result of White systematically
misplacing his pieces after winning
material on move 27.

44 ... c1=♕ 45 ♘xc1 ♕xc1 46 a6
♕f1+ 47 ♔a5 ♕a1+ 48 ♔b6 ♕d4+

Black exchanges queens in order
to safely play ... g6-g5 and obtain
his own passed pawn.

49 ♕xd4 ♗xd4+ 50 ♔c7 g5! 51
hxg5 h4 52 b5
The b-pawn must go to b6 in
order to shield the a7 square from
Black's bishop.

52 ... h3 53 b6 h2 54 a7 ♗e5+ 55
♔d7 h1=♕ 56 a8=♕

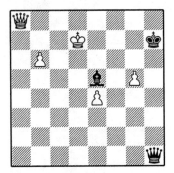

Reaching an endgame which
should really be drawn. Of course
White will have whatever practical
chances are going on account of his
passed pawns.

56 ... ♕h3+ 57 ♔e7 ♕h4 58 ♔e6
♕xg5 59 ♕f8 ♗g3 60 ♕f7+ ♔h8
61 ♕f6+ ♕xf6+ 62 ♔xf6 ♗b8

62 ... ♔g8 fails because of 63 e5!
♗f2 64 b7 ♗a7 65 ♔e7 ♗b8 66 e6
followed by 67 ♔d7 and 68 e7.

63 ♔f7 ♗e5 64 ♔e6 ♗b8 65 ♔f7
♗e5 66 ♔e6 ♗b8 67 ♔d7
A 'winning attempt' of no conse-
quence. But perhaps HIARCS had
an eye on the clock situation when it
repeated the position.

67 ... ♔g7 68 ♔e7 ♗e5 69 b7
♗b8 70 ♔e6 ♔f8 71 ♔d7 ♔f7 72
♔c6 1:0
Presumably on time. After 72 ...
♔e6 the position is a simple draw.

22/4: 1) White to play

22/4: 2) Black to play

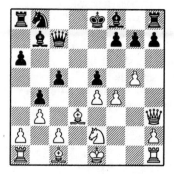

22/4: 3) White to play

22/4: 4) White to play

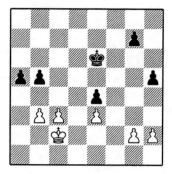

A22/4: a) White to play

A22/4: b) White to play

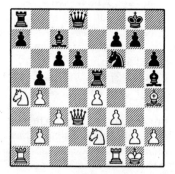

11 The Opening

How one should approach the opening is one of the most thorny issues on the chessboard. Should one play the sharpest and most principled variations, just go for logical development, try and put you opponent on his own resources, surprise him?

All these approaches have their pros and cons and most Grandmasters will use a combination of one or more of them in their games. Let's examine each method in turn:

Month 23/Week 1:
Razor Sharp Theory

With the notable exception of Anatoly Karpov, most of the current leading players play the sharpest and most principled lines. They no doubt feel that these moves are the 'best' and offer the best chance to get something with White or equalise with Black.

Bobby Fischer was the man who started this approach and in his day almost everyone was afraid of his highly analysed variations of the Sicilian Najdorf and King's Indian Defence. Garry Kasparov took this approach even further by assembling a team of analysts.

The following game shows the extent to which the tentacles of sharp opening theory have extended.

Kasparov - Timoshenko
USSR Ch, Frunze 1981

1 d4 d5 2 c4 c6 3 ♘f3 ♘f6 4 ♘c3 e6 5 ♗g5 dxc4 6 e4 b5 7 e5 h6 8 ♗h4 g5 9 ♘xg5 hxg5 10 ♗xg5 ♘bd7 11 exf6 ♗b7 12 g3 c5 13 d5 ♕b6 14 ♗g2 0-0-0 15 0-0 b4 16 ♘a4

I have not commented on the first 16 moves simply because they are such standard theory in this, the Botvinnik Variation of the Semi-Slav Defence. White has alternatives in 16 dxe6 and the amazing 16 ♖b1!?, but the knight move used to be the main line.

16 ... ♕b5 17 a3 ♘b8 18 axb4 cxb4 19 ♗e3 ♗xd5 20 ♗xd5 ♖xd5 21 ♕e2 ♘c6 22 ♖fc1

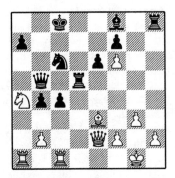

22 ... ♘a5?!

At the time of the game this was a 'TN' (theoretical novelty) which Timoshenko had evidently prepared at home. Against a lesser opponent it might well have succeeded but Kasparov finds a brilliant answer.

Two years later Mikhail Tal improved on Black's play with 22 ... ♘e5!, the game Kasparov-Tal, Moscow 1983 continuing with 23 b3 (23 ♗xa7?! ♕b7 24 ♗e3 ♖d3 gives Black counterplay) 23 ... c3 24 ♘xc3 bxc3 25 ♖xc3+ ♔b8! 26 ♕c2 ♗d6 27 ♗xa7+ ♔b7 28 b4 and now 28 ... ♖d3 would have equalised. This in turn led White to search for improvements such as 19 ♕d4!? and 19 ♕f3. When Black found ways of dealing with these he turned back to the currently fashionable 16 ♖b1!?.

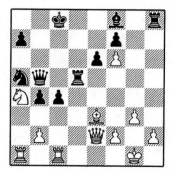

23 b3! c3 24 ♘xc3!

At first sight it doesn't look as if White will have enough for his sacrificed piece but Black's exposed king proves to be a long-term problem. It requires very subtle handling by White to keep the flames of his attack alight.

24 ... bxc3 25 ♖xc3+ ♔d7 26 ♕c2 ♗d6 27 ♖c1 ♕b7 28 b4!

Opening up more files on the queenside along which White's heavy artillery will penetrate. For the time being Black defended himself very accurately according to Kasparov.

28 ... ♕xb4! 29 ♖b1 ♕g4

30 ♗xa7!!

Remarkably cool play. The a-pawn is a valuable defensive piece in that it closes the access of White's pieces along the a-file, but to use a valuable tempo to capture this pawn requires delicate judgement.

30 ... e5

Freeing the e6 square for his king but loosening the position of his rook on d5 Kasparov immediately takes advantage of this.

31 ♕a2! ♖d1+

According to Kasparov 31 ... ♕f5 was a better defence though apparently inadequate because of 32 f3!.

32 ♖xd1 ♕xd1+ 33 ♔g2 ♕h5 34 ♕a4+ ♔e6 35 h4!

The winning move, after 35 ... e4 36 ♕xe4+ ♕e5 37 ♕g4+ ♕f5 38 ♖e3+ ♗e5 39 ♕e2 Black cannot meet all of White's threats.

35 ... ♕e2 36 ♕xa5 ♖a8 37 ♕a4!

An object lesson in winning a won game. White drives home his advantage.

37 ... ♔xf6 38 ♕d7 ♔g7 39 ♖f3 ♕c4 40 ♕xd6 ♖xa7 41 ♕xe5+ ♔h7 42 ♖f5 ♕c6+ 43 ♔h2 1:0

For anyone but a full-time professional it is difficult to recommend variations such as this, simply because of the time required to learn them. Not only is the main line massively complicated, there are numerous equally complicated sidelines. The assessment of any of these lines can be completely overturned by a single strong move.

In the following game Lev Polugaevsky put a massive hole in one of these sub-variations with his inspired seventeenth move.

Polugaevsky - Torre
Moscow 1981

1 d4 d5 2 c4 c6 3 ♘f3 ♘f6 4 ♘c3 e6 5 ♗g5 dxc4 6 e4 b5 7 e5 h6 8 ♗h4 g5 9 ♘xg5 hxg5 10 ♗xg5 ♘bd7 11 exf6 ♗b7 12 g3 c5 13 d5 ♘b6 14 dxe6 ♕xd1+ 15 ♖xd1 ♗xh1 16 e7 a6

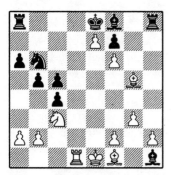

All this had been seen before in the game Belyavsky-Bagirov, USSR 1981 in which White, naturally enough, captured the bishop on f8 with check. No doubt Polugaevsky analysed this game at home and he now comes up with a truly incredible idea.

17 h4!! ♗h6 18 f4!!

Brilliantly imaginative yet very logical. White's kingside pawns are an immensely powerful force once they start to advance.

18 ... b4 19 ♖d6! ♖b8

19 ... bxc3 20.♖xb6 cxb2 21 ♖xb2 leaves Black unable to free himself.

20 ♘d1 ♗xg5 21 fxg5 ♘d5 22 ♗xc4 ♘xe7 23 fxe7 ♔xe7 24 ♖f6!

An important move which ties Black to the defence of f7. White is winning.

24 ... ♖hf8 25 ♘e3 ♗e4 26 ♖xa6 ♖bd8 27 ♖f6 ♖d6 28 ♖f4 ♖d4 29 h5 ♗d3 30 ♘d5+ ♔d6 31 ♖xd4 cxd4

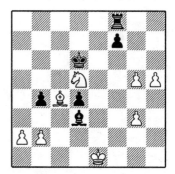

32 ♗b3?

Rather spoiling a brilliant game. 32 ♗xd3! ♔xd5 33 h6 ♖g8 34 h7 ♖h8 35 ♔d2 ♔d6 36 ♔c2 ♔e7 37 ♔b3 ♔f8 38 ♔b4 ♔g7 39 ♔c4 would have been a more fitting and deadly conclusion.

32 ... ♗c2 33 ♗xc2 ♔xd5 34 ♗b3+?

34 h6! would have still won.

34 ... ♔e5 35 g4 ♔f4?

Losing without a struggle. 35 ... d3! would have been far more difficult for White to refute.

36 g6 ♔e3 37 g7 ♖c8 38 ♔f1 d3 39 ♔g2 ♔f4 40 h6 1:0

KM23/1: 1) White to play

KM23/1: 2) White to play

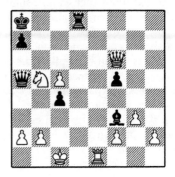

KM23/1: 3) White to play

KM23/1: 4) White to play

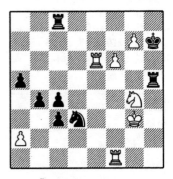

A23/1: a) White to play

A23/1: b) White to play

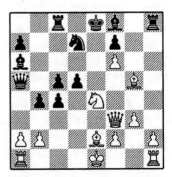

Month 23/Week 2:
Meat and Potato Systems

For players at club level it is impossible to be up-to-date with the very latest theory which causes many of them to switch to tricky, off-beat lines which have little justification from a strategic point of view. I don't recommend this because I think that it tends to lead to a tricky, off-beat approach to the game and limits a player's potential to develop.

A far better approach is that used by Grandmasters such as Anatoly Karpov, Paul Keres, Boris Spassky, Svetozar Gligoric and Lajos Portisch who specialise in durable logical opening systems which lead to playable and interesting middle-game positions. Such lines have stood the test of time, will not be refuted by a single sharp move. They rely on positional understanding rather than memory, home analysis or an up-to-date computer database.

One such line is the Closed Variation of the Sicilian Defence which Spassky has used with success throughout his career. White builds a solid middlegame formation with aggressive potential, aiming to outplay his opponent in the later stages. Here are two heavyweight encounters from the Closed Sicilian duel between Spassky and Portisch:

Spassky - Portisch
Geneva Cm 1977

1 e4 c5 2 ♘c3 ♘c6 3 g3 g6 4 ♗g2 ♗g7 5 d3 d6 6 f4 e5

Adopting the Botvinnik formation. Black leaves a hole on d5 but argues that White will be unable to establish a piece on this square. Meanwhile Black ensures that he will have a strong grip on the centre.

7 ♘h3 exf4 8 ♗xf4 ♘ge7 9 0-0 h6 10 ♖b1 0-0 11 a3 ♗e6 12 ♗e3

Inhibiting Black's projected 12 .... d5 and preparing to bring the knight on h3 to f4 In this early part of the game the two contestants artfully jockey for position.

12 ... ♘e5 13 ♘f4 ♗d7 14 ♔h1 ♖c8 15 ♕d2 ♔h7 16 h3 ♗c6 17 g4 ♕d7 18 ♖f2 b6 19 ♖bf1 ♗b7 20 ♕e2 ♖ce8 21 ♗c1 ♔g8 22 ♕e3 b5 23 ♕g3 b4 24 axb4 cxb4 25 ♘d1 d5

Things have suddenly come to life with Black fulfilling his strategic objective, the freeing ... d6-d5 advance. But Spassky turns out to be well prepared and post-mortem analysis indicated that Black should probably have saved time with a 20 ... b5 (rather than 20 ... ♖ce8) and later prepared ... b5-b4 with 23 ... a5 This would have ensured that Black doesn't lose control of the d4 square, a factor that White immediately exploits.

26 d4! ♘5c6 27 exd5 ♘xd4 28 c4! bxc3 29 bxc3 ♘b3?

The final mistake in a difficult position. 29 ... ♖c8 had to be tried

after which 30 ♗a3 is met by 30 ...
♘b5!. Now White's bishop comes
to a3 and supports a decisive advance of his d and c- pawns.

30 ♗a3! ♖c8 31 c4!

The advance of the pawns is combined with the threat of 32 ♕xb3
Black's position is hopeless against
a player such as Spassky who finishes the job with some nice attacking play.

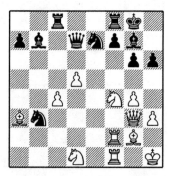

31 ... ♘a5 32 ♖e2 ♖fe8 33 ♖fe1

33 ♕e1 was quicker, forking the
two knights on a5 and e7. But
Spassky has something more spectacular in mind.

33 ... ♗f8 34 ♘h5! ♘xd5

The immediate 34 ... gxh5 is answered by 35 gxh5+ ♔h7 36 ♗xe7
♗xe7 37 ♗e4+ f5 38 ♗xf5+ ♕xf5
39 ♖xe7+ followed by mate. Portisch tries desperately to bail out but
the attack comes crashing through.

**35 cxd5 gxh5 36 gxh5+ ♗g7 37
♗b2 f6 38 ♗xf6 ♖xe2 39 ♖xe2
♕f7 40 ♖e6! 1:0**

The threat is 40 ♗xg7 ♕xg7 41
♖g6 and 40 ... ♖c1 is met by 41
♖e8+!.

In this second game Portisch
switches to a more conservative system of development in which Black
inhibits the possibility of White ever

playing f4-f5 with 6 ... e6 and 7 ...
♘ge7. This is generally considered
to be Black's best line against
Spassky's favourite 6 f4.

**Spassky - Portisch
Toluca Izt 1982**

**1 e4 c5 2 ♘c3 d6 3 g3 ♘c6 4
♗g2 g6 5 d3 ♗g7 6 f4 e6 7 ♘f3
♘ge7 8 0-0 0-0 9 ♗e3 ♘d4 10 ♖b1**

White's aim in this position is to
remove Black's knight from d4 and
this protects the b2 pawn in preparation for 11 ♘e2 Spassky has also
tried 10 ♗f2 which intends 11
♘xd4 whilst 10 e5 is a sharp attempt to seize the initiative.

**10 ... ♖b8 11 ♘e2 ♘xf3+ 12
♗xf3 b6 13 g4 f5!**

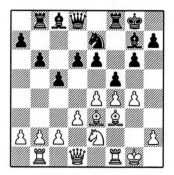

A key defensive manoevre which
prevents White's planned f4-f5
thrust and makes 13 g4 look dubious in Portisch's opinion. Over
the following moves we see a fierce
battle for the centre.

**14 ♘g3 ♗b7 15 gxf5 exf5 16 c4
♕d7 17 ♕d2 ♖be8 18 ♖be1 ♘c6
19 ♗g2**

White's e4 pawn is coming under
pressure. 19 exf5 is answered by 19
... ♘d4! 20 ♗xd4 ♗xd4+ and ...
gxf5.

19 ... ♘d4 20 ♔h1 fxe4 21 dxe4 h5!

A powerful move which intensifies the pressure on e4 through the threat of 22 ... h4. Portisch has correctly judged that he can afford the weakening of his kingside.

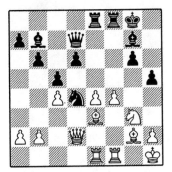

22 ♕d3 h4 23 ♗xd4 cxd4!

Precise play by Portisch. After 23 ... ♗xd4 White could try 24 ♘e2! ♗xb2 25 ♖g1 with a dangerous attack for the sacrificed pawn.

24 ♘e2 h3 25 ♗f3 ♕e7 26 ♕d2

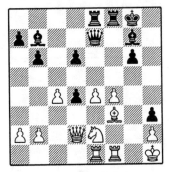

26 ... g5!

Once again Portisch has assessed the position very deeply and seen that he can afford to move his kingside pawns. One of the points is that 27 fxg5 is answered by 27 ... ♖xf3! etc.

27 ♔g1 gxf4?

An unfortunate slip after his previous fine play. As Portisch pointed out in his notes he could have won immediately with 27 ... d3! 28 ♕xd3 ♗xe4 29 ♗xe4 ♕xe4 30 ♕xh3 ♖xf4!-+.

28 ♘xd4 ♕f6 29 ♘b5

And not 29 ♘f5? because of 29 ... ♕g5+ followed by 30 ... ♖xf5.

29 ... ♖d8 30 ♘xa7 ♖a8 31 ♘b5 ♖xa2 32 ♕xd6 ♖xb2 33 ♕xf6 ♖xf6 34 e5 ♖g6+ 35 ♔h1 ♗xf3+ 36 ♖xf3 ♗xe5 37 ♖xh3

37 ... f3!

Despite the reduction in material Black has a winning attack. The attempt to simplify with 38 ♖g1 fails against 38 ... ♖bg2 39 ♖xg2 fxg2+ 40 ♔g1 ♖g4! 41 ♖h5 ♗b8 followed by ... ♔g7 when White suddenly finds himself without any moves.

38 ♖f1 ♖bg2! 39 ♖d1 ♗f4! 40 ♘d4

40 ♖f1 is met by 40 ... ♗e3 41 ♖g3 ♖2xg3 42 hxg3 ♖h6#.

41 ... f2 41 ♘f3

If 41 ♘e2 there is 41 ... f1=♕ or 41 ♖g3 ♖xh2+! etc.

41 ... ♗e3 42 ♖d8+ ♔g7 43 ♖d7+ ♔f6 0:1

KM23/2: 1) White to play

KM23/2: 2) White to play

KM23/2: 3) White to play

KM23/2: 4) White to play

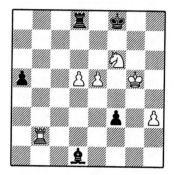

A23/2: a) White to play

A23/2: b) White to play

Month 23/Week 3:
Anti-Theory

In addition to the established theoretical lines there are many other playable moves which have not been studied at all. Players attracted to such possibilities will be motivated by the thought that they do not want to enter into a sharp theoretical line (week one) or even a standard, meat and potatoes middle-game position (week two). They want to create something unusual in which brain work will take precedence over homework and willingly enter the uncharted realm of anti-theory.

In the 1960s Larsen won one tournament after another despite the presence of many of the leading Soviets. In the opening he tended to adopt unusual lines which had the effect of utterly confounding many of his opponents.

His patented 1 b3 became known as 'Larsen's Opening'.

Larsen - Donner
San Juan 1969

1 b3 e5 2 ♗b2 d6 3 g3 ♘f6 4 ♗g2 g6 5 e4 ♗g7 6 ♘e2 0-0 7 0-0 ♘h5?!

Thrown on his own resources Donner makes a serious mistake. Larsen's reply really rules out Black's projected ... f7-f5 and the knight on h5 is shown to be offside.

8 d4! ♘c6 9 ♘a3 ♕e7

The logical follow-up to 7 ... ♘h5!? would be 9 ... f5 but according to Larsen this is better for White after 10 exf5 gxf5 11 ♗xc6! bxc6 12 dxe5 dxe5 13 f4!. Nevertheless this would have been a more consistent approach as now Donner finds himself with a very passive position.

10 ♘c4 exd4?!

A further mistake, giving up the centre. He should hang tough with 10 ... ♖e8.

11 ♘xd4 ♘xd4 12 ♗xd4 ♗e6 13 ♘e3 c6 14 ♗xg7 ♘xg7 15 ♖e1 ♕c7 16 ♕d4

After just 16 moves White has obtained an excellent game with more space plus weaknesses on d6 and on the dark squares around Black's king. Could he have obtained such a position with more orthodox methods?

16 ... a5 17 ♖ad1 ♖ad8 18 ♖d2 f5?!

This attempt to free Black's position only serves to create more weaknesses. Of course it isn't easy to sit tight and get tortured.

19 exf5 ♘xf5??

The decisive mistake after which White's rooks are able to penetrate on the e-file. Black had to recapture with the bishop.

20 ♘xf5 ♗xf5 21 ♖de2

The winning move. 21 ... ♖d7 loses a piece after 22 g4 and 21 ... ♕g7 is met by 22 ♕b6.

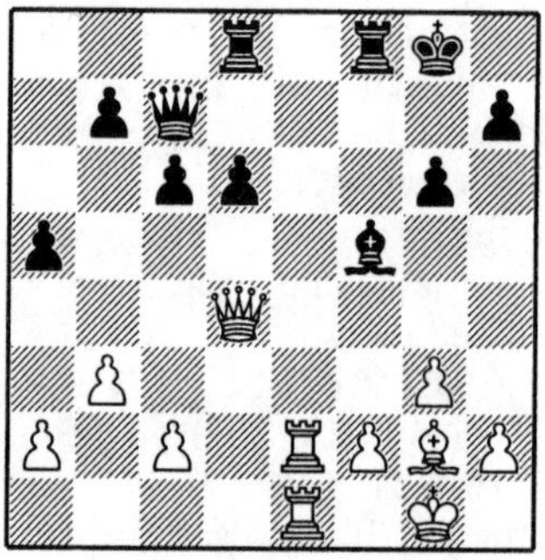

21 ... ♕f7 22 ♖e7 c5

After 22 ... ♖fe8 White can choose between 23 ♕b6 and 23 ♕h4.

23 ♕h4 g5 24 ♕xg5+ ♕g6 25 ♕d2 1:0

It is certainly a brilliant success to beat a player like Donner in just 25 moves. So would I recommend playing such 'anti-theory' to club players?

This may seem very tempting in that it avoids the chore of studying a lot of theory. But there are also a couple of serious drawbacks.

The first is that it is much easier to learn classical middlegame technique by obtaining classical middlegame positions in your own games. The second is that not everybody has the positional understanding of a Larsen and being thrown on one's own resources might have unfortunate results. In fact even Larsen had some problems in this respect after getting Spassky 'out of the book' in the following famous game:

Larsen - Spassky
USSR-Rest of the World,
Belgrade 1970

1 b3 e5 2 ♗b2 ♘c6 3 c4

Going for a kind of reversed Sicilian. 3 e3 (intending 4 ♗b5) is more common and arguably more logical.

3 ... ♘f6 4 ♘f3 e4

Taking up the gauntlet, 4 ... d6 would be more compact.

5 ♘d4 ♗c5 6 ♘xc6 dxc6 7 e3 ♗f5 8 ♕c2 ♕e7 9 ♗e2 0-0-0 10 f4?

Larsen optimistically pursues strategic objectives by denying Black use of the e5 square but sadly neglects his development. He should develop with 10 ♘c3 with an interesting middlegame in prospect.

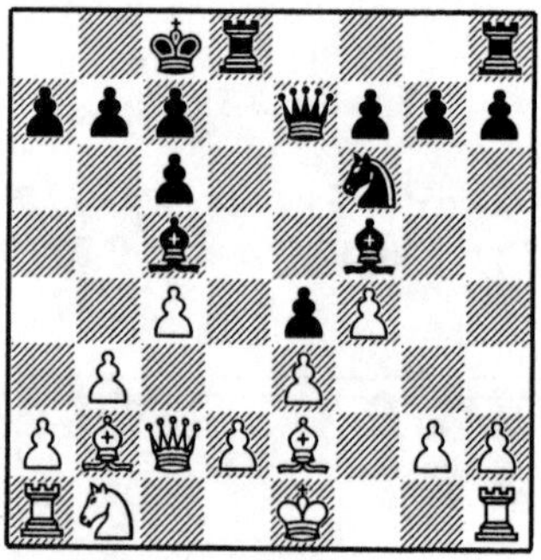

10 ... ♘g4!

Seizing the initiative. Black now threatens 11 ... ♕h4+ 12 g3 ♕h3 and 11 ... ♖xd2 is another interesting idea.

11 g3 h5

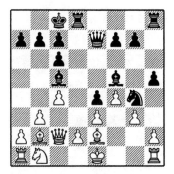

12 h3

White is already in desperate straits as the attempt to develop with 12 ♘c3 runs into the shattering 12 ... ♖xd2! 13 ♕xd2 (13 ♔xd2 is met by 13 ... ♗xe3+ 14 ♔d1 ♖d8+ 15 ♔e1 ♗f2+ etc) 13 ... ♗xe3 14 ♕d1 (or 14.♕c2 ♗f2+ 15 ♔d2 e3+) 14 ... ♗f2+ 15 ♔f1 h4! followed by 16 ... hxg3. Larsen must now have been hoping that Spassky would retreat his knight after which 13 g4 would be rather good for him.

12 ... h4!

This brilliant reply destroys all White's illusions. The knight is sacrificed for a huge passed g-pawn.

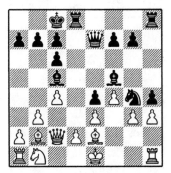

13 hxg4

The line 13 ♗xg4 ♗xg4 14 hxg4 hxg3 15 ♖g1 ♖h1!! is similar to the game, after 16 ♖xh1 g2 17 ♖g1 ♕h4+ 18 ♔e2 ♕xg4+ 19 ♔e1

♕g3+ 20 ♔e2 (or 20 ♔d1 ♕f2 21 ♔e1 ♗e7!) 20 ... ♕f3+ 21 ♔e1 ♗e7! Black obtains a mating attack.

13 ... hxg3 14 ♖g1

Played instantly. How can Black continue his attack?

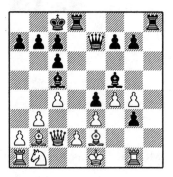

14 ... ♖h1!!

The sensational climax of Spassky's brilliant combination. White must capture the rook because 15 ♔f1 is met by 15 ... ♖xg1+ 16 ♔xg1 ♕h4 followed by mate.

15 ♖xh1 g2

16 ♖f1

If 16 ♖g1 there follows 16 ... ♕h4+ 17 ♔d1 ♕h1 18 ♕c3 ♕xg1+ 19 ♔c2 ♕f2 20 gxf5 ♕xe2 21 ♘a3 ♗b4 winning the queen.

16 ... ♕h4+ 17 ♔d1 gxf1=♕+ 0:1

Mate is forced after 18 ♗xf1 ♗xg4+. A truly sensational game.

KMP23/3: 1) Black to play

KMP23/3: 2) White to play

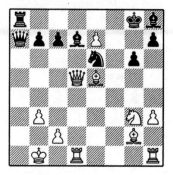

KMP23/3: 3) White to play

KMP23/3: 4) White to play

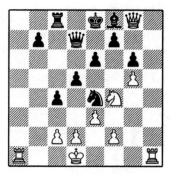

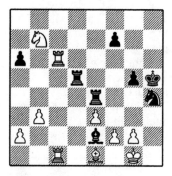

A23/3: a) White to play

A23/3: b) White to play

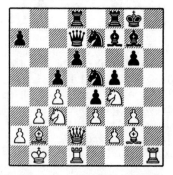

Month 23/Week 4:
Surprise Weapons

It is very useful to have one or two surprise lines in your opening repertoire to play on an occasional basis. Having this option available can be very useful if, for example, you don't like what your opponent plays against your usual repertoire. It can also throw your opponent on his own resources which can be useful against players who know 'theory' very well but may not be so adept at thinking for themselves.

The Trompowsky Opening (1 d4 ♘f6 2 ♗g5) is a good example of a highly effective surprise line which has the great advantage that you can play it on move two after the most popular first move sequence!

GMs such as Ivan Sokolov and Joe Gallagher use the 'Tromp' occasionally with great effect but the arch-guru of this opening is Julian Hodgson. Because Hodgson uses it in virtually every game it does not have any surprise value for him at all. Yet he still makes very good results with it because it leads to unusual positions in which he can use positional understanding rather than knowledge.

Hodgson - van der Wiel
Amsterdam 1994

1 d4 ♘f6 2 ♗g5 c5

The 'main line' is 2 ... ♘e4, avoiding doubled pawns. Of course the text move is quite playable but in allowing doubled pawns Black takes on more responsibilities.

3 ♗xf6 gxf6 4 d5 ♕b6 5 ♕c1 ♗h6 6 e3 f5 7 c4 f4?!

A thematic move which liquidates the doubled pawns and Van der Wiel evidently prepared for the following exchange sacrifice. Unfortunately for him there is a flaw in his calculations.

8 exf4 ♗xf4 9 ♕xf4! ♕xb2 10 ♘e2 ♕xa1 11 ♘ec3 ♕b2

Van der Wiel's innovation which attempts to improve on the 11 ... d6 of Alexandrov-Frolov, Saint Petersburg 1994 Hodgson is quick to point out the drawback of the move.

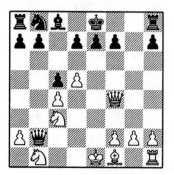

12 d6!

A powerful blow which cuts Black's position in two. It is difficult to know exactly what Van der Wiel missed as after three more moves his position is hopeless. He had probably hoped that 12 d6 would give his knight a good square on c6 but this turns out to be a minor consideration.

12 ... ♘c6 13 ♗d3 exd6 14 0-0 ♘e5 15 ♕f6

With all White's pieces participating in the attack and Black's development so retarded it is difficult to see the slightest prospect of defence. 15 ... ♖g8 is met by 16 ♘d5, winning on the spot.

15 ... 0-0 16 ♘d5 ♖e8 17 ♕g5+

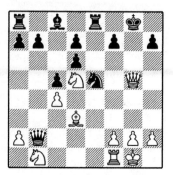

17 ... ♘g6

After 17 ... ♔h8 Hodgson intended 18 ♘f6! ♘xd3 19 ♕h6 ♕xf6 (forced) 20 ♕xf6+ ♔g8 21 f4! with a winning attack.

18 ♘f6+ ♔f8 19 ♕h6+

Both 19 ♗xg6 and 19 ♘xe8 also win but Hodgson wants marks for artistic merit.

19 ... ♔e7 20 ♘d5+ ♔d8 21 ♗xg6 hxg6 22 ♘bc3 1:0

There's no good defence to the threat of 23 ♕g5+.

Hodgson has played many such brilliant games with his beloved 'Tromp' but there is a danger in playing such openings too often. The first problem is that insufficient variety can be detrimental to ones development as a player, the second is that being too predictable can enable the opponent to prepare.

At club level it's unlikely that one will be faced with an innovation as stunning as Gelfand's new move in the following game. But just knowing what to expect can make an opponent feel more comfortable and better prepared for the coming struggle from a psychological point of view.

Hodgson-Gelfand
Groningen 1996

1 d4 ♘f6 2 ♗g5 ♘e4 3 ♗f4 c5 4 f3 ♕a5+ 5 c3 ♘f6 6 ♘d2

Personally speaking I would prefer to take space with 6 d5 and I suspect that Hodgson now agrees with this sentiment.

6 ... cxd4 7 ♘b3 ♕b6 8 cxd4 ♘c6!

Apparently Gelfand had prepared this move for his 1994 match against Michael Adams but did not get the chance to use it. Hodgson turns out to be the unfortunate recipient.

9 e4 e5!

The point of Black's previous move. White is behind in development and there is a certain weakness on the a7-g1 diagonal so it makes sense to blast the position wide open.

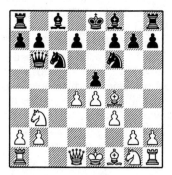

10 dxe5 ♗b4+ 11 ♔e2!

Despite the unpleasantness of having been caught in a prepared line, Hodgson defends very accurately. Both 11 ♘d2 ♘h5! and 11 ♗d2 ♘xe5 favour Black whereas the text should equalise with continued good defence.

11 ... ♘xe5 12 ♕d4

12 ♗xe5 is just bad for White after 12 ... ♕b5+ 13 ♔f2 ♕xe5 due to the crippling weakness of his dark squares.

12 ... ♘g6! 13 ♗e3 d5 14 exd5 0-0

15 a3?!

After this White is worse due to the insecure position of his knight on b3. He should have played 15 ♔f2! after which 15 ... ♕xd4 16 ♗xd4 ♘xd5 is about equal.

15 ... ♕xd4 16 ♗xd4 ♗e7 17 ♔f2 ♘xd5 18 ♘e2 ♗e6 19 ♘c5 ♗xc5 20 ♗xc5 ♖fc8 21 ♖c1 ♘e5 22 ♘d4 b6 23 ♘xe6 fxe6 24 ♖e1 ♘xf3 25 gxf3 ♖xc5 26 ♖xe6 ♖f8 27 ♖e4

According to Gelfand 27 ♖e2 intending ♖d2 was better. Even after the text the position may be objectively drawn but in practice the defence is very difficult indeed.

27 ... ♖c2+ 28 ♔g3 ♘f6 29 ♖e2 ♘h5+ 30 ♔f2 ♖fc8 31 b3 ♔f8 32 ♖g1 ♖8c3 33 ♖g5 g6 34 ♖b5 ♘f4 35 ♖xc2 ♖xc2+ 36 ♔e3 ♘e6 37 ♗c4 ♘c7 38 ♖e5 ♖xh2 39 a4 ♖h1

40 ♔f4 ♖h4+ 41 ♔e3 ♖h1 42 ♔f4 a5 43 ♔g4 ♖g1+ 44 ♔h3 ♖d1 45 f4 ♖d7 46 ♖e4 ♔g7 47 ♔g4 ♔f6 48 ♔f3 ♖d6 49 ♗g8 h5 50 b4 ♖d3+ 51 ♔f2 ♖d8 52 ♖c4 ♘a6 53 ♖c6+ ♔g7 54 ♖xb6 ♘xb4 55 ♗e6 ♘d5 56 ♗xd5 ♖xd5 57 ♔e3 h4

58 ♖b5

This leads to a queen endgame which may be lost. It was better to keep rooks on with 58 ♔f3.

58 ... ♖xb5 59 axb5 a4 60 b6 a3 61 b7 a2 62 b8=♕ a1=♕ 63 ♔f3 ♕c3+ 64 ♔g2 ♔h6 65 ♕d6 ♕g3+ 66 ♔h1 ♕h3+ 67 ♔g1 ♔h5 68 ♕d4

68 ♔f2 was the last chance to stay in the game. Black's next move effectively decides matters.

68 ... ♕f5! 69 ♔g2 ♔g4 70 ♕d1+ ♔xf4 71 ♕d2+ ♔g4 72 ♕d1+ ♔g5 73 ♕d8+ ♔h5 74 ♕h8+ ♔g5 75 ♕d8+ ♕f6 76 ♕d2+ ♔h5 77 ♕e2+ ♔h6 78 ♔h3 ♕f4 79 ♔g2 ♕g3+ 80 ♔h1 ♕h3+ 81 ♔g1 ♕f5 82 ♔h2 g5 83 ♕e8 ♕f6 84 ♕c8 ♕f4+ 85 ♔h1 ♔h5 86 ♕e8+ ♔g4 87 ♕e6+ ♕f5 88 ♕c4+ ♔g3 89 ♕c7+ ♕f4 0:1

KMP23/4: 1) White to play

KMP23/4: 2) White to play

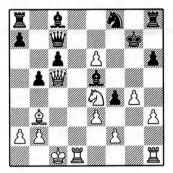

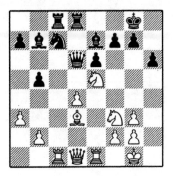

KMP23/4: 3) White to play

KMP23/4: 4) White to play

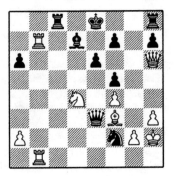

A23/4: a) White to play

A23/4: b) Black to play

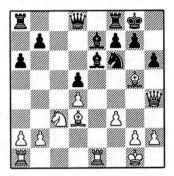

12 The Elements of Mastery

In this final month of the Power-Chess Program I want to review the elements of chess mastery which the course is designed to foster.

In my view there are four main qualities that an aspiring player of any age needs to develop: vision, intuition, creativity and mental toughness. Let's look at these in turn.

Month 24/Week 1:
Vision

The reason that most players give for their defeats is that they 'didn't know the opening'. In actual fact the majority of chess games are decided when one player misses a move or idea that his opponent has seen and this holds true both at club level and Grandmaster level alike.

How does one develop vision? Unfortunately this attribute is impossible to learn and tends to be a function of natural ability. Yet even players with limited talents in this department can improve their vision with practice. One way, which has featured heavily on this course, is to analyse positions for yourself, against the clock and preferably without moving the pieces on the board. Another useful method is blindfold chess.

One player who always impressed me with the depth and clarity of his

vision was the Estonian Grandmaster, Paul Keres. In the following two games we see his brilliant vision in evidence.

Keres - Kotov
Budapest Ct 1950

1 e4 c5 2 ♘f3 d6 3 d4 cxd4 4 ♘xd4 ♘f6 5 ♘c3 a6 6 ♗e2 ♕c7 7 ♗g5 ♘bd7 8 0-0 e6 9 ♗h5 ♕c4?

Allowing a brilliant combination which Kotov might be forgiven for having overlooked. Black should play 9 ... g6 with a very reasonable game.

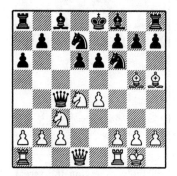

10 ♘xe6! ♕xe6

10 ... ♘xh5 is answered by the amazing 11 ♕d5!! when 11 ... ♘b6 (11 ... ♕xd5 12 ♘c7#)12 ♕xc4 ♘xc4 13 ♘c7+ ♔d7 14 ♘xa8 wins.

11 ♘d5! ♔d8

Once again the only chance. 11 ... ♘xd5 12 exd5 ♕f5 is met by 13 ♕e1+! ♘e5 14 f4+-.

12 ♗g4 ♕e5

Or 12 ... ♕e8 13 ♕d2! with the threat of 14 ♕a5+.

13 f4 ♕xe4

After 13 ... ♕xb2 White has simply 14 ♖b1 ♕a3 15 ♗xd7

14 ♗xd7 ♗xd7

If 14 ... ♔xd7 there follows 15 ♗xf6 ♔c6 16 c4 gxf6 17 ♕a4+ b5 18 cxb5+ ♔xd5 19 ♖ad1 etc.

15 ♘xf6 gxf6

Kotov tries to complicate the issue by giving up the exchange. 15 ... ♕c6 is met by 16 ♘d5+ ♔c8 (or 16 ... f6 17 ♘xf6) 17 ♖f3 ♔b8 18 ♖c3+- and 15 ... ♕g6 loses elegantly to 16 ♘d5+ f6 17 ♕d4! fxg5 18 ♕b6+ ♔e8 19 ♖ae1+ ♔f7 20 ♕xb7 ♖d8 21 ♕c7.

16 ♗xf6+ ♔c7 17 ♗xh8 ♗c6 18 ♕d2 ♗h6 19 ♖ae1 ♕g6 20 ♖e7+ ♔d8 21 ♖fe1 a5 22 ♗d4 ♖a6 23 ♕f2

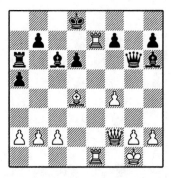

Decisively renewing the threat of 24 ♗b6+. If 23 ... ♗xf4 there follows 24 ♗b6+ ♔c8 25 ♖c7+ ♔b8 26 ♖xc6! bxc6 27 ♖e8+ ♔b7 28 ♖e7+ ♔c8 (or 28 ... ♔b8 29 ♗c7+) 29 ♕xf4 ♖xb6 30 ♕d4! ♔d8 31 ♖a7 with a mating attack.

23 ... ♗f8 24 ♗b6+ ♔c8 25 ♖e8+ ♗xe8 26 ♖xe8+ ♔d7 27 ♖xf8 1:0

In the next game we see Keres punishing a mistake in the opening. After 9 ... a6 it almost looks like a forced win for White!

Keres - Szabo
USSR-Hungary, Moscow 1955

1 e4 c5 2 ♘f3 d6 3 d4 cxd4 4 ♘xd4 ♘f6 5 ♘c3 ♘c6 6 ♗g5 e6 7 ♕d2 ♗e7 8 0-0-0 0-0 9 f4 a6

A normal-looking 'Sicilian' move but in this position a serious mistake. Black should take measures against White's threatened 10 e5 with 9 ... ♘xd4 or 9 ... e5.

10 e5! dxe5 11 ♘xc6 bxc6

After 11 ... ♕xd2+ 12 ♖xd2 bxc6 13 fxe5 ♘d5 14 ♗xe7 ♘xe7 White gets a serious plus with 15 ♗d3!, preparing to capture Black's knight should it attack e5 from the g6 square.

12 fxe5

12 ♕xd8 would not be so effective as after 12 ... ♖xd8 13 ♖xd8+ ♗xd8 14 fxe5 Black has 14 ... h6 15 ♗h4 g5.

12 ... ♘d7

12 ... ♘d5 13 ♗xe7 ♕xe7 14 ♘e4 gives Black a truly miserable position in which White's knight on e5 has unchallengable control over

the central dark-squares. Black must aim for counterplay against the weak e5 pawn and was no doubt hoping for something like 13 ♗xe7 ♕xe7 14 ♕f4 ♕c5 15 ♖e1 Keres comes up with a far more incisive line.

13 h4! ♖b8 14 ♕e3 ♖e8 15 ♖h3 ♕a5

Exchanging queens with 15 ... ♕b6 would bring Black little relief; 16 ♕xb6 ♖xb6 17 ♗xe7 ♖xe7 18 ♖hd3 gives White a huge plus with unchallengeable control of the d-file and severe weaknesses in the opposing camp. Keeping queens on the board also has its drawbacks as White's attack proves to be the more potent.

16 ♗xe7 ♖xe7 17 ♖g3!

Swinging into action along the third rank the rook sets Black serious problems. 17 ... g6 weakens the dark squares even further and sliding off the g-file with 17 ... ♔f8 is met by 18 ♖e1 h6 19 ♕e4! meeting 19 ... ♕b4 with 20 ♕h7! ♕xb2+ 21 ♔d2 etc. Szabo's next move is an attempt to make the least possible concession but it runs into a stunning combinative finale.

17 ... ♖e8

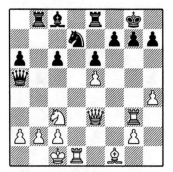

18 ♖xd7!

Eliminating one of Black's key defenders after which White's attack crashes through. The difficulty of this combination lies in its unforced nature; all Black's defensive options have to be considered.

18 ... ♗xd7 19 ♗d3 h6

White can show that 19 ... ♕b4 is a rather empty threat by calmly proceeding with his own attack: 20 ♕g5 ♕xb2+ 21 ♔d2 g6 22 h5 sets up decisive sacrificial threats against the g6 square. Szabo's move prevents 20 ♕g5 but the attack is already too strong.

20 ♕f4

20 ♕e4 would also be very powerful but Keres chooses a more subtle approach. The threat now is 21 ♕f6.

20 ... ♔f8

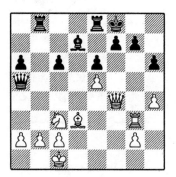

21 ♖xg7!

The second sacrifice strips away the last defensive ramparts. Black is forced to accept.

21 ... ♔xg7 22 ♕f6+ ♔f8

Or if 22 ... ♔g8 there follows simply 23 ♕xh6 f5 24 exf6 with no good defence againt the threat of 25 ♕g7#.

23 ♗g6 1:0

After 23 ... ♖e7 there is 24 ♕h8#.

KMP24/1: 1) White to play

KMP24/1: 2) White to play

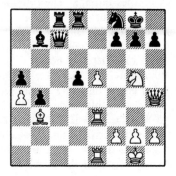

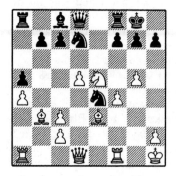

KMP24/1: 3) Black to play

KMP24/1: 4) White to play

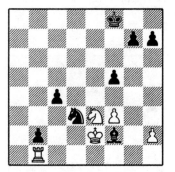

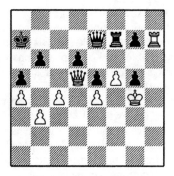

A24/1: b) White to play

A24/1: b) Black to play

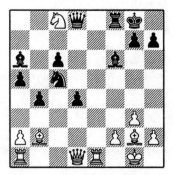

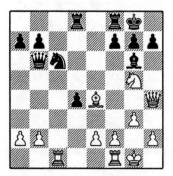

Month 24/Week 2:
Intuition

It is difficult to decide whether vision or intuition is the most important facet of a chessplayer's make-up. These two modes of thought are intertwined at every moment of a game. Intuition, for example, tells us which candidate moves to calculate and sometimes not to calculate at all.

These days I am inclined to trust intuition over lengthy calculations. If my 'gut instinct' tells me that a move is right or wrong I know from experience that this is probably the case.

A player's intuition grows richer as he gains experience. It is impossible to acquire such positional feeling overnight or by reading a book on the subject. It is rather acquired over a period of time when you immerse yourself in the art of chess.

Alexander Alekhine had the most finely developed intuition, especially when it came down to a trade-off between material and position. In the following game he sacrifices a whole rook on largely intuitive grounds:

Alekhine - Book
Margate 1938

1 d4 d5 2 c4 dxc4 3 ♘f3 ♘f6 4 e3 e6 5 ♗xc4 c5 6 0-0 ♘c6 7 ♕e2 a6 8 ♘c3 b5 9 ♗b3 b4?

This proves to be loosening and neglects Black's development. Subsequent games showed that 9 ... ♗b7 is better.

10 d5!

A suprising coup which tears the position open whilst Black's king is uncastled. 10 ... exd5 11 ♘xd5 ♘xd5 12 ♖d1 (followed possibly by 13 e4) and 10 ... bxc3 11 ♗a4 ♕xd5 12 e4 both recover the material with advantage.

10 ... ♘a5 11 ♗a4+ ♗d7 12 dxe6 fxe6 13 ♖d1!?

Leonid Shamkovich later found another strong line in 13 ♘e5 bxc3 14 ♘xd7 ♘xd7 15 ♕h5+ ♔e7 (15 ... g6 16 ♕e5) 16 ♖d1 ♖a7 17 e4. Alekhine's idea also seems good but he is about to make his material investment into a whole rook.

13 ... bxc3 14 ♖xd7! ♘xd7 15 ♘e5 ♖a7 16 bxc3!

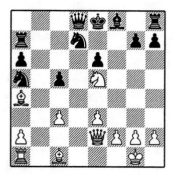

Alekhine had no doubt seen this position when embarking on this line. It isn't easy to ascertain whether White has enough from calculation alone, Alekhine felt that he had good compensation due to the difficulty Black faces with his development.

16 ... ♔e7

Alekhine pointed out that 16 ... g6 is answered by 17 ♕d3 ♔e7 18 e4 ♘f6 19 ♕f3 and that 16 ... ♗d6 is met by 17 ♕h5+ g6 18 ♘xg6 hxg6 19 ♕xh8+ ♗f8 20 e4 with a continuing attack. Black's last move breaks the pin on the a4-e8 diagonal so Alekhine promptly sets up another one.

17 e4! ♘f6 18 ♗g5 ♕c7 19 ♗f4

Finally White is starting to generate direct threats but the development of White's initiative has been a distinctly gradual process.

19 ... ♕b6

19 ... ♔d8 20 ♘c6+ wins Black's queen but still leaves White behind on material. But his initiative continues unabated after either 20 ... ♘xc6 21 ♗xc7+ ♔xc7 22 e5 ♘d7 23 f4 or 20 ... ♕xc6 21 ♗xc6 ♘xc6 22 ♖d1+ ♘d7 23 e5 Another defensive try is 19 ... ♕b7 but then 20 ♕e3! ♔d8 (or 20 ... ♘xe4 21.♗g5+) 21 ♕d3+ ♔c8 22 ♖b1 ♕xe4 23 ♘f7!! wins in spectacular style.

20 ♖d1 g6 21 ♗g5 ♗g7 22 ♘d7 ♖xd7 23 ♖xd7+ ♔f8 24 ♗xf6 ♗xf6 25 e5 1:0

In the following game Alekhine sacrifices just a pawn and the exchange but it seems by no means clear that he can catch Black's king in the centre.

Alekhine - Junge
Prague 1942

1 d4 d5 2 c4 e6 3 ♘f3 ♘f6 4 g3 dxc4 5 ♕a4+ ♘bd7 6 ♗g2 a6 7 ♕xc4 b5 8 ♕c6 ♖b8 9 0-0 ♗b7 10 ♕c2 c5 11 a4!

Attempting to open files on the queenside at the cost of a pawn. Black should have declined with 11 ... b4 but Junge decides he can safely take it.

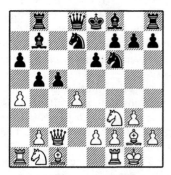

11 ... ♗xf3?! 12 ♗xf3 cxd4 13 axb5 axb5 14 ♖d1 ♕b6 15 ♘d2 e5

A more cautious approach is 15 ... ♗c5 in order to get castled as soon as possible.

16 ♘b3 ♘c5

Once again Black should think about king safety with 16 ... ♗e7. The text gives Alekhine that glimmer of opportunity he needs to catch Black's king in the centre.

17 ♘xc5 ♗xc5

This runs into a stunning reply but by now there was little choice. After 17 ... ♕xc5 18 ♕f5 White threatens things like 19 ♗c6+ (19 ... ♕xc6 20 ♕xe5+) and 19 e3.

18 ⌶a6!!

A brilliant exchange sacrifice that could only be made on intuitive grounds. Black's king is caught in the centre for just long enough.

18 ... ♕xa6 19 ♕xc5 ♕e6

19 ... ♘d7 is answered by 20 ♗c6 with a strong attack after either 20 ... ⌶c8 21 ♕xe5+ ♔d8 22 ♗xd7 or gives 20 ... f6 21 ♕d6.

20 ♗c6+

20 ... ♘d7

After 20 ... ♔d8 White continues his attack with 21 ♗d2 b4 22 ♕a5+ when 22 ... ♔c8 is met by 23 ⌶c1 After 22 ... ♔e7 White can choose between 23 ♕c7+ ♘d7 24 ♗xd7 ♕xd7 25 ♕xe5+ ♕e6 26 ♕xg7 and 23 ♗xb4+ ⌶xb4 24 ♕xb4+ ♕d6 25

♕b7+ with a strong attack in either case.

21 ♗xd7+ ♔xd7 22 ♕a7+

22 ... ♔c6

Having come under such a ferocious attack it is hardly surprising that Black stumbles. 22 ... ♔c8 is bad because of 23 ♗g5 which threatens 24 ⌶c1+ but he had a better defence in 22 ... ♔d6!. White could force a draw with 23 ♗f4 exf4 24 ⌶xd4+ ♔c6 25 ⌶d1 ⌶hc8 26 ⌶c1+ etc and he might try to improve on this by throwing in the moves 23 f4 f6 24 fxe5+ fxe5 before sacrificing a piece with 25 ♗f4 (25 ... exf4 26 ♕xd4+ ♔c6 27 ⌶c1+ ♔b7 28 ♕xg7+ ♔a6 29 ⌶a1+ ♔b6 30 ♕a7+ and 26 ... ♔e7 27 ♕xg7+ ♕f7 28 ⌶d7+ both win Black's queen).

23 ♗d2! ⌶hc8 24 e4!

Taking away the d5 square. The net is gradually tightening around the Black monarch.

24 ... ♕b3 25 ⌶a1! b4

25 ... ⌶b6 is answered by 26 ⌶c1+ and 25 ... ♔d6 by 26 ⌶a6+.

26 ⌶a6+ ♔b5 27 ⌶a5+ ♔c6

Or 27 ... ♔c4 28 ♕a6+ etc.

28 ♕c5+ ♔d7 29 ⌶a7+ 1:0

KMP24/2: 1) White to play

KMP24/2: 2) White to play

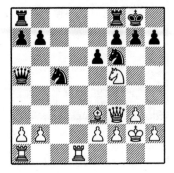

KMP24/2: 3) Black to play

KMP24/2: 4) Black to play

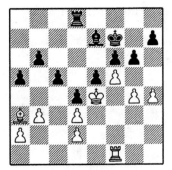

A24/2: a) White to play

A24/2: b) White to play

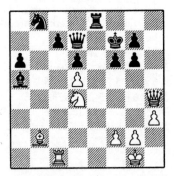

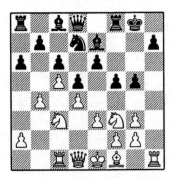

Month 24/Week 3:
Creativity

Creativity is a fundamental aspect of chess mastery in that the process by which we come to understand the game is essentially a creative one. It's no good simply reading a book which explains where to put your rook and which pawn lever to use. In order to make this dead knowledge into living understanding you have to ask questions, play about with the position, test and probe the different possibilities until you know what makes it work. Only then will you really start to understand exactly what is happening.

David Bronstein has one of the most brilliantly creative minds of any chessplayer that I've met. Bronstein loves the dynamics of argument which is fundamental to the creative process and has enabled him to produce so many original ideas. Never accepting the status quo, he is for ever trying to reinvent the wheel.

Bronstein's nature is such that he is unable to play the same way, game after game. As a result he has frequently found himself at a disadvantage against players who have a limited but thoroughly worked out repertoire, at least in the early stages. Yet his lively mind is forever asking questions to which there are no standard answers.

Bronstein - Gligoric
Moscow 1967

1 e4 e5 2 ♘f3 ♘c6 3 ♗b5 a6 4 ♗a4 ♘f6 5 0-0 ♗e7 6 ♗xc6

Bronstein varies from the standard 6 ♖e1 in order to create a different set of problems. Gligoric responds well and in the early stages builds up an excellent position.

6 ... dxc6 7 d3 ♘d7 8 ♘bd2 0-0 9 ♘c4 f6 10 ♘h4 ♘c5 11 ♘f5 ♗xf5 12 exf5 ♖e8 13 b3 ♕d5 14 ♗b2 e4!?

A dynamic move which aims to activate Black's pieces. Black had a solid continuation in 14 ... ♖ad8.

15 ♘e3 ♕f7 16 d4 ♘d7 17 ♕g4 c5

Continuing in the same dynamic style, giving up a pawn for play along the d- and e-files.

18 ♕xe4 cxd4 19 ♗xd4 c6 20 ♖ad1 ♘c5 21 ♕g4 ♗f8 22 ♘c4 ♖ad8 23 ♗e3 b5 24 ♘d2 ♖d5 25 c4 ♖dd8 26 cxb5 cxb5 27 ♘f3 ♖d5 28 ♘d4 ♖ee5 29 ♖d2!?

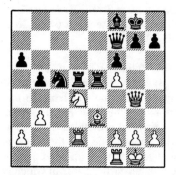

A dubious move according to the notes in *Informator 3* but Bronstein is laying a beautiful trap by luring Black into pinning the knight on d4.

29 ... ♕d7 30 ♖c1 b4 31 h3!?

Continuing to pursue the brilliant idea that Bronstein conceived on his 29th move. Objectively speaking White should simplify with 31 ♘f3.

31 ... ♘e4 32 ♖dc2 ♖xd4 33 ♖c7 ♕d5?

The trap has been laid and Gligoric falls right into it. In fact he could have played 33 ... ♘c3! after which 34 ♖xd7 ♖xg4 35 ♖xc3 bxc3 36 hxg4 c2 37 ♖xc7 ♗c5 even wins for Black.

34 ♗xd4 ♕xd4 35 ♖xg7+!!

A shattering blow which leads to mate.

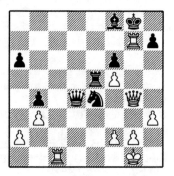

35 ... ♗xg7 36 ♖c8+ ♔f7 37 ♕h5+ ♔e7 38 ♕e8+ ♔d6 39 ♖c6+ ♔d5 40 ♕d7+ 1:0

The following game has been deeply analysed, not least by exponents of Alekhine's Defence. Bronstein adopts the Four Pawns Attack, White's most principled line. Ljubojevic adopts one of the sharpest counters, armed with an improvement on an earlier game in which he had played White.

Bronstein - Ljubojevic
Petropolis Izt 1973

1 e4 ♘f6 2 e5 ♘d5 3 d4 d6 4 c4 ♘b6 5 f4 dxe5 6 fxe5 c5

A less usual option to the more standard 6 ... ♗f5 Ljubojevic's treatment is highly provocative and I can't help questioning the wisdom of playing this way against a Bronstein.

7 d5 e6 8 ♘c3 exd5 9 cxd5 c4!

This move stems from one of the great specialists in Alekhine's Defence, Vladas Mikenas. Black opens up squares for his king's bishop.

10 ♘f3 ♗g4

Quite recently the move 10 ... ♗b4 has become fashionable though whether this is only a temporary phenomena remains to be seen. Lines such as this are subject to dramatic changes, depending on the assessment of the latest new move.

11 ♕d4 ♗xf3 12 gxf3 ♗b4 13 ♗xc4 0-0 14 ♖g1 g6!

Ljubojevic's new move, improving on the game Ljubojevic-Honfi, Cacak 1971 which went 14 ... ♕c7 15 e6 f6 16 ♗h6 ♕xc4 17 ♖xg7+ ♔h8 18 ♖g8+!! ♔xg8 19 ♕g1+1:0.

15 ♗g5 ♕c7 16 ♗b3 ♗c5 17 ♕f4! ♗xg1 18 d6

Calmly opening up the a2-g8 diagonal and driving a wedge into Black's position.

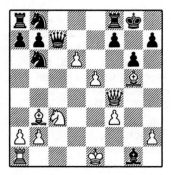

It was in this position that the search for improvements for Black was the most diligent, with Black (Ljubojevic included) having tried 18 ... ♕c5 in a number of later games. It would take a brave man indeed to state definitively that this is bad for Black anyway though the onus is on Black to save himself after 19 ♘e4 ♕d4 20 ♖d1 ♕xb2 21 ♘f6+ ♔h8 22 ♖d2. In any case 18 ... ♕c5 is better than 18 ... ♕c8.

18 ... ♕c8?!

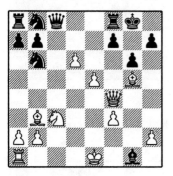

19 ♔e2?!

In such a complex position it is hardly suprising that the players make mistakes. There was a stronger continuation in 19 0-0-0 ♗c5 20 e6! fxe6 21 ♕e5 ♖e8 22 ♗h6 ♕d7 23 ♘e4 ♘c6 24 ♘f6+ etc. Ljubojevic should now have played 19 ... ♕c5 meeting 20 ♘e4 with 20 ... ♕b5+ and 20 e6 with the remarkable 20 ... ♘8d7!!.

19 ... ♗c5? 20 ♘e4 ♘8d7 21 ♖c1 ♕c6

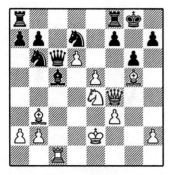

22 ♖xc5!

By giving up the other rook Bronstein penetrates the dark squares around Black's king.

22 ... ♘xc5 23 ♘f6+ ♔h8 24 ♕h4 ♕b5+

25 ♔e3!!

In the thick of battle White sees that the safest place for his king is in the centre! After 25 ... ♕d3+ 26 ♔f2 Black's checks are running out.

25 ... h5 26 ♘xh5 ♕xb3+

A desperate throw but there is little else Black can do. Even with White's knight on h5, 26 ... ♕d3+ 27 ♔f2 is safe enough for White (27 ... ♘e4+ 28 fxe4 ♕d4+ 29 ♔g2 ♕xb2+ 30 ♔h3 ♕c3+ 31 ♘g3+ is curtains).

27 axb3 ♘d5+ 28 ♔d4 ♘e6+ 29 ♔xd5 ♘xg5 30 ♘f6+ ♔g7 31 ♕xg5 ♖fd8

Had Bronstein not been in time-trouble, Ljubojevic would surely have resigned.

32 e6 fxe6+ 33 ♔xe6 ♖f8 34 d7 a5 35 ♘g4 ♖a6+ 36 ♔e5 ♖f5+ 37 ♕xf5 gxf5 38 d8=♕ fxg4 39 ♕d7+ ♔h6 40 ♕xb7 ♖g6 41 f4 1:0

A truly amazing game!

KMP24/3: 1) Black to play

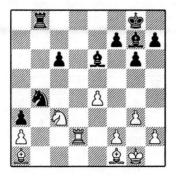

KM24/3: 2) Black to play

KM24/3: 3) White to play

KM24/3: 4) White to play

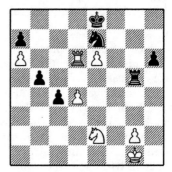

A24/3: a) Black to play

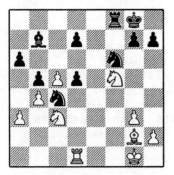

A24/3: b) Black to play

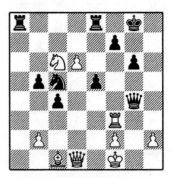

Month 24/Week 4:
Mental Toughness

I have met many players with vision, intuition and creativity yet they can be unable to make the most of these qualities without the requisite mental toughness. Chess is quite unique in the way that it preys upon fear, indecision and lack of confidence.

In the thick of battle do you trust that your opponent has everything worked out? How do you cope with situations in which you need to win your final game? Can your nerves take it if your team needs a draw from you to win the match?

At these times we need to trust our head rather than listen to our fears and this can make the difference between victory and defeat.

The following two games featured crucial match situations with quite different requirements. In the first game Spassky needed only a draw in order to win his match with Keres outright. In the second Kasparov had to win to hold onto his World Championship crown.

Keres - Spassky
Riga Cm 1965

1 d4 ♘f6 2 c4 g6

Already a major surprise. 2 ... g6 is usually associated with sharp, fighting chess rather than 'playing for a draw' but Spassky knew exactly what he was doing. As Krogius pointed out in his book *Psychology In Chess* it is very dangerous just to play for a draw:

"In thinking only of safety the chess player involuntarily exaggerates his opponent's chances and deliberately curbs his own aggressive tendencies, thereby paralyzing and impoverishing his own play. Fear and uncertainty accompany moods of this kind. In the meantime the opponent, greatly encouraged, makes cheeky attacks which can scarcely be beaten off without making a sortie from the stronghold."

Seen in this light Spassky is doing exactly the right thing by going for a full-blooded struggle from the outset.

3 ♘c3 ♗g7 4 e4 d6 5 f4 c5 6 d5 0-0 7 ♘f3 e6 8 ♗e2 exd5 9 cxd5 b5

Yet again Spassky chooses a razor-sharp move. 9 ... ♗g4 has become established as a reliable defence for Black.

10 e5 dxe5 11 fxe5 ♘g4 12 ♗f4

A new move at the time, 12 ♗g5 or 12 ♗xb5 having been played in earlier games. Spassky reacts with great energy, knowing full well that passivity or indecision would spell disaster in such a sharp position.

12 ... ♘d7 13 e6 fxe6 14 dxe6 ♖xf4!

14 ... ♘b6 would favour White after 15 ♕xd8 ♖xd8 16 e7 ♖e8 17 ♗d6.

15 ♕d5

Winning the exchange but conceding the initiative.

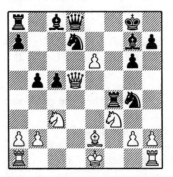

15 ... ♔h8 16 ♕xa8
16 0-0-0 would be dubious because of 16 ... ♖b8 17 ♕d6 ♗h6!.
16 ... ♘b6 17 ♕xa7 ♗xe6 18 0-0 ♘e3

19 ♖f2
Another big decision. Keres had considered playing 19 ♖ad1 but then 19 ... ♘xd1 20 ♖xd1 ♗d4+ 21 ♔h1 b4 22 ♘b5 ♗d5! sets in motion a counterattack. Another idea was 19 ♗xb5!? but then 19 ... ♘xf1 20 ♖xf1 ♖f7 gives Black compensation for his pawn.
19 ... b4 20 ♘b5
In a later game (Bartis-Smetan, 1970) White tried to improve at this point with 20 ♘d1 but instead of Smetan's 20 ... ♘g4 (which was answered by 21 ♘g5! threatening 22 ♕xg7+!) Spassky intended first 20 ... ♖f7! 21 ♕a5 and only then 21 ... ♘g4 with a strong attack.
20 ... ♖f7 21 ♕a5 ♕b8 22 ♖e1 ♗d5! 23 ♗f1 ♘xf1 24 ♖fxf1 ♘c4 25 ♕a6 ♖f6 26 ♕a4 ♘xb2! 27 ♕c2?
The losing move. White should play 27 ♕a5 when the position remains very tense.
27 ... ♕xb5 28 ♖e7
Keres had missed the fact that 28 ♕xb2 is refuted by 28 ... ♖xf3.

28 ... ♘d3 29 ♕e2 c4 30 ♖e8+ ♖f8 31 ♖xf8+ ♗xf8 32 ♘g5 ♗c5+ 33 ♔h1 ♕d7 34 ♕d2 ♕e7 35 ♘f3 ♕e3 0:1

Needing a win at all costs, many players would be tempted to lurch towards their opponent's kingside and throw everything into the attack, including the kitchen sink. In the next game Kasparov handles things quite differently, opening the game in very quiet style and aiming above all to keep the tension. This is psychological torture for a player who needs only a draw.

Kasparov - Karpov
Seville WCh 1987

1 c4 e6 2 ♘f3 ♘f6 3 g3 d5 4 b3 ♗e7 5 ♗g2 0-0 6 0-0 b6 7 ♗b2 ♗b7 8 e3 ♘bd7 9 ♘c3 ♘e4 10 ♘e2
Kasparov keeps the tension at a maximum by avoiding exchanges.
10 ... a5 11 d3 ♗f6 12 ♕c2 ♗xb2 13 ♕xb2 ♘d6 14 cxd5 ♗xd5 15 d4 c5 16 ♖fd1 ♖c8?!
Already a slight mistake after which Black has to exchange off his bishop. 16 ... ♕e7 was a better choice.

17 ♘f4 ♗xf3 18 ♗xf3 ♕e7 19
♖ac1 ♖fd8 20 dxc5 ♘xc5 21 b4!

Exposing Black's b6 pawn as a
target. 21 ... ♘ce4 is met by 22
♖xc8 ♖xc8 23 ♕d4! according to
Taimanov.

**21 ... axb4 22 ♕xb4 ♕a7 23 a3
♘f5 24 ♖b1 ♖xd1+ 25 ♖xd1 ♕c7
26 ♘d3! h6?!**

26 ... g6 was a better way to make
'luft' for his king.

27 ♖c1 ♘e7 28 ♕b5 ♘f5 29 a4!

Kasparov tightens his grip, the advance of the a-pawn underlining the
insecurity of the knight on c5.

**29 ... ♘d6 30 ♕b1 ♕a7 31 ♘e5!
♘xa4?**

31 ... ♘f5 was a better defensive
try.

32 ♖xc8+ ♘xc8

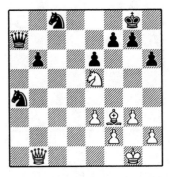

33 ♕d1?

As the time-control approaches
both sides make some errors. 33
♕b5! was better as now Black could
have equalised with 33 ... ♘c5!.
After missing this opportunity Karpov slips into a nightmarish
endgame.

**33 ... ♘e7? 34 ♕d8+ ♔h7 35
♘xf7 ♘g6 36 ♕e8 ♕e7 37 ♕xa4
♕xf7 38 ♗e4 ♔g8 39 ♕b5 ♘f8 40
♕xb6 ♕f6 41 ♕b5 ♕e7 42 ♔g2 g6**

**43 ♕a5 ♕g7 44 ♕c5 ♕f7 45 h4
h5?**

45 ... ♔g7 was a better defence
but Black would have the most miserable defensive chore in any case.

**46 ♕c6 ♕e7 47 ♗d3 ♕f7 48
♕d6 ♔g7 49 e4 ♔g8 50 ♗c4 ♔g7
51 ♕e5+ ♔g8 52 ♕d6 ♔g7 53 ♗b5
♔g8 54 ♗c6 ♕a7 55 ♕b4 ♕c7 56
♕b7 ♕d8**

57 e5!

The winning move. Black's
pieces are completely tied up.

**57 ... ♕a5 58 ♗e8 ♕c5 59 ♕f7+
♔h8 60 ♗a4 ♕d5+ 61 ♔h2 ♕c5
62 ♗b3 ♕c8 63 ♗d1 ♕c5 64 ♔g2**

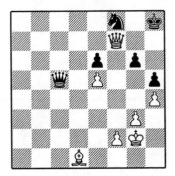

1:0

The winning line is 64 ... ♕d5+
65 ♗f3 ♕c5 66 ♗e4 ♕a3 67 ♔h3!
♕b4 68 f3 ♕b8 69 f4 ♕d8 70 ♗xg6
♘xg6 71 ♕xg6 ♕xh4+ 72 ♔g2!+-.

KM24/4: 1) Black to play

KM24/4: 2) White to play

KM24/4: 3) Black to play

KM24/4: 4) White to play

A24/4: a) Black to play

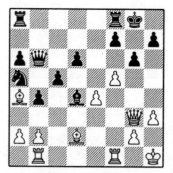

A24/4: b) Black to play

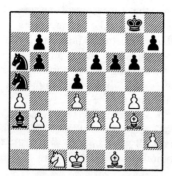

Key Moves Solutions

Months 13-24

KM13/1

1) 1 ♘xe5! ♗xd1 2 ♘d7! ♗e7 3 ♘exf6+ ♗xf6 4 ♖e8+ ♕xe8 5 ♘xf6# **Kazic-Vukovic, Yugoslavia 1970**

2) 1 ♕h7+!! ♔xh7 2 ♘f6+ ♔h8 (2 ... ♔xh6 3 ♖h3+ ♔g5 4 ♖g3+ ♔h6 5 ♖g6# or 4 ... ♔f4 5 ♘h5#) 3 ♗xg7+ ♔xg7 4 ♖g3+ ♔xf6 (4 ... ♔h6 5 ♖g6#, 4 ... ♔f8 [or h8] 5 ♖g8#) 5 ♖g6# **1:0 Engles-Beratende, 1943**

3) 1 ... f5+ 2 exf6 (2 ♔h4 ♕h1#) 2 ♕f5+ 3 ♔h4 ♕f5# 0:1 **Borisenko-Simagin, Moscow 1955**

4) 1 ... ♘h1+! 2 ♖xh1 ♖df2, 3 ... ♖8f3#, **Dietrich-Bauer, Austria 1967**

KM13/2

1) 1 ... ♘f3+ 2 gxf3 ♗xf3 0:1 (3 hxg3 ♖h1#, 3 h3 ♖xh3, 4 ... ♖h1#) **Zollner-Velasco, Munich 1934**

2) 1 ♗b4! forces 1 ... ♕xb4 as 1 ... axb4 leads to mate after 2 ♘e7+ ♔h8 3 ♕xh7+ ♔xh7 4 ♖h2#

3) 1 ♕xh6! gxh6 2 ♘f6+ ♔h8 3 ♘xd7+ ♔g8 (3 ... ♔h7 4 ♘xf8+, 5 ♘d7+-) 4 ♖e8! ♘c6 5 dxc6 ♕a7 6 c7 1:0 **Spassky-Kholmov, USSR tch, Rostov 1971**

4) 1 ♖c6+! ♔xd5 2 ♗g2# **Straonttinch-Zauerman, corr 1984**

KM13/3

1) 1 ♘f6+ gxf6 2 ♖xe8+ 1:0 (2 ... ♕xe8 3 ♗xf6; 2 ... ♗xe8 3 ♕h6 [threatening 4 ♗xf6] 3 ... ♕d7 4 ♕xf6 ♔f8 5 ♖e1+-) **Tompa-Herrou, Val Thorens 1980**

2) 1 ♕h6! 1:0 (1 ... gxh6 2 ♘xh6# or 1 ... ♗f6 2 ♗xf6) **Spassky-Marszalek, World Student Cht 1955**

3) 1 ... ♖xh3! -+ (2 ♖xh3 ♖c4#, 2 ♖xc7 ♖b3# or 2 ♖fc2 ♖c4+ 3 ♖xc4 ♖b3#) **Pines-Gabis, USSR 1955**

4) 1 ♗g5!! 1:0 (1 ... fxg5 2 ♔g6 or 1 ... g1=♕ 2 ♗xf6+ ♔g8 3 h7+ etc) **Perenyi-Brandics, Budapest 1985**

KM13/4

1) 1 ♖f4! 1:0 (1 ... ♕xf4 2 ♕xh7# or 1 ... ♕xd3 2 ♖xf8#) **Belov-Ongemakh, Narva 1984**

2) 1 ♖xe5! fxe5 2 ♘g5 ♗f6 (2 ... ♗c8 3 ♗xg7, 4 ♕xh7+) 3 ♘xe6 1:0 **Tal-Timman, Nice Ol 1974**

3) 1 ... ♗f5!! 2 ♕xa8 ♕d6+ 3 ♔c1 ♘a1! (threatening 4 ... ♘b3#) 4 ♕xb7 (4 b4 ♕c6+ 5 ♔b2 ♕c2+ 6 ♔xa1 ♕b1#; 4 ♗c4 ♕c5 5 b3 ♘xb3+) 4 ♕c7+!! 0:1 (5 ♕xc7 ♘b3#) **Vaganian-Planinc, Hastings 1974-5**

4) 1 ♖xf7+ ♗xf7 2 ♘f5+ ♔e6 (2 ... ♔e8 3 ♖d8#) 3 ♘g7+ ♔e7 4 ♗d8# **Hever-Siklaj, Hungary 1975**

KM14/1

1) 1 ♕g5+! ♗xg5 2 hxg5+ ♔xh5 3 g4# Sherzer-Mate, Budapest 1989

2) 1 ... ♕c6! 2 ♕xc6 (2 ♖xc6 ♖a1+ 3 ♗f1 ♗h3) 2 ... bxc6 3 ♗f3 ♗h3-+ Barcza-Keres, Tallinn 1969

3) 1 ... ♖h1+! 2 ♔xh1 ♗xf2-+ (3 ... ♖h8#) Cevallos-Mohring, Tel Aviv 1964

4) 1 ... ♖e3+! 2 ♔d4 ♔e6 (threatening 3 ... ♘f5#) 3 c5 ♘f5+ 4 ♔c4 b5+! 5 ♔xb5 ♖xb3+ -+ Prins-Denker, Hastings 1945-46

KM14/2

1) 1 ♕xg8+!+- (1 ... ♔xg8 2 ♖exg7+ ♔h8 3 ♖g8+ ♔h7 4 ♖2g7#) Alapin-Levitsky, St Petersburg 1911

2) 1 ... ♖e1+ 2 ♔g2 ♖g1+! 3 ♔xg1 ♕e1+ 4 ♔g2 ♕f1+! 5 ♔xf1 ♗h3+ 6 ♔g1 ♖e1# Netto-Abente, Peru 1983

3) 1 ... ♘b6! 0:1 Popov-Emelyanenko, Corres. 1984-85

4) 1 ♘e5! (threatening 2 ♗g5, 2 ♖f7 and 2 ♘g6) +- Benjamin-Dlugy, New York 1988

KM14/3

1) 1 ♕xf7+ ♔xf7 2 ♗d5# Pape-Stanke, Wernogerode 1980

2) 1 ... ♖b1+ 2 ♔g2 ♘f4+! 3 ♔f3 (3 ♕xf4 ♕xa6; 3 gxf4 ♕xg4+) 3 ... ♘e6 = Engelbert-Hofmann, Schleusingen 1961

3) 1 ♗xe4+! fxe4 2 ♖e5+! (2 ♖xe4? ♖e2+) = Lisitsin-Bondarevsky, Leningrad 1950

4) 1 ... ♘f5+ 2 ♔d3 ♖xc3+ 3 ♔xc3 ♘e3! 4 ♖xf2 ♘d1+! 5 ♔d4 ♘xf2-+ Pirc-R Byrne, Helsinki Ol 1952

KM14/4

1) 1 ♕h6! (1 ... gxh6 2 ♘xh6#)+- Kotronias-King, New York 1990

2) 1 d5! (1 ♘xe8 ♖xe8 is less clear) 1 ... ♘xd5 2 fxe4 ♗xe4 3 ♘xf7 (threatening 4 ♘h6+) 3 ... ♕xf7+- Davies-Wessman, Katrineholm 1995

3) 1 ♖h8+ ♔g6 2 f5+ exf5 3 ♕xh6+ gxh6 4 ♖ag8# Bernstein-Kotov, Groningen 1946

4) 1 ♖d8!+- (1 ... ♖xd8 2 c7+; 1 ... ♗g7 2 ♖b7#) Sznapik-Bernard, Poznan 1971

KM15/1

1) 1 ... ♗e6 2 ♖xa5 ♗xb3 = Cebalo-Nogueiras, Taxco Izt 1985

2) 1 ♕a8! ♖xa8 2 fxe7+- Paglilla-Carbone, Argentina 1985

3) 1 g5+! fxg5 2 ♕xh7+! ♔xh7 3 ♘xg5+, 4 ♘xh3+- Maroczy-Rubinstein, Prague 1908

4) 1 ♖xf2! gxf2 2 ♖xf5! ♔xf5 3 g4+ ♔xg4 4 ♔g2+-

KM15/2

1) 1 ... f5! prevented White from taking the initiative with e2-e4 in **Karpov-Kasparov, London/Leningrad WCh 1986**

2) 1 ... h5! 2 ♖ef1 ♖h6! prevented White from taking the initiative on the kingside with g2-g4 in **Kupchik-Capablanca, Lake Hopatcong 1926**. Black later took the initiative on the queenside with an advance of his a- and b- pawns.

3) 1 a4! ♔g7 2 g6 ♔g8 3 ♔f6 ♔f8 4 g7+ ♔g8 5 ♔g6+-

4) 1 ... h5! should be played in order to prevent h4-h5 by White. In **Korchnoi-Antoshin, Erevan 1954**, White to play won after 1 h5 ♖a5 2 g4 ♖a7 3 ♖c6 ♖a3 4 f3 ♖a5 5 ♖c8+ ♔h7 6 f4 ♖a2+ 7 ♔f3 ♖a3+ 8 ♔f2

罝a2+ 9 ♔e3 罝a3+ 10 ♔d4 罝g3 11
罝f8 f6 12 e5 罝xg4 13 e6 罝xf4+ 14
♔d5 罝f5+ 15 ♔d6 罝xh5 16 e7 罝e5
17 e8=♕ 罝xe8 18 罝xe8 ♔g6 19
♔d5 ♔f5 20 罝e1 h5 21 罝f1+ ♔g4
22 ♔e4 g5 23 罝xf6 h4 24 ♔e3 ♔g3
25 ♔e2 g4 26 ♔f1 ♔h2 27 罝f4 h3
28 罝xg4 ♔h1 29 ♔f2 h2 30 ♔g3
♔g1 31 ♔h3+ 1:0

KM15/3

1) 1 ... f5! prevents g2-g4 and
f4-f5 and controls e4

2) 1 a4! b4 (1 ... bxa4 2 ♘xa4 and
3 b3 also blockades the queenside) 2
♘b5 d5 3 c4 bxc3 4 bxc3 killed
Black's queenside play in **Spassky-
Larsen, Malmo Cm 1968**

3) 1 ... ♔e8! 2 ♗xb6 ♔e7 brought
about a blockade **Kobaidze-
Cereteli**, USSR 1969

4) 1 ♕d2! (1 ♘xb6+?? cxb6 2 h4
gxh4 3 ♕d2 h3! 4 gxh3 h4! brought
about a blockade in **A.Petrosian-
Hazai, Belgium 1970**) followed by
2 ♔b3, 3 ♘c3, 4 ♔a4 and
♘a2-c1-b3xa5 wins for White.

KM15/4

1) 1 ... ♘c3! (2 bxc3 ♗a3#) 0:1
**Rosenthal-Makogonov, Moscow
1936**

2) 1 ... 罝f3+! 0:1 (2 gxf3 ♕e3+ 3
♔g3 ♕xf3+ and 2 ♔g1 ♕e1+ 3
♔h2 ♕g3+ 4 ♔g1 罝e1+) **Kmoch-
Rubinstein, Semmering 1926**

3) 1 ... ♔c6! (1 ... ♔e6 2 ♔g3
♔f6 3 h3 ♔g6 4 ♔h4 makes steady
progress) 2 ♔g3 (2 g5 罝b5=) 2 ...
♔b6 3 罝a8 ♔b5 4 h3 ♔b4 5 ♔f4
罝c2 6 罝b8+ ♔c3 7 罝a8 ♔b4 ½-½
**Reshevsky-Alekhine, Amsterdam
1938**

4) 1 ♔g6! (1 ♔f6 c4 2 bxc4 bxc4
3 ♔e5 c3 4 bxc3 a3-+) 1 ... ♔xh4 2
♔f5 ♔g3 (2 ... c4 3 bxc4 bxc4 3

♔e4 c3 4 bxc3 a4? 5 ♔d3!+-) 3
♔e4 ♔f2 4 ♔d5 ♔e3 5 ♔xc5 ♔d3
6 ♔xb5 ♔c2 7 ♔xa5 ♔xb3 ½-½
**Lasker-Tarrasch, St Petersburg
1914**

KM16/1

1) 1 ♕xf8+ 罝xf8 2 罝xh7+ ♔xh7
3 罝h1# **Skuja-Rosenberg, Riga
1962**

2) 1 ♗e6!! 1:0 (1 ... ♕xh4 2
罝xf8+, 1 ... 罝xf3 2 ♕xd8+ or 1 ...
罝e8 2 ♕xd8, 3 罝f8+) **Pisarsky-Markushev, Novosibirsk
1983**

3) 1 ♕e1+! 1:0 (1 ... 罝xe1 2 g3#)
**Stahlberg-Becker, Buenos Aires
1944**

4) 1 h4! 罝b4+ 2 ♔xe5 罝xh4 3 f4!
罝xf4 4 罝xg7+ ♔xg7 5 罝xg5+, 6
♔xf4+- **Khalomeyev-Isakov,
Simferopol 1947**

KM16/2

1) 1 a4! set about obtaining a
passed a-pawn in **Smyslov-
Duckstein, Zagreb 1955**

2) 1 ... ♕b4! 2 ♕xb4 axb4 3 ♘e4
♗xe4 4 fxe4 罝xa4 5 ♗xc7 f5! 6 e5
罝c8 7 ♗d6 ♘g4 8 e3 罝a1+ 9 ♔e2
罝c2+ 10 罝d2 b3! 0:1
**Sajtar-Smyslov, Moscow-Prague
1946**

3) 1 a4! improved the position of
White's a-pawn and prevented
Black from gaining counterplay by
bringing his rook to a6 at some
moment **Reti-Romanovsky,
Moscow 1925**

4) 1 ... h5! prevented White from
exchanging the powerful knight on
d5 (with ♘e5-g4-e3) in **Zakharov-
Dvoretsky, USSR 1978**. Black
went on to win after 2 罝d2 f6 3 ♘f3
罝c4 4 b3 罝c6 5 h4 g4 6 ♘e1 ♘c7 7
罝xh5 ♔g6 0:1

KM16/3

1) 1 ... ♗g3! (1 ... ♕xd1+ 2 ♔h2)
2 ♕b5 ♕xd1+ 3 ♕f1 ♗h2+ 4 ♔f2
♗g3+ = **Lengyel-Davies, Budapest
1993**

2) 1 ♖e8+! ♘xe8 2 ♕h7+! ♔xh7
3 ♘f8+ ♔h8 4 ♘g6+ =
Neumann-NN, 1956

3) 1 ♖xe5! ♖xe5 2 g3 f4 3 g4+-

4) 1 g4+! hxg4 (1 ... ♔e4 2 ♖d4#)
2 ♖d5+! exd5 3 ♕c8+! ♕xc8 =
Zazdis-Zemitis, Riga 1936

KM16/4

1) 1 ♖xf8+ ♗xf8 2 ♕g8+! ♔xg8
3 ♘h6+ ♔h8 4 ♘f7+ =
Kratkovsky-Lapienis, USSR 1982

2) 1 ♗e5!! (1 ... ♖xe5 2 ♕xg7#; 1
... ♗xe5 2 ♕xe8+ ♔h7 3 ♕g6+
♔g8 4 ♖d8#) 1:0 **Miles-Pritchett,
London 1982**

3) 1 ... ♕g4+! 2 ♔h6 (2 ♔xg4 =)
2 ... ♕g5+ (3 ♔f6 ♕e6+) ½-½
Portisch-Lengyel, Malaga 1964

4) 1 ♖h8+! ♔xh8 (1 ... ♔g6?? 2
♕e6#) 2 ♖b8+ ♔h7 3 ♖h8+ ♔xh8
4 ♕xg7+ = **Stolberg-Pimenov,
Rostov-on-Don 1941**

KM17/1

1) 1 ♘e4! ♘xe4 2 ♖xd7+-
**Gligoric-Stahlberg, Zurich Ct
1953**

2) 1 ♖d5! ♖xd5 (1 ... ♖c4 2 b3
♖d4 3 ♔e3 f6 4 ♘a4 ♔e7 5 ♘c5
♖xd5 6 exd5 ♘b4 7 d6+ is also
good for White) 2 exd5 ♘d4+ 3
♔d3 ♔e7 4 f4! f6 5 fxe5 fxe5 6
♔e4 ♔d6 7 ♖f1 ♖c8 8 ♖f7+-
**Rubinstein-Mieses, St Petersburg
1909**

3) 1 ... ♗xe4 2 ♗xe4 ♘e5
produced a position in which
Black's queen and knight were
stronger than queen and bishop in
**Znosko Borovsky - Tartakower,
Paris 1933**

4) 1 ♗xa6! (1 ♕e3 ♕c5 2 ♕xc5
♘xc5 3 ♖fb1 ♖fd8 4 ♗f1 ♖d6 was
very bad for White in **Kasparov-
Korchnoi, London Cm 1983**)
produces a position in which White
has good drawing chances as there
are only major pieces on the board.

KM17/2

1) 1 ... ♖a4! 2 ♖xa4 bxa4 3 ♔f3
(Or 3 f5 ♔f7 4 ♔f4 ♔f6 5 ♔e4 ♔e7
6 ♔d4 ♔f6 7 ♔c4 ♔xf5 8 ♔b4 ♔e6
9 ♔xa4 ♔d7=) 3 ♔f5 4 ♔e3 ♔f6 5
♔d4 ♔f5 6 ♔c5 ♔xf4 7 ♔b5 ♔e5
8 ♔xa4 ♔d6 ½-½ **Speelman-
Chandler, Hastings 1987-88**

2) 1 a4! (**Guliev-Tukmakov,
Nikolaev 1993** went 1 ♔e3?? ♔d6
2 ♔e4 c4 3 a4 c3 4 ♔d3 ♔xd5 0:1)
1 ... ♔d6 2 a5 c4 (2 ... ♔xd5 3 a6!,
4 b6!) 3 a6! (3 b6? a6!=) 3 ... ♔c5 4
d6! ♔xd6 5 b6+-

3) 1 ♖c7!! b1=♕ 2 ♖d8! ♕e4 (2
... d1=♕ 3 ♖b8+ ♔a3 4 ♖a7+, 5
♖xa4+, 6 ♖xb1; 2 ... ♕f1 3 ♖b8+
♕b5 4 ♖xb5+, 5 ♖d7) 3 ♖b8+ ♔a3
4 ♖a7+ ♕a4 5 ♖xa4+ ♔xa4 6
♖d8+- (From a study by
Olmoutsky, 1964)

4) 1 ... ♗xe4! 2 ♗xe4 ♔a4 3 ♗f5
♔b3 4 ♗xg4 e4 5 ♗xh3 ♔xc3 6 g4
♔d2 0:1 **Bisguier-Fischer, New
York 1967**

KM17/3

1) 1 ♖d5! (zugzwang) 1 ... ♖a3 (1
... ♗f8 2 ♖d7+ ♔e8 3 ♖c7 ♗e7 4
♔g6 ♗f8 5 ♖c8+ etc) 2 ♗xc5 ♗xc5
3 ♖xc5 ♖xb3 4 ♖c7+ ♔f8 5 ♔g6
♖f3 6 ♖f7+ ♔e8 7 ♖xg7 ♖f4 8 h5
♖xc4 9 ♔xh6+- **Capablanca-
Kostic, Havana 1919**

2) 1 ♗e8! (zugzwang) 1 ... ♔d8 2
♗xg6! ♘xg6 3 ♔xb6 ♔d7 4 ♔xc5
♘e7 5 b4 axb4 6 cxb4 ♘c8 7 a5
♘d6 8 b5 ♘e4+ 9 ♔b6 ♔c8 10

♔c6 ♚b8 11 b6 1:0 Fischer-Taimanov, Vancouver Cm 1971

3) 1 ♖b2!! (zugzwang) 1 ... f4 2 ♗xf4 ♖f5+ 3 ♔h6 b5 4 ♗d6 b4 5 g4 ♖xf3 6 g5 ♘e6 7 ♔xg6 ♖d3+- Fischer-Tal, Curacao Ct 1962

4) 1 ... ♖b1! (1 ... ♘b4 2 ♖d2 ♖b1 3 ♘b2 ♖xb2 4 ♖xb2 ♘d3+ 4 ♔e2 ♘xb2 5 ♔d2 =) 2 ♔e2 (2 ♔e1 ♘a5 3 ♔d2 ♖xb3 4 ♖xb3 ♘xb3+ 5 ♔c3 was tougher) 2 ... ♖xb3!-+ Lasker-Capablanca, Havana WCh 1921

KM17/4

1) 1 ♔g2! calmly improved White's position in **Karpov-Gligoric, Leningrad Izt 1973**

2) 1 ... ♗d4! (preventing White from using his king actively unless he further weakened his kingside with f2-f3 or f2-f4) 2 ♔e2 ♔g7 3 f3 ♗d5 4 h3 ♔f6 5 ♘e8+ ♔f7 6 ♘d6+ ♔e6 7 f4 ♗c6 8 g4 ♗b6 9 ♘c8 ♗d8 10 ♔e3 ♗b7 11 ♘d6 ♗b6+ 12 ♔d3 ♗a6+ 13 ♔c3 ♗c7 14 gxf5+ gxf5 15 ♘e8 ♗xf4 and Black won in **Darga-Portisch, Beverwijk 1964**

3) 1 h3! calmly strengthened White's position in **Botvinnik-Langeweg, Hamburg 1965** and he went on to win after 1 ... ♘fe8 2 ♔g2 ♔f8 3 ♔g3 ♔e7 4 ♖a5 ♘c8 5 ♖e5+ ♔d8 6 ♗b5 ♖e7 7 ♖xe7 ♔xe7 8 ♗xe8 ♔xe8 9 ♔f4 ♔d7 10 ♗c5 1:0

4) 1 ... a5! improved Black's position in **Averbakh-Keres, USSR Ch, Moscow 1950** and he won after 2 ♔h4 ♘xd4 3 ♗h6 ♘e6 4 ♗e3 c5 5 ♔h5 ♔e5 6 ♗c1 ♘d4 7 ♗h6 ♔f6 8 ♗g5+ ♔e6 9 ♗h6 gxh6 10 ♔xh6 ♘c6 11 g7 ♘e7 12 ♔h7 ♔f7 13 ♔h6 ♔g8 14 f4 ♔f7 0:1

KM18/1

1) 1 ♖xe7! (1 ... ♖xe7 2 f6+ +-) 1:0 **Brooks-Kornfeld, Chicago 1982**

2) 1 ... ♖xc3! 2 ♕xc3 ♕xc3 3 bxc3 ♖c8 gave Black excellent compensation for the exchange in **Holmes-Ward, London 1991**

3) 1 c4! e5 (1 ... bxc4 2 ♗xc4; 1 ... ♘c7 2 ♗e4) 2 ♗e4! ♘c7 3 ♗xb7 ♖xb7 4 ♗e3+- **Beliavsky-Watson, London 1985**

4) 1 h6! ♗f8 (1 ... ♗h8 2 ♖h1) 2 ♔c3 (2 g5 seems strong after 2 ... ♖a5 3 ♖b1 ♖xa2 4 c5+- or 3 ... ♖a3+ 4 ♖b3) 2 ... fxg4 3 ♗xg4 ♔f7 4 ♗e6+ ♔f6 5 ♗g8 ♖c7 6 ♗xh7 e6 7 ♗g8 exd5 8 h7 ♗g7?? (8 ... ♖xc4+ 9 ♔d3 ♗g7) 9 ♗xd5+- ♗h8 10 ♔d3 ♔f5 11 ♔e3 ♖e7+ 12 ♔f3 a5 13 a4 ♖c7 14 ♗e4+ ♔f6 15 ♖h6 ♖g7 16 ♔g4 1:0 **Karpov-Kavalek, Nice Ol 1974**

KM18/2

1) 1 ... c5! left White with horrific dark-square weaknesses in **Guseinov-Muratov, Moscow 1995**

2) 1 ... d3 2 ♗xd3 ♗xb2 3 ♖ab1 ♗e5-+ **Martin-Ivkov, Buenos Aires 1955**

3) 1 ... g5! 2 g3 (Or 2 fxg5 ♗xe5) 2 ... gxf4 2 gxf4 ♗h6 0:1 **Serebro-Frolov, Kherson 1990**

4) 1 ... b5! 2 bxc5 bxc4 gave Black a strong initiative in the game **Knezevic-I.Zaitsev, Dubna 1976**

KM18/3

1) 1 ♗xc6! gave Black permanent structural weaknesses in **Larsen-Huebner, Leningrad Izt 1973**

2) 1 ♗d6! (1 ♗a3 ♘f6 Davies-Kinsman, Wrexham 1997) keeps Black tied up as 1 ... ♘f6 2 ♗xc6 wins the e5 pawn

3) 1 ♖b5! is an excellent technical move which tied Black down to the a-pawn in **Polugaevsky-Ivkov, Hilversum 1973**

4) 1 ♗xe4! ♖dxe4 2 ♖xe4 ♖xe4 3 ♖xa6+ ♔h5 4 f3! (threatening 5 g4) 1:0 **Rubinstein - Gruenfeld, Semmering 1926**

KM18/4

1) 1 b6! axb6 2 a7! ♖xa7 3 ♖g7+ +- **Buchers-Petri, Correspondence 1958**

2) 1 ♔g7 h4 2 ♔f6 ♔b6 (2 h3 3 ♔e6 h2 4 c7 ♔b7 5 ♔d7=) 3 ♔e5! h3 4 ♔d6! h2 5 c7= (Reti, 1921)

3) 1 a4 ♔b3 2 a5 ♔c4 (After 2 ♔c3 White should play 3 ♔b1! ♔d4 4 a6 ♔e3 5 ♔f1+- rather than 3 a6 ♔d2! when Black draws) 3 a6 ♔d3 4 a7 f2 5 a8=♕ f1=♕ 6 ♕a6+ and 7 ♕xb1+- (Rinck, 1922)

4) 1 ... b4! 2 axb4 ♖xh4! 3 gxh4 c3+ 4 bxc3 a3 0:1 **Lund-Nimzowitsch, Oslo 1921**

KM19/1

1) 1 ♘xe4!! ♘xe4 2 ♕g6+ ♔d8 3 ♖xd5+! 1:0 (3 ... ♔c7 4 ♕f7+ ♔b8 5 ♖b3 ♕xb3 6 ♘c6#) **Spielmann-Oskam, Scheveningen 1923**

2) 1 e5! (threatening e5-e6 followed by g2-g4 and h3-h4) 1 ... fxe5 2 f6! ♖e6 (2 ... ♖xf6 3 ♖xf6 gxf6 4 ♕g6+; 2 ... ♖xf6 3 ♕xe8+) 3 f7+ ♔h8 4 ♕f5 e4 5 ♕xe6 exd3 6 ♖ad1 1:0 **Spielmann-Speijer, Hamburg 1910**

3) 1 f5! ♗d6 2 ♗f4 brought the bishop to a highly effective post in **Spielmann-Reti, Moscow 1925**

4) 1 g4! fxg4 2 ♗xg4 ♗f7 3 ♘e4 h5 4 ♘f6! ♔e7 5 ♘xh5+- **Spielmann-Saemisch, Karlsbad 1929**

KM19/2

1) 1 ... ♘xh2! (2 ♗xh2 ♕xd4; 2 ♔xh2 ♗xb4!, 3 ... ♕h4#) -+ **Sigurjonsson-Stein, Reykjavik 1972**

2) 1 g7+! ♘xg7 2 h7! 1:0 **Stein-Kholmov, USSR Ch, Leningrad 1963**

3) 1 ... c3! (1 bxc3 b3) 0:1 **Furman-Stein, USSR Ch, Leningrad 1963**

4) 1 ... ♗h8! (2 ♔f7 f5! 3 ♔g8 ♗a1) 0:1 **Antoshin-Stein, Havana 1968**

KM19/3

1) 1 ♕xd7+ ♔xd7 2 ♘c5+ **Tal-Tringov, Munich Ol 1958**

2) 1 ♗a4! ♖c8 2 ♗d7!+- **Tal-Vasiukov, USSR Ch, Kharkov 1967**

3) 1 ♗f8! ♔xf8 2 ♖h8+ ♔e7 3 ♖xa8 ♔d6 4 f6 gxf6 5 g7 ♘ce7 6 ♖xa6+ 1:0 **Tal-Tauve, Riga 1965**

4) 1 ♘xc8 ♖xc8 2 a4! bxa4 3 ♖xa4+- **Tal-Benko, Portoroz Izt 1958**

KM19/4

1) 1 ♘xg7! ♗xg7 2 ♗h6 1:0 **Kasparov-Najdorf, Bugojno 1982**

2) 1 ♘c8! ♘c6 (1 ... ♖xc8 2 ♕f5 xc8, h7) 2 ♘xa7 ♘xa7 3 ♗d5 1:0 **Kasparov-Ligterink, Malta Ol 1980**

3) 1 ♖xd5! exd5 2 ♘a6+ ♔b7 3 ♘xb8 ♔xb8 4 ♔e3 ♔c7 5 ♔d4 ♔c6 6 a4 ♔b6 7 ♔xd5 ♔a5 8 ♔d6 ♔xa4 9 ♔e7 f5 10 ♔f7 1:0 **Kasparov-Galle, Wattignies 1976**

4) 1 ♖xc4! ♗a3? (1 ... ♘xc4 2 ♘xc4 ♗c5) 2 ♖xc7 ♗xb2 3 ♖c5! (3 ... ♘b7 4 ♖c8+ ♔f7 5 ♖c7+) 1:0 **Kasparov-Kharitonov, Leningrad 1977**

KM20/1

1) 1 ♖f8+! ♗xf8 2 d6+ ♗e6 3 ♗xe6# Steinitz-Wilson, London 1862

2) 1 ... ♕h4! 2 ♖g2 (2 ♖xh4 ♖g1#) 2 ... ♕xh2+ 3 ♖xh2 ♖g1# Rainer-Steinitz, Vienna 1860

3) 1 ... ♖e3+! (1 ... ♖xd5 2 cxd5 ♔g6 3 c4=) 2 ♔f2 ♖c3! 3 ♖xc5 ♖xc2+ 4 ♔f3 ♖xh2 5 ♖c8 ♖c2 6 c5 ♖c3+ 0:1 Gelbfuhs-Steinitz, Vienna 1873

4) 1 ♗xe7! ♘xe7 2 ♗f7! ♔d6 3 ♔e3 ♔c5 4 ♔f4 ♔d6 5 b3 ♔c5 6 ♗xg6 ♘xg6+ 7 ♔xf5 1:0 Steinitz-Chigorin, Vienna 1898

KM20/2

1) 1 ♘xe5! (1 ... fxe5 2 ♕xe5 ♗f6 3 ♕xf6!+-)+- Nimzowitsch-Rubinstein, Semmering 1926

2) 1 ♗f6!! ♕xf6 2 ♖he1+ ♗e7 (2 ... ♗e6 3 ♕d7#) 3 ♗xc6+ ♔f8 (3 ... bxc6 4 ♕d8#) 4 ♕d8+! ♗xd8 5 ♖e8# Nimzowitsch-Alapin, St Petersburg 1913

3) 1 ... ♗xh3! 2 ♗f1 (2 ♔xh3 ♖h1#; 2 gxh3 ♘f3+ 3 ♕xf3 ♕g1#) 2 ... ♗d7 3 ♔g1 ♗b5 4 ♖d1 ♕xe3!! 5 ♕xe3 ♖xd1 6 ♕b6 ♘g4 7 g3 ♗xf1 0:1 Asztalos-Nimzowitsch, Bled 1931

4) 1 ... g5! 2 ♖c2 (2 ♖xb2 axb2 3 ♔c2 f4-+) 2 ... f4! 3 gxf4 gxf4 4 ♖c5+ ♔d6 5 exf4 ♖xa2 6 ♖a5 e3 7 ♔e1 ♖a1+ 8 ♔e2 a2 9 f5 ♖h1 10 ♔xe3 a1=♕ 11 ♖xa1 ♖xa1 0:1 Tartakover-Nimzowitsch, London 1927

KM20/3

1) 1 ... ♗xd6! (2 ♗xd6 b2-+) 0:1 Verlinsky-Botvinnik, Moscow 1931

2) 1 ♖xg7+! ♔xg7 2 ♘h5+ ♔g6 (2 ... ♔g8 3 ♘xf6++-) 3 ♕e3! 1:0

Botvinnik-Keres, World Ch Tournament 1948

3) 1 ♕g3! fxe5 2 ♕g7 ♖f8 3 ♖c7 ♕xc7 (3 ... ♕d6 4 ♖xb7 d3 5 ♖a7 ♕d8 6 ♕xh7+-) 4 ♕xc7+- 1:0 Botvinnik-Euwe, World Ch Tournament 1948

4) 41 ♘f7+! (41 b7?? ♖b3 42 ♘f7+ ♔h7 43 ♘d8 a5 44 d6 a4 45 d7 a3 46 ♘c6 a2-+) 1:0 (41 ♔g7 42 b7 ♖b3 43 ♘d8 a5 44 d6 a4 45 d7 a3 46 ♘e6+- or 43 ♔f8 44 h5! ♔e8 45 h6 ♔xd8 46 h7+-) Botvinnik-Tal, Moscow WCh 1960

KM20/4

1) 1 ... ♖xc4! 0:1 Tal-Petrosian, Curacao Ct 1962

2) 1 ♕h8+! 1:0 (1 ... ♔xh8 2 ♘xf7+) Petrosian-Spassky, Moscow WCh 1966

3) 1 ♖xg6! ♕e5 (1 ... fxg6 2 ♕c3+) 2 ♕xh5# 1:0 Petrosian-Korchnoi, Ciocco Cm 1977

4) 1 ♔xc4! ♔b2 2 ♖e1 a1=♕ 3 ♖xa1 ♔xa1 4 b5 ♗d7 5 b6 ♗c8 6 ♔d4 ♔b2 7 ♔e5 ♔c3 8 ♔xf4 ♔d4 9 ♔g5 ♔e5 10 ♔xh5 ♔f6 11 g4 ♗b7 12 ♔h6 1:0 Petrosian-Smyslov, Moscow 1951

KM21/1

1) 1 ♘xh7! f5 2 ♘hg5! 1:0 Capablanca-Becker, Karlsbad 1929

2) 1 ♖e1+!! ♗e5 2 d6+! ♔e6 (Or 1 ... ♔d8 2 ♕b6+ ♗c7 3 ♕xa6+ etc) 3 ♕b3+ ♔f5 4 ♕d3+ ♔g5 5 ♕e3+ ♔f5 6 ♕e4+ ♔e6 7 ♕c4+ ♔xd6 8 ♖d1+ ♔e7 9 ♖xd7+ ♔xd7 10 ♕xa6 +- Capablanca-Zubarev, Moscow 1925

3) 1 ♗xg6! ♔xg6 (1 ... ♘xg6 2 ♘f5++-) 2 ♕c2+ ♔f6 3 ♕f5+ ♔g7

4 ♕xg4+ ♔h7 was Capablanca-Kan, Moscow 1935 and now 5 ♖e5! ♘f6 (or 5 ... ♕g7 6 ♖h5+ ♔g8 7 ♖g5+-) 6 ♕h4+ ♔g8 7 ♖g5+ was the quickest way to win

4) 1 ♘xb7! ♖xb7 2 ♗xc6+ ♖d7 3 c5 ♔e7 4 ♗xd7 ♘xd7 5 c6+- Capablanca-Lilienthal, Moscow 1936

KM21/2

1) 1 ♘xf7! ♘xf7 2 ♗b6 ♕d7 3 ♗xd8 ♔h7 4 ♗xf7 ♕xd8 5 ♗g6+ 1:0 Smyslov-Ljublinsky, USSR Ch, Moscow 1949

2) 1 ... ♘e5! 2 dxe5 (2 ♕f4 ♘d3+) 2 ... ♕xe5+ 3 ♔f1 ♕xg5 4 ♗f3 ♕f6 5 ♗xd5 (desperation) 5 ... ♕xf7-+ Tolush-Smyslov, USSR Ch, Leningrad 1947

3) 1 a6 bxa6 2 ♖c7+ ♔g6 3 ♖d7 ♘e7 4 ♗b4 ♘f5 5 ♖xd5!+- Smyslov-Letelier, Venice 1950.

4) 1 ♖b6! (1 ♔d6 ♘e8+ 2 ♔xe6 ♖e7+, 3 ... ♖xe3) 1 ... ♔c8 (1 ... ♖f5+ 2 ♔d6 ♘e8+ 3 ♔c6; 1 ... ♔e7 2 e4, 3 ♖b7) 43 ♔d6 ♖f2 44 ♔c6 ♖c2 45 ♖b7 ♘e8 46 ♖a7 ♔b8 47 ♖e7 1:0 Smyslov-Simagin, USSR Ch, Moscow 1951

KM21/3

1) 1 ♗xc5! bxc5 2 ♖xe6+ 1:0 Fischer-Hook, Siegen Ol, 1970

2) 1 g6! fxg6 2 ♖h1 ♕d4 3 ♕h7+ 1:0 Fischer-Gligoric, Bled Ct 1959

3) 1 e5! dxe5 (1 ... bxc3 2 exf6 ♗xf6 3 ♗xf6 gxf6 4 ♘e4 ♕f5 5 ♘xd6 ♕g6 6 ♖f3+-; 2 ... gxf6 3 ♗h6) 2 ♗xf6 gxf6 (2 ... bxc3 3 ♘e4 ♕b4 4 ♕g4 gives a strong attack) 3 ♘ce4 ♕d4 4 ♕h5 ♘xb3 (4 ... exf4 5 ♘f5! exf5 6 ♖xf4! +-) 5 ♕h6! exf4 6 ♘h5 f5 7 ♖ad1! ♕e5 8 ♘ef6+ ♗xf6 9 ♘xf6+ ♕xf6 10 ♕xf6 ♘c5 11 ♕g5+ ♔h8 12 ♕e7

♗a6 13 ♕xc5 ♗xf1 14 ♖xf1 1:0 Fischer-Benko, Bled Ct 1959

4) 1 ... ♖xd3 (2 ♘xd3 ♖xc2+ 3 ♔e1 ♗g3+) 0:1 Grossguth-Fischer, Philadelphia 1956

KM21/4

1) 1 ... ♖e1+! 2 ♖f1 (2 ♘xe1 ♖xe1+ 3 ♖f1 ♕f3 4 ♖xe1 ♕h1+ 5 ♔f2 ♕g2+ 6 ♔e3 ♕f3#) 2 ... ♖xf1+ 3 ♔xf1 ♕xh2 4 ♖d5 ♗xd5 5 cxd5 ♕xg3 6 fxg5 ♕f3+ (7 ♕f2 ♕d3+ 8 ♔g1 ♕b1+) 0:1 Ljubojevic-Karpov, Linares, 1993

2) 1 ♘f6! ♔xf6 (1 ... ♕xf3 2 ♘xe8+) 2 ♗e5+! ♔xe5 3 ♕xe4+ ♔xe4 4 ♖e1+ ♔f5 5 ♖xe8 ♗e6 6 ♖xf8 ♗xa2 7 ♖c8 1:0 Karpov-Topalov, Dos Hermanas 1994

3) 1 a4 crippled Black's queenside pawn majority in Karpov-Yusupov, Dortmund 1997

4) 1 ... ♖xb1! 0:1 (2 ♖xb1 c3) Lautier-Karpov, Linares 1995

KM22/1

1) 1 ♖xc8! ♖xc8 2 ♗xf5 1:0 Lasker-Janowsky, Hastings 1895

2) 1 ... g5! 2 ♕a2 (2 fxg5 ♘e5! 3 ♗c5 ♖d1-+) 2 ... gxf4 3 ♖e2 ♕g6 4 ♕c2 ♔h7 5 ♕c3 ♖g8 6 ♔h1 ♕h5 7 ♖d2 fxg3 8 ♗xg3 ♖xg3 9 ♕c6 ♘e5 10 ♕e4+ ♔g8 11 ♖df2 ♖g5 12 ♖c2 ♖d8 0:1 Tartakower-Lasker, St Petersburg 1909

3) 1 ♕d6+ ♔g7 2 ♕d4++- Lasker-Von Freyman, St Petersburg 1909

4) 1 h4! b4 2 ♖ab7 b3 3 ♔h2 ♖d2 4 ♖xb3 ♖e8 5 ♖bb7 ♖xd3 6 ♖xg7 ♖d8 (Or 6 ... ♖e6 7 ♖gd7 ♖g6 8 ♖d8+ ♖g8 9 ♖d6+-) 7 ♖h7+ ♔g8 8 ♖xh6 ♖e3 9 ♖hh7 d4 10 ♖hd7 ♖ee8 11 h5 d3 12 h6 ♖xd7 13 ♖xd7 ♖e6 14 ♖xd3 1:0 Lasker-Eliskases, Moscow 1936

KM22/2

1) 1 Nxh7! Re8 (13 ... Kxh7 14 Qh6+ Kg8 15 Qxg6+ Kh8 16 Qh6+ Kg8 17 Be4 f5 18 Bd5+ Rf7 19 Qg6+) 2 Qh6 Ne3 3 Ng5 Bxg5 4 Bxg5 Qxg5 5 Qxg5 Bxd5 6 0-0 Bxc4 7 f4 1:0 Korchnoi-Karpov, Moscow Cm, 1974

2) 1 Bxe7! Qxe7 2 Nxd5 Qe6 (2 ... Bxd5 3 Qxd5 Ra7 4 Qxe4) 3 Bxe4 Rd8 4 Nf6+! (4 Nc3? Qxb3 5 axb3 Bxe4 6 Nxe4 Rxd4) 4 ... Bxf6 5 Qxe6 fxe6 6 Bxb7 Ra7 7 Bg2 Rxd4 8 Nd3 +- Korchnoi-Epishin, Madrid 1995

3) 1 Ra7! Rb8 2 h5 Kg8 3 Rxa4 Rb7 4 Kg4 Kg7 5 Ra2 Kh6 6 Kf5 Rb6 7 e4 Rc6 8 f4 exf4 9 gxf4 Rc5+ 10 Kxf6 Kxh5 11 e5 Kg4 12 f5 h5 13 Ra4+ Kg3 14 e6 h4 15 e7 Rc8 16 Kf7 1:0 Korchnoi-Tal, Moscow Cm, 1968

4) 1 ... h5! 2 Ke2 Kc2 3 Ke3 Kc3 4 Kf3 Kd3 0:1 Smyslov-Korchnoi, USSR Ch, Leningrad 1960

KM22/3

1) 1 Bh6+! 1:0 Shirov-Leko, Belgrade 1995

2) 1 Rxd6! Qxd6 2 Qxg7+ Kb6 3 Qxh8 Qd1+ 4 Bf1 1:0 Shirov-Hertneck, Bundesliga 1995

3) 1 e5! dxe5 2 Ne4 Re8 3 g5 Nxe4 (3 ... Nh5 4 Rxh5 gxh5 5 Nf6+ Kh8 6 Qxh7#) 4 fxe4 exd4 5 Rxd4 1:0 Shirov-Ljubojevic, Monte Carlo 1995

4) 1 Bd8! (threatening 2 Nf6+) 1 ... Rf1+ 2 Kc2 Rf2+ 3 Kb3 Bc5 4 Nf6+ Nxf6 5 Rg7+ Kf8 6 gxf6 Rf3+ 7 Kc2 Rf2+ 8 Kd1 Rf1+ 9 Ke2 Rf2+ 10 Ke1 Rxa2 11 Be7+ Bxe7 12 fxe7+ Ke8 13 d6 1:0 in Shirov-Kamsky, Linares 1993

KM22/4

1) 1 g6! fxg6 2 Bb2 Qd7 3 Qe3!+- "Virtual Chess"-"Junior", Computer World Ch , Paris 1997

2) 1 ... Rh4+!! 2 Kxh4 (2 gxh4?? Qg2#) 2 ... Qh2+ 3 Kg5 (3 Kg4?? Qh5#) 3 ... Qxg3+ 4 Rg4 Qe5+= "Nimzo 3" - "MChess Pro", Computer World Ch, Paderborn 1995

3) 1 h4! gxh4 2 Kf3 Ke8 3 Kf4 Kd7 4 Kg5 1:0 Anand-"Pentium Genius2", London 1994

4) 1 h3? (1 h4!=) 1 ... h4! 2 Kb2 Kd5 3 Ka3 Kc5 4 Kb2 a4-+ "Gandalf" - "Chess Genius", Computer World Ch, Paderborn 1995

KM23/1

1) 1 Qd6+! (1 ... Kxd6 2 Nxc4+; 1 ... Ke8 2 Qb8+) 1:0 Gonzales-Villamayor, Philippines 1996

2) 1 Qxd8+! (1 ... Kxd8 2 Re8 Qxe8 3 Nc7+ etc) 1:0 Frohne-Rosenberger, Dortmund 1995

3) 1 Rxc5 Rxc5 (1 ... fxe5 2 Rxc8+ Kb7 3 Bxe4++-) 2 Qxc5 Rd1+ 3 Bf1 1:0 Beliavsky-Palac, Bled 1996

4) 1 Re8!! (1 f7 Kxg7 2 Re8 Rh8) 1 ... Rxe8 2 f7 Rg8 3 Nf6+ 1:0 Fedorowicz-Wolski, San Francisco 1997

KM23/2

1) 1 Rxg6! Kxg6 (1 ... Bxd5 2 Nxf5) 2 Nxf5 Kf7 (2 ... Bxd7 3 Ne7+) 3 Nfe7 Qb7 4 Qg2 Rhg8 5 Qe4 Rg7 6 Re1 1:0 Spassky-Ostl, Bundesliga 1989-90

2) 1 Rxg7! (1 ... Kxg7 2 Rc1 Qxe3 3 Rc7+) 1:0 Spassky-Gipslis, USSR Ch, Baku 1961

3) 1 Bxh5!! gxh5 2 Qxh5 (threatening 3 Rh6, 4 Rh8#) 2 ...

♘f8 3 ♖h6 ♖h7 4 ♖ee6! ♕d7 5
♖xh7 ♘xh7 6 ♖g6+ ♔h8 7 ♖h6 e6
8 g6 1:0 Spassky-Robatsch,
Bundesliga 1983-4
4) 1 ♖b7! f2 2 e6! ♖xd5+ 3 ♔h6!
(3 ♘xd5?? f1=♕ 4 e7 ♔f7!) 3 ...
♖h5+ (3 ... f1=♕ 4 ♖f7#; 3 ... ♗h5
4 ♖b8!+-) 4 ♔g6 1:0 Spassky-
Larsen, Malmo Cm 1968

KM23/3
1) 1 ... ♕a1+! 0:1 Sahovic-
Matulovic, Belgrade 1969
2) 1 ♖xf7! ♔xf7 2 ♖f1+ ♗f6 3
♗xf6 1:0 Larsen-Eley, Hastings
1972
3) 1 ♘xg6! (1 ♖h7 ♘xg5) 1 ...
fxg6 2 ♖h7 1:0 Gulko-Korelov,
Odessa 1972
4) 1 f3! ♖xe3 2 g4# 1:0 Larsen-
Pomar, Palma de Majorca 1971

KM23/4
1) 1 ♖d7+ (1 ... ♗xd7 2 ♕e7+, 3
♕f7#) 1:0 Hodgson-Martin,
British Ch 1992
2) 1 ♘xf7! ♔xf7 2 ♘e5+ ♔g8 (or
2 ... ♔f8 3 ♕h5 etc) 3 ♕h5 ♗f6 (3
... ♖f8 is met by 4 ♕g6) 4 ♕f7+
♔h8 5 ♘g6+ ♔h7 6 ♘e7+ ♔h8 7
♕g6 ♕xe7 8 ♕h7# 1:0
Hodgson-Trevelyan, Paris 1995
3) 1 ♘xf5! exf5 2 ♕d6 ♕e6 (2 ...
♕e7 3 ♕d4, f2, h8) 3 ♕d4 1:0
Hodgson-Lukacs, Kecskemet 1988
4) 1 ♖b8+! (1 ... ♕xb8 2 ♕h8+)
1:0 Hodgson-Cerrajeria, Zara-
gosa 1993

KM24/1
1) 1 ♘xh7! ♘xh7 2 ♖h3 ♕c1 3
♕xh7+ ♔f8 4 ♖e3 d4 5 ♕h8+ ♔e7
6 ♕xg7 ♖f8 (6 ... ♗d5 7 ♕f6+ ♔d7
8 ♗xd5, 9 ♕xf7#; 6 ... ♔f8 7 e6) 7
♕f6+ ♔e8 8 e6 (8 ... dxe3 9 exf7+
♔d7 10 ♗e6+; 9 ... ♖xf7 10 ♗xf7+

♔d7 11 ♗e6++-) 1:0 Keres-Fine,
Ostend 1937
2) 1 d6! ♘xe5 (1 ... ♘xd6 2 g6!
hxg6 3 ♘xg6 ♖e8 4 ♕h5!, 5 ♕h8#;
1 ... cxd6 2 ♘xf7 ♖xf7 3 ♗xf7+
♔xf7 4 ♕d5++-) 2 fxe5 (2 ... ♘xc3
3 ♕d3+-; 2 ... ♗h3 3 ♖xf7!; 2 ...
cxd6 3 exd6 ♘xd6 [3 ... ♘xg5 4
♗xg5 ♕xg5 5 d7+-] 4 ♗c5+-) 1:0
Keres-Lilienthal, USSR Absolute
Ch, Moscow/Leningrad 1941
3) 1 ... c3! 2 ♘c2 (2 ♔xd3 ♗xe3
3 ♔xe3 c2; 2 ♔xc3 ♗c1-+) 2 ...
♘e1! 3 ♘a3 (3 ♘xe1 ♗xe1 4 ♔d3
♗d2-+) Fine-Keres, Amsterdam
1938 and now 3 ... ♗h4!-+ (4 ♖xe1
♗xe1 5 ♔xe1 c2!)
4) 1 b4! axb4 2 a5 ♕b7 50 ab+
♔xb6 51 ♕xd6+ ♔a7 52 ♕xe5 b3
53 ♖h3 ♖f6 54 ♕d4+ ♖b6 55 ♖xb3
1:0 Keres-Euwe, Amsterdam 1939

KM24/2
1) 1 ♘e5+ (1 ... ♘xe5 2 ♖a7+
♔c6 3 ♕e4#) 1:0 Alekhine-
Bogoljubov, World Ch, 1929
2) 1 ♘xg7! ♔xg7 (1 ... ♘ce4 2 b4
♕xb4 3 ♘h5+-) 2 ♗d4! ♘e4 (2 ...
♘d7 3 ♗c3+-) 2 ♕xe4 ♕f5 3 ♕xf5
exf5 4 ♖ac1 ♖fe8 5 ♖c7 ♖xe2 6
♖xb7 ♔g6 7 ♗xf6 ♔xf6 8 ♖d6+ (8
... ♔g7 9 ♖dd7 ♖f8 10 ♔f3 ♖c2 11
♖dc7 ♖d2 12 ♔e3+-) 1:0
Alekhine-Rabar, Prague 1942
3) 1 ... ♗h3! 2 ♖d8+ (2 ♗xh3
♕e3+ 3 ♔h1 ♕f3+ 4 ♔g1 ♕f2+ 5
♔h1 ♕xh2#) 2 ... ♕xd8 3 ♗xh3
♕xa8 0:1 Opocensky-Alekhine,
Prague 1942
4) 1 ... h5! 2 fxg6+ (2 g5 fxg5 3
hxg5 ♗xg5 4 fxg6+ ♔xg6 5 ♔xe5
h4-+) 2 ... ♔xg6 3 gxh5+ ♔f7! (3 ...
♔xh5 4 ♔f5!) 4 h6 (4 ♔h5 ♖h8 5
♔g4 ♔e6) 4 ... ♔e6 5 ♖g1 ♖h8 6
♖g6 ♗f8 0:1 Wolf-Alekhine,
Karlsbad 1923

KM24/3

1) 1 ... ♘xa2! 2 ♘xa2 ♗xa1 3 ♗d3 ♖d8 4 ♖d1 ♗b2 0:1 Baturinsky-Bronstein, Moscow 1946

2) 1 ... ♘xa3! 2 ♕f3 (2 ♕xa3 ♗xf1 3 ♔xf1 ♕xh3+) 2 ... ♘c2! 3 de de 4 ♗xb5 cxb5 6 ♕f1 ♘d4 7 ♔g2 a3 8 ♗d2 a2 9 ♕a1 ♘e3+ 10 ♔g1 ♕e2 11 ♕xa2+ ♔h7 0:1 Zagorjansky-Bronstein, Moscow 1947

3) 1 ♗f7! ♕xf7 (1 ... ♘xf7 2 ♕xb8 xa7 +-) 2 ♕xb8+ ♘e8 3 ♕b7 ♕h5 4 h3 ♔h7 5 ♕xa7 e5 6 ♗e3 e4 7 ♕e7 1:0 Bronstein-Szabo, Zurich Ct 1953

4) 1 ♖b6! ♖d5 (1 ... axb6 2 a7) 2 ♖b7 ♘c6 3 ♘c3 ♖xd4 4 ♘xb5 ♖d1+ 5 ♔f2 c3 6 ♘xc3 ♖d2+ (6 ... ♖a1 7 ♘b5 ♖a5 8 ♘d6+ ♔f8 9 ♖f7+ ♔g8 10 ♘e8+-) 7 ♔g1 ♘d8 8 ♖xa7 1:0 Bronstein-Taimanov Moscow 1951

KM24/4

1) 1 ... ♖xe3! (2 ♕xe3 ♗f4) won a piece and the game in Botvinnik-Pachman, Moscow 1947

2) In Kotov-Euwe, Groningen 1946 White could have won immediately with 1 ♕c8! fxe6 (2 ... ♖c2 3 ♔f1! ♖xc3 4 ♘c7) 2 ♖xe6 3) 1 ... ♗xd6 2 ♗xd6 ♖d8! (2 ... ♖xd6 3 ♗xh7+) 3 ♗e2 ½-½ Vidmar-Capablanca, San Sebastian 1911

4) 1 ♔g2! (1 ... ♖xe4 2 ♔f3) +- Alekhine-Capablanca, Buenos Aires WCh, 1927

Analysis Positions Solutions

Month 13

A13/1

a) Tal-Simagin, Leningrad 1956. White is ahead in development and Black's king is still in the centre at the moment.

White's Plan: Do I have a way to attack Black's uncastled king?

Black's Plan: I need to get my king to a safer place.

Candidate Moves: 12 ♘xe6; 12 f5; 12 ♘xf7.

Analysis: 12 ♘xf7! ♚xf7 13 f5 dxe5 (13 ... ♘xe5 14 ♔h1; 13 ... ♚g8 14 fxe5 ♘xe5 15 ♔h1 ♘g6 16 ♕h5 ♘e7 [16 ... ♚h7 17 ♖f7+-] 17 ♕f7+ ♚h7 18 ♖f6+-) **14 fxe6+ ♚xe6 15 ♖b1!** (Black escapes after 15 ♕g4+ ♔d6 16 ♗a3+ ♔c7 17 ♖ab1 ♕a6 or 15 ♕c4+ ♔d6 16 ♗a3+ ♔c7 17 ♖ab1 ♗xa3 18 ♖xb6 axb6) **15 ... ♕xb1 16 ♕c4+ ♔d6** (Or 16 ... ♚e7 17 ♗a3+ ♔d8 18 ♖xb1 ♗xa3 19 ♖xb7 ♖b8 20 ♖xa7 ♖b1+ 21 ♔f2 ♖f8+ 22 ♚e2 ♗e7 23 ♕xc6 etc) **17 ♗a3+ ♔c7 18 ♖xb1 ♗xa3 19 ♕b3 ♗e7 20 ♕xb7+ ♔d6** and now 21 ♖d1! threatening 22 d5 and 22 dxe5+ would have been the simplest.

Assessment: White has a winning attack.

b) Averbakh-Kotov, Zurich Ct 1953. White has more space on the queenside but his king looks vulnerable.

White's Plan: After safeguarding my king I might eventually be able to organise a queenside break-through based on the b2-b4 lever.

Black's Plan: I want to attack White's king position and h3 looks like the jelly-spot.

Candidate Moves: 30 ... ♖h6; 30 ... ♕xh3+!?

Analysis: 30 ... ♕xh3+!! 31 ♚xh3 ♖h6+ 32 ♚g4 ♘f6+! (32 ♖f8?! 33 ♘xf4 ♘f6+ 34 ♔f5 ♘g4+ 35 ♚xg4 ♖g8+ 36 ♘g6+ ♖gxg6+ 37 ♔f5 ♖h5+ 38 ♖g5 ♗xg5 39 ♚g4! is not that clear) **33 ♔f5** and now 33 ... ♘g4 would have been the quickest way to win.

Assessment: 30 ... ♕xh3+ gives Black a winning attack.

A13/2

a) Gurgenidze-Lein, USSR Ch, Tbilisi 1966. Black's king is in the centre but the position is presently closed.

White's Plan: If I can open the centre I might exploit Black's un-castled king.

Black's Plan: I need to complete my development and get my king into safety.

Candidate Moves: 11 ♘xf5; 11 g4.

Analysis: 11 ♘xf5!! ♘a5 (11 ... ♗b7 is hopeless after 12 ♘d6+ ♗xd6 13 exd6, 11 ... exf5 12 e6 ♕xf4 [12 ... d6 13 e7 ♗xe7 14

Bxd6 Qd7 15 Qd5 Rf8 16 Bxe7 Nxe7 17 Qxa8+-] 13 exd7+ Kd8 14 Re8+ Kc7 15 d8=Q+ Nxd8 16 Qxd8+ or and 11 ... gxf5 12 Qh5+ Kd8 13 Rad1 followed by 14 Bxe6 will catch Black's king in the crossfire) 12 Bd5! (12 Nd6+ Bxd6 13 ed Qc6 14 Bd5 is also quite enough, but the text is more beautiful) 12 ... Bb7 (12 ... exd5 13 Nd6+ Kd8 14 Qxd5 leaves Black facing too many threats) 13 Nd6+ Bxd6 14 exd6 Qc8 (Or 14 ... Qd8 15 Bxe6 dxe6 16 Rxe6+ Kf7 17 Re7+ Kg8 18 Bh6) 15 Bh6! Rg8 16 Qf3 Bxd5 17 Qxd5 Nc6 18 Rad1 (threatening 19 Rxe6+ fxe6 20 d7+) 18 Nd8 19 Qg5 Nc6 20 Qf6 g5 21 Re5 1:0 (21 Qd8 22 Rxe6+).

Assessment: White can break through with a winning attack.

b) Vladimirov-Doda, Leningrad 1967. White is two pawns down but has a big lead in development and a strong passed pawn on d6.

White's Plan: I have to exploit my advantage in development before Black consolidates.

Black's Plan: If I can complete my development I should have a winning game.

Candidate Moves: 17 Rxf5; 17 Bxf7+; 17 Nb5.

Analysis: 17 Bxf7+ (17 Rxf5! gxf5 18 Bxf7+! was a more accurate move order and Black in turn should avoid this with 17 ... Qxc3 18 Bxf7+ Kg7 19 Rf3 Qd4+! [19 ... Qxa1 20 Rxa1 Bxa1 21 Bxe8] 20 Qxd4 Bxd4+ 21 Kf1 Rf8 22 Re1 Nc6! [22 ... Rxf7 23 Rxf7+ Kxf7 24 Re7+ Kg8 25 Re8+ Kf7 26 d7] 23 Bd5! when White has a dangerous initiative for the pawn) 17 ... Kxf7 18 Rxf5+ gxf5? (18 ...

Kg7! [18 ... Kg8 19 Qd5+ Kh8 20 Re1! Bd4+ 21 Qxd4+-] 19 d7 [19 Rf3 Bxc3 20 Rb1 Rxb1! 21 Qxb1 Re1++] 19 Nxd7 20 Qxd7+ Kh8 21 Rxe5 Qxa1+ when White would have to fight for a draw after 22 Qd1 [22 Kf2? Rf8+ 23 Ke2 Qxc3] 22 Qxd1+ 23 Nxd1 Rxe5 24 Bf6+ Kg8 25 Bxe5 Re8) 19 Qh5+ Kf8 (and not 19 ... Kg7? 20 Bh6+ Kf6 21 Rf1 when 21 ... Qc2 fails to 22 Nd5+! Ke6 23 Qxe8+ Kxd5 24 d7! Nxd7 25 Qxd7+ Kc4 26 Rc1+- and 21 ... Bd4+ to 22 Kh1 Re5 23 Qg5+ Kf7 24 Rg7+ Ke8 25 Nd5! Nd7 26 Qg8+ Nf8 27 Nf6+!) 20 Rf1! Bd4+ 21 Kh1 Re6 22 Rxf5+ Bf6 23 Bh6+ Kg8 24 Qg5+! Kf7 (24 ... Bxg5 25 Rf8#; 24 ... Kh8 25 Bg7+ Kg8 [25 ... Bxg7 26 Qd8+] 26 Bxf6+ Kf8 27 Bg7+ Ke8 28 Rf8+ Kd7 29 Qd8+ Kc6 30 Qc7#) 25 Rxf6+! Rxf6 26 Qg7+ Ke6 27 Qe7+ 1:0 (27 ... Kf5 28 Qe4#).

Assessment: A complex struggle in which 17 Rxf5! is the best.

A13/3

a) Nezhmetdinov-Tal, USSR Ch, Baku 1961. Black's structure looks quite nice but he is unable to castle kingside.

White's Plan: I should open it up before Black makes his king safe.

Black's Plan: I must get my king to safety.

Candidate Moves: 17 Nd5; 17 g5; 17 Rxf6; 17 Nxf7.

Analysis: 17 Rxf6! (17 Nd5 would be met by 17 ... Nxd5 18 exd5 Nf4 and 17 g5? is bad because of 17 ... Bxh6) 17 Bxf6 18 Nd5 Qd8 (18 ... Bxd5 19 exd5 Nd4 20 Qf2 gives White dual threats of 21 d6 and 21 Qxf6 and neither 20 ... Qb6 21 Be3+- nor 20 ... Qd6 21

g5+- is an adequate defence) **19 ♕f2 ♘f4 20 ♗xf4 ef 21 e5!** (21 ♕xf4 allows Black to escape after 21 ... ♗xd5 22 exd5 ♕b6+ 23 ♔h1 0-0-0 24 ♘xf7 ♗xb2 25 ♖b1 ♖hf8 26 ♖xb2 ♖d7) **21 ... ♗xe5** (21 ... ♗h4! was better [and not 21 ... ♗g7 22 ♘f6+ ♗xf6 23 exf6 ♗xg2 24 ♖e1+- or 21 ... ♗xd5 22 exf6 ♗e6 23 ♗c6+ ♔f8 24 ♕c5+-] when 22 ♕c5 is met by 22 ... ♖c8 and 22 ♘f6+ by 22 ... ♕xf6 23 exf6 ♗xf2+ 24 ♔xf2 ♗xg2! [24 ... 0-0-0? 25 ♗xb7+ ♔xb7 26 ♘xf7 ♖d2+ 27 ♔e1+-] 25 ♖e1+ ♔f8 26 ♔xg2 ♖e8 27 ♖d1 leaves White with a bind but nothing very clear) **22 ♖e1 f6 23 ♘xf6+! ♕xf6 24 ♕d4 ♔f8** (Or 24 ... ♗xg2 25 ♖xe5+ ♔f8 26 ♖f5!) **25 ♖xe5 ♕d8** (25 ... ♖d8 26 ♖e8+) **26 ♖f5+ gxf5 27 ♕xh8+ ♔e7 28 ♕g7+ ♔e6 29 gxf5+ 1:0**
Assessment: 17 ♖xf6! set a dangerous attack in motion but there were defensive resources.

b) Kavalek-Matulovic, Bucharest 1966. There is a whiff of a combination against the vulnerable f6 square if only Black's queen can be distracted.
White's Plan: I should look at things which try to exploit the loose-looking position of Black's pieces.
Black's Plan: When White defends against the threat of 19 ♘g4 I can consolidate with ♖f8 and try to plant a minor piece on e5.
Candidate Moves: 19 ♘xf6+; 19 ♖xf6.
Analysis: Kavalek won with **19 ♖xf6! ♗xf6 20 ♘f5! gxf5 21 g3 ♗c3** (21 ... ♕h3 22 ♘xf6+ ♔f7 23 ♗f1! wins Black's queen) **22 bxc3 ♕d8 23 exf5 ♘g7** (23 ... ♘f8 24

♗g5 ♕a5 25 ♗f6 is not an improvement) **24 ♗g5 ♕f8 25 ♘f6+ ♔h8 26 ♘xd7 ♕f7 27 ♘f6 ♘h5 28 ♘xh5 ♕xh5 29 ♗f6+ ♔g8 30 ♗e4 h6 31 ♕xd6 ♖e8 32 ♗d5+ 1:0**
Assessment: 19 ♖xf6 wins by force.

A13/4
a) Tarrasch-Alekhine, Baden-Baden 1925. White is temporarily a pawn up but Black can recapture either the pawn on a4 or play 21 ♗xh3. Black's pieces are quite active and he has the two bishops, White's knight on b3 seems particularly poorly placed.
White's Plan: I would like to free myself with exchanges.
Black's Plan: I can win my pawn back in several different ways but would like to maintain the initiative whilst doing so. This looks like a rather calculative position in which I need to find the most effective looking sequence of moves.
Candidate Moves: 21 ... ♕xa4; 21 ... ♗xh3; 21 ... ♗f5; 21 ... ♖xe1.
Analysis: 21 ... ♗f5! (21 ... ♗xh3 22 gxh3 ♕xf3 23 ♗g2) **22 ♗d3** (22 ♕d2 ♕xa4 23 ♘c1 ♗c2 24 ♖xe8+ ♖xe8 25 ♖e1 ♘e4 26 ♕f4 c4 27 ♘d4 ♗xd4 28 cd ♕b4! is good for Black according to Alekhine's analysis) **22 ♗xh3** (22 ... ♗xd3 23 ♕xd3 c4 24 ♕d2) **23 ... gxh3 ♕xf3 24 ♖xe8+** (24 ♗f1 ♖xe1 25 ♖xe1 ♕xd5 is also good for Black) **24 ... ♖xe8 25 ♗f1 ♖e5 26 c4 ♖g5+ 27 ♔h2 ♘g4+ 28 hxg4 ♖xg4 0:1**
Assessment: Black has a strong if not decisive initiative.

b) Kholmov-Bronstein, USSR Ch, Kiev 1964. White's pieces are in menacing positions around

Black's king, Black has a tremendous knight on e5 and the only dark-squared bishop on the board.

White's Plan: I must act immediately for if Black defends against my kingside pressure his positional trumps will dominate.

Black's Plan: In the short term I need to drive back White's aggressively placed pieces and safeguard my king position.

Candidate Moves: 18 ♘e2; 18 ♖d3!?; 18 ♘c6!?.

Analysis: 18 ♘c6! ♘xc6 19 e5! ♗g5+ (19 ... dxe5 20 ♘e4 ♗g5+ 21 ♘xg5 f6 22 ♘xh7+-; 19 ... ♘xe5 20 ♘e4 ♘g6 [20 ... ♘d7 21 ♖xd6 exf5 22 ♖xf6 ♖g8 23 ♖xg8+ ♔xg8 24 ♖xf5 ♘f8 25 ♘f6+ ♔h8 26 ♖e5! ♗e6 27 ♖g5+-] 21 ♘xf6 ♕xf6 22 fxg6 ♕g7 23 ♕xg7+ ♔xg7 24 gxf7+ ♔xf7 25 ♖xd6; 19 ... ♗xe5 20 f6 ♗xf6 21 ♗d3 ♗g5+ 22 ♖xg5 f5 [22 f6 23 ♖g3 bxc3 24 ♗xh7+-] 23 ♖dg1 ♖a7 24 ♘e2 ♘e5 25 ♘f4 ♖c7 26 ♗xf5 ef 27 ♘d5+-) 20 ♖xg5 f6 21 exd6 ♕f7 22 ♖g3 bxc3 23 ♗c4 cxb2+ 24 ♔b1 ♘d8 and now 25 d7! ♗xd7 26 ♖xd7 was the most efficient way to win.

Assessment: 18 ♘c6!! gives White a winning attack.

Month 14

A14/1
a) Alekhine - Capablanca, Buenos Aires WCh 1927.
White's position looks slightly preferable because of the poorly placed knight on b6, the vulnerable pawns on e5 and a7 and the slight weakness of Black's kingside.

White's Plan: I would like to create pressure on the dark squares where Black has some weaknesses.

Black's Plan: I would like to simplify the position.

Candidate Moves: 21 ♖fd1; 21 ♕e3; 21 ♕d2.

Analysis: 21 ♕d2! ♗e6? (Black's best defence was 21 ... ♘a4 according to Emanuel Lasker; 21 ... ♗c6 favours White after 22 ♘h4! ♗xe4 23 ♕e3!, 22 ... ♗d7 23 ♕a5 or 22 ... ♘xe4 23 ♘hf5+ gxf5 24 ♘xf5+ ♔f6 25 ♕xh6+ ♔xf5 26 g4#) **22 ♗xe6 ♕xe6 23 ♕a5 ♘c4 24 ♕xa7 ♘xb2 25 ♖xc8 ♖xc8 26 ♕xb7** winning a pawn and later the game.

Assessment: 21 ♕d2 gives White a strong initiative.

b) Alekhine-Weenink, Prague Ol, 1931.
White's pieces look menacingly placed and Black's king position seems vulnerable, especially on the light squares.

White's Plan: The position cries out for action on the kingside yet how exactly do I break through?

Piece pressure alone may not be enough, could I use my pawns as well?

Black's Plan: I need to defend and exchange some pieces.

Candidate Moves: 22 ♕g6; 22 ♗xh6; 22 g4.

Analysis: 22 g4! ♕d6 23 ♗g6! (and not 23 g5? ♕d5) **23 ... ♖f8 24 g5 ♗xd4 25 gxh6 ♘df6 26 hxg7+ ♔xg7 27 ♕h6+ ♔h8** (27 ♔g8 28 ♘xd4 ♕xd4 29 ♖g3+-) **28 ♘xd4 ♕xd4 29 ♗b2! 1:0** (29 ♕d7 30 ♖d3! ♕g7 31 ♗xf6+-)

Assessment: 22 g4! sets about demolishing Black's kingside.

A14/2
a) Fine-Denker, U.S.A. Ch 1940.
Black's pieces are directing their fire towards White's queenside but he does have weaknesses on b5 and d6.

White's Plan: If I can defuse Black's initiative I can set about attacking the d6 pawn.

Black's Plan: My position might turn sour if my initiative comes to nothing because the overall structure is preferable for White. This looks like the time to act.

Candidate Moves: 24 ... ♕a6; 24 ... ♖xc4.

Analysis: 24 ... ♖xc4! (Denker chose 24 ♕a6 and after 25 ♖xb3 ♖xc4 26 ♖xb7! ♕xb7 27 ♕xc4 ♖c8 28 ♕d3 ♗f8 29 ♕c2 ♖b8 left Black a pawn down, though this proved very difficult for White to use because his bishop is tied to the defence of b2) **25 ♕xc4 ♘xc1 26 ♖xc1 ♕xb2 27 ♖aa1 ♖c8 28 ♕f1 ♗xc3 29 ♖ab1 ♕a3 30 ♖xb7 ♗xa4** leaves Black with excellent compensation for the exchange.

Assessment: Black would have been better had he sacrificed on c4, after 24 ♕a6 White is on the positive side of the position.

b) Stein-Tal, USSR Cht, Moscow 1961. A Sicilian structure in which Black has taken the slightly unusual step of castling queenside where his king lacks pawn cover.

White's Plan: I would like to find a way to exploit the shaky position of Black's king, perhaps by exchanging a defender or two.

Black's Plan: Given time I may be able to play ♔b8 and ♖c8 to create counterplay on the c-file.

Candidate Moves: 15 ♘d5; 15 ♗d5; 15 b4.

Analysis: 15 ♗d5! b4 (15 ... ♖d7 might have been advisable) **16 ♗xb7+ ♔xb7 17 ♘d5!! exd5** (17 ... ♗f8 18 ♕h5 ♕xa2 19 ♘c6!!; 17 ... b3! 18 axb3 ♕a1+ 19 ♔d2 ♕xb2 20 ♘c3 ♖c8 21 ♕f3 ♘d7 was best with wild complications) **18 exd5 ♖d7 19 ♘c6 ♕xa2** (19 ... ♕c7 20 ♕xb4+ ♔c8 21 ♕g4 ♔b7 22 b4 ♘a4 23 ♕xd7 ♕xd7 24 ♖xe7 ♕xe7 25 ♘xe7 ♘c3 26 ♖d3 ♘xa2+ 27 ♔b2 ♘xb4 28 ♖b3+-) **20 ♕xb4+ ♔c7 21 ♘xe7 ♖b8 22 ♕a3 ♕c4 23 ♘c6 ♖b3** (23 ... ♖b5 was more tenacious) **24 ♕a5+ ♖b6 25 ♔b1 ♘a4 26 ♖d4 ♘xb2 27 ♔c1 ♕c5 28 ♖e3 ♔b7 29 ♖c3 ♖b5 30 ♕a3 ♕xa3 31 ♖xa3 ♖xd5 32 ♘a5+ 1:0**

Assessment: After 15 ♗d5 Black must play very accurately to stay on the board.

A14/3

a) Denker-Baker, U.S.A. 1937. White has two bishops and a mighty pawn centre but it is presently coming under tactical pressure with Black threatening both e4 and d4.

White's Plan: I must either defend my central pawns or attack Black's king.

Black's Plan: I want to take one of those centre pawns!

Candidate Moves: 16 d5; 16 ♘f5; 16 dxc5.

Analysis: 16 dxc5! (16 d5? ♘xd5! 17 exd5 ♕xd5) **16 ... ♕d4+ 17 ♔h1 ♕xa1 18 ♕e2 ♕e5** (White was threatening 19 ♗b2 ♕a2 20 ♗c4) **19 ♗b2 ♕g5** (19 ... ♕xc5 20 ♘f5 has the deadly threats of 21 ♘xg7 or 21 ♗xf6 gxf6 22 ♕g4+ and 20 ♘e8 loses to 21 ♕g4 g6 22 ♘h6#) **20 ♖f5 ♕g4** (20 ... ♕g6 21 e5 ♘d5 22 ♖h5 ♘f4 23 ♗xg6 ♘xe2 24 ♗xh7+-; 20 ... ♕h4 21 ♖xf6 gxf6 22 ♘f5 ♕f4 23 ♘e7+ ♔h8 24 g3 ♕g5 25 h4 ♕h6 26 ♕f3+-) **21 ♕xg4 ♘xg4 22 ♖g5! ♘f2+ 23 ♔g1 f6** (23 ... ♘xd3 24 ♖xg7+ ♔h8 25 ♗f6 h6 26 ♘f5 decisively threatens 27 ♖xf7+ ♔g8 28 ♘xh6#) **24 ♗c4+ ♔h8** (24 ♖f7 25 ♗xf6+-) **25 ♘h5! ♘d1** (25 ... fxg5 26 ♗xg7#; 25 ... ♘xe4 26 ♖xg7 ♗c6 27 ♖c7 ♗e8 28 ♘f4 etc) **26 ♗a1 ♗xe4 27 ♖xg7 ♗g6 28 ♖g8+! 1:0** (28 ... ♖xg8 29 ♗xf6+ ♖g7 30 ♗xg7#)

Assessment: 16 dxc5 gives White a decisive initiative.

b) Zilberman-Davies, Rishon-le-Zion 1994. A Sicilian-type structure in which White has a slight space advantage and pressure against Black's isolated a-pawn, Black has pressure against e4

White's Plan: I want to capture Black's a-pawn or at least force Black's pieces into passive positions in his attempts to defend it

Black's Plan: My a-pawn is a problem, do I defend it or counterattack?

Candidate Moves: 20 ... ♕c8; 20 ... a5; 20 ♘c5.

Analysis: 20 ... ♘c5! 21 ♗xc5 (21 ♖a3 ♘cxe4 22 ♘xe4 ♘xe4 23 ♘xa6 ♕xc2) **21 ... dxc5 22 ♘xa6 ♕b6 23 ♗f1 ♖ed8 24 ♕a3 ♗f8** (defending the pawn on c5 which imprisons White's knight-with his next move White tries to bail out into the endgame but Black's initiative continues unabated) **25 ♕b3 ♕xb3! 26 cxb3 ♖d2! 27 ♖ea1 ♖xb2 28 ♘xc5** (28 ♘c7 ♖xa4 29 ♖xa4 ♖xb3 wins a pawn) **28 ... ♗xc5! 29 ♖xa8+ ♗xa8 30 ♖xa8+ ♔g7 31 ♖a2 ♖xa2 32 ♘xa2 ♘xe4 33 ♔g2 ♘xf2 34 ♘c3 f5 35 ♘a4 ♗d4 36 b4 ♘d1 37 ♔f3 ♘e3 38 ♗d3 e5 39 b5 ♘d5 40 ♗c4 e4+ 41 ♔e2 ♘b6 42 ♘xb6 ♗xb6 43 ♗d5 ♔f6 44 ♗g8 h6 45 ♗d5 g5 46 ♗c6 ♔e5 47 ♗e8 f4 48 gxf4+ gxf4 49 ♗h5 ♔f6 0:1**

Assessment: 20 ... ♘c5! gives more than enough for the pawn.

A14/4

a) Stein-Petrosian, USSR Ch, Moscow 1961. A Winawer French in which it is not clear where Black's king will find safety.

White's Plan: My pawn structure has been weakened but my pieces

are very active. I want to bring my bishop to a3.

Black's Plan: I would like to play ... ♗a4 on my next move in order to prevent White's queen's bishop from ever emerging via a3.

Candidate Moves: 19 ♖a1; 19 a4.

Analysis: 19 a4!! (19 ♖a1 ♗a4) **19 ... ♗xa4 20 ♖a1 b5** (an unfortunate necessity as now Black's queen's bishop will be permanently shut out of play) **21 ♗a3 ♕d7 22 ♖f2!** (quietly strengthening the pressure) **22 ♖b7 23 ♖af1 ♕d8 24 ♕d1!!** (another quiet move with devastating effect White's queen is now positioned to leap into Black's kingside) **24 ... ♖h6 25 ♗c1 ♖h7 26 ♗xe6! 1:0** (26 ... fxe6 27 ♕g4 is devastating)

Assessment: The opening of the a3-f8 diagonal with 19 a4, renders Black's position well-nigh indefensible.

b) Stahlberg-Stein, Erevan 1965. White's king looks insecure but should the queens be exchanged this will not be an important factor.

White's Plan: I want to exchange queens after which the occupation of d5 should give me a good game.

Black's Plan: I would like to avoid the exchange of queens and put my knight on that inviting e5 square.

Candidate Moves: 14 ... ♘g4; 14 ... ♘d7.

Analysis: 14 ... ♘d7!! 15 ♗xf8 (15 ♗f2 ♕g5 16 00 ♘e5 gives Black a strong initiative without any material investment) **15 ... ♕h4+ 16 ♔d2** (16 g3 fxg3-+; 16 ♔f1 locks in the rook on h1) **16 ... ♗xf8 17 ♕e1 ♕e7 18 ♔c2 ♘e5 19 ♖c1 ♗g7 20**

♘d5 ♕c5 21 ♕g1 (21 b3 would loosen the dark squares) 21 ... ♕xc4+ 22 ♔b1 ♕d3+ 23 ♖c2 (23 ♔a1 ♘c4) 23 ... ♗e6 24 ♗e2? (Black maintains his initiative after 24 ♕d1 ♕a6 [25 ♘c7?? ♕xa2+] though the outcome is still far from clear) 24 ... ♕xe4 25 ♘c3 ♕f5 26 ♕c1 ♘c6 27 ♔a1 ♘b4 28 ♖d2 ♘xa2! (forcing the return of the exchange after which Black is left with a simple material advantage) 29 ♘xa2 ♕a5 30 ♗c4 ♗xc4 31 ♕xc4 ♕xd2 32 ♖b1 ♖d8 33 ♘c3 ♕xg2 34 ♘e4 h6 35 ♕c7 ♖d3 36 ♔a2 ♕xe4 0:1

Assessment: 14 ... ♘d7! gives Black good compensation for the exchange.

Month 15

A15/1

a) Capablanca - Alekhine, Buenos Aires WCh 1927. White's pieces are more actively placed and Black's queenside pawns are a bit weak.

White's Plan: I would like to use my superior mobility to attack Black's weakened queenside.

Black's Plan: I need to reduce White's piece activity with exchanges.

Candidate Moves: 17 ... ♗e7; 17 ... ♘e4.

Analysis: 17 ... ♘e4! (17 ... ♗e7 18 ♘a4 b5 [18 ... ♘e4? 19 ♗xe7 ♘xd2 20 ♗xf8 ♘xf1 21 ♗b4] 19 ♗xf6 ♗xf6 20 ♘c5 is better for White) **18 ♘xe4 ♗xh4!** (18 ... ♗xe4?! 19 ♗xd8 ♖fxd8 20 ♖fd1! takes control of the d-file) **19 ♘d6 ♗d5 20 e4 ♖fd8! 21 ♘xf7 ♔xf7 22 exd5 ♖xd5 23 ♖xd5 exd5 24 ♖d1 ♗f6!** (24 ... ♔e6?! 25 ♗g4+ ♔e5 26 g3 ♗f6 27 f4+) **25 ♗f3 ♖c8 26 ♗xd5+ ♔e7 27 b3 ♗b2 28 a4 ♖c1 29 ♖xc1 ♗xc1 30 ♗c4 ½-½**

Assessment: 17 ... ♘e4 simplifies the position and allows Black to hold the balance.

b) Tal-Nunn, USSR-Rest of the World, London 1984. White is ahead in development, he threatens 20 ♖ae1 and Black's f-pawn is weak.

White's Plan: I would like to use my advantage in development to infiltrate Black's position; ♘f3-h4 is a strong idea.

Black's Plan: I must find a way to neutralise White's initiative before things get out of hand.

Candidate Moves: 19 ... ♕e3+; 19 ... ♘e3.

Analysis: 19 ... ♘e3! (Nunn rejected 19 ... ♕e3+ because of 20 ♕xe3 ♘xe3 21 ♖f2 ♗d7 22 ♖e1 ♘g4 23 ♖fe2) **20 ♖ae1** (20 ♖fe1 f4 allows Black to take the initiative after either 21 ♘e2 ♗g4 22 ♘xf4 ♖xf4 23 ♖xe3 ♕f7 or 21 ♘e4 ♖g6 22 ♘h4 ♖g4 23 ♘xd6 ♕h5) **20 ... f4 21 ♘d1** (21 ♘e4 ♖g6 22 ♘h4 ♖g4 23 ♖xf4 ♖xf4 24 ♕xe3 ♗d4 25 ♕xd4 cxd4 26 ♘f6+ ♖xf6 27 ♖xe8+ ♔g7 was an unclear queen sacrifice pointed out by Tal) **21 ... ♗g4 22 ♘xe3 fxe3 23 ♖xe3 ♕h5 24 ♗e4** (24 h3 ♗xf3 25 ♖exf3 ♖af8 gets nowhere) **24 ... ♖af8 25 ♕d3 ♗xf3 26 ♗xf3 ♕g5 27 ♔h1?!** (27 ♖e6!? ♖f4 28 ♖xd6 [28 ♖g6 ♖xf3 29 ♖xf3 ♖xf3 30 ♖xg7+ ♔xg7 31 ♕xf3 ♕c1+=; 28 g3!?] 28 ... ♖xf3 29 ♖xf3 ♕c1+ 30 ♔f2 ♕xb2+ 31 ♕e2 ♗d4+ 32 ♔f1 ♕c1+=) **27 ... ♖f4 28 b3** (28 ♖e6 ♖d4 29 ♕c2 ♖d2 30 ♕e4 ♖d4) **28 ♖h4 29 ♖e4** (29 ♕f5 30 ♖fe1 ♗e5 31 ♖g4+ ♖xg4 32 ♕xf5 ♖xf5 33 ♗xg4 ♖f2=) **½-½**

Assessment: Black can defend himself with accurate play.

A15/2

a) Lasker-Steinitz, New York WCh, 1894. White has an extra piece but his king is exposed.

White's Plan: I need to safeguard my king even if that means returning some material.

Black's Plan: The material situation is quite hopeless so I have to keep the initiative.

Candidate Moves: 31 ♕e2; 31 b3.

Analysis: 31 b3! (covering the light squares on the queenside. Lasker rejected 31 ♕e2 because of 31 ... ♕d5) **31 ... ♖e8 32 ♕e2 ♕h3** (32 ... ♕d5 33 c4) **33 ♔d1 ♖a8 34 ♖f2 ♖a2 35 b5!** c5 (otherwise White's knight would establish itself on the d4 square) **36 ♘xg7 d5 37 ♔c1 ♕d3** ("On 37 c4 there would have followed 38 bc or 37 ♘d3+ 38 ♔b1 with exchanges to follow"—Lasker) **38 ♕xd3 ♘xd3+ 39 ♔b1 ♖b2+ 40 ♔a1 ♖xb3 41 ♖f3 c4 42 ♘e8 ♘b4 43 ♖g3 ♖a3+ 44 ♔b1 ♖b3+ 45 ♔c1 ♘d3+ 46 ♖xd3!** and White won.

Assessment: 31 b3 snuffs out Black's attack.

b) Karpov-Gligoric, Milan 1975. White has more space, the more homogeneous pawn structure and there are weak pawns in Black's camp on a6 and d6. Black has some temporary piece activity.

White's Plan: After driving Black's pieces to less active squares I can play for the thematic b2-b4 lever.

Black's Plan: This position could turn against me if I cannot make something of my active pieces.

Candidate Moves: 28 ♘c1; 28 ♗e1.

Analysis: 28 ♗e1! ♕e7 (28 ... ♘f6 29 f4! exf4 30 ♘xf5) **29 ♖xb3 ♖xb3 30 ♘c1 ♖b8 31 ♘d3 ♖b3 32 f3** (32 ♕c2 ♕b7 33 ♗c3 ♗h6 is unconvincing) **32 ... ♕g5** (32 ... ♗h6 is better) **33 ♔h2 ♘f6 34 ♕c2 ♖b8 35 b4!** with a powerful initiative for White.

Assessment: After dampening down Black's piece activity White can take the initiative with a later b2-b4.

A15/3

a) Bondarevsky-Lilienthal, USSR Ch, Moscow 1941. White has a large space advantage and the pin on the knight on f6 is very unpleasant.

White's Plan: I want to bring a rook or two to the f-file in order to increase the pressure against the pinned knight on f6.

Black's Plan: This is looking nasty, I desperately need to find a way to break this pin on my knight.

Candidate Moves: 19 ... ♕f8; 19 ... exf4.

Analysis: 19 ... exf4! (19 ... ♕f8 20 ♗xf6) **20 gxf4 g5! 21 fxg5** (21 ♗g3 gxf4 22 ♗xf4 ♘g4 23 h3 ♕f6 24 ♖f1 ♘e5 25 ♕h5 was White's best attempt to exploit Black's weakened kingside) **21 ... ♘g4 22 e5! ♘xe5 23 ♕h5 hxg5 24 ♗xg5 f6 25 ♗h4 ♕g7 26 ♗g3 ♗g4 27 ♕h4 ♔f7!** when Black had turned the tables as was suddenly threatening 28 ... ♖h8!.

Assessment: 19 ... exf4 and 20 ... g5 gets Black out of trouble.

b) Yusupov-Timman, Tilburg 1986. White has the two bishops and a dangerous looking pawn centre but his c-pawns are doubled and make his position inflexible.

White's Plan: I would like to use my pawn centre as a battering ram and open the position up for the two bishops.

Black's Plan: I need to restrict the activity of White's bishop pair by keeping lines closed and then attack his weak pawns.

Candidate Moves: 13 ... ♕e7; 13 ... f4; 13 ... fxe4.

Analysis: 13 ... fxe4! (Timman played 13 ... ♕e7?! when White developed a strong initiative after 14 e5 ♘f7 15 f4 g5 [15 ... d6!?] 16 d5! gxf4 17 ♘f3 ♘h8 18 ♖ae1 ♘g6 19 ♗c1 ♔h8?! (19 ... ♖ae8) 20 ♕f2 ♕g7 21 h4! ♕h6 [21 ♖g8!?] 22 ♘g5! ♕xh4 23 ♕xh4 ♘xh4 24 ♖xf4 ♘g6 25 ♖f3 ♖ae8 26 ♖h3; 13 ... f4 14 ♗e2!, 15 ♘d3) **14 fxe4 ♖xf1+ 15 ♔xf1 e5! 16 ♘f3 ♘f7** would have kept the bishop pair firmly under control and given Black the somewhat better game.

Assessment: Black can keep the position closed when White will struggle to find full compensation for his pawn weaknesses.

A15/4

a) Neikirkh-Botvinnik, Leipzig Ol 1960. White is poised to launch a fierce attack on Black's king with moves like ♖h3, ♕h5 and f4-f5 though his centre is in danger of collapse.

White's Plan: If I can't inflict immediate damage this position might turn against me.

Black's Plan: If I survive the immediate danger the weaknesses in White's game should leave him open to a counterstroke.

Candidate Moves: 12 ... ♘xb3; 12 ♗b7; 12 ... g6.

Analysis: 12 ... ♘xb3! (12 ... ♗b7 13 ♖h3 ♘xb3 14 ♕h5 h6 15 ♘xb3 leaves White threatening 16 f5 followed by 17 ♗xh6) **13 ♘c6** (13 axb3 ♗b7 14 ♖h3 g6! safeguards the kingside and would therefore favour Black) **13 ... ♕d7 14 ♘xe7+ ♕xe7 15 axb3 f6! 16 exd6?** (according to Botvinnik White should have waited for Black to exchange pawns on e5) **16 ... ♘xd6 17 ♖d3 ♘f5 18 ♖a4 ♕e8!** (18 ... ♗b7 19 ♖d7!) **19 ♘e4** (19 ♖e4 ♗b7 20 ♖e1 was relatively best) **19 ... b5 20 ♖a5?** (20 ♖a1) **20 ... ♗b7 21 ♘d6** (21 ♘c5 ♗xg2+ 22 ♔xg2 ♕c6+) **21 ♘xd6 22 ♖xd6 ♖d8!** (threatening 22 ... ♕c6!) **23 ♕d2** (23 ♖xd8 ♕xd8 24 ♕e1 ♕d5 25 ♕e2 ♖d8 26 ♗e3 ♕d1+ 27 ♕xd1 ♖xd1+ 28 ♗g1 ♖d2-+) **23 ♖xd6 24 ♕xd6 ♕d8 25 ♕xe6+ ♖f7 26 ♕e1 ♖e7 0:1**

Assessment: Black can defend and then take the initiative.

b) Smirin-Davies, Tel Aviv 1991.
White threatens 30 ♗b6 or take the knight on e5 which defends f7. On the other hand Black's pieces are quite actively placed in the centre.

White's Plan: Continue my tactical threats.

Black's Plan: I need to survive the next move!

Candidate Moves: 27 ... ♘7c6; 27 ... ♘g8.

Analysis: 29 ... ♘7c6!? (Lev Psakhis accused me of having a "too complicated brain" in the post mortem and pointed out that Black can also play 29 ... ♘g8 after which 30 ♗b6 ♕e7 31 ♗xd8 ♖xd8 leaves both of White's rooks under threat after ♘xc4 followed by either ♗e5 or ♗xa1) 30 ♗b6 ♕d7 31 ♗xd8 ♘d4! 32 ♗d1?! (32 ♕d2) 32 ... ♘xc4 33 ♗f6? (33 bxc4) 33 ... ♖xe4 34 ♕xe4 ♗xe4 35 ♗xh8 ♘e5 36 ♖c1 f5 37 f4 ♘ec6 38 h4 ♘e6 39 ♗f3 ♘xf4! 40 ♗xe4 ♘e2+ 41 ♔h2 ♘xc1 42 ♗xf5 gxf5 43 ♖g8+ ♔e7 44 ♖g7+ ♔d8 45 ♖xd7+ ♔xd7 46 ♘xf5 ♘xb3 47 g4 ♘c5 48 h5 ♘e5 49 g5 b3 0:1

Assessment: Black's position contains suprising resources, after 29 ... ♘g8 he stands no worse and 29 ... ♘7c6!? is also interesting.

Month 16

A16/1

a) Flohr-Keres, Moscow 1950. White has an extra pawn, strong pressure against e6 and d7 and Black's king stuck in the centre.

White's Plan: Can I strike before Black recaptures on c5 or should I let him do this and put pressure on the d-file?

Black's Plan: I hope to recover my pawn with 16 ... bxc5 and then consolidate with 17 ... d6.

Candidate Moves: 16 ♖d2; 16 ♘d4; 16 b4.

Analysis: 16 b4! (Better than Flohr's quiet 16 ♖d2 after which 16 bxc5 17 ♖fd1 d6 was reasonably solid for Black; 16 ♘d4! ♗xc5 17 ♕a4 or 17 ♕c1!? was a quiet but effective plan) **16 ... ♘c6** (16 ... ♘xc4 17 ♕xa7! ♗d5 [17 ... ♗c6 18 ♗xe6+ ♔xe6 19 ♘d4+ ♔f7 20 ♘xc6 ♖xc6 21 ♖xd7 ♕e8 22 cxb6 ♘xe3 23 fxe3+-; 17 ... ♘xe3? 18 fxe3 ♗xf3 19 ♖xd7+-] 18 ♖xd5 exd5 19 ♕b7 ♔e8 20 ♕xd5 ♘xe3 21 fxe3 ♕c7 22 ♖d1 ♖d8 23 cxb6 ♕c6 24 b7 ♖xd5 25 ♖xd5 ♔f7 26 b5) **17 cxb6 axb6 18 ♕b3 ♘xb4** (18 ... ♗xb4 19 c5) **19 ♗xe6+ ♔xe6 20 ♗xb6 ♕xb6** (20 ... ♕e8 21 c5+ ♘d5 22 e4) **21 c5+ ♗d5 22 ♖xd5 ♗xc5 23 ♖fd1! ♗xf2+ 24 ♔g2 ♘xd5 25 ♕xd5+ ♔e7 26 ♕xd7+ ♔f8 27 ♕xc8+** wins.

Assessment: By taking decisive action White can obtain a winning position.

b) Stahlberg-Keres, Helsinki 1935. Black is a whole piece up but his king is sitting with the wind in his hair.

White's Plan: I need to find a way through to Black's king.

Black's Plan: I will have to deal with the threats as and when they arise.

Candidate Moves: 30 ♖b3; 30 ♖f3.

Analysis: 30 ♖f3! (Stahlberg got nowhere with 30 ♖b3? ♘b6 31 ♗d3 when Black could have consolidated immediately with 31 ... ♕g5! 32 ♕xg5 hxg5 33 ♗b5 ♗d5; 30 ♗xd5?! ♗xd5 31 ♖xd5? is bad because of 31 ... ♕a1+) **30 ... ♘f4** (30 ... ♕g7 31 ♗xg6+; 30 ... ♕e7 31 ♗xg6+) **31 ♕b5** wins for White according to Keres.

Assessment: The right sequence gives White a winning game.

A16/2

a) Karpov-Kasparov, London-Leningrad WCh 1986. White is the exchange up but both 25 ... ♘xd2 and 25 ... ♗b5 are threatened.

White's Plan: If I cannot maintain my advantage of the exchange I need to give it back so as to ensure the later advance of the d-pawn.

Black's Plan: It looks as if I should win back the exchange after which I need to blockade the d-pawn.

Candidate Moves: 25 ♖d1; 25 ♗f4; 25 ♗h6.

Analysis: 25 ♗f4! (25 ♖d1 ♗a4) **25 ... ♗b5 26 f3 g5** (26 ... ♗xf1 27 ♔xf1 ♘f6 28 ♖xe8+ ♘xe8 29 ♗e5!, 30 d6, 31 d7) **27 ♗xg5 ♗xf1 28 ♔xf1 ♘d6 29 ♗e7!** (29 ♖xe8+ ♘xe8 30 ♗e7 f5 31 ♗xc5 b6 32 ♗d4 ♔f7 might keep Black alive) **29 ... ♘c8** (29 ... ♘c4 30 d6 ♘b6 31 ♖b1, 32 ♖xb6, 33 d7) **30 ♗xc5 ♖d8 31 ♖e5 f6 32 ♖f5 b6** (32 ♔f7 33 g4 ♘e7 34 ♖h5 ♖h8 also leaves Black miserably placed) **33 ♗d4 ♘e7 34 ♗xf6 ♖xd5 35 ♖g5+ ♖xg5 36 ♗xg5 ♘c6 37 ♔e2 ♔f7 38 ♔d3 ♔e6 39 ♔c4 ♘e5+ 40 ♔d4 ♘c6+ 1:0**

Assessment: With accurate play White should win

b) Alekhine-Saemisch, Baden-Baden 1925. White has an extra pawn but his king is exposed and Black's combination of queen and knight work very well together.

White's Plan: The immediate advance of my b-pawn would expose my king so I should create a second weakness on the other flank by advancing my kingside pawns.

Black's Plan: If White pushes his b-pawn I will harrass his with my queen and knight.

Candidate Moves: 34 ♕d4.

Analysis: 34 ♕d4! ♕e7 35 ♗d3! ♕c7 36 g4 ♔f7 37 h4 ♘b6 38 h5! gxh5 39 gxh5 ♕c6 40 ♗e4! (40 ♗xh7? ♕xf3 41 ♕xb6 ♕d1+=) **40**

... ♕b5 41 h6 ♕b3 42 ♗c2! ♕b5 43 ♕d3! (exchanging queens under the most favourable circumstances) **43 ♕xd3 44 ♗xd3 ♘c8 45 ♗xh7 ♘e7 46 ♔c1 f5 47 b4 ♘d5 48 b5 ♔e6 49 ♔d1 ♔d6 50 f4 ♘xf4 51 ♗xf5 ♘d5 52 ♗e4 1:0**

Assessment: With fine technique White should be able to win.

A16/3

a) Vadasz-Davies, Budapest 1993. Black's pieces look loose, his queen is en prise and the pins on the h1-a8 diagonal mean that the pawn on d4 will probably drop.

White's Plan: When Black moves his queen I'll take the knight on f5 and then recover the pawn on d4.

Black's Plan: Desperate times call for desperate means, I need to mix it at any cost.

Candidate Moves: 18 ... ♕d7; 18 ... ♖e4.

Analysis: 18 ... ♖e4!! 19 ♘xf5 (19 ♗xe4 ♕xe4 20 ♘xf5 ♘e5 21 f3 ♘xf3+ 22 ♖xf3 ♕xf3 23 ♘h6+ ♔g7 24 ♘f4 ♕h1+ 25 ♔f2 ♕xh2+ 26 ♔e1 ♕xb2 etc) **19 ... ♕xf5 20 ♘xd4 ♘xd4 21 exd4 ♖e7! 22 ♗xb7 ♖xb7 23 ♖ad1 ♖d8 24 ♖d2 ♖bd7= 25 ♕c3 ♕f6 26 ♖fd1 ♖d5 27 ♕e3 ♔g7 28 ♕e4 ♖8d7 29 ♖d3 ♕d6 30 ♖e1 ♖xd4 31 ♖xd4 ♕xd4 32 ♕xd4+ ♖xd4 33 ♖e7 a5 34 ♖b7 ½-½**

Assessment: 18 ... ♖e4! puts a large spanner in the works

b) Juhasz-Davies, Budapest 1993. Black's position is full of holes and weaknesses and he is threatened with both 25 ♘xb4 and 25 e5.

White's Plan: When Black retreats his rook from b4 I'll crush him completely with 25 e5.

Black's Plan: I would do anything to complicate matters.

Candidate Moves: 24 ... ♘xe4.

Analysis: 24 ... ♘xe4! 25 ♗xe4 ♖xe4 26 ♘xb4 ♗d4+ 27 ♔h1 cxb4 28 ♘xd6 ♕xd6 29 ♖xc8+ ♔g7 30 f5 f6 31 ♗h6+ ♔f7 32 ♖h8?! g5 33 ♖c1 (33 ♖xh7+ ♔g8 34 ♖g7+ ♔h8 leaves both rook and bishop are in no man's land) 33 ... ♘c5 34 ♗f8 (34 ♖c4? ♕xh2+! 35 ♔xh2 ♖h4+ 36 ♔g3 ♘e4+ 37 ♔f3 ♘xd2+; 34 ♕xb4 ♖h4 35 h3 ♖xh3+ 36 gxh3 ♕xd5+ 37 ♔h2 ♕e5+ 38 ♔g2 ♕e4+ 39 ♔h2 ♗e5+) 34 ... ♕e5 35 ♗xc5 ♗xc5 36 ♖c8 (36 ♖xh7+ ♔g8 37 ♖h3 ♖e2 38 ♕d1 ♕e4 39 ♕f1 ♖f2 40 ♕g1 ♖c2 41 ♕f1 ♕xg2+) 36 ... ♗d6 37 g3 ♖e2 38 ♕d3 ♕xb2 39 ♕f3 g4 40 ♕f1 ♕e5 0:1

Assessment: White must surely be winning, or is he? But in White's shoes I would not have let Black take on e4 in the first place.

A16/4

a) Vukovic-Iovcic, Yugoslavia 1956. White is a pawn up and has a three to one majority on the kingside. His bishop can simultaneously blockade the a-pawn and support the advance of his kingside pawns.

White's Plan: I want to create two connected passed pawns on the kingside and shepherd them towards the 8th rank.

Black's Plan: I need to break up White's pawn majority before he improves the position of his pieces. One hope is that his h-pawn is the opposite colour to his bishop and cannot promote on its own.

Candidate Moves: 35 ... h5.

Analysis: 35 ... h5! 36 g5+ (36 gxh5 would allow Black to sacrifice his knight for White's f-pawn as even an extra bishop White would be unable to promote one of his two h-pawns should Black's king hide on h8) 36 ... ♗f5 37 ♔e3 ♔g4 38 g6 ♘f6 39 g7 ♔xh4 40 g8=♕ ♘xg8 41 ♗xg8 and now **Black** actually resigned in a drawn position! Black would indeed be lost after 41 ... ♔g4? 42 ♗e6+ ♔g3 43 f5 h4 44 f6 h3 45 f7 h2 46 f8=♕ h1=♕ 47 ♕f4+ ♔g2 48 ♕f2# but with 41 ... ♔g3! he would put White in unusual zugzwang and Black would draw after either 42 f5 ♔g4 43 f6 ♔g5 44 f7 a2 or 42 ♗d5 h4 43 f5 h3 44 f6 h2 45 f7 h1=♕! 46 ♗xh1 a2 47 f8=♕ a1=♕.

Assessment: A draw!

b) Tarrasch-Lasker, Dusseldorf WCh 1908. Things look grim for Black as after 15 ... ♔xg7 16 ♘f5+ recovers the piece with a big advantage.

White's Plan: I've won a pawn and Black's kingside is shattered. I wonder where I'll dine this evening.

Black's Plan: Objectively speaking I'm lost but I'm going to make it as difficult as I can.

Candidate Moves: 15 ... ♔xg7; 15 ... ♘xf2.

Analysis: 15 ... ♘xf2! (15 ... ♔xg7 16 ♘f5+ ♔h8 17 ♕xg4) 16 ♔xf2?! (16 ♕d4! ♘g4 [16 ... c5 17 ♕xf2 ♔xg7 18 ♘h5+ is hopeless after either 18 ... ♔h6 19 ♖e3 or 18 ... ♔h8 19 ♕xf7] 17 ♘f5 ♕e6 18 ♕xa7 [18 h3?! ♗f6; 18 ♕c3 ♗f6 19 ♗xf6 ♕xf6 20 ♕g3 ♕g6 21 ♕xg4] 18 ... d5?! 19 h3 ♘f6 20 ♘xe7+, 21 exd5+-) 16 ... ♔xg7 17 ♘f5+ ♔h8

18 ♕d4+ f6 19 ♕xa7 ♗f8 20 ♕d4 ♖e5 21 ♖ad1 ♖de8 22 ♕c3 ♕f7! 23 ♘g3? (bringing the knight to a passive position, he should play 23 ♕f3 intending 24 c4) 23 ... ♗h6 24 ♕f3 (here White should bring his knight back to f5) 24 ... d5 25 exd5 ♗e3+ 26 ♔f1 cxd5 27 ♖d3? (27 ♘f5 was necessary but then 27 ... d4 would leave Black with adequate play for his pawn) 27 ... ♕e6 28 ♖e2 f5 29 ♖d1 (29 ♔e1 f4 30 ♘f1 ♗f2+!-+) 29 ... f4 30 ♘h1 d4 31 ♘f2 ♕a6 32 ♘d3 ♖g5! 33 ♖a1 ♕h6 34 ♔e1 ♕xh2 35 ♔d1 ♕g1+ 36 ♘e1 ♖ge5 37 ♕c6 ♖5e6 38 ♕xc7 ♖8e7 39 ♕d8+ ♔g7 40 a4 f3 41 gxf3 ♗g5 0:1

Assessment: White is winning but it isn't easy.

Month 17

A17/1

a) Chernin-Petursson, Norway 1979. White's bishops are potentially very strong due to the open nature of the position.

White's Plan: If I could neutralise Black's temporary activity the bishop pair would give me an edge.

Black's Plan: I need to use my temporary activity before White's bishops become a problem.

Candidate Moves: 45 ♗e4; 45 g4; 45 ♗e5; 45 ♖e5.

Analysis: 45 ♖e5! (45 g4 ♘e6 46 ♔f2 ♖a5 gives Black counterplay against f3 and a2) 45 ... ♖xe5 (45 ... ♖c1+ 46 ♔f2 ♖a1 47 ♖e2 drives Black's rook from its irritating position) 46 ♗xe5 ♗xf3 47 ♗b8 a6 48 ♗c8! (48 ♗c7 b5 49 ♗c8 b4, 50 ... ♗d5) 48 ... ♗d5 49 a3 ♗c4+ 50 ♔f2 ♘g6 51 ♔e3! (51 ♗c7 ♘e7) 51 ... ♘e7 52 ♗b7 a5 53 ♔d4 ♗e6 54 ♗c7 ♘c8 55 ♔e5 ♔g7 56 ♗d8 ♗h3 57 ♗e4 ♗e6 58 ♗d3 ♗h3 59 ♗e2 ♗e6 60 g4 ♗b3 61 ♗a6 ♗e6 62 ♗e2 ♗b3 (after 62 ... h6 White plays for g4-g5, creating a passed h-pawn) 63 g5 ♗e6 64 h4 ♗h3 65 h5 ♗e6 66 ♗d3 ♗g4 67 h6+ ♔g8 68 ♗c7 ♗f3 (Black should be careful to avoid either 71 ... ♔f8? 72 g6+- or 71 ... ♔h8? 72 ♗xc8 ♗xc8 73 ♔xf7+-) 69 ♗c4 ♗g4 70 a4?! (White should have avoided this as a fantastic defensive idea is now possible) 70 ... ♗d1 71 ♔f6 ♗h5 72 ♗b5 ♗g4 73 ♗c4 ♗h5 74 ♗d5 ♗g6 (Or 74 ♔f8 75 ♗e4 ♔g8 76 ♗f5 etc) 75 ♗b7 ♗c2! 76 ♗c6 (Dvoretsky pointed out that White could also have won with 76 ♗xc8, ultimately infiltrating Black's fortress) 76 ... ♗d3 77 ♗d7 ♗c2!! 78 ♗e8 ♗b3 79 ♗d7 ♗c2 80 ♔e5 ♗d1 81 ♔d4 ♗b3 82 ♔c3 ♗e6 83 ♗xe6 fe 84 ♔c4 ♔f7 85 ♔b5 ♔g6 86 ♗xb6 ♔xg5 87 ♔xa5? (87 ♗c5) 87 ... ♔f6 (87 ... ♘xb6! 88 ♔xb6 e5=) 88 ♗c5 e5 89 ♔b5 ♔e6 90 ♔c6 e4 91 a5 ♘e7+ 92 ♔c7 ♘d5+ 93 ♔b7 1:0

Assessment: 45 ♖e5! gives White excellent winning chances.

b)   Azmaiparashvili-Yurtaev, Pavlodar 1982. Black has a central majority, White's knight blockades his isolated b-pawn.

White's Plan: How can I maintain my knight on b4?

Black's Plan: After the exchange of minor pieces I will be no worse.

Candidate Moves: 24 ♘xc6; 24 ♗xc6.

Analysis: 24 ♗xc6! ♗xc6 25 ♖c1 ♗d7 (25 ... ♗e4 26 ♖dd1! [26 ♖xc8 ♖xc8 27 f3 ♖c1+ 28 ♔f2 ♗f5 29 e4 ♗e6 30 ♖c2 ♖h1 31 h4 h6 32 ♖c7 ♔f6 33 ♖b7 ♖h2+ 34 ♔e3 ♖g2 35 ♖xb5 ♖xg3]) 26 ♖dc2 e6 27 ♔f1 ♔f6 28 ♔e1 d5 (28 ... ♔e7) 29 ♖xc8 ♖xc8 30 ♖xc8 ♗xc8 31 ♔d2 ♗d7 32 ♔c3 ♔e5 33 ♘c2 ♔d6 34

♔b4 ♔c6 35 ♘d4+ ♔b6 36 f4 f6 37 a4! (creating a passed pawn) 37 ... bxa4 38 bxa4 e5 39 fxe5 fxe5 40 ♘f3! e4 41 a5+ ♔a6 42 ♘d4 (threatening 43 e3 followed by ♘b3-c5) 42 ... e3 43 ♘c2 ♗b5 44 ♘xe3 ♗xe2 45 ♘xd5 ♔b7 46 ♘f6 h5 47 h4 ♔c6 48 ♔c3 (48 ... ♔b5 49 ♘d5 wins Black's remaining pawns) 1:0

Assessment: 24 ♗xc6! keeps an edge for White.

A17/2

a) Von Gottschall-Nimzowitsch, Hannover 1926. White's c5 pawn is weak because of the insecure position of his bishop on f2 Black's pieces are actively placed, especially the rook on f3.

White's Plan: Ideally I would like to exchange rooks but I would settle for neutralising my opponent's plans.

Black's Plan: I can't win this position with my passed e-pawn alone so I need to manoevre against White's weaknesses on c5 and his kingside pawns. But first of all I can further improve my king position.

Candidate Moves: 38 ... ♔d5; 38 ... ♔e5.

Analysis: 38 ... ♔e5! (losing a tempo, after 38 ... ♔d5 39 ♖b4 it isn't clear how Black can continue) 39 ♖b4 ♔d5! 40 h4 (40 ♖d4+ ♔xc5 41 ♖xe4 ♖xf2+-+; 40 ♖b6 h4 41 gxh4 gxh4 42 ♗xh4 ♔xc5-+) 40 ... gxh4 41 gxh4 ♖h3 42 ♖d4+ ♔e5 43 ♖d8 ♗d5 44 ♖e8+ ♗e6 45 ♖d8 ♔f4 46 ♖f8+ ♗f5 47 ♖f7 ♖h2 48 ♖e7 ♗g4+ 49 ♔e1 ♔f3 50 ♖f7+ ♔g2 51 ♔d2 ♔f1 52 ♔e3 ♗f3 53 ♗g3 ♖xb2 54 ♗d6 ♖b3+ 55 ♔d4 ♔f2 56 ♖g7 e3 57 ♗g3+ ♔f1 58 ♖f7 e2 59 ♖e7 ♗c6 0:1

Assessment: White can gradually be run out of moves.

b) Von Holzhausen - Nimzowitsch, Hannover 1926. Black is a pawn up but at present the extra pawn is blockaded by White's knight on e3.

White's Plan: I can't undertake much in the way of positive action so I need to sit tight.

Black's Plan: White is tied to my passed e-pawn but to win I need to open up a second front on the queenside.

Candidate Moves: 32 ... a6; 32 ... ♖h6.

Analysis: 32 ... ♖h6! (starting the process of softening up White's kingside) 33 h3 ♖g6 34 ♖e2 a6 35 ♖f4 b5 36 b3 ♖g5 37 g4 ♖ge5 38 ♔c3 a5! 39 ♖ef2 a4 40 bxa4 bxc4! 41 ♖f8 ♖5e7 42 ♖xe8 ♖xe8 43 ♘xc4 ♘xc4 44 ♔xc4 ♖a8 45 ♖f7 (45 ♔b3? ♔d5!-+) 45 ... ♖xa4+ 46 ♔b3 (46 ♔c3 was better) 46 ... ♖b4+! 47 ♔c3 ♖b7 48 ♖f5 ♖a7 49 ♔c4 ♖a4+ 50 ♔b3 ♖d4 51 ♖e5 ♔d6 52 ♖e8 ♖d3+ 53 ♔c4 ♖xh3! (finally taking advantage of the weakness created some 20 moves earlier) 54 ♖xe4 ♖a3 55 ♖e2 ♖a4+ and Black went on to win.

Assessment: The breakthrough on the queenside should prove decisive once White's kingside has been softened up.

A17/3

a) Nimzowitsch - Capablanca, New York 1927. White is tied down to the weak pawns on d4 and f4 and his king looks rather exposed.

White's Plan: Hang on to my d-pawn and pray.

Black's Plan: I can increase the pressure by advancing my b-pawn, on b3 it would provide an outpost on c2.

Candidate Moves: 38 ... ♕c1; 38 ... b5.

Analysis: 38 ... b5! 39 ♔g1 b4 40 axb4 axb4 41 ♔g2 ♕c1! 42 ♔g3 (42 h3 b3 43 ♔h2 ♖e1 44 ♔g2 ♕b1 45 ♖e2 ♖c1 and 46 ... ♖c2-+) **42 ♕h1! 43 ♖d3** (43 ♖e2 ♖xe2 44 ♕xe2 ♕g1+-+, 43 ♕g2 ♕xg2+ 44 ♔xg2 [or 44 ♖xg2 ♖xd4] 44 ♖xf4 or 43 ♕f3 h4+ 44 ♔f2 ♕e1+-+) **43 ... ♖e1** (threatening 44 ... ♖f1 45 ♕e3 ♖g1+-+) **44 ♖f3 ♖d1 45 b3** (45 ♔h3 ♖d2 46 ♕g3 h4-+; 45 ♖b3 ♕e4 46 ♖xb4 ♖d3+ 47 ♔h4 ♖f3-+; 45 h3 ♖g1+ 46 ♔h4 ♖g4#) **45 ... ♖c1! 46 ♖e3** (46 ♔h4 ♖c2 47 ♕xc2 ♕xf3 48 h3 ♕xf4#; 46 h3 ♖g1+ 47 ♔h4 ♖g4#, 46 ♕e2 ♖c2! 47 ♕xc2 h4+ 48 ♔xh4 ♕xf3 49 h3 ♕xf4# or 46 ♕d2 h4+ 47 ♔xh4 [47 ♔f2 ♖f1+] 47 ... ♕xf3-+) **46 ... ♖f1 0:1** (47 ♕e2 ♕g1+ 48 ♔h3 ♖f2-+)

Assessment: White is defenceless against the gradual infiltration of his position.

b) Andersson-Franco, Buenos Aires 1979. White's pieces dominate the position and Black has serious weaknesses on c7 and e5 as well as a very bad bishop.

White's Plan: To break through I like the idea of c4-c5 for which my knight should be on d3.

Black's Plan: I have no active plan so I must wait and hope for the best.

Candidate Moves: 33 ♘b2.

Analysis: 33 ♘b2! ♔e8 (33 ... ♖d6 34 ♖xd6 ♔xd6 35 c4, 36 ♘d3, 37 c5+, 38 ♔c4+-) **34 ♘d3 ♗g7** (34 ... c6 35 ♖dd7 cxb5 36 ♘b4+-) **35**

c4 ♗f6 36 c5 bxc5 37 ♘xc5 ♖e7 (37 ... ♖b6 38 ♘d7!) **38 ♖a6!** (preventing 38 ... c6 and securing e6 for his knight) **38 ... ♗h8 39 ♔c4!** (once again preferring to improve the position rather than try to force matters prematurely) **39 ♗g7 40 f3 ♖b8 41 ♘e6 ♗f6 42 ♖c6 1:0** (42 ... ♖b7 43 ♖d8+ ♔f7 44 ♖f8#; 42 ... ♖c8 43 b6)

Assessment: Black is helpless if White proceeds methodically.

A17/4

a) Ribli-Kavalek, Tilburg 1980. Black has a weak pawn on e6 and the inferior pawn structure. The open f-file and bishop on c5 gives him counterplay against f2.

White's Plan: If I can't win the e6 pawn I would like to blockade it with my knight on e4.

Black's Plan: I would like to create counterplay against f2.

Candidate Moves: 20 ♖xe6; 20 ♗e3; 20 ♗g5.

Analysis: 20 ♗g5! (20 ♖xe6 ♘g4! 21 ♘e4 ♗d4! [21 ... ♗xf2+ 22 ♘xf2 ♘xf2 23 ♗d2; 21 ... ♘xf2 22 ♘xc5 bxc5 23 ♗d2] 22 ♖d6 ♗e5 23 ♖d1 ♗xh2+; 20 ♗e3 ♗xe3 21 ♖xe3 ♘d5! 22 ♖xe6 ♘xc3 23 bxc3 ♖ac8 24 ♖e3 ♖f4 [threatening to repeat the position with 25 ... ♖fc4 26 ♖c1 ♖a4] 25 h3 ♖fc4 26 ♖c1 ♖8c7 27 ♔f1 ♖a4 28 ♖a1 ♖ac4 29 ♖d1 h6 ½-½ was the game continuation) **20 ... ♖ad8!?** (20 ... ♘g4 21 ♗h4!; 20 ... ♘d5 21 ♘e4, 20 ... ♔f7 21 ♖d1) **21 ♗xf6!** (and not 21 ♖xe6 ♗xf2+ 22 ♔xf2 ♘e4+ 23 ♔g1 ♘xg5=) **21 ... ♖xf6 22 ♘e4 ♖f5 23 g3** keeps and edge for White.

Assessment: White can maintain a small advantage with 20 ♗g5.

b) **Korchnoi-Karpov, Moscow Cm 1974.** White's rook is well placed on the 7th rank and his king well centralised. White's kingside majority contains a useless doubled pawn, Black's passed d-pawn is firmly under control.

White's Plan: I would like to round up that d-pawn and then turn my attention to the other Black weaknesses.

Black's Plan: White is in command at the moment but I might hope for counterplay with my d-pawn.

Candidate Moves: 44 ♔d4; 44 h4.

Analysis: 44 h4! (systematically improving White's position rather than blundering into 44 ♔d4 ♖c8 45

♖xa5? d2) **44 ... h5 45 a3 ♗a6 46 ♔d2** (46 ♖xa6 ♖xc3 47 ♖xa5 g6 48 ♖a7 ♖b3 49 a4 ♖a3 50 a5 ♔g8 leaves White unable to make progress) **46 ... ♖c6 47 ♖d7** (threatening 48 ♖d5) **47 ♗c4** (Or 47 ... ♖b6 48 ♘d1) **48 ♘d1 ♗b5 49 ♘e3 g6 50 ♖d5!** (forcing the reply) **50 ... ♖b6 51 ♘d1!** (immediately trying to win the d-pawn) **51 ... ♔f7 52 ♘b2! ♗a6** (52 ... ♗c6 53 ♘c4 52 ♗c6 ♘c4) and now Korchnoi should have played **53 ♘xd3!** (rather than 53 ♘a4?!) **53 ... ♗xd3 54 ♖xd3 ♖b2+ 55 ♔c3 ♖xf2 56 ♔b3** followed by 57 ♔a4, winning the a-pawn and the game.

Assessment: With accurate play White's advantage should be decisive.

Month 18

A18/1

a) Karpov-Miles, London 1982.

White has an advanced passed a-pawn but his other pawns look rather weak.

White's Plan: I need to find a way to advance my a-pawn.

Black's Plan: Stop the a-pawn and harass White's king.

Candidate Moves: 29 ♖e2?; 29 ♖xd5!?.

Analysis: 29 ♖xd5! ♖xd5 30 ♖c3! ♖d8 (30 ... ♖xc3+ 31 ♔xc3 ♖c5+ 32 ♔b4 ♖c7 33 ♗g2 threatens ♗b7, a7; 30 ... ♖a8 31 ♗g2 e6 32 ♗xd5 exd5 33 ♖c6+-) **31 ♖c7!** (31 ♗g2? ♖d4 32 a7 d5; 31 a7 b4 32 axb4 ♖d1 33 ♗a6 ♖a1 34 b5 ♖a8) **31 ... ♖d1 32 ♗xb5 e5 33 a7 exf4 34 ♖b7 ♖b1+ 35 ♔a4 ♖xb5 36 ♖xb5 f3 37 ♖b8 f2 38 ♖xd8+ 1:0**

Assessment: White has a forced win.

b) Miles-Keene, London 1982.

White's rooks are very active and Black's king badly placed.

White's Plan: I would like to find a way to attack Black's king before he safegaurds it with 34 ... ♔e8.

Black's Plan: With level material in a rook endgame I should be able to draw, but only if my king doesn't have trouble. Given time I will play 34 ... ♔e8 and 35 ... ♔d7.

Candidate Moves: 34 ♖h8+; 34 b3!?.

Analysis: 34 b3! ♖xa3 35 ♖h8+! ♔g7 36 ♔e4! e6 (36 ... ♖c5 37 f5, 38 ♖4h7#) **37 ♖b8!** (threatening 38 ♖4h8, 39 ♖bg8#) **37 ... d5+?** (37 ... ♖b5? 38 ♖hh8 f5+ 39 ♔d3 ♖bxb3 40 ♖hc8 ♔g6 41 ♖c7! threatening 42 ♖h8; 37 ... ♖c5 seems to hang on after 38 ♖hh8 f5+ 39 ♔d4 ♖d5+! [39 ... ♖c7? 40 ♖bg8+ ♔f7 41 g6+ ♔f6 42 ♖h7+-] 40 ♔c4 b5+ 41 ♔b4 ♖a2) **38 ♔d3!** (38 ♔e3 e5) **38 ... ♖xf4** (38 ... f6 39 ♖xb7+ ♔g8 40 g6+-) **39 ♖xf4 ♖xb3 1:0**

Assessment: 34 b3 poses very difficult problems.

A18/2

a) Gruenberg-Glek, Tallinn 1986.

Black is a piece up, White has a passed pawn on b7.

White's Plan: I am threatening 23 ♗xd8 followed by 24 ♖a8 and when Black moves the rook on d8 I can play 23 ♗c7.

Black's Plan: I must stop that a-pawn even if it means returning some material.

Candidate Moves: 22 ... ♖d7; 22 ... ♖dc8; 22 ... ♖xb7; 22 ... ♗f8.

Analysis: 22 ... ♗f8! (22 ... ♖dc8 23 bxc8=♕+ ♗xc8 24 ♗c7 ♖b5 25 ♖a8 is good for White) **23 ♔h1** (23 ♖b1 ♖d7! 24 ♗xd7 ♘xd7 25 ♗c7? ♗c5+) **23 ... ♖dc8!?** (23 ... ♗d6 24 ♗xd8 ♖xd8 25 ♖d1 [25

Ra8 Rb8] 25 ... b2 26 Ra8 Rb8 27 Rxb8+ &xb8 28 Rb1 &f8 29 Rxb2 &e7 30 Rc2 &d8 31 &a6=) **24 bxc8=W &xc8 25 &d8! Rxb5 26 &xf6 b2 27 Rb1 Rc5 28 &g5= h6 29 &e3 Rc3 30 Ra8** (30 &d2 Rc2=) **30 ... &g7 31 h3 &xh3** (31 ... Rxe3 32 Rxc8 Rb3=) **32 Rxf8!** (32 gxh3 Rxe3 33 Rxb2 Rxf3 leaves Black with all the chances) **32 ... &xg2+! 33 &xg2 Rc2+ 34 &g3 &xf8 35 &xh6+ &e7 36 &g7?** (36 &e3 f5=) **36 ... f6 37 &h6 g5 38 &g4 Rh2 39 &f5 &f7 40 &f8??** (40 &xg5 fxg5 41 &xe5) **40 Rh4 0:1**

Assessment: 22 ... &f8! leads to a double-edged position which should be drawn with best play.

b) Chekhov-Karsa, Lvov 1983. White has a passed a-pawn, Black is attacking the b4 pawn.

White's Plan: I need to support my passed a-pawn's advance.

Black's Plan: I need to blockade that dangerous a-pawn.

Candidate Moves: 23 a6; 23 &d2; 23 b5!?.

Analysis: 23 b5! (23 a6 &xb4) **23 ... cxb5 24 a6 &c4 25 &xc4 bxc4 26 &c3 &c5** (26 ... b5 27 a7 Ra8 28 &xb5) **27 &xc5 &xc5 28 a7 Ra8 29 &d5! c3** (29 ... b5 30 &b6 Rxa7 31 Rxa7 c3 32 Rc7 stops Black's c-pawn) **30 &xc3 &b3 31 Ra6 &d4** (31 ... &c5 32 Ra3+-) **32 &d5 &c6 33 Rxb6 &xa7 34 Ra6 1:0**

Assessment: 23 b5! gives White's knight access to the crucial b5 and d5 squares after which he can decisively advance his a-pawn.

A18/3

a) Smyslov-Benko, Monte Carlo 1969. Black's knight on a4 is out of

play and White's rook is well placed on the 7th rank.

White's Plan: Can I launch an attack on f7 with my rook and knight?

Black's Plan: I would like to simplify make a draw.

Candidate Moves: 25 &c6; 25 f4.

Analysis: 25 &c6! Rd2 (25 ... &c3? 26 &e7) **26 &e5 Rxe2 27 &xf7** (threatening 28 &g5+) **27 ... h5 28 &g5+ &f6** (28 ... &f8 29 &f1 Re5 30 f4 Re3 31 &f2 wins the e6 pawn) **29 &f1! Rxf2+** (29 ... Rb2 30 f4 &f5 31 h3, 32 Rf7#) **30 &xf2 &xg5 31 &e3 &g4 32 b5 &h3 33 Rc4 &b2** (33 ... &c5 34 Rxc5 bxc5 35 b6+-) **34 ... Rc2** (34 ... &a4 35 &f4 h4 36 gxh4 &xh4 37 &e5+-) **1:0**

Assessment: In this deceptively quiet position White can launch a winning attack.

b) Spassky-Fischer, Sveti-Stefan m 1992. Material is level and the pawn structure more or less symmetrical.

White's Plan: I wonder if I can exploit the position of Black's king on the a3-f8 diagonal by sacrificing the exchange.

Black's Plan: If White retreats his bishop I can exchange on f3 and bring my knight to e5. The f4 square looks ripe for occupation.

Candidate Moves: 20 &b2; 20 Rxc5.

Analysis: 20 Rxc5! &xc5 21 &xb4 Rhd8? (Seirawan suggested 21 ... gxf4 22 gxf4 Rhg8 23 &d2 &d7 24 &c4 &a8 intending 25 ... Rg6, 26 ... Rcg8 and 27 ... &f6) **22 &a3! gxf3 23 gxf3 &d7** (23 ... e5? 24 &f5+; 23 ... &f8? 24 &xc5+

Xxc5 25 ♘xe6+-; 23 ... ♔e8 24
♘c4 ♘h5?! 25 e5+-) 24 ♘c4
(threatening 25 ♘a5) 24 ... ♗a8 25
♔f2 Xg8 26 h4 Xc7 27 ♘c2 Xb8?!
(27 ... ♔f6) 28 ♗a3 h5? (28 ... Xg8)
29 Xg1! ♔f6 30 ♔e3 a5 31 Xg5 a4
32 b4 ♘b7 33 b5 (33 ♗b2+! ♔e7
34 ♘2a3, 35 ♘b5) 33 ... ♘bc5 34
♘d4 e5 35 ♘xe5 ♘xe5 36 Xf5+
♔g7 37 Xxe5 ♘xe4 38 ♗d3 (38
fxe4 Xc3+ 39 ♔f4 Xxa3) 38 ... Xc3
39 ♗b4 Xxd3+ 40 ♔xd3 ♘f6 41
♗d6 Xc8 42 Xg5+ ♔h7 43 ♗e5
♘e8 44 Xxh5+ ♔g6 45 Xg5+ ♔h7
46 ♗f4 f6 47 Xf5 ♔g6 48 b6 Xd8
49 Xa5 ♗xf3 (49 ... ♗c6 50 ♔e3)
50 h5+ (50 ... ♔g7 51 Xa7+ ♔g8 52
b7) **1:0**
Assessment: The exchange sacrifice is quite promising though not
necessarily decisive.

A18/4
a) Uhlmann-Karpov, Skopje
1976. Black is a piece up but has no
less than three pieces attacked by
White's knight.
White's Plan: I will win the exchange and take the e5 pawn. I think
that my rook and pawn will be no
worse than the two minor pieces.
Black's Plan: Defending my
bishop seems to leave me with nothing. Perhaps I can let it go whilst
activating my position!?
Candidate Moves: 29 ... X8e7;
29 ... ♘f4!?.
Analysis: 27 ... ♘f4! (27 ... X8c7
28 ♘xc4 Xxc4 29 Xxe5=) 28 ♘xb7
(28 ♘xc8 Xxc8 29 Xxe5 ♘xg2-+)
28 ... ♘d3 29 ♘d6! ♘xe1 30 ♘xc4
(30 ♘xc8?? ♘c2-+) 30 ... ♘c2 31
♘d6 Xd8 (31 ... Xc6 32 ♘f5 Xf6
33 Xc1 or 32 ... ♘xa1 33 ♘e7+ lets
White escape) **32 ♘b7 Xd2 33 Xc1**
(although it is normally better to

play actively in endgames, 33 Xb1
was better in this case) **33 ... ♘d4**
34 Xc8+ ♔h7 35 h4 Xxb2 36 Xa8
♘e2+ (36 ... Xa2 37 Xxa7 b4-+) 37
♔h2 ♘f4 38 ♔g1 ♘d3 39 ♘d6
♘xf2 40 Xxa7 ♘g4 (threatening 41
... Xb1#) **41 g3** (41 Xf7 ♘e3 42
♘f5 [42 Xf2? Xb1+ 43 ♔h2 ♘g4+]
42 ... Xxg2+ 43 ♔h1 Xf2 44 ♘xh6
Xf6! 45 Xxf6 gxf6 46 ♘f7 ♘c4) 41
... ♘e3 42 ♔h1 ♔g6 43 Xb7 (43
♘e8 ♔f5 44 ♘xg7+ ♔g4-+) **43 ...**
Xd2 44 ♘xb5 ♘f5 45 g4 ♘xh4 46
♔g1 (Black was threatening 46 ...
♘f3 and 47 ... Xh2#) **46 Xg2+ 47**
♔f1 Xxg4 48 Xa7 ♘f5 49 a4 h5 50
a5 h4 51 Xa8 h3 0:1
Assessment: Black has all the
chances though 33 Xb1 might have
held.

b) Kavalek-Rogoff, Oberlin
1975. Black is a pawn up but White
will capture f5. After that both f7
and h5 will be weak.
White's Plan: I want to attack
Black's pawn weaknesses and tie
him down.
Black's Plan: I don't want to defend passively, can I activate my
forces somehow?
Candidate Moves: 32 ... Xh8; 32
... Xe8; 32 ... f6!?.
Analysis: 32 ... f6!! 33 Xe6+ (33
Xxf6 ♗d4! 34 Xe6+ [34 Xxf5
Xf8-+] 34 ... ♔d5 35 Xa6 ♗xf6 36
Xxf6 ♔e4! when Black's active
king supports the advancing f-pawn)
33 ... ♔d5 34 Xxf6 ♔e4 (Black's
king has become menacingly active
and the passed pawn on f5 is turning
into a monster) **35 Xf7 Xc7! 36 Xf8**
(36 Xxc7 ♗xc7 37 ♔c2 f4 38 ♔d2
♔f3!, 39 ... ♔g2, 40 ... f3-+) 36 ...
♗c5! 37 Xf6 ♗d4 38 Xf8 ♗g7!
(chasing White's rook from its

optimal location behind the passed pawn) **39 ♖e8+ ♔f3 40 ♖e1 ♗d4!** (supporting Black's king and pawn) **41 b4 ♔g4 42 ♖d1** (42 ♖f1 ♗e5 43 ♖g1+ ♗g3, 44 ... f4) **42 ♗f2 43 ♖d5 ♖f7** (now it is Black's rook that comes behind the passed pawn) **44 ♔c2 f4!** (44 ... ♗xh4 was less good) **45 ♔d1 f3 46 a4 ♗g3! 47 ♖d4+ ♔h3 48 ♗e3 f2 49 ♗xf2 ♗xf2 50 ♖e4 ♗xh4 51 a5 ♗f2 52 b5 h4 53 ♔e2 ♔g2 54 b6 ab 55 ab h3 56 ♖g4+ ♗g3 0:1**

Assessment: 32 ... f6!! turns the tables by allowing Black to activate his king.

Month 19

A19/1

a) Spielmann-Forgacs, Hamburg 1910. White is a pawn down but has menacing kingside piece activity. Black's queen is very active, White's knight on a3 is badly placed and his back rank is weak.

White's Plan: In order to capitalise on my active pieces I would like to cause serious damage to Black's king position.

Black's Plan: I need to combine cool-headed defence with counterplay.

Candidate Moves: 20 ♘xf7; 20 ♘xe6; 20 d5.

Analysis: **20 d5!** (20 ♘xf7 ♗xf7 21 ♕xf7+ ♔h8 or 20 ♘xe6 fxe6 is less dangerous) **20 ... hxg5 21 dxe6 fxe6 22 ♕f7+ ♔h7 23 ♖ac1! ♕xa3** (23 ... ♕d3 24 ♖f3+-) **24 ♖xc7 ♕f8** (24 ... ♖g8 25 ♕h5#) **25 ♕h5+ ♔g8 26 ♖xf8+ ♖xf8 27 h4! ♖ac8 28 b6! ♖xc7 29 bxc7 ♖c8 30 ♕d1 1:0**

Assessment: White has a winning attack.

b) Spielmann - Hoenlinger, Vienna 1933. White has a slight lead in development and pressure against f7.

White's Plan: My bishop on b3 is about to be exchanged and Black is catching up in development. I must act now.

Black's Plan: I want to exchange that bishop on b3 or complete my development with 19 ... ♗f5.

Candidate Moves: 19 ♗c4; 19 ♗d5; 19 ♗xf7+!?.

Analysis: **19 ♗xf7+! ♖xf7 20 ♘xf7 ♔xf7 21 ♖d5! ♘e6 22 ♖fd1 ♕c6** (22 ... ♘f8 23 ♖d8 keeps Black bottled up) **23 ♕b3 b5 24 ♖d6 ♕e4 25 ♕c3! ♔e7** (25 ... ♗b7 26 f3) **26 ♕h8 g5** (26 ... ♕xg2+ 27 ♔xg2 ♗b7+ 28 ♔f1 ♖xh8 29 ♖d7+, 30 ♖xb7) **27 f3 ♕g6 28 ♖d8 ♕c2** (28 ... ♘xd8 29 ♕xd8+ ♔f7 30 ♕d5++-) **29 ♖e8+ ♔f7 30 ♕g8+ ♔f6 31 ♖e1** (31 ♖f8+! ♘xf8 32 ♕xf8+ ♔e6 33 ♖d6+ ♔e5 34 ♕f6#) **31 ... ♕c6 32 h4 h6** (32 ... gxh4 33 f4!, 34 ♖1xe6+) **33 h5 1:0**

Assessment: Sacrificing two pieces for a rook and a pawn increases White's initiative to decisive proportions.

A19/2

a) Stein-Hort, Los Angeles 1967. White has a passed c-pawn and Black a central pawn majority. Black's bishop on d5 is impressive but his pieces look slightly loose.

White's Plan: Black's pieces have come to effective squres and he threatens my knight on a5. If I'm going to exploit the fact the looseness of Black's position it has to be now.

Black's Plan: After White exchanges on c6 I will play for a central advance with e5-e4.

Candidate Moves: 22 ♘xc6; 22 ♘xd4; 22 ♘xe5.

Analysis: 22 ♘xe5! (22 ♘xd4 ♗xg2 23 ♘xb5 ♕b8 24 ♘xc6 ♕xb5-+) 22 ... ♘xb4 (22 ... ♖xe5 23 ♗xd5+ ♖xd5 and now both 24 ♕b3 ♘xb4 25 ♗a3! and 24 ♕f3! ♘xb4 25 ♗a3 leave Black with enough pieces hanging to compensate for the sacrificed piece) 23 ♘xd7 ♕xd7 24 c6 ♕f7 25 ♖xe8+ ♖xe8 26 ♘b7 and White a strong game without material investment.

Assessment: 22 ♘xe5 leads to wild complications which look promising for White.

b) Savon-Stein, Sarajevo 1967. From a strategic point of view White seems to be doing well but Black's pieces are active and there are gaping holes in White's lines.

White's Plan: Having played c4-c5 I'd like to keep tight control of the position whilst aiming for that weak pawn on c7.

Black's Plan: I think I can stir up trouble if I open the position. My immediate problem is the rook on a7 but maybe I can sac the exchange somehow.

Candidate Moves: 23 ... dxc5.

Analysis: 23 ... dxc5! 24 ♘b5 ♖a5 25 ♗xc5 ♕d8 26 ♗xf8 ♕xf8 27 gxh5!? (after 27 ♘c3 a sample line is 27 ... ♖a3 28 gxh5 ♘gxh5 29 ♖a2 ♖xa2 30 ♘xa2 ♘f4 intending 31 ... ♕h6; 27 ♘xc7? is met by 27 ... ♖c5) 27 ... ♘fxh5 (27 ... ♗xb5 28 ♗xb5 ♖xb5 29 hxg6 fxg6 30 ♘e6 ♘xe6 31 ♖xg6+ etc) 28 ♖b2 ♘f4 29 ♗f1 ♗xb5 30 ♗xb5 (30 ♖xb5 ♖xb5 31 ♗xb5 ♕d8! wins the

knight on g5) 30 ... ♗xg5! 31 ♕c3 (31 ♖xg5 ♕a3! leaves White unable to deal with the threats of ♖xb5 and ♕xf3+) 31 ... ♖a3 32 ♕xe5 ♘h3 33 ♖f1 ♗f4 34 ♕d4 ♕e7 35 ♖e2 ♗e5 36 ♕c4 ♘h5 37 ♖a2 ♘5f4 38 ♖xa3 ♕xa3 39 ♗d7 ♕b2 40 ♗xh3 ♘xh3 0:1

Assessment: The inspired exchange sacrifice gives Black tremendous pressure.

A19/3

a) Averbakh-Tal, Riga 1958. Black has very active pieces, at least for the time being. In the long term the d6 pawn may become weak.

White's Plan: I want to dampen down Black's temporary piece activity with a2-a3 and then fix my attention on his weak d6 pawn.

Black's Plan: I might do something dramatic with my temporarily active pieces.

Candidate Moves: 12 ... ♘h5; 12 ... ♘xe4.

Analysis: 12 ... ♘xe4! (12 ... ♘h5 13 ♗g5 f6 14 ♗e3 f5 15 a3! fxe4 16 axb4 exf3 17 ♗xf3 cxb4 18 ♘e4 would have been good for White according to Tal's second Koblents) 13 ♘xe4 ♗f5 14 ♘fd2 ♘xd5 15 ♗xd6? (the best line was 15 ♗g3 ♕e7 16 ♗b5 when 16 ... ♗xe4 17 ♘xe4 ♕xe4 18 ♗xe8 ♕xe8 19 ♗xd6 ♕c6 20 ♗g3 c4 when Black has good compensation for the exchange; 16 ♗f3 would be met by 16 ♖ad8) 15 ... ♘f6! 16 ♗f3 (16 ♗xc5 ♘xe4 17 ♘xe4 ♗xe4) 16 ... ♘xe4 17 ♘xe4 ♗xe4 18 ♗xe4 ♕xd6 19 ♕c2 ♖e7 20 ♗f3 ♖ae8 21 ♖ad1 ♗d4 22 a4 b6 23 b3 ♖e5 24 ♖d2 h5 25 ♖e2 ♖xe2 26 ♗xe2 h4 27 ♔h1 ♕f4 28 g3 ♕f6 29 ♕d1 ♖d8 30 ♗g4 ♗xf2! 31 ♕e2 ♖d2! 32

♕e8+ ♔h7 33 gxh4 ♕d4 34 ♗h3
♕d3 35 ♗g2 ♖d1 0:1
Assessment: Black gets excellent
compensation for his piece.

b) Tal-Gligoric, Bled Ct 1959.
Black has an extra pawn but is behind in development and unable to
bring his king to safety. White's
pieces are quite menacingly placed.
White's Plan: I really want to get
at that Black king. How do I set
about opening it up?
Black's Plan: I must get my king
to safety after which the extra pawn
would be significant.
Candidate Moves: 22 ♘g6; 22
♗e6.
Analysis: 22 ♗e6! (threatening
23 ♕f5) 22 ... ♖g8 23 ♗c4! (23
♕f5 d5) 23 ... ♔f8 (23 ... 0-0-0 24
♕f5+ ♘d7 25 ♗xf7 threatens to
trap Black's queen with 26 ♖c4) 24
♗b5 ♕c5 25 ♖c4 ♕e5 26 ♖xc7 recovering the pawn with continuing
pressure.
Assessment: The stunning 22
♗e6! sets the position alight and
poses Black very serious defensive
problems.

A19/4
a) Kasparov-Gheorghiu, Mos-
cow Izt 1982. Black's king is still in
the centre and White has a central
pawn majority.
White's Plan: I would like to
catch Black's king whilst it is lan-
guishing in the centre.
Black's Plan: I want to bring my
king to safety and try to create
counterplay on the c-file.

Candidate Moves: 14 d5.
Analysis: 14 d5! exd5 15 exd5
♗xd5 16 ♗b5 a6 (16 ... ♗e6 17
♕a4 ♖d8 18 ♗f4 ♕c8 19 ♘e5+-)
17 ♗f4! ♕xf4 18 ♗xd7+ ♔xd7 19
♖xd5+ ♔c7 (19 ... ♔c8 was a better
try) 20 ♖e1 ♗d6 (20 ... ♗f6 21
♖e4+-) 21 ♖f5 ♕c4 22 ♖e4! ♕b5
23 ♖xf7+ ♔b8 24 ♖e6! ♖d8 25 c4
♕c6 26 ♘e5 ♕c8 27 ♕b1! 1:0
Assessment: 14 d5 gives White a
strong if not decisive attack

b) Kasparov-Anand, Amsterdam 1996. White has more space
and manoeuvrability but Black's
position seems quite solid.
White's Plan: I would like to direct my attention towards the opposing king position with ♗d3, ♗c2
and ♕d3 but Black will be able to
defend against this with ... f7-f5
and then gain counterplay with ...
b7-b6. Perhaps I need to take account of these defensive resources
and proceed quite subtly.
Black's Plan: My main idea is
queenside counterplay with ...
b7-b6.
Candidate Moves: 13 ♖e1; 13
♗d3; 13 ♖c1.
Analysis: 13 ♖c1!! ♖e8! (13 ...
b6 14 c4! bxc5 15 dxc5 dxc4 16
♗xc4 ♗xc5 17 ♗b5 wins material)
14 ♖e1 ♗f6 after which Kasparov
later claimed he should have played
15 ♗d3 intending ♗b1 followed by
♕d3 with a slight initiative.
Assessment: The subtle 13 ♖c1
keeps a slight initiative.

Month 20

A20/1

a) Steinitz-von Bardeleben, Hastings 1895. Black has an extra pawn but his king is under fire in the centre from White's actively placed forces. White's queen and knight are both hanging.

White's Plan: With Black's pieces so loose and his king exposed I need to analyse forcing sequences.

Black's Plan: If I can survive the immediate pressure my extra pawn might count for something.

Candidate Moves: 22 ♖xe7+; 22 ♘e6.

Analysis: 22 ♖xe7+!! ♔f8! (22 ... ♔xe7 23 ♖e1+ ♔d6 24 ♕b4+ ♔c7 25 ♘e6+ ♔b8 26 ♕f4+-; 23 ... ♔d8 24 ♘e6+ ♔e7 25 ♘c5+-) **23 ♖f7+! ♔g8 24 ♖g7+! ♔h8** (24 ... ♔f8 25 ♘xh7+) **25 ♖xh7+ ♔g8 26 ♖g7+ ♔h8 27 ♕h4+! ♔xg7 28 ♕h7+ ♔f8 29 ♕h8+ ♔e7 30 ♕g7+ ♔e8 31 ♕g8+ ♔e7 32 ♕f7+ ♔d8 33 ♕f8+ ♕e8 34 ♘f7+ ♔d7 35 ♕d6#**

Assessment: White can force the win.

b) Chigorin-Steinitz, Hastings 1895. Black is two pawns up and a potentially powerful bishop pair On the other hand he is under serious pressure right now from White's active knights.

White's Plan: I'm going to drive Black's queen from the defence of c6 and then fork his king and rook.

Black's Plan: Perhaps I can buy my way out of trouble by returning just some of the material.

Candidate Moves: 20 ... ♕d5; 20 ... ♕b5.

Analysis: 20 ... ♕b5! 21 ♕xb5 cxb5 22 ♘xb6 axb6! (22 ... ♖d2 23 a4!) **23 ♘c6+ ♔b7 24 ♘xd8+ ♖xd8** Black had more than enough compensation for the exchange.

Assessment: After 21 ♕b5 Black is clearly better.

A20/2

a) Nimzowitsch - Alekhine, Semmering 1926. Both kings are coming under attack, a wild-looking position.

White's Plan: With Black storming through the centre I need to hit him first on the kingside.

Black's Plan: On my next move I'll take on e4 when White's king looks hopelessly exposed.

Candidate Moves: 33 ♖xc3; 33 ♘g6+.

Analysis: 33 ♘g6+! (33 ♖xc3 ♗xc3 34 ♕xc3 ♕f2-+) **33 ... hxg6 34 ♕g4! ♖f7?** (34 ... ♖g8 produces mind-boggling complications: 35 fxg6 ♔g7 36 ♖d7+ ♗xd7 37 ♕xd7+ ♔xg6 38 ♗d3 ♔h6 39 ♕h3+ ♔g7 40 ♖g1+ ♕xg1+ 41 ♔xg1) **35 ♖h3+ ♔g7 36 ♗c4! ♗d5 37 fxg6 ♘xe4 38 gxf7+ ♔f8 39 ♖xe4 ♗xe4+ 40 ♕xe4 ♔e7 41 f8=♕+ ♖xf8 42 ♕d5 ♕d6** (Or 42 ...

♕c6 43 ♖h7+ ♔e8 44 ♗b5+-) 43 ♕xb7+ ♔d8 44 ♖d3 ♗d4 45 ♕e4 ♖e8 46 ♖xd4 1:0

Assessment: Who knows?

b) Bogoljubow-Nimzowitsch, San Remo 1930. With opposite side castling violent mutual attacks can be expected.

White's Plan: After 12 ... ♗xc3 13 ♗xc3 I will try to open the g-file with g2-g4 to launch an atttack against Black's king.

Black's Plan: I want to open lines against White's king which means prising away his pawn cover The main target would seem to be c4 which I could attack with moves like ♗a6 and ♖c8 etc. My first problem is my bishop on b4, do I have to capture on c3?

Candidate Moves: 12 ... ♗a6; 12 ... a4.

Analysis: 12 ... a4!! 13 ♘b5 (13 axb4 ♘xb4 14 ♕b1 ♘b3#) 13 ... ♗xd2+ 14 ♘xd2 ♘a5 15 ♗f3 d5! 16 cxd5 ♗a6! and Black's queenside initiative was developing at speed.

Assessment: Black has the better attacking chances.

A20/3
a) Lundin-Botvinnik, Groningen 1946. Black is a pawn up and his knight on d4 is a powerhouse.

White's Plan: When Black's rook retreats I'll restore material parity.

Black's Plan: Perhaps I can sacrifice the exchange to keep the b4 pawn, relying on my mighty knight to give me compensation.

Candidate Moves: 46 ... c5.

Analysis: 46 ... c5! 47 ♗xa4 ♘xf3+! 48 ♔f2 ♗xg4! 49 ♗d1

♘e5! 50 ♗xg4 ♘xg4+ 51 ♔g1 (51 ♔f3 ♘e5+-+) 51 ... ♖xh5 52 ♖g2 ♗f6 0:1

Assessment: The sacrifice of the exchange gives Black a crushing position.

b) Stoltz-Botvinnik, Groningen 1946. White's king is in the centre and Black's bishop on d3 is magnificently placed.

White's Plan: After Black moves his rook I want to bring my bishop back to f3 and then get castled.

Black's Plan: I want to exploit White's king position by coming to the e-file as quickly as possible.

Candidate Moves: 15 ... ♖b8; 15 ... 0-0.

Analysis: 15 ... 0-0! (15 ... ♖b8 allows 16 ♗f3 0-0 17 0-0) 16 ♗f3 (16 ♗xa8 ♕xa8 is terrible for White as is 16 ♗xh6 ♗xh6 17 ♕xh6 ♘f5! 18 ♕d2 ♗xe2 etc) 16 ... g5! 17 0-0 ♘g6! (preparing to bring his knight to e5 and d3) 18 ♖e1 (18 ♗xa8 ♕xa8 19 ♖e1 ♘e5-+) 18 ... ♘e5 19 ♗g2 ♗a6 20 ♕d1 ♘d3 21 ♕a4 ♕f6 22 f4 ♖ae8 23 ♗c6 ♘xe1 24 ♗xe8 ♘f3+ 25 ♔f2 ♘xd2 26 ♗c6 ♗xe2 27 ♔xe2 dxc3 28 bxc3 ♕xc3 29 ♖d1 ♖d8 30 ♗e4 gxf4 31 gxf4 ♕h3 32 ♖g1 ♕h5+ 33 ♔e3 ♕h3+ 34 ♔e2 ♕xh2+ 35 ♖g2 ♕h5+ 36 ♔e3 ♕h3+ 37 ♔e2 ♕e6 0:1

Assessment: With precise play Black's attack looks decisive.

A20/4
a) Keres-Petrosian, Bled Ct 1959. Black has strong pressure on the g-file and a passed e-pawn. Black's light-squared bishop is inhibited by his pawns on e4 and f5, his king looks rather exposed and several of his pawns are weak.

White's Plan: I would like to have my knight on e3 to cover g2 and blockade the e-pawn and then attack d6 pawn along the d-file. I doubt that I have time for this so I should probably try to open it up with 47 b4.

Black's Plan: How do I intensify the pressure on the kingside before White gains counterplay? One idea that springs to mind is to sacrifice a rook on g3 in order to open the h-file.

Candidate Moves: 46 ... ♖g3; 46 ♕d8.

Analysis: 46 ... ♕d8! 47 b4 ♖g3!! 48 hxg3 (48 ♕e2 ♘d3-+; 48 ♕c1 ♘d3 49 ♗xd3 ♖xd3 gives Black a clear advantage) **48 ... hxg3 49 ♖fd2** (49 bxc5 ♕h4 50 ♗d3 ♕h2+ 51 ♔f1 ♕h1+ 52 ♔e2 gxf2 53 ♖b1 exd3+ 54 ♕xd3 ♕xg2 55 ♖f1 dxc5 56 ♘c2 ♗c6-+) **49 ... ♕h4 50 ♗e2 ♖h7! 51 ♔f1?** (51 ♗h5 ♖xh5 52 ♔f1 axb4 53 axb4 ♘d3 54 ♖xd3 ♕h1+ 55 ♕g1 exd3 56 ♘f3 ♗e6! 57 c5 ♗c4 58 ♘d2 ♖h4!-+; 54 ♖b1 ♕xf4+! 55 ♕xf4 ♖h1+ 56 ♔e2 ♘xf4+ 57 ♔e3 ♖xb1 58 ♔xf4 ♖f1+!-+) **51 ... ♕xf4+!! 0:1**

Assessment: Black can develop a decisive attack.

b) Fischer-Petrosian, Bled Ct 1959. Black has established control over the important e5 square and the bishop on g2 is quite bad. The pawn on d3 can become weak once Black's knight is on e5.

White's Plan: If I cannot get my bishop into play I will be condemned to a long and difficult defence.

Black's Plan: I really want my knight on e5 after which White will be tied to the defence of his d3 pawn.

Candidate Moves: 27 ... ♕e7; 27 ... ♕d6; 27 ... ♕c7.

Analysis: 27 ... ♕e7! 28 ♖b1 (28 bxc5 ♘e5! 29 ♖xd4 ♘xd3; 28 ♖d1 ♘e5 29 ♖xc5 ♖xc5 30 bxc5 ♕xc5) **28 ... ♘e5 29 ♖xc5 ♖xc5 30 bxc5 ♘xd3** and Black's passed pawn was the most important factor in the position. Petrosian went on to win a dramatic struggle.

Assessment: Black is clearly better.

Month 21

A21/1

a) **Capablanca-Oskam, Rotterdam 1920.** White has a passed d-pawn which is firmly blockaded by the bishop on d6.

White's Plan: To get that d-pawn moving I need to remove the blockader from d6. How?

Black's Plan: I must keep that d-pawn under lock and key. It might even become weak in some positions.

Candidate Moves: 19 ♕d2; 19 ♕d1; 19 ♕xe8+.

Analysis: 19 ♕xe8+! ♘xe8 20 ♖xe8+ ♘f8 (20 ... ♔h7 21 ♘e4 [threatening 22 ♘xd6 and 23 ♗g3] 21 ... f5 22 ♘xd6 ♕xd6 23 ♗g3 f4 24 ♗d3+ g6 25 ♗xf4 ♕xf4 26 ♖e7+ ♔g8 27 ♖xd7-; 21 ... ♘e5 22 ♘xe5 ♗xe5 23 ♗d3! f5 24 ♖e7 ♕b8 [24 ... ♕d8 25 ♖xg7+ ♔xg7 26 ♗xd8 fxe4 27 ♗xe4 ♗xb2 28 ♗xb6 c4 29 d6 ♗xe4 30 d7 ♗f6 31 ♗d4 etc] 25 ♘f6+! ♔g6 [25 ... ♗xf6 26 ♗xf6 ♔g6 27 ♗e5] 26 g4 ♗c8 27 ♘d7 ♗xd7 28 ♖xd7+-) 21 ♘e4 g5 22 ♗g3 ♗xg3 23 hxg3 ♔g7 24 ♘e5 b5 25 axb5 axb5 26 d6! ♕a5 27 ♖e7 ♕e1+ 28 ♔h2 ♗xe4? (28 ... ♕xe4!) 29 ♖xf7+ ♔h8 (29 ... ♔g8 30 ♘g4!! bxc4 31 ♘xh6+ ♔h8 32 ♖xf8+ ♔g7 33 d7! ♔xf8 34 d8=♕+ ♔g7 35 ♕xg5++-) 30 ♖xf8+ ♔g7 31 ♖f7+ ♔h8 32 d7 **1:0**

Assessment: The queen sacrifice gives White a clear advantage.

b) **Capablanca - Bogoljubow, Moscow 1925.** Black's king has been forced to make a run for it but he is threatening the e3 pawn.

White's Plan: My aim is to butcher Black's king.

Black's Plan: The exchange of queens will help my king's chance of survival.

Candidate Moves: 17 ♕f7; 17 h4; 17 ♕xb6.

Analysis: 17 ♕xb6 (17 ♕f7 ♕f8; 17 h4 ♕xe3+ 18 ♔f1 gxf4 19 g5+ ♔h5 20 gxf4+ ♔g4 21 ♕e6+ ♔f3-+) 17 ... axb6 18 ♖d1 but now in fact he played the mistaken 18 ... ♖g8? (18 ... gxf4! would have been good for Black after 19 g5+ ♔g7 20 gxf6+ ♘xf6 21 ♖xf4 [21 ♖g5+ ♔f7 22 exf4 h6!] 21 ... ♖a5!) 19 ♘fd5! ♘xg4 (19 ... ♖g6 20 ♘e7 ♘c5 21 ♖d8!) 20 ♘e7 ♖g7 21 ♖d6+ ♔h5 22 ♖f3! ♘gf6 23 ♖h3+ ♔g4 24 ♖g3+ ♔h5 25 ♘f5 ♖g6 (25 ... ♘xd5? 26 ♖h6+! ♔xh6 27 ♖h3#) 26 ♘e7 g4? (26 ... ♘c5! 27 ♘xg6 ♘fxe4!) 27 ♘xg6 ♔xg6 28 ♖xg4+ ♔f7 29 ♖f4 ♔g7 30 e5 ♘e8 31 ♖e6 **1:0**

Assessment: White is having to struggle to maintain his initiative.

A21/2

a) Smyslov-Koenig, USSR-Great Britain 1946. Black is a pawn up but White's pieces are lurking in the vicinity of his king.

White's Plan: I really must capitalise on my attacking chances, this is not a position for the faint-hearted.

Black's Plan: If I can defuse White's attack my extra pawn will be important.

Candidate Moves: There are various attacking tries but the first thing I should look at is the explosive 31 ♘xg7!?.

Analysis: Smyslov played 31 ♘xg7!! the point of which is that 31 ... ♔xg7 gives White a winning attack after 32 ♘f5+ ♔g8 33 ♗f6 ♖d6 34 ♘h6+ ♔h7 35 ♕h4 ♖xf6 36 ♘g4+ ♔g8 37 ♘xf6+ ♔g7 38 ♘e8++- or 32 ... ♗xf5 33 exf5 ♖d4 (33 ... ♘g6 34 ♕h5!) 34 f6+! ♔h7 35 ♗f4! ♘e6 36 ♕h5+ ♔g8 37 ♔h2 In the game Black made an enterprising bid for counterplay with 31 ... ♗xf2+ but after 32 ♖xf2 ♕xc4 33 ♘e8 White had serious threats in any case The final moves were 33 ... ♘h7 34 ♘f6+ ♔g7? (presumably overlooking the reply Black's last chance to stay on the board was with 34 ♘xf6 35 ♗xf6 ♖d6 36 ♕h4 ♖xf6) 35 ♗h6+! ♔h8 (35 ... ♔xh6 36 ♘f5+ ♗xf5 37 ♘g8 or 37 ♖h2#) 36 ♘xd7 ♕d4 37 ♘xe5 1:0

Assessment: 31 ♘xg7! gives Black difficult if not insurmountable problems.

b) Smyslov-Reshevsky, Hague/Moscow WCh 1948. Black's d6 pawn looks weak and White is ahead in development.

White's Plan: I would like to get at the d6 pawn before Black is fully mobilised.

Black's Plan: I want to complete my development with 26 ♘d7 when the position looks fine for me.

Candidate Moves: 26 ♕e2; 26 ♖d2; 26 ♕h4!?.

Analysis: 26 ♕h4! (26 ♖d2 ♘d7 [27 ♗c7? ♘f6]; 26 ♕e2 ♘d7 27 ♗c7 d5 28 exd5 exd5 29 ♖xd5 ♘f6 gives Black some counterplay) 26 ... ♕d7 (26 ... ♕xh4 27 gxh4 wins the d6) 27 ♕d8+! ♕xd8 28 ♗xd8 ♘d7 29 ♗c7 ♘c5 30 ♖xd6 won a pawn and later the game.

Assessment: After 26 ♕h4 White has a decisive advantage.

A21/3

a) Fischer-Petrosian, USSR-Rest of the World, Belgrade 1970. Black's king is stuck in the centre and must try to reach safety on the queenside.

White's Plan: I need to keep Black's king in the middle. My feeling is that I need more control over the dark-squares.

Black's Plan: In order to safeguard my king I like the idea of 32 ... ♖c7 and 33 ... ♖e7.

Candidate Moves: 32 ♖e6; 32 ♕f4; 32 ♕e5.

Analysis: 32 ♕e5! ♖c7 (32 ... ♕c7 33 ♕xd5+!) 33 b4! ♕c6 34 c4! dxc4 35 ♗f5 ♖ff7 36 ♖d1+ ♖fd7 (36 ... ♘d7 37 ♖fe1) 37 ♗xd7 ♖xd7 38 ♕b8+ ♔e7 (38 ... ♕c8 39 ♖xd7+ ♘xd7 40 ♕d6) 39 ♖de1+ 1:0

Assessment: There is no way out for Black's exposed king.

b) Robert Byrne-Fischer, U.S.A. Ch 1963. Black's pieces are very active but if the knight on d3 retreats the d5 pawn will fall. White's pawns on f2 and e3 don't look well guarded which suggests the possibility of a combination.

White's Plan: This looks good for me, when Black moves his knight I'll take his d-pawn.

Black's Plan: This is no time to retreat, my d5 pawn is too weak I have to attack.

Candidate Moves: 15 ... ♘xf2.

Analysis: 15 ... ♘xf2! 16 ♔xf2 ♘g4+ 17 ♔g1 ♘xe3 18 ♕d2 ♘xg2! (after 18 ... ♘xd1 19 ♖xd1 White picks up the d5 pawn) 19 ♔xg2 d4! 20 ♘xd4 ♗b7+ 21 ♔f1 (21 ♔g1 ♗xd4+ 22 ♕xd4 ♖e1+! 23 ♔f2 ♕xd4 24 ♖xd4 ♖xa1-+; 21 ♔f2 ♕d7 22 ♗b2 ♕h3 23 ♘f3 ♗h6 24 ♕d3 ♗e3+ 25 ♕xe3 ♖xe3 26 ♔xe3 ♖e8+ 27 ♔f2 ♕f5 etc) 21 ... ♕d7 (22 ♕f2 ♕h3+ 23 ♔g1 ♖e1+ 24 ♖xe1 ♗xd4 25 ♕xd4 ♕g2#) 0:1

Assessment: 15 ... ♘xf2 gives Black a winning attack.

A21/4

a) Karpov-Portisch, Torino 1982. A fairly quiet looking position in which White has the two bishops and some pressure against f7.

White's Plan: My most dangerous bishop is the one without an opponent on a2. Can I do something to intensify the pressure against f7? Maybe I need to eject Black's queen from its strong position.

Black's Plan: The only thing that worries me is White's bishop on a2. I'd like to neutralise it by putting my knight on c4.

Candidate Moves: 22 ♖e3; 22 g4.

Analysis: 22 g4! ♕d7 (22 ... ♕f4 23 ♗xd6 ♕xd6 [23 ... cxd6 24 ♗d5!] 24 ♕f3 ♕d7 25 ♗b1!) 23 ♗xf7+! ♔h8 (23 ... ♔xf7 24 ♖xa5 ♖xa5 25 ♕b3+ ♔g6 26 ♖e6+) 24 ♗xd6 ♕xf7 25 ♖e7 ♕f8 26 ♗c5 ♕f4 27 ♕e2 h6 28 ♖e4 ♕f7 29 ♖e5 ♘c4 30 ♖xa8 ♖xa8 31 ♖f5 ♕g6 32 ♕e4 ♔h7 33 h3 ♖a1+ 34 ♔g2 ♖c1 35 ♗b4 ♘d6 36 ♗xd6 cxd6 37 ♕d3 d5 38 f3 1:0

Assessment: The surprising 22 g4! gives White a clear advantage.

b) Karpov-Rogers, Bath 1983. Black's own bishop on d5 is a source of strength where it stands but doesn't have anywhere to go should White play c2-c4.

White's Plan: I would like to embarrass the bishop on d5 by threatening c2-c4.

Black's Plan: I need to get my king safe and secure the position of my bishop on d5.

Candidate Moves: 18 ♘xd7; 18 ♗e1!?.

Analysis: Karpov played the immediate **18 ♗e1!!** (after 18 ♘xd7 ♔xd7 the king doesn't look so bad). Threatened with 19 c4 Rogers tried **18 ... ♘xe5** (after 18 ... ♗xa2 there is 19 ♖a3 ♗d5 20 ♗a5 trapping the queen) **19 dxe5 ♘f5** but after **20 ♖h3** his position was hopeless. The game ended with **20 ... 0-0-0** (20 ... c5 is refuted by 21 ♖xd5 exd5 22 ♕xf5) **21 c4 ♕c5 22 b4 ♗f3 23 ♖xd8+ ♖xd8 24 ♕xf3 ♕xe5 25 ♗c3 ♕d6 26 ♗d3 ♘d4 27 ♕xf7 ♘f5 28 ♗xf5 ♕f4+ 29 ♖e3 1:0**

Assessment: 18 ♗e1!! is a winning move.

Month 22

A22/1

a) Lasker-Pirc, Moscow 1935.
White is well ahead in development and Black's king is still in the centre.

White's Plan: I would like to use my lead in development to launch and immediate attack, can I find a way to breach Black's defences?

Black's Plan: If I can get safely castled I should stand quite well.

Candidate Moves: 13 ♖xf6.

Analysis: 13 ♖xf6! gxf6 14 ♕h5+ ♔d8 (14 ... ♔d7 15 ♕f7+ ♗e7 16 ♘f5! ♖e8 17 ♖d1 d5 18 ♘xd5; 14 ... ♔e7 15 ♘f5+! exf5 16 ♘d5+ ♔d8 17 ♗b6+ ♔d7 18 ♕f7+ ♔c6 19 ♕c7++-) **15 ♕f7 ♗d7** (15 ... ♗e7 16 ♘f5! ♕c7 17 ♘a4! ♖f8 18 ♕xh7 ♔e8 19 ♗b6 ♕d7 20 ♕h5+ ♖f7 21 ♘g7+ ♔f8 22 ♕h8#; 16 ... ♖e8 17 ♘xd6! ♗xd6 [or 17 ... ♕c6 18 ♘xe8 ♕xe8 19 ♗b6+ ♔d7 20 ♖d1+] 18 ♗b6+ ♗c7 19 ♖d1++-) **16 ♕xf6+ ♔c7 17 ♕xh8 ♗h6 18 ♘xe6+! ♕xe6 19 ♕xa8 ♗xe3+ 20 ♔h1 1:0**

Assessment: 13 ♖xf6 gives White a winning attack.

b) Euwe-Lasker, Zurich 1934.
White's pawn on e5 controls f6 and gives Black's king some cause for concern.

White's Plan: My pieces are quite well positioned for an attack on Black's king I can use f6 as a

pivot for my attack and my queen might come into play after g2-g3 and ♕h3.

Black's Plan: Such a critical position normally requires crisp play. Public enemy number one is the pawn on e5, do I have a way to eliminate it?

Candidate Moves: 35 ... ♕xe5.

Analysis: 35 ... ♕xe5!! 36 ♘f6+ ♕xf6 37 ♖xf6 and now the cold-blooded **37 ... ♘xe1!** should have been played. After Lasker's **37 ... ♘xf6** White could have defended himself with **38 ♖e2! ♖d1 39 ♖xc2 ♖xf1+ 40 ♔xf1.**

Assessment: Black's queen sacrifice gives him the initiative.

A22/2

a) Korchnoi-Novikov, Antwerp 1997. A difficult and tense position in which Black's last move (20 ... e5) built a broad pawn centre and threatened the knight on d4. On the other hand it surrenders the f5 square.

White's Plan: Can I take pot-shots at Black's expanded centre?

Black's Plan: I want to intensify the pressure against Black's backward c2 pawn.

Candidate Moves: 21 ♘df5; 21 ♘gf5.

Analysis: 21 ♘gf5! ♗xf5? (21 ... ♗f8 22 ♘b5 ♖c5! 23 d4!? exd4 24 ♗xd4 produces a complex game) **22**

♘xf5 ♗f8 23 ♘g3 ♕e6 24 d4
exd4?! (Black should keep it closed
with 24 ... e4!) 25 ♗xd4 ♘e4 26
♘h5! ♘c3 27 ♗xc3 ♖xc3 28 ♘f4
♕a6 29 ♗xd5 ♘f6 30 ♖xb7 ♕xe2
31 ♗xf7+ ♔h8 32 ♘xe2 ♖xa3 33
♖xa3 ♗xa3 34 ♖a7 ♖xc2 35 ♖a8+
♔h7 36 ♘f4 ♖c1+ 37 ♔g2 g5 38
♗g6+ ♔g7 39 ♖a7+ ♔g8 40 ♘e6
♖c8 41 ♖xa4 ♗b2 42 ♖a7 ♘d5 43
♗h7+ ♔h8 44 ♗f5 1:0

Assessment: 21 ♘gf5! is the best
with chances for both sides.

**b) Korchnoi-Greenfeld, Beer-
Sheva 1995.** White's h1 rook is *en
prise.* Black's knights are not securely placed.

White's Plan: If I defuse the immediate threats my position would
be very attractive.

Black's Plan: I must keep the initiative as White's structure is better.

Candidate Moves: 10 ♕c2; 10
♕b3; 10 ♕a4; 10 h3.

Analysis: 10 h3! ♘f3+ (10 ...
♕xh1 11 hxg4, 12 ♘c7+, 12 ♗xe5)
11 ♔e2 ♘ge5 12 b3 g5 (12 ... a6 13
♗g2) 13 ♗g2 gxf4 14 exf4 a6 15
fxe5 axb5 16 ♗xf3 ♕c5 17 ♘xb5
♕xe5+ 18 ♔f1 ♗g7 and now 19
a4! would have been the best, White
having a clear advantage after 19 ...
♕xa1 20 ♕xa1 ♗xa1 21 ♘c7+
♔d8 22 ♘xa8 ♗d4 23 ♔e2.

Assessment: The cool 10 h3 defuses Black's transitory activity.

A22/3

**a) Salov-Shirov, Amsterdam
1995.** White has an extra pawn but
the powerful bishop on b5 prevents
him from castling kingside. Black
has a slight lead in development.

White's Plan: After I coordinate
my pieces this position will be good

for me. The main problem is king
safety.

Black's Plan: I have a temporary
lead in development for my pawn
minus but I need to strike now.

Candidate Moves: 16 ... b6; 16 ...
♘f4.

Analysis: 16 ... ♘f4!? (16 ... b6
17 ♗c3 ♘f4 [17 ... ♘xc3 18 dxc3
♗d3 19 ♕b2] 18 ♕f5! ♘xg2+ [18
... ♘d3+ 19 ♔f1] 19 ♔d1 is also far
from clear) 17 ♗xd8 ♖xd8 18 ♕c3!
(18 ♕e4 ♘d3+ 19 ♔e2 ♕f6-+; 18
0-0-0? ♘d3+ 19 ♔b1 ♘xf2) 18 ...
♕e6! (18 ... ♘d3+ 19 ♔f1) 19 f3?
(19 ♔d1 19 ♘d3 20 ♖f1 ♘e5! 21
♖g1 ♖d3! is messy) 19 ... ♖d3 20
♕xc5 ♘xg2+ 21 ♔d1 ♘xe3+! 22
♔c1 b6! 23 ♕c7 ♖d6! 24 ♕b8+
♗e8 25 ♘e4 ♖c6+ 26 ♘c3 ♘d5 27
♖a2 ♖c8 28 ♕g3 ♘xc3 29 dxc3
♕xb3 30 ♖c2 ♗a4 31 ♕f2 ♕xa3+
32 ♔b1 ♗xc2+ 33 ♕xc2 ♖xc3 0:1

Assessment: 16 ... ♘f4 is certainly the sharpest way to play it, but
may not necessarily be stronger than
16 ... b6.

**b) Korchnoi-Shirov, Madrid
1996.** White is a pawn down but he
will win d4, has a nice central pawn
chain and two bishops. Black's
pieces are aggressively posted but
there are no obvious inroads into
White's camp.

White's Plan: After recovering
the pawn on d4 I'd like to organise
an eventual c4-c5 to free my duo of
central pawns

Black's Plan: In the long run
White's position could become very
good I'd like to use my active
pieces immediately.

Candidate Moves: 20 ... g5; 20 ...
♘xe4.

Analysis: 20 ... ♘xe4! 21 fxe4 ♕g4 (threatening 22 ... f3 and 22 ... e4) **22 h3?** (22 ♕h3 f3 23 ♕xg4 ♗xg4 24 h3 ♗h5 25 ♗h1 ♖xe4 gives compensation for the piece but nothing special) **22 ... ♕g5 23 ♔h1 ♕h4 24 ♔g1 ♖f6 25 ♗xd4 ♖g6 26 ♔h1 ♖xg2! 27 ♔xg2 ♖xe4 28 ♗g1** (28 ♗f2 ♖e2) **28 ... ♖e2+ 29 ♔h1 ♗g6! 30 ♗f2 ♗e4+ 0:1**

Assessment: After 20 ♘xe4 Black gets good compensation for his piece.

A22/4

a) "MChess Pro" - "Quest", Computer World Ch , Paderborn 1995. White is about to lose the trapped knight on a4, Black's pieces on the kingside are quite clumsily placed and there is a pin on the knight on f6.

White's Plan: I need to do something to compensate me for the loss of the knight on a4. An advance of my f and e-pawns seems like the thing to do.

Black's Plan: I want to take White's knight!

Candidate Moves: 18 f4; 18 ♘g3.

Analysis: 18 ♘g3! (18 f4 ♗xe2) **18 ... g5!?** (18 ... bxa4 19 f4! ♖b5 20 c4 g5 21 fxg5 hxg5 22 cxb5 gxh4 23 ♘xh5 ♘xh5 24 ♕f3!) **19 f4! gxh4 20 fxe5 hxg3 21 ♖xf6 gxh2+ 22 ♔h1 bxa4 23 ♖af1 ♕f8** (23 ... dxe5 24 ♕g3+ ♔f8 25 ♖xh6) **24 e6!** (24 exd6 ♗d8!) **24 ... ♕g7 25 exf7+ ♔f8 26 ♕a6! ♗b6 27 ♕b7 ♖d8 28 ♖e6!** (28 ... ♗xf7 29 ♖ef6; 28 ... ♕g5 29 ♕d7!!) **1:0**

Assessment: White's has more than enough for the knight.

b) "Dragon" - "Stobor", Computer World Ch, Paderborn 1995.

The players have castled on opposite wings and there are opposite colour bishops. Black has weakened his kingside with h5.

White's Plan: How do I open lines on the kingside?

Black's Plan: I need to concentrate first and foremost on defence.

Candidate Moves: 28 ♗xh5.

Analysis: 28 ♗xh5!! gxh5 29 ♘f5 ♖xf5 30 exf5 ♖xf5 31 ♕e4! ♕f8 (31 ... ♖f8 is met by 32 ♕d5+ ♔h7 33 ♖g5 with a continuing attack and 31 ... ♖f6 would be answered by 32 ♕a8+ ♔h7 33 ♕xa6) **32 ♖xd6! ♕xd6?!** (32 ... ♖f1+! 33 ♖d1 ♖xd1+ was better) **33 ♕xf5 ♕d3+ 34 ♕xd3 ♘xd3 35 ♖g6! ♘c5 36 ♖g5 ♘e6 37 ♖xh5 ♗f6 38 a4! bxa4 39 ♖a5 ♗xh4 40 ♖xa4 ♗e7 41 ♖xa6 ♔f7 42 b4 ♔f6 43 ♔c2 ♔e5 44 ♖a1 ♘f4 45 b5 ♗c5 46 ♖a8 ♘g2 47 ♔b3 ♘f4 48 ♖b8 ♘e6 49 ♔c4 ♗d6 50 ♖a8 ♗c5 51 ♖a2 ♗e3 52 ♖e2 ♔e4 53 ♖e1 ♘d8 54 b6 ♘b7 55 ♔b5 ♔f3 56 ♖d1 ♘c5 57 ♖d8 ♔f2 58 ♔c6 ♘a6 59 ♖f8+ ♔g3 60 ♖a8 ♘c5 61 b7 ♘xb7 62 ♔xb7 ♔f4 63 ♔c6 ♗d2 64 c4 ♔e5 65 c5 ♔f6 66 ♔d7 1:0**

Assessment: 28 ♗xh5 creates in-roads into Black's position after which White enjoys a prolonged initiative.

Month 23

A23/1

a) Ivanchuk-Shirov, Wijk aan Zee 1996. Black's pawns are more advanced but his king is more exposed.

White's Plan: Black's bishop on f8 is overworked in that it is needed to defend both g7 and the knight on c5. Do I have a combination?

Black's Plan: My long term prospects should be good because of my advanced queenside pawns and passed d-pawn.

Candidate Moves: 21 ♘xc5; 21 ♕g7.

Analysis: 21 ♕g7!! ♗xg7 22 fxg7 ♖g8 23 ♘xc5 d4?! (23 ... ♖c7 24 ♘xb7 ♖xb7 25 ♖fd1! and now 25 ... ♖xg7 26 ♖xd5 ♕e8 27 ♖c5+ ♖c7 28 ♖xa7! ♖xc5 29 ♖a8+ ♔d7 30 ♖xe8 and 25 ... ♖d7 26 ♗h3 f5 27 ♗xf5 ♖gxg7 28 ♖xa7 ♔d8 29 ♗xd7 ♖xd7 30 ♖a8+ favour White) **24 ♗xb7+ ♖xb7 25 ♘xb7 ♕b6** (25 ... ♔xb7 26 ♗xd4 a5 27 ♖fe1+-) **26 ♗xd4! ♕xd4 27 ♖fd1 ♕xb2 28 ♘d6+ ♔b8 29 ♖db1 ♕xg7 30 ♖xb4+ ♔c7 31 ♖a6! ♖b8 32 ♖xa7+ ♔xd6 33 ♖xb8 ♕g4 34 ♖d8+ ♔c6 35 ♖a1 1:0**

Assessment: The queen sacrifice is very strong if not winning for White.

b) Kramnik-Ehlvest, Riga 1995. Black's pawn mass is more advanced. On the other hand his long term king safety seems to be more of a problem as queenside castling has been ruled out.

White's Plan: Black's king seems very precariously placed, how can I open lines in the centre?

Black's Plan: I want to evacuate my king from the centre.

Candidate Moves: 17 0-0-0; 17 ♕f5.

Analysis: 17 ♕f5! (17 0-0-0 ♕xa2) **17 ... dxe4 18 0-0-0 ♖c7** (18 ... ♖d8? 19 ♕xe4+; 18 ... ♕c7 19 ♗g4) **19 ♗g4 ♗b5 20 ♕xe4+ ♔d8 21 ♗xd7! ♗xd7 22 ♖he1** (threatening 23 ♕e8#) **22 ♗h6 23 ♕a8+ ♖c8 24 ♖xd7+! ♔xd7 25 ♕d5+ 1:0** (after 25 ... ♔c7 there follows 26 ♖e7+ and 27 ♕b7#)

Assessment: White has a winning attack.

A23/2

a) Spassky-Gufeld, Wellington 1988. White's hanging pawns on d4 and c4 control a lot of terrain and his pieces are much more active.

White's Plan: I would like to attack Black's king, can I eliminate his dark-squared bishop?

Black's Plan: I would like to get some kind of counterplay against the d- and c-pawns and White's vulnerable looking king.

Candidate Moves: 31 ♖xf6.

Analysis: 31 ♖xf6 ♖xf6 32 d5 ♔f7 (32 ... ♖d6 33 ♕d4+-) **33 ♘e6**

♖xe6 (33 ... ♖d7 34 ♘d4+-) 34 dxe6+ ♚xe6 35 ♖e1+ ♚f7 36 ♕d4 ♕xa4 37 ♕g7 ♚e8 38 ♗f6 ♚d8 39 ♕f8 ♕e8 40 ♖d1 ♖d7 41 ♗e7 ♚c7 42 ♕e8 1:0

Assessment: The exchange sacrifice gives White a winning attack.

b) Spassky-Geller, Sukhumi Cm 1968. Black has queenside pressure, White is trying to break through on the other flank.

White's Plan: I need to find a way to break through, how can I eliminate some of Black's defenders?

Black's Plan: Besides threatening 26 ... ♘xb3 I have strong pressure against c2. If I can force White onto the defensive this position should turn in my favour.

Candidate Moves: 26 ♗xd4; 26 ♕h4; 26 ♘d5.

Analysis: 26 ♘d5! (I doubt that Spassky even considered 26 ♗xd4 cxd4 27 ♕xd4 and in fact this is met by 27 ... ♘d5! 28 ♕f2 ♘xf4 29 ♕xf4 ♗b2) **26 ... ♘xb3 27 e5!** ♘xc1 (27 ... dxe5 28 ♘xf6+ exf6 29 ♗xb7 ♘xc1 30 ♗xc8 ♘xd3 31 ♕f3 fxg5 32 cxd3 e4 33 de ♖a3 and a rather equal final position) and now 28 exf6 was the right move with a strong attack. Spassky played the mistaken **28 ♗xc1?** and after **28 ... ♗xd5 29 ♗xd5 ♘xd5 30 ♕h4 ♘f6 31 exf6 exf6 32 ♕h7+ ♚f8 33 ♘e4 ♕e5 34 ♗f4 ♕d4+ 35 ♚h1** would have been in serious trouble had Black now played correctly with 35 ... ♖d8.

Assessment: After Spassky's 26 ♘d5 both sides have chances in a complicated struggle.

A23/3

a) Larsen-Kavalek, Lugano 1970. The position is blocked but opposite side castling suggests violence. Who will open lines first?

White's Plan: I would really like to lever Black's kingside open with something like f2-f3 or g3-g4 Unfortunately Black's knight on e5 seems to stop these ideas or does it? I have to watch out for 20 ♗xc4.

Black's Plan: It isn't easy for me to lever open White's king with pawn advances but I might well be threatening to sacrifice a piece with 20 ♗xc4.

Candidate Moves: 20 ♘cd5; 20 ♕e2; 20 g4.

Analysis: 20 g4! ♘xg4 21 f3! exf3 22 ♗xf3 ♘e5 (22 ... ♘f6 23 ♕h2 ♖fe8 24 ♘b5 ♘c8 25 ♗xf6 ♗xf6 26 ♕h7+ ♚f8 27 ♗d5 etc) 23 ♕h2 ♗xc4!? (23 ... ♖fe8 24 ♘b5 ♘c8 25 ♕h7+ ♚f8 26 ♗d5+-) **24 bxc4 ♘xf3 25 ♕h7+ ♚f7 26 ♘cd5 ♖g8 27 ♘xe7 ♖b8 28 ♚a1** (28 ♚c1!+-) **28 ... ♕xe7 29 ♕xg6+ ♚f8 30 ♘e6+ ♕xe6 31 ♗xg7+!** (31 ♕xe6?? ♗xb2+ 32 ♚b1 ♗a3+ 33 ♚c2?? ♖g2+ etc) **31 ... ♚e7 32 ♗f8+! ♖bxf8** (32 ... ♖gxf8 33 ♖h7+ ♖f7 34 ♖xf7+ ♕xf7 35 ♕xd6+ ♚e8 36 ♕xb8+ ♚e7 37 ♕d8+ ♚e6 38 ♕d6#) **33 ♖h7+** (33 ... ♖f7 34 ♖xf7+ ♕xf7 35 ♕xd6+ ♚e8 36 ♕d8#) **1:0**

Assessment: 20 g4! gives White a winning attack.

b) Fischer-Andersson, Siegen Ol, 1970. Black has more space, White has more centre pawns.

White's Plan: Probably Black can prevent the thematic breakthroughs with either b3-b4 or d3-d4.

Another idea is to try and establish a knight on e4 and secure it against ... f6-f5 with g2-g4.

Black's Plan: I have more space but it's difficult to see how I should breach White's position.

Candidate Moves: 13 ♖fd1; 13 ♖fe1; 13 ♔h1.

Analysis: Fischer established his knight on e4 and supported it with g2-g4: **13 ♔h1!? ♕d7 14 ♖g1 ♖ad8 15 ♘e4 ♕f7 16 g4 g6 17 ♖g3 ♗g7 18 ♖ag1 ♘b6 19 ♘c5 ♗c8 20 ♘h4 ♘d7 21 ♘e4 ♘f8 22 ♘f5 ♗e6 23 ♘c5 ♘e7 24 ♘xg7 ♔xg7 25 g5 ♘f5 26 ♖f3 b6 27 gxf6+ ♔h8 28 ♘xe6 ♖xe6 29 d4 ed 30 ♗c4 d3 31 ♗xd3 ♖xd3 32 ♕xd3 ♖d6 33 ♕c4 ♘e6 34 ♗e5 ♖d8 35 h4 ♘d6 36 ♕g4 ♘f8 37 h5 ♘e8 38 e4 ♖d2 39 ♖h3 ♔g8 40 hg ♘xg6 41 f4 ♔f8 42 ♕g5 ♘d6 43 ♗xd6+ 1:0**

Assessment: Fischer's 13 ♔h1 is a highly original concept and does create some problems.

A23/4

a) Hodgson-Pia Cramling, Bern 1995. White has an impressive build-up of forces on the kingside.

White's Plan: Can I sacrifice on h6?

Black's Plan: I need to defend my king.

Candidate Moves: 22 ♗xh6.

Analysis: **22 ♗xh6! ♘e4** (22 ... gxh6 23 ♕xh6, 24 ♖e5; 23 ... ♕b6 24 ♔h1! ♕xd4 25 ♖ad1; 23 ♘g4 24 ♗g1!+-) **23 ♕h5 ♘f6** (23 ... g6 24 ♕e5 ♗f6 25 ♕f4 ♗xd4+ 26 ♔f1 g5 27 ♗xg5! ♗xg5 28 ♖xe4 ♕xf4 29 ♖xf4 ♗e5 30 ♖h4** leaves White

with an extra pawn and good winning chances) **24 ♕g5 ♘e8 25 ♕e3 ♗f6 26 ♗f4 ♕b6 27 ♗e5 ♗xe5 28 ♕xe5 ♕xb2 29 ♘a4 ♕a3 30 ♘c5 ♘f6 31 ♘xe6 ♖ae8 32 ♗f5 fe 33 ♗xe6+ ♔h8 34 ♖e3 ♕b2 35 ♖ae1 ♘h7 36 ♕h5 g6 37 ♕xd5 ♘f6 38 ♕e5 ♔g7 1:0**

Assessment: 22 ♗xh6 is winning for White

b) Hodgson-Jonsson, Reykjavik 1989. A wild position in which both players' kings are coming under pressure.

White's Plan: I'd like to get my king off the e-file—it's starting to look very draughty.

Black's Plan: If I can open a few more lines I might catch White's king in the crossfire.

Candidate Moves: 22 ... ♗xc4; 22 ... d5; 22 ... g5.

Analysis: **22 ... g5! 23 ♖xb7** (23 fxg5 ♕xg5, 24 ... ♕g3+) **23 ... ♕xb7 24 fxg5 ♗g4!!** (24 ... ♘h7 25 ♕h5 ♗f5! 26 g6 ♗xd4 27 ♔d1! ♖f1+ 28 ♔d2 ♖f2+= [29 ♗e2? ♖xe2+ 30 ♕xe2 ♗xg6+] 25 gxf6! ♗xd1 26 f7+ ♔xf7 27 ♖h7+ ♔e6 28 ♖xb7 ♗g4 29 ♖xa7 ♖a8 30 ♖g7 ♖g8 31 ♖xg8 ♖xg8 32 a4 ♗h5 33 ♔f2 ♗d1 34 a5 ♖b8 35 ♔e3 ♖b3 36 ♔d2 ♖a3 37 g3 ♗b3 38 g4 ♖a4 39 g5 ♔f7 40 e5 dxe5 41 ♗xe5 ♗xc4 42 g6+ ♔g8 43 ♗xc4+ ♖xc4 44 ♔d3 ♖g4 45 a6 ♖a4 46 a7 ♖xa7 47 ♔c4 ½-½**

Assessment: After 22 g5! the position explodes into action, objectively speaking Black is probably winning.

Month 24

A24/1

a) Keres-Book, Kemeri 1937. White has an extra rook for just two pawns but the knight on c8 looks trapped Black's other pieces are displaying a menacing level of activity.

White's Plan: Can I get my knight out safely or profitably let it go?

Black's Plan: After capturing White's knight on c8 I might generate threats based on my passed d-pawn and the invasion of my knight on the d3 square.

Candidate Moves: 22 ♘a7; 22 ♕h5; 22 ♕c2; 22 ♖c1; 22 ♘e7+; 22 ♗xd4.

Analysis: 22 ♕h5! (Keres rejected 22 ♘a7 because of 22 ♕b6 23 ♘xc6 ♘d3. White could have brought about a favourable endgame with 22 ♘e7+ ♗xe7 23 ♕xd4) **22 ... ♘a4** (22 ... ♘d3 23 ♗e4 g6 24 ♗xg6 hxg6 25 ♕xg6+ ♔h8 26 ♘e7 ♗xe7 27 ♖xe7 ♕xe7 28 ♗xd4+ ♘e5 29 ♕h5+ ♔g8 30 ♗xe5+-) **23 ♗e4! g6** (23 ... h6 24 ♕g6) **24 ♗xg6 hxg6 25 ♕xg6+ ♔h8 26 ♘e7! ♗xe7 27 ♖xe7!** (27 ... ♕xe7 28 ♗xd4+-) **1:0**

Assessment: White wins most easily by playing for the attack.

b) Ivkov-Keres, USSR-Rest of the World, Belgrade 1970. Black's d4 pawn has a cramping effect on White's position whilst White's pieces are singlemindedly pointing towards the h7 square.

White's Plan: I want to give mate on h7.

Black's Plan: If I defuse the immediate threats my extra space and active pieces should count for something.

Candidate Moves: 19 ... h6; 19 ... ♘e5.

Analysis: 19 ... ♘e5! (19 ... h6 20 ♗xg6 fxg6 21 ♘e6) **20 ♘xh7?!** (20 ♗xg6 ♕xg6 21 ♕f4 was given by Ivkov when 21 ... ♘c6! is fine for Black) **20 ... ♖fe8 21 ♘g5** (21 ♗xg6 ♕xg6 22 ♘g5 d3! is also good for Black) **21 ... d3! 22 exd3 f5 23 ♗g2 ♖d4 24 ♕h3 ♘xd3 25 ♘f3?** (25 ♖c2! ♘e1 26 ♖c1 ♖d2 allows 27 ♗d5+!) **25 ♘xc1 26 ♘xd4 ♕xd4 27 ♖xc1 ♖e2 28 ♖f1 ♖xb2 29 ♗f3 ♖xa2 30 ♗xb7 a5 31 ♕g2 ♗f7 32 ♕f3 g6 33 h4! ♖a1 34 ♖xa1 ♕xa1+ 35 ♔h2 ♕e5 36 ♗c6** and now 36 ... ♕c5 would probably have won.

Assessment: White's kingside threats have more bark than bite.

A24/2

a) Alekhine-Prils and Braut, Antwerp 1923. Black has two extra pawns but his pieces are passively placed and there is a big hole on e6. His king looks vulnerable too.

White's Plan: I have excellent compensation for my two pawns and I'd like to attack Black's king.

Black's Plan: We have two extra pawns but our position is rather uncomfortable. It would be nice to exchange some pieces and push that passed a-pawn.

Candidate Moves: 29 ♘e6; 29 ♖c4.

Analysis: 29 ♖c4! (29 ♘e6 ♖xe6!) **29 ... ♖e5 30 ♘e6 ♖h5** (30 ... ♖xe6 31 dxe6+ ♕xe6 32 ♖e4! ♕f5 33 ♗xf6!+-; 30 ... ♖xd5? 31 ♘xg7!+-) **31 ♕e4 ♕e7 32 ♕d3 ♗b6** (32 ... ♘d7 33 ♖e4 ♘e5 34 ♕xa6 ♗b6 35 ♕c8 +-) **33 ♖e4 ♕d7 34 g4 ♖h8 35 ♖f4! ♖e8 36 ♗xf6! gxf6** (36 ... ♖xe6 37 dxe6+ ♕xe6 38 ♗d4+ ♔g8 39 ♗xb6 cxb6 40 ♖d4!+-) **37 ♖xf6+! ♔xf6** (37 ... ♔e7 38 ♕xg6+-) **38 ♕c3+ 1:0**

Assessment: By first preparing ♘d4-e6, White obtains a winning attack.

b) Alekhine-Bogoljubow, Hastings 1922. Black has advanced his kingside pawns before White has castled on that flank.

White's Plan: Black's king position looks rather draughty to me, I wonder if I can exploit it by opening lines.

Black's Plan: If I can consolidate my king position my long-term prospects should be good because of my space and bishop pair.

Candidate Moves: 13 g4; 13 ♕c2; 13 ♗d3.

Analysis: 13 g4! (13 ♗d3 and 13 ♕c2 are met by 13 ... g4) **13 ... fxg4 14 ♘e5 ♘xe5 15 dxe5 ♕c7 16 ♕d4 ♖f5** (otherwise White would proceed with 17 ♗e2, 18 ♗xg4 and 19

f4) **17 ♗d3! ♕xe5 18 ♕xe5!** (18 ♗xf5 ♕xf5 gives Black two pawns for the exchange and a safe king) **18 ... ♖xe5 19 ♖xh7 ♗f6 20 ♔d2 ♗g7 21 ♖ch1 ♖b8 22 ♘a4 ♖f5 23 ♗xf5 exf5 24 ♖7h5 ♗e6 25 ♖xg5 d4 26 exd4 ♖d8 27 ♔c3 ♔f8 28 ♖d1 ♔f7 29 ♘b6 ♖h8 30 ♖xg7+ ♔xg7 31 a4 ♖h2 32 ♖g1 f4 33 d5 cxd5 34 ♔d4 g3 35 f3 ♔f6 36 b5 axb5 37 axb5 ♖h5 38 c6 bxc6 39 bxc6 ♔e7 40 c7 ♔d6 41 c8=♕ ♗xc8 42 ♘xc8+ ♔d7 43 ♖c1 ♖h2 44 ♖c2 1:0**

Assessment: 13 g4 gives White excellent attacking chances.

A24/3

a) Botvinnik-Bronstein, Moscow WCh 1951. Black has an exra pawn but his structure is badly weakened. The pawn on d5 looks doomed.

White's Plan: After winning back the pawn on d5 I will attack d7 and maybe a6.

Black's Plan: Can I make it difficult for White to recapture on d5?

Candidate Moves: 30 ... ♘xa3; 30 ... ♔h8.

Analysis: 30 ... ♔h8! 31 ♖e1 (31 ♘xd5 is bad because of 31 ... ♗xd5 32 ♗xd5 ♘xd5 33 ♖xd5 g6 34 ♖xd7 [34 ♘d6 ♘e3] 34 ... gxf5 35 c6 ♘e5 36 ♖c7 ♖f7 37 ♖c8+ ♔g7 38 c7 ♔f6 39 ♔f2 ♘c6 40 ♔e3 ♘a7 etc) **31 ... ♘xa3 32 ♘d6 ♗c6 33 ♖a1 ♘c2 34 ♖xa6 d4!** (stronger than 34 ... ♘xb4-the passed pawn wins the game for Black) **35 ♘cxb5 ♗xg2 36 ♔xg2 ♘g4 37 ♘f5** (Or 37 ♘e4 d3) **37 d3 38 ♖d6 ♖xf5 39 ♖xd7 ♘ce3+ 0:1**

Assessment: 30 ... ♔h8 created problems for White in what seemed like a strong position for him.

b) Tolush-Bronstein, USSR Ch, Riga 1958. Black is the exchange up and White's king is exposed.

White's Plan: This position is desperate so I should try to stir up trouble with my d-pawn and against Black's king.

Black's Plan: How can I finish things off?

Candidate Moves: 30 ... ♘d7; 30 ... e4.

Analysis: 30 ... e4 (after 30 ... ♘d7 31 ♘e7+ Black has to play 31 ... ♔h8 because other king moves are answered by 32 ♖xf7+) **31 ♘e7+ ♖xe7! 32 dxe7 exf3! 33 ♕d8+ ♔h7 34 e8=♕ ♕h3+ 35 ♔e1 ♘d3+ 36 ♔d2 ♕h6+ 37 ♔c3 ♕xc1+** (38 ♔d4 ♕xb2+–+) **0:1**

Assessment: Black can win quite cleanly with some sharp play.

A24/4

a) Bronstein-Keres, Budapest Ct 1950. Black has an extra pawn but is faced with a very dangerous attack on his king.

White's Plan: My main attacking plan is based on playing f5-f6 to cramp Black's king and bring my queen to the h-file.

Black's Plan: This looks very dangerous, I need to reinforce my kingside defences and then hopefully create counterplay on the queenside.

Candidate Moves: 25 ... c4; 25 ... ♘c4.

Analysis: 25 ... ♘c4? (25 ... c4! was better with the idea of sacrificing the exchange after 26 ♗h6 ♘b7!) **26 ♗h6?** (26 ♗c1 would have been the best, threatening 27 ♗b3 ♘e5 28 ♗d5) **26 ... ♗g7?**

(Black should definitely leave the rook on f8 to its fate with 26 ... ♘xb2) **27 ♗xg7 ♔xg7 28 f6+ ♔h8 29 ♕g5 b3?** (29 ... ♖g8 30 ♖f4 ♕d8 31 ♖h4 ♕f8 32 ♖h6, 33 ♕h4) and now Bronstein could have won nicely with **30 ♖f4 bxa3 31 ♕h6 axb2+ 32 ♔h2 ♖g8 33 ♕xh7+** etc.

Assessment: The exchange sacrifice allows Black to defend.

b) Botvinnik-Bronstein, Moscow WCh 1951. White has the slight advantage of two bishops. Black's structure is slightly weakened.

White's Plan: I want to open the position up for my bishops.

Black's Plan: Should I sit tight or win that b3 pawn?

Candidate Moves: 35 ... ♗xc1; 35 ... ♔f7.

Analysis: 35 ... ♗xc1? (Black should play 35 ... ♔f7 after which White could hardly hope to break through, the text wins a pawn but allows White to open it up) **36 ♔xc1 ♘xb3+ 37 ♔c2 ♘a5 38 ♔c3 ♔f7 39 e4 f5? 40 gxf5 gxf5 41 ♗d3 ♔g6 42 ♗d6?!** (42 ♗b1) **42 ♘c6 43 ♗b1 ♔f6?** (Black could still draw with 43 ... ♘a7 44 exd5 exd5 45 ♗a2 b5) **44 ♗g3 fxe4 45 fxe4 h6 46 ♗f4 h5 47 exd5 exd5 48 h4 ♘ab8 49 ♗g5+ ♔f7 50 ♗f5 ♘a7 51 ♗f4 ♘bc6 52 ♗d3 ♘c8 53 ♗e2 ♔g6 54 ♗d3+ ♔f6 55 ♗e2 ♔g6 56 ♗f3 ♘6e7 57 ♗g5 1:0** (57 ... ♘c6 58 ♗xd5 ♘d6 59 ♗f3 ♔f5 60 ♗c1! b5 61 ♗xc6 bc 62 a5 wins for White)

Assessment: If Black sits tight he should draw without difficulty.